THE
GREAT BOOK OF
MAGIC

By
WENDY RYDELL
with
GEORGE GILBERT

THE GREAT BOOK OF
MAGIC

Including

150 Mystifying Tricks You Can Perform

HARRY N. ABRAMS, INC., PUBLISHERS, NEW YORK

Created by: **Plenary Publications International, Inc.**
300 East 40th Street
New York, N.Y. 10016

ISBN 8109-1306-2
Library of Congress Catalog Card Number: 76-12665

Printed and bound in the United States

TABLE OF

	PAGE

THE MAGIC OF MAGIC — 11

A brief introduction to magic and magic-making, highlighting the timelessness and universality of magic as a performing art.

CHAPTER 1–BLACK MAGIC, WHITE MAGIC — 12

The growth and development of magic from prehistory to the age of science. The primitive magician—the rites of imitative and contagious magic and the uses of black and white magic—the astrologer-priests of Chaldea—the magic-making of ancient Egypt, Greece, and Rome—the monotheistic Israelites—the rise of Christianity and the elevation of Satan—the Cabala—the growing conflict between magic and religion—the Church versus sorcery, witchcraft, Satanism, and all manner of pagan beliefs—the Inquisition—the tribulations of the conjurer and the alchemist—black magic scourged and the conjurer moved to center stage.

CHAPTER 2–FROM THE FIRST MAGICIANS... — 35

Dedi the Egyptian and the first recorded conjuring feat—the clever magic-cum-science of the ancient Egyptian and Greek temple priests—the mystery of the cups and balls—conjuring in the New World—the gory machinations of Europe's medieval conjurers and the first exposés of their techniques—the Indian Rope Trick and other fabled magic of the Orient—Vaucanson, von Kempelen, and the automata of the industrial era—the magicians themselves: Jacob Philadelphia, Isaac Fawkes, Philip Breslaw, Gustavus Katterfelto, Giovanni Giuseppi Pinetti, and the dashing charlatan Giuseppi Balsamo, Alessandro, Conte di Cagliostro.

CHAPTER 3–...TO THE MASTERS OF MAGIC — 59

The glorious golden age of magic, highlighting the lives—and greatest tricks—of its most masterful conjurers, including...

THE INNOVATOR—JEAN EUGÈNE ROBERT-HOUDIN and his contemporaries, — 60
The Great Bosco, Comus, Louis Comte, Philippe, Signor Blitz, Joseph Michael Hartz, Robert Heller, John Henry Anderson.

THE NEW WORLD RECONQUERED—THE BROTHERS HERRMANN, including — 71
Carl, Alexander, and the rest of the conjuring Herrmann family, along with the Davenport Brothers, Professor Pepper and his fabulous "ghost," and the inventions of Joseph de Kolta.

CONTENTS

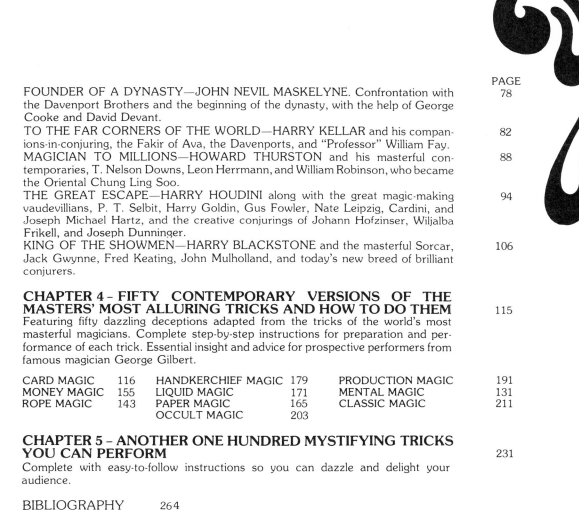

PAGE

FOUNDER OF A DYNASTY—JOHN NEVIL MASKELYNE. Confrontation with the Davenport Brothers and the beginning of the dynasty, with the help of George Cooke and David Devant. — 78

TO THE FAR CORNERS OF THE WORLD—HARRY KELLAR and his companions-in-conjuring, the Fakir of Ava, the Davenports, and "Professor" William Fay. — 82

MAGICIAN TO MILLIONS—HOWARD THURSTON and his masterful contemporaries, T. Nelson Downs, Leon Herrmann, and William Robinson, who became the Oriental Chung Ling Soo. — 88

THE GREAT ESCAPE—HARRY HOUDINI along with the great magic-making vaudevillians, P. T. Selbit, Harry Goldin, Gus Fowler, Nate Leipzig, Cardini, and Joseph Michael Hartz, and the creative conjurings of Johann Hofzinser, Wiljalba Frikell, and Joseph Dunninger. — 94

KING OF THE SHOWMEN—HARRY BLACKSTONE and the masterful Sorcar, Jack Gwynne, Fred Keating, John Mulholland, and today's new breed of brilliant conjurers. — 106

CHAPTER 4 – FIFTY CONTEMPORARY VERSIONS OF THE MASTERS' MOST ALLURING TRICKS AND HOW TO DO THEM — 115
Featuring fifty dazzling deceptions adapted from the tricks of the world's most masterful magicians. Complete step-by-step instructions for preparation and performance of each trick. Essential insight and advice for prospective performers from famous magician George Gilbert.

CARD MAGIC	116	HANDKERCHIEF MAGIC	179	PRODUCTION MAGIC	191
MONEY MAGIC	155	LIQUID MAGIC	171	MENTAL MAGIC	131
ROPE MAGIC	143	PAPER MAGIC	165	CLASSIC MAGIC	211
		OCCULT MAGIC	203		

CHAPTER 5 – ANOTHER ONE HUNDRED MYSTIFYING TRICKS YOU CAN PERFORM — 231
Complete with easy-to-follow instructions so you can dazzle and delight your audience.

BIBLIOGRAPHY — 264

INDEX — 265

JOSEPH
PINETTI

THE MAGIC OF MAGIC

The ability of magic to fascinate the human imagination is almost as ancient as man himself. Even today, in an age when science offers convincing rational explanations for all manner of natural phenomena, the purveyors of magic — whether of the occult or of the spectacular stage illusion — continue to hold a firm grip on the imagination.

By definition magic is any mysterious or seemingly inexplicable or extraordinary power to control events or to produce marvelous effects. Such a definition applies equally to the centuries-old rituals of the tribal shaman, to the esoteric rites of the modern-day high priest of the occult, and to the entertaining deceptions of the stage conjurer. Yet this definition somehow seems much too superficial to encompass the full scope of this oldest of human inventions.

Magic was man's first religion; it was his first attempt to understand and control the world around him. It may well have laid the groundwork for his early endeavors in science, medicine, technology, and the creative arts.

Even during man's so-called civilized centuries, when magic and formalized religion coexisted uneasily and then confronted each other in open opposition, magic retained its powerful hold on the imaginations of millions.

Today technology has brought to modern man the kind of power to control his world that not even the wiliest ancient magician dared to imagine. But the inexorable march of technology has also brought an era of stress and anxiety, which, in turn, has brought about a questioning of the moral prohibitions that through the ages have circumscribed human belief and behavior. As a result increasing numbers of people are turning back to magic in a search for answers that modern religions seem unable to supply to them.

Many others, shunning these twentieth-century rituals of the occult, nevertheless seek to divine the future through the ancient arts of astrology or numerology, or they take an interest in other manifestations of the occult, such as spiritualism, palmistry, dream interpretations, Tarot readings, and extrasensory perception. Still others, claiming to be too wise or sophisticated to give credence to ancient rites of magic, are delighted to escape from present-day stress by watching the performance of a skilled conjurer or even by learning to practice his amusing trickery themselves.

Although no single volume can fully document so vast a subject as magic and its many applications, this book attempts to trace some of the reasons underlying its amazing renaissance in this technological age of anxiety. The ancient roots of ritual magic are examined along with its growth and development over the centuries and its almost inevitable eclipse as a result of the forces let loose by the Inquisition.

In addition, performing magic — the art of conjuring as entertainment — is traced from its prehistoric origins, through its early centuries of development under the pall of the Inquisition, and finally to its emergence into a glorious golden age highlighted by the marvelous machinations of the great masters of the conjuring art.

A separate section of this book is devoted to fifty updated versions of the greatest tricks of the master magicians, complete with illustrated instructions for performing them. Also included are one hundred simpler tricks, which are just as enjoyable and mystifying.

Wendy Rydell

BLACK MAGIC, WHITE MAGIC

Magic—and man's need to believe in it— is probably as old as man himself. It was held in awe long before it was given a name; it was feared far more than any of the natural catastrophes that were part and parcel of prehistoric man's perilous life.

Magic was man's first attempt to understand and master the world around him. It represented power— power to control what he could not understand. It was, in short, his first religion.

When did man first discover the need to believe in magic? Probably not long after he emerged—an apelike creature—from the uplands of East Africa about two million years ago.

By all rights this primitive being should have become as extinct as the dinosaur. Certainly of all the creatures who lived in prehistoric times, none was as poorly equipped to survive as he. Yet this vulnerable creature did survive because inside his large and wondering brain were the seeds of logic and reason and the capacity to develop an imagination.

At first prehistoric man's survival was a random thing. He was buffeted about by forces he could not understand and preyed upon at least as much as he was predator himself. But soon, as time on earth is measured, he began casting about for some way to control his destiny. He started to examine the only thing in the world he knew anything about — himself.

Prehistoric man found himself to be a creature of many needs, many fears, many hungers, and many weaknesses as well as a few dimly perceived strengths and aspirations. With this rudimentary knowledge of himself he began to look more closely at the other living things that shared his world. He realized that all of life — man, bird, animal, tree, plant — shared a common force which could be snuffed out instantly and arbitrarily for reasons he could not explain.

He had no idea what this life force might be or why it could be killed so capriciously. Yet, if all living things shared this mysterious force, they must also share the same characteristics he had come to discover in

himself. So prehistoric man took the next reasoning step: he personified every living thing and gave it a spirit and personality not unlike his own.

The spirit of the tiger was brave; that of the hyena was strong but cowardly. The river spirit was usually calm and weak, but when it was hungry, it became a rampaging force which swallowed up everything it touched. The sun spirit, provider of heat and light, was the most powerful of all.

After peopling every element of his world with spirits, both good and evil, prehistoric man took what seemed to him to be the next logical step. If everything on earth had a unique personality and spirit, as he had himself, then everything on earth could be influenced in the

same ways he was. If the river flooded its banks, it was because the river spirit was hungry and needed to be fed—just as he needed food when he was hungry. If the rains did not fall, it was because the sky spirits were offended—just as he might be offended by the actions of another man. If the sun darkened ominously during the day, the shadow demon that covered its face must be frightened away—just as a marauding animal had to be frightened away from the tribal camp.

Gradually, over uncounted centuries, prehistoric man took his theory that like produces like and developed rituals of magic—with suitable rites and incantations—which he hoped would control the forces that threatened his tenuous little world.

Since powerful magic was needed to make the spirits bend to the will of the tribe in matters of grave importance, like guaranteeing a continuing food supply or averting a natural catastrophe, the whole tribe usually took part in these ritual ceremonies. But prehistoric man also needed magic to succeed in his day-to-day affairs—to bring him a safe journey or a healthy child or a cure for his pain or even an extra bit of dexterity when he sat by the fire and manipulated a few small stones for the amusement of his family.

Obviously it was impractical for the whole tribe to lay aside its work and take part in a ritual ceremony every time an individual needed to invoke a bit of everyday magic. So, inevitably the job of making magic for the tribe was turned over to one man—the tribal magician.

The tribal magician might have been the son of a magician, inheriting the secret knowledge of generations of magician-ancestors. Or he might have

been the oldest member of the tribe and wise in the ways of dealing with the spirits. Or he might even have been the laziest member of the tribe, coveting the job because he knew it relieved him of all other responsibilities—and was surely easier than hunting or fishing or fighting tribal enemies. But no matter how or why he got the job, the magician kept it because he was shrewd and clever in his understanding of human nature.

As the practice of magic became more complex and stylized, the magician became the most powerful member of the tribe. He was its high priest, leading them through the ritual magic performances intended to control the external realities of their lives. He was also the tribal seer and diviner of the future; as such, he was its most influential adviser, and no one—not even the chief—dared to embark on an undertaking of any importance without first consulting him.

At first the magician made what has come to be called white magic—spells and rites and incantations and medicines aimed at doing good. He was the tribal ambassador to good spirits and was expected to call upon them to protect the tribe from the wrath of evil spirits, or demons. At almost the same time the magician also began to deal in what has come to be called black magic—using his power to bring harm to one man or one tribe at the request of another.

At first the line between white magic and black magic was a thin one. The distinction between the two kinds of magic revolved around the intent of the magician and whether he wielded the awesome but neutral power of magic for good or for evil.

That thin line between the two kinds of magic widened considerably when the magician, being all too human, saw black magic as a way to gain more profit, power, and honor for himself by accepting the bribes of those who wanted harm done to an enemy. So, for a price, the magician was willing to invoke the spirits of evil and command them to do his bidding.

Yet even the boldest magician feared the evil spirits. As much to protect himself as to enhance his own power and prestige, he gradually evolved a set of taboos for his tribe to follow as a means of keeping the evil spirits quiescent. These taboos varied with each tribe, each culture—even with each magician. But in all cultures the magician alone was the arbiter of how taboos were to be obeyed and how transgressors were to be punished.

Meanwhile, the magician continued to polish and perfect his many rituals of magic, while always making sure that he and he alone knew the precise manner and method to carry them out.

In general primitive magic fell into two distinct categories: imitative magic and contagious magic. Both categories, depending on the intent of the magician, could be made to produce white or black magic.

Imitative magic was rooted in the age-old theory that

A 15,000-year-old cave drawing from Les Trois Frères in southern France shows a sorcerer disguised as a stag. This prehistoric ritual of imitative magic was designed to lure herds to the forest and is still practiced today among primitive tribes.

Diorama of a Cro-Magnon artist at work. Cave paintings like these may have been part of the prehistoric practice of magic.

Cave painting (right) of a deer hunt, uncovered in Castellón, Spain, shows typical stylized silhouettes of Spanish culture of 8000-9000 B.C.

Colorful representation of Mani (left), the hunting god of the Wape tribe, Papua New Guinea. Wape tribesmen believe that Mani is the spirit who assures good hunting.

Ancient Egyptian terra-cotta disk (right) is incised with Greek zodiac symbols. The disk was probably used by Greek scholars working in Alexandria.

like produces like. That theory gave rise to such rites as the stag dance of the prehistoric magician, who donned a deer skin and antlers in hopes that, by taking on the appearance and characteristics of the stag, he could draw the herd toward the attacking hunters.

That particular magic rite, captured by a Stone Age artist, appears in a drawing on the wall of a cave in the Ariège district of France and shows a prehistoric magician—wearing skins and antlers—performing a stag dance.

The theory that like produces like underscored countless prehistoric rituals of magic. The witch doctor, by simulating the agonies of the patient and then simulating his own recovery, made the patient follow the same procedure. The voodoo practitioner, by mutilating or destroying the image of an enemy, caused similar harm to the enemy himself.

Contagious magic was based on the principle that the part of the whole is as good as the whole—that things which have once been in contact with each other continue to exert an influence, one on the other, even after physical contact has ended.

To primitive man this meant that any extension of himself—his teeth, hair, saliva, nails, even his footprints—could be used by an enemy to wield powerful magic over him. Because of his colossal dread of contagious magic, a tribesman always burned or buried his discarded clothes, weapons, and anything that had once been a part of his body, as, for example, his hair or his teeth.

Prehistoric man over countless generations became totally bound up in his myths and his magic. They became more than his religion; they were an integral part of his life, to be believed in and practiced day in and day out from birth to death. As a result, the magician, with his knowledge of magic and magic-making, became the most powerful member of his tribe. His power stemmed logically from man's desperate need to control a world he could not understand—a need that had led to man's first religion, magic.

The magician helped to establish the efficacy of that belief in magic by devising rites and rituals of his own, many of which are practiced almost unchanged today among primitive tribes as diverse and far-flung as the Haidas of British Columbia, the Chuckchi of Siberia, the Ainu of Japan, and the Bantu of South Africa.

He laid the cornerstones of uncounted taboos and superstitions, whose remnants survive in the superstitious practices of even today's most advanced technological societies.

He enhanced his powers with an occasional spectacular success based more on the law of averages than on any magic formula and covered his many failures by convincing his followers that *their* actions—and not his—had called down stronger magic to work against them. He even chose to direct the power of magic in evil ways so he could gain personal glory.

When primitive man took his first halting steps toward becoming civilized man, the magician went right along with him, all the while maneuvering himself into his accustomed position of power and prestige.

Man's earliest civilizations sprang up in the area known as the Fertile Crescent, not far from the Mediterranean Sea. Here a series of ancient peoples known as the Mesopotamians built the world's first cities.

Astrology, which arose from the ancient civilization of Mesopotamia, may have been man's first formal codified religion. It was surely his oldest art of divination—the first of perhaps sixty or seventy divinatory arts which the human imagination would devise in later generations.

The first astrologers were Chaldeans, heirs to the civilizations of ancient Sumer and Assyria, who came to power in the Fertile Crescent sometime after 1000 B.C. By that time they were already highly knowledgeable in the science of astronomy and had elaborated a complex system of numerology. These two, in combination, became the basis of a new divinatory art, astrology, which the Chaldeans regarded as an exact science.

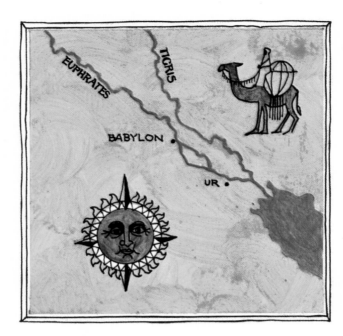

The cradle of civilization—the Fertile Crescent watered by the Tigris and Euphrates rivers—was the site of man's first cities.

Chaldean astrologer-priests were convinced that human destiny was somehow intertwined with the heavens and that the earth was the center of the universe. They had, in fact, formulated an entire quasi-scientific cosmology from which came a kind of national faith in the efficacy of the stars and their bearing on human destiny.

Their observations of the heavens had deep religious meaning for all Chaldeans; their planets were named after Chaldean gods and the movements of those planets were assumed to represent the movements of the gods themselves.

With their firm belief that the future could be read in the stars, Chaldean astrologer-priests drew up horoscopes which plotted the positions of the sun, moon, and planets in the twelve houses of the zodiac, according to their positions at the moment of an individual's birth. They then interpreted these positions and relationships in conformity with well-defined rules, in the belief that they could divine answers to the mysteries of the universe and reveal the character and future of a human being on earth.

At about the same time that the Chaldeans had developed their religious beliefs, a parallel civilization had sprung up in Egypt with a similar system of belief, which also combined ceremonial magic and religious rites.

Both religious systems were based on well-developed myths of creation; both developed an elaborate pantheon of gods, goddesses, spirits, and demons, whose names often changed from culture to culture but whose powers remained the same in all the ancient cultures of the Fertile Crescent.

Enlil, the mythical Sumerian storm god who was credited with creating the universe, became known as Marduk during the Babylonian first dynasty. The Sumerian mother goddess, Innini, was renamed Ishtar by the Babylonians and was worshiped as Astarte in Egypt. Below these all-powerful deities were a host of lesser gods who could be evoked to protect against the forces of evil, as well as other gods who represented those evils.

In accordance with the primitive belief that only a chosen few could address these mighty spirits directly, the magician—already experienced in the ways of bending the gods to his will—simply took the title of priest and continued acting in his customary capacity.

In some religious systems, however, where the magician's imperious commands to the gods had not brought the desired results, the belief slowly began to surface that it might be more judicious to beg for the favors of the gods. This change of technique brought about the emergence of the high priest and the demotion of the magician to a less prominent position in the religious scheme of things.

Even as the high priest enhanced his own religious powers—at the cost of the magician's domination—the magician was far from an outcast. He was still widely sought out to intercede with the gods for clients who wanted harm done to another, or a cure for an illness, or assurances of a desired outcome for a particular undertaking.

In addition, his divinations and astrological predictions helped him retain his position as official adviser on the affairs of state; there was hardly a ruler who undertook an important enterprise without first

Symbol of the Persian deity Mithras (right), *who represented the sun, light, and truth. Babylonian demon of disease and evil (far right).*

The Tower of Babel (below) *by Pieter Bruegel, the Elder. The architectural form is that of a Babylonian ziggurat, or storeyed tower; inside the massive structure there was only a small temple designed to receive the honored deity.*

Statue of Isis (left), Egyptian goddess of fertility, preparing to nurture an infant on her lap. The goddess wears a crown combining cow's horns and the symbolic sun disk.

Statue of Osiris (right), Egyptian god of the lower world and judge of the dead. Osiris was presumed by ancient Egyptians to rule over paradise.

Detail of drawing (right) from an Egyptian Middle Kingdom tomb at Beni Hasan shows one of several passes made by ancient cups-and-balls manipulators.

seeking his court magician's advice.

In Egypt, as in the Mesopotamian cultures, where magic and religion were inextricably combined, the position of the magician was honored and secure. The Egyptians particularly revered Osiris and Isis, the mythical husband and wife who were their chief deities of industry and fertility. They considered the goddess Isis a magician supreme, with powers to perform great miracles. According to Egyptian myth, those marvelous powers enabled her to reunite her husband's body after it had been dismembered by his brother Set, the god of evil. From this myth came the cult of necromancy, the art of foretelling the future by communicating with the dead—an art that evolved into the modern spirit séance.

The elevated position of Isis in the Egyptian pantheon and her honored calling as a magician emphasized the pervasiveness of magic in ancient Egyptian society. Effigies, painted images, incantations, and amulets—the stock-in-trade of magicians—were part of almost every religious ritual; religious rituals were almost always part of every rite of magic.

Another rite—of a somewhat different kind of magic—also appears to have surfaced in ancient Egypt. A drawing on the wall of a burial chamber in the town of Beni Hasan—probably made about 2000 B.C.—portrays two men performing what appears to be a conjuring trick with several cup-shaped bowls. The hieroglyphs describing the drawing—which have been translated as "Up from under"—seem to confirm that an unseen ball or other small round object is hidden under one of the bowls and is about to be magically produced.

The discovery of such a drawing suggests that this conjuring deception was common in ancient Egypt. Archaeological findings of groups of small, round, carefully matched pebbles on the sites of several prehistoric cultures suggest that the Egyptian cups-and-balls trick may have had its origins as early as the Stone Age.

While civilization spread out beyond the confines of the Fertile Crescent, bringing the religions of the Mesopotamians and Egyptians with it, a strange, new religion was developing among the wandering desert tribes of Israel. Led by the patriarch Abraham, these nomadic Israelites had come out of the Mesopotamian city of Ur some time around 2000 B.C. Many of them had once worshiped the ancient Phoenician god Baal along with other deities and had been, in fact, believers of magic.

Sometime during their desert wanderings, the Israelites began to center their religion around a single deity, Yahweh—Jehovah—an abstract god who controlled the entire universe; a god who could be contemplated and loved by his followers but who could not be influenced by even the wiliest magician.

The unique monotheistic religion, which rose unaccountably out of a sea of polytheism, shunned all formalized rites of magic. Yet it was constantly being threatened by the prevailing belief in magic of the other cultures that surrounded it. As a result, backsliding into polytheism, idol worship, and the standard rituals of magic was common among individual Israelites and even among their leaders, who now and then consulted with magicians or practiced magic themselves.

One particularly spectacular bit of magic related among the Old Testament recordings of miracles involved the Israelite Aaron, brother of Moses. According to the biblical account, Aaron cast down his rod at the feet of the mighty pharaoh, Ramses II. Instantly the rod turned into a wiggling serpent before the pharaoh's astonished eyes. Not to be outdone, the pharaoh's own magicians, Jannes and Jambres, duplicated Aaron's feat with their own rods. Even as they did, Aaron's serpent swallowed theirs—an action that Ramses quite naturally took to be an evil omen.

The rod that turned serpent may, in fact, have been a *Naja haja*, an Egyptian species of cobra that can be made motionless by applying pressure to a point just below its head. When the pressure is released, the serpent instantly regains its mobility.

Jannes and Jambres, as court magicians, would certainly have been aware of this peculiar characteristic of the *Naja haja*. But it is somewhat surprising that Aaron, a believer in Yahweh, should have been well versed in the ways of magic.

The Israelites struggled to keep the worship of Yahweh untainted by the prevailing rituals of magic. The ancient Greeks, however, reveled in the dualistic celebration of magic and religion. They, too, had evolved their own pantheon of gods, including the magicians Circe and Medea, but they were also influenced by the beliefs, rituals, and deities of other cultures.

From Persia—especially in the writings of Zoroaster—came the concept of Ahriman, the adversary, who would later become entwined with Baal, the enemy of Yahweh, and be recast as Satan, Prince of Darkness. From Egypt came the cult of necromancy and from Mesopotamia came the cult of astrology. From within Greece itself came the cult of Hecate, patroness of sorcerers, whose followers were automatically assumed to be magicians.

The ancient Greeks also devised their own arts of divination, such as chiromancy—from the Greek *cheir*, meaning hand—in which the practitioner divined the future by reading the lines on the palm of the hand. According to the chiromancer, both the shape of the hand and the lines on it could be read to indicate character, fortune, and even length of life.

Another ancient art of divination, numerology—foretelling the future by the use of certain numbers—gained added impetus from the works of the Greek philosopher Pythagoras and came into widespread use. According to the numerologist, the potency of numbers derived from the fact that every heavenly body was associated with a number and every letter of the alphabet was also associated with a number. By combining and interpreting the numbers associated with an individual—such as his date of birth and the letters of his name—the numerologist was able to divine the individual's future.

Ancient Greece was also the home of scientific speculation, and for the first time in human experience the power of magic began to be questioned. Astrology, with its premise that the earth was the center of the universe, came into conflict with the science of astronomy and the realization that the astrological maps of the Chaldeans were erroneous. The mathematical concepts of Euclid and others flew in the face of numerology. The study of physics and the laws of natural phenomena substituted scientific findings for magic formulas. Medicine, raised to a science by Hippocrates and other physicians, confronted the healing rituals of magic. So in ancient Greece the battle between science and magic was joined. It would become an epic struggle for the control of men's hearts and minds for generations to come.

Another, somewhat different kind of battle was also going on between the maker of conjuring magic as entertainment and those who watched him perform. Some of these wandering street conjurers had become marvelously adept in their performance of tricks using sleight of hand; so adept, in fact, that their

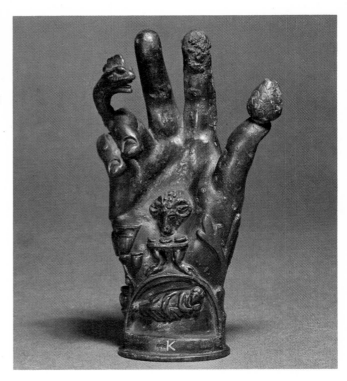

Roman bronze magic hand, probably owned by a follower of Gnosticism, who used it to ward off evil.

audiences—even as they enjoyed watching their deceptions—were instantly distrustful of anyone whose hands were quick enough to fool the eye.

The greater the conjurer's skill, the more distrustful his audience became—and the more difficult for the conjurer to eke out a livelihood, which depended on the few coins thrown at his feet as he performed.

While the Greek intellectual pitted science against magic, often finding magic to be the loser, the citizens of ancient Rome firmly believed in the efficacy of magic. Black magic flourished along with the official religions of Rome. The ancient rities of contagious magic—such as piercing someone's name with a nail or sticking pins in a wax image of an enemy to do him harm—continued unabated. The worship of evil spirits, the invocation of evil curses, and the casting of malicious spells were common.

At first the Roman religion had no formal pantheon of its own; instead, the Romans believed in national deities that had evolved out of the myths of the founding of Rome. As the Roman armies spread out to conquer the world, they brought back the cults of other provinces. The Greek pantheon took the place of the original national deities; the Greek festivals of Bacchus and Dionysus were celebrated along with the Roman

Saturnalian festivals; Greek deities were given Roman names and worshiped with as much fervor in Rome as they had been worshiped in Greece. In fact, much of this fervor was orgiastic in nature and set patterns of worship which would be followed for many centuries.

Afraid their own powers would be undermined by the growing power of magicians over the masses, the emperors of Rome eventually made strenuous efforts to control the practice of magic. It became a capital offense to consult a magician. The practice of magic was punished by torture. Even the mere knowledge of the occult arts could bring banishment, hard labor, or death.

The Roman emperors had not suddenly become disbelievers in magic. On the contrary, they were highly superstitious; they wore magic amulets to ward off evil and often consulted with astrologers before making any decisions. Their attempts to suppress the practices of magic were based on their desire to keep its benefits for themselves. But, for all their stringent laws, magic still flourished. It had been practiced for too many generations to be easily given up by its followers. Not even the birth of still another religion, Christianity, would erase the ancient beliefs by which men had lived for countless centuries.

In the first years after the crucifixion of Jesus Christ, the Church fathers struggled to gain converts to Christianity. Their ultimate goal was to replace the ancient beliefs with their own religion. But their progress was painfully slow, and they were forced to live in a kind of uneasy coexistence with pagan religions and mystic cults that they universally condemned.

They sought ways to compete with the old gods and idols, ways to dramatize and inculcate their own beliefs. They found what they were looking for when they reached back into ancient lore and reintroduced the devil as the Prince of Darkness and progenitor of all evil, the eternal adversary of Christ in the battle for the hearts and souls of mankind.

The devil was not a Christian invention. He had been Pazuzu, king of the evil spirits of the air, in Mesopotamia; he reappeared as Baal-zebub, lord of the flies, among the Philistines; he was Ahriman, the adversary in Zoroastrianism; he was the Israelite Satan, ruler of the underworld but subject to the will of Yahweh. In each of these roles he had been a demon and a representation of evil, but in none of them had he been elevated to such overwhelming prominence as the Church fathers now gave him.

They compiled a complete theology of the Devil. They insisted that he and his evil horde lay in wait at

Roman representation of Tempus, the god of time (above left). *Roman representation of Mors, the god of death* (above right). *Thirteenth-century Bohemian representation of Satan* (right).

every turn to ensnare the innocent into sinning. Unremittingly they reiterated the evils of the Devil with such fervor and determination that they created the kind of fear and loathing of him they needed.

But their spectacular success had a darker side. As Christians came to hate and fear the Devil, they also began to personify him, to identify him, to build up a mystique of names, faces, events, and fantasies which made him so loathsome that some became fascinated with him and raised him as the god of still another religion, the antichristian cult of Satanism.

The Satanists based their beliefs on their own interpretation of the Christian gospels—in particular, the Gospel of Matthew, in which Satan tempted Jesus with an offer of dominion over the world in return for Christ's adoration. Such an offer, according to the Satanists, could have been made only if Satan were indeed powerful enough to dominate the world. It was

A fifteenth-century engraving by Martin Schongauer depicts the temptation of Saint Anthony.

to that all-encompassing power that they dedicated themselves and their profane rituals.

One of the most loathsome of all Satanist rituals—in the view of the Church—was the celebration of the Black Mass, a perverse parody of the Christian mass, in which the Christian cross was hung upside down, inverted Christian prayers were chanted, and animal sacrifices were made on the altar steps.

The Black Mass horrified and inflamed the leaders of the Church and made them intensify their efforts to wipe out every vestige of Satanism. But the medieval world was rife with religious sects, cults, rituals, and beliefs that were anathema to the leaders of Christianity. One of them was the practice of theurgy, an occult art that called on the magical intervention of benign spirits to perform miracles of goodness. The theurgists based their cult on the Chaldean Oracles, a compilation of the sayings of the semidivine Persian religionist Zoroaster. They were also deeply influenced by the idealistic concepts of the Greek philosopher Plato.

The theurgists never doubted the ultimate triumph of good over evil, and in that respect they were not unlike the followers of Christianity. But their practice of image animation and their claim that they could enjoin the gods to appear visibly before them made them a serious threat to Christianity.

Another cult unacceptable to the Church fathers was Gnosticism, practiced by dissident Christians who initially proclaimed that the world and everything in it was irredeemably evil, although later they accepted the view of the Persian monk Mani that the struggle between good and evil was forever in doubt. The persuasive logic of Manichaean concepts drew many converts to Gnosticism, and inevitably it was branded a heresy by the Church.

Another sect that plagued the Church rose out of the ninth-century research of a number of rabbis who believed that the ancient Hebrew scriptures contained a series of hidden meanings—obscured by a kind of code—that offered insights into all of science and nature. They sought to decode the ancient writings by juggling the letters in the name of Jehovah and multiplying them in an infinite variety of combinations until they found the right combination to unlock the secrets of the universe.

These rabbinical searchers for truth were nothing more nor less than scholars seeking pure knowledge. They recorded their findings in two collections—the *Sefer Yezirah* ("Book of the Creation") and the *Sefer Zohar* ("Book of Splendor"). Together these collections became known as the Cabala. No matter what their original purpose had been, the books of the Cabala became the textbooks of magic for those who turned them into the basis of a new cult, Cabalism.

The cabalistic movement was immensely successful. Its followers claimed that the books of the Cabala—with

Magic circles and symbols (above) *used by the notorious sixteenth-century German magician Johann Faust, according to Scheible's* Das Kloster.
Faust confronts Mephistopheles (left), *from Christopher Marlowe's* The Tragical Historie of Doctor Faustus. *According to legend, Faust signed a pact with Mephistopheles (the Devil), who was to become his servant for twenty-four years. In return, Faust was to give up his soul to Mephistopheles when the pact ended.*

their formulas, their figures, their arithmetic combinations of letters and numbers—contained every charm for making every conceivable kind of magic and sorcery. They even ascribed to the Cabala ancient roots in Egyptian sorcery, which, of course, it never had.

For those who believed in magic, the symbols of the Cabala gained an honored place beside more-ancient magical symbols—the magic circle; the triangle with its three infinities; the interlocked triangles that symbolized the faith of the Israelites but also represented the footprint of the trud demon (a special demon whose symbol sorcerers used to call up and repel other demons); the cross, which became the symbol of Christianity as well as the magical representation of man standing at the center of the universe; the Sanskrit

swastika, which represented the four winds and the four seasons; and the most powerful of all magic symbols, the five-sided pentagram.

Although the books of the Cabala were never intended to be primers of magic, other medieval books were written specifically for that purpose. These books were the grimoires—they were more commonly known as black books—and they offered their readers a kind of do-it-yourself manual for calling up the spirits.

The most widely known of these black books was the *Clavicula Salomonis*, the Key of Solomon. Unlike the Cabala, the Key of Solomon is often considered to have been of ancient origin, dating before the Christian era. Updated, with new magical formulas added to it, the Key of Solomon found popularity during the

In a dramatic painting by Pedro Berruguete, Saint Dominic and members of the Inquisition tribunal watch as two heretics are tortured by secular authorities.

turbulent medieval period and, along with other black books such as the *Sacred Magic of Abra-Melin the Mage* and the *Lemegeton*, helped to trigger an upsurge in the practice of sorcery.

To thousands of suffering, downtrodden people in the Europe of the eleventh and twelfth centuries, the lure of sorcery was tremendous. It offered them—as the practice of magic had always offered its practitioners—a way to achieve personal power and aggrandizement at a time when they could see only poverty and despair ahead of them.

Many flocked to the established sorcerers to request that magic spells be performed for them. Others begged to be taken on as apprentices so that they, too, could learn to invoke the power of demons.

As sorcerers' apprentices they had much to learn. There were chants to be memorized, magic symbols to be learned, techniques for harnessing the awesome power of the occult to be mastered. Above all, there was the Pact—the agreement written in blood that bound the apprentice's immortal soul to Satan. Only then could the apprentice become a full-fledged sorcerer and take up his life's work—the invocation of the forces of Satan to do whatever he commanded of them.

During the first ten centuries of its existence, Christianity, still weak and few in numbers, suffered the continuing belief in magic, although it had first proscribed its practice and rituals as early as 305 at the Council of Elivira and then at subsequent councils— at Laodicea in 366, Orleans in 511, and Auxerre in 570.

By the eleventh century, when the practice of magic became more sinister and the Church had become more powerful, the Christian fathers launched an all-out campaign to be rid of magicians and wipe out all traces of the practice of magic.

The campaign began with the papal bull of 1233, in which Pope Gregory IX established the *Inquisitio hereticae pravitatis*—the Inquisition, a tribunal specifically for the suppression of heresy. It continued in 1258 with the papal bull of Pope Alexander IV condemning all forms of black magic. This papal letter methodically listed the reasons for condemnation: sorcerers deny God; they blaspheme; they commit incest; they kill people and then boil and eat them; they worship Satan and swear by his name; they consecrate their children to Satan and often sacrifice them to him; and, in all ways they serve as Satan's slaves.

With an ardor so intense that it seemed almost diabolical, the inquisitors went about their brutal business. They snatched at every rumor, every suggestion—real or imagined—that a specific heresy existed. Even if the heresy was never proved, they meted out punishments that they believed were suitable—imprisonment for life, torture, burning at the stake.

The inquisitors did not actually carry out the sentences they imposed. Because of the ecclesiastic

Following the ceremonial lighting of candles, a modern witch (right) is ready to proceed with an invocation to Satan.

Despite strong efforts by the Church to suppress it, the antichristian cult of Satanism continues even today. Modern Satanists (below) celebrate one of their rituals, led by their high priestess.

Anton Szandor La Vey, (above) who founded his Church of Satan in 1966, is a leading modern Satanist and is often called the Black Pope.

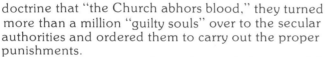

With ancient pentagram in background, Satanists (right) blaspheme Church in Satanic Ritual Chamber.

doctrine that "the Church abhors blood," they turned more than a million "guilty souls" over to the secular authorities and ordered them to carry out the proper punishments.

Whether to ingratiate themselves with the powerful inquisitors or to satisfy their own bloodlust, those in charge of meting out punishment devised a number of barbaric tortures. Pincers fitted with iron spikes were clamped around the arms and legs of those deemed to be heretics and slowly tightened until the victims collapsed in screaming agony. Torture collars were strapped to the necks of presumed sorcerers while the soles of their feet were roasted slowly over white-hot charcoals. Another commonplace torture was the forcible swallowing of boiling oil. Not surprisingly, many thousands—whether guilty or not—admitted to having committed lesser heresies in order to avoid the special tortures reserved for those judged guilty of major heresies.

Among the innocents caught by the fury of the Inquisition were a number of persons doing nothing more than practicing the ancient art of sleight of hand. A young girl who ripped apart and restored a handkerchief—a classic conjuring trick—was tried for witchcraft in Cologne. Wandering street magicians were barred from working or residing in a number of cities. Some who dared to ply their trade were persecuted by the inquisitors because their deceptions were presumed to be aided by evil spirits; therefore, they must be heretics.

Of all the heretics so passionately ferreted out by the Inquisition, none were more eagerly interrogated, tortured, convicted, and punished than those women accused of practicing witchcraft.

The practice of witchcraft was nothing new to the experience of mankind. Prehistoric tribal magicians often used real or imagined witches as scapegoats when their rites had failed to bring the desired results. Ancient cults honored their ancient witches—Hecate, Medea, Canidia, Sagana, Circe. Members of the pagan fertility cults of ancient England were regarded as witches.

By the time of the early Middle Ages witches were assumed to belong to two distinct categories; the wicca, or white witch, and the Satanist, or black witch. The wicca, especially in Britain—the name itself is an old English word meaning wise and referred to both male and female witches—was a kind of folk doctor who worshiped the pagan gods of ancient Druidic cults. Wiccas, or white witches, were considered to be wise and cunning. They used their knowledge of herbs, inherited from forebears, to brew potions and salves to cure the sick. Although they often lived somewhat apart from the rest of the Christian community and were regarded as different from other citizens, it was generally felt that they had no connection with Satan and the forces of evil.

An occasional wicca might claim special magical powers beyond those attributed to most wiccas—the ability to fly was a frequent boast—but, beyond that, wiccas were consulted to use their magic power to do good works; for example, to stimulate fertility for a barren client or prepare love philtres for those who had been spurned or to serve as a midwife to the poor.

The Satanist, or black witch, was quite another matter. Like the sorcerer, the black witch had presumably signed the Pact with Satan by squatting down on the ground, placing one hand on her head and the other under the soles of her feet, and swearing to Satan, "I give thee all that is between my hands." To seal the Pact, Satan would then nip her skin with his teeth in some inconspicuous place and brand her with the devil's mark, the unmistakable badge of the black witch. From that moment on, the black witch was a worshiper of the power of evil over good and a sworn follower of Satan, with the diabolical ability to simply think of an evil action in order to make it come to pass—or so it was believed.

The black witch was credited with any major or minor crime that a human being could invent. She was held responsible for curdling milk, for making hens stop laying, for causing a ripening field of grain to suddenly shrivel up and die. She was reportedly able to make a neighbor sicken and die for no explainable reason. She had the power to make people fall in or out of love. She could turn living beings into toads or the other way around.

Yet for all her evil ways, the most loathsome practice of the black witch was her celebration of the sabbat, or witches' sabbath—a depraved orgy in which, it was rumored, the witch ended up having sexual relations with Satan himself. Perhaps this practice more than any other caused Innocent VIII to issue his papal bull of 1484—entitled *Summis desiderantes affectibus*—condemning witchcraft. It was the supposed sabbat with its diabolical implications that inflamed the sensibilities of the inquisitors and made them fanatically eager to destroy every vestige of witchcraft.

In continental Europe the search for witches was generally conducted by the inquisitors. In England witch-hunting was usually directed by the Puritans. Their ardor in seeking out and punishing witches was no less than that of the inquisitors; like the inquisitors, they made no distinction between white and black witches or between innocence and guilt. In the three hundred years between 1400 and 1700, an estimated

The Compendium Maleficarum, *compiled by the friar Francesco-Maria Guaccio and published in Milan in 1626, presented a seventeenth-century Church view of Satan and his works. The etching (below) from the* Compendium *shows Satan marking a newcomer with the imprint of his claw.*

A fifteenth-century etching (right) shows two witches, whose heads have been changed to sheeplike form, being escorted to a sabbat by a demon.

Cornelius Agrippa von Nettesheim, a brilliant fifteenth-century alchemist, was believed to be a master magician. He always traveled with two huge dogs, popularly assumed to be demons in canine form.

Paracelsus, the sixteenth-century physician-alchemist who has been called the father of modern medicine, was also reputed to be the founder of the Rosicrucians, an association formed to study the occult.

one million persons were punished for witchcraft, sorcery, magic, and other heresies.

The Puritan witch-hunting mania carried over to the New World and to the Massachusetts colony, which the Puritans first settled. It reached a peak of madness in 1692 with an outburst of witch persecutions that lasted for eight months and culminated in the deaths of at least twenty so-called witches.

Meanwhile in Europe the forces let loose by the Inquisition continued to pervade all things. Certain practices having nothing to do with Satan and with black magic — practices like alchemy and conjuring as entertainment — were assumed to have an evil basis and a secret intent and were automatically suspect.

Conjurers, for example, claimed no pact with the Devil, no satanic skills, no assistance from demons or imps of Satan. Whatever assistance they needed during the performance of their tricks usually came from a concealed — but very human — confederate.

But because conjurers often clothed themselves in wizard's garb; because they enhanced their tricks with strange gibberish not unlike the incantations of witches and sorcerers; because they often performed amazing tricks and displayed skills so adept, many who watched them perform were convinced that they were servants of Satan. So conjurers, by the very nature of their trade, became a ready object of scorn and mistrust.

Another common target of medieval suspicion was the alchemist — practitioner of a primitive kind of chemistry — who hoped to find the philosopher's stone, a mystical substance that could turn anything it touched into purest gold and give back youth to the aged.

Although alchemy seems to have had its roots in the work of ancient Egyptian metallurgists and in the pseudoscientific writings of the Persian mystic Zoroaster, it was not widely practiced in Europe until sometime during the middle of the fourteenth century. Even then it was practiced at the risk of condemnation by the Church authorities.

The alchemist tried to be a scientist, a seeker of absolute truth and perfection. But he was operating in an era when magic, science, and religion were anathema to each other. He could not easily base his research on the findings of his predecessors — the ancient Greek, Arab, and Hebrew scientists; the Church had long banned ancient and medieval writings which did not conform to its prescribed doctrines of faith.

Since he was a product of his times, the alchemist could not help being influenced by the claims and counterclaims of the opposing forces of magic and religion. So in the secrecy of his laboratory he worked to find his panacea — his philosopher's stone — or he experimented to discover the marvelous elixir of life or the universal solvent that would dissolve all substances and return them to their pure essences.

Not all alchemists were unknown and unsung. Cornelius Agrippa von Nettesheim, born in Germany in 1486, was a brilliant alchemist who also dabbled in astrology, medicine, politics, and theology. Agrippa's ability to live by his wits brought him into royal and Church circles; it also led him into debtors' prison. Although many of the details of his life are unknown, he was believed by many of his contemporaries to be a master magician.

The sixteenth-century German-Swiss alchemist and

physician Paracelsus was credited with performing a number of astonishing cures; today he is often described as the father of modern medicine. Other alchemists also managed to make important scientific discoveries in their laboratories. Blaise de Vigenère is credited with the discovery of benzoic acid, and the German Johann Kunckel von Löwenstern was able to isolate phosphorus.

Eventually chemistry, metallurgy, and other sciences took over from these first early efforts of the alchemist. But neither science nor religion could slake man's compelling desire to divine his future or prevent his imagination from creating new arts of divination.

Several of the major arts of divination—astrology, numerology, and chiromancy—had been practiced for many centuries. Other divinatory arts, which had been popular in ancient times, had fallen into disuse in medieval Europe, although they are still practiced by a number of primitive tribes. They include haruspicy, divination from the entrails of animals; cleromancy,

divination by casting lots; aeromancy, divination by observing atmospheric conditions; crystallomancy, divination by means of crystal gazing; rhabdomancy, divination by the use of small sticks or divining rods; and geomancy, divination by throwing handfuls of dirt into the air and predicting the future by the way they fall to earth.

Late in the fourteenth century another major art of divination—cartomancy, or divination by Tarot cards—came into use in Europe. Although they were used principally for fortune-telling, the Tarot cards were also used for card games and are the oldest surviving playing cards. The origins of the Tarot are shrouded in mystery. Some claim Tarot cards were developed in Asia and brought to Europe by fourteenth-century traders, while others believe that they were brought

The Tarot cards (below) have been reproduced from the Visconti-Sforza deck which dates from mid-fifteenth-century Milan. Pictured from left to right are the cards which represent, in order, the Wheel of Fortune, the Hanged Man, and Death.

back by returning crusaders who received them from the Saracens and Moors of North Africa. Still others suggest that a French painter named Gringonneur painted the first pack of Tarot cards in 1392 to help his king, Charles VI, relieve his long sieges of madness.

According to some students of the Tarot, the twenty-two major cards of the Tarot—known as the major arcana—were derived from the *Book of Thoth* of the ancient Egyptians. According to others, they represent the twenty-two paths of the Cabala. Whatever its origins, the Tarot pack quickly became an almost indispensible divining tool of the witch and at the same time the fashionable means by which European aristocracy peered into the future.

In its most elaborate form the Tarot deck was made up of seventy-eight cards—twenty-two cards comprised the major arcana and fifty-six the minor arcana. Each of the all-important major arcana had a special significance: the cards numbered one to twenty-one were decorated with figures that represented natural laws, elements, virtues, and vices; the twenty-second card was unnumbered and represented the fool or madman (comparable to the modern joker).

The special significance of the fifty-six cards of the minor arcana was based on suit and number. The four suits (roughly resembling those of the modern playing deck) were wands or batons (clubs), cups (hearts), swords (spades), and pentacles or money (diamonds). Each suit was comprised of ten numbered cards—ace to ten—and four court cards—king, queen, knight, and page. The modern playing deck of fifty-two cards, which is known as the French deck and is now standard throughout the world, evolved from the numbered suits of the Tarot deck.

To the cartomancer reading the deck as a serious matter of divination, the significance of each card turned up was qualified by the cards immediately surrounding it and by his own interpretations of their meaning, which, in turn, were often colored by the expectations of the client for whom he was divining.

Fascination with the Tarot pack did not stop with fashionable society. For those conjurers who could afford to buy a pack, it became an extensive source of all kinds of tricks and sleight of hand and increased their repertoires considerably.

By the end of the sixteenth century the fires of inquisitorial fervor began to be banked considerably, perhaps because—according to the French dramatist-philosopher Voltaire—witches ceased to exist as soon as men stopped burning them.

Europe was witnessing a renaissance of thought, a rebirth of intellectual curiosity and mechanical experimentation that had not been evident since the time of ancient Greece and Rome. Writers, painters, philosophers, and composers benefited from this new frame of mind. So did scientists and artisans and men of commerce, who were learning to deal with a world

vastly expanded by discovery and conquest of previously unknown lands.

Science was at the threshold of a new age; its mechanical miracles would fire the human imagination as the works of black magic had once fired the medieval imagination. This is not to say that interest in and superstitious fear of the occult had suddenly faded. On the contrary, new forms of divination or modernized forms of ancient ones continued to appear; for example, metoposcopy—divination from the markings of the forehead—and physiognomy—divination from characteristics and expressions of the human face.

A German-Austrian physician named Franz Anton

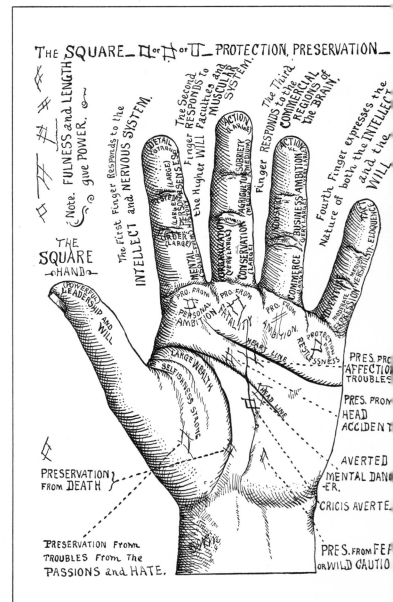

Chiromancy is one of the ancient arts of divination still practiced today. This nineteenth-century diagram of the hand was the chiromancer's guide to divination. It features the chief lines, mounts, and signs used in palmistry.

Frontispiece of an early seventeenth century grimoire filled with invocations to the demons. Various magic talismans appear above the title.

Mesmer, born in 1734, claimed to have the power—he called it animal magnetism—to heal with his hands. Mesmer's techniques were referred to as mesmerism, and out of this work developed hypnosis and faith healing and the beginnings of research into telepathy and spiritualism. The mysteries of clairvoyance and clairaudience—seeing and hearing that which is beyond the range of ordinary perception—traced back to the ancient Greek oracles and even beyond. Renewed interest in them in the eighteenth and nineteenth centuries would lead to later scientific research into many baffling phenomena of extrasensory perception. Even the practices of black magic, scourged as they were during the cataclysmic upheavals of the medieval era, would be resurrected in later times.

As this climate of change set the stage for the coming industrial age, it also set the stage for the conjurer. He slowly freed himself from the suspicions that had surrounded him and had often engulfed him in the fury directed against the practitioners of black magic. He began to be accepted for what he was—an entertainer, an actor, a performer of tricks and illusions, a presenter of deceptions designed simply to amuse and amaze his audience. He carried on an ancient tradition, one that seems to date back to prehistory.

The age of the black magician—follower of the secret and evil arts—was coming to an end. A new magician—an entertainer—was ready to take center stage.

Centuries-Old Rites and Rituals of Magic

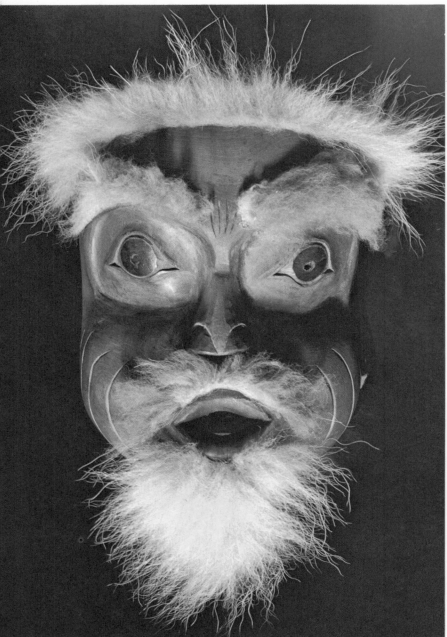

Symbols and ritual figures of magic in cultures around the world today include: feather-adorned Tsimshian mask (left) of the wind spirit; warrior-magician Bhima (above), a ritual figure from the Indian epic Ramayana, displayed by the priest in a temple compound in Bali, Indonesia; celebration of the eve of Saint Nicholas in the Austrian village of Bad Mitterndorf follows ancient pre-Christian rites, with figures dressed as supernatural creatures (below).

FROM THE FIRST MAGICIANS...

To Henry Westcar, archaeologist and admirer of the great and powerful kingdoms of ancient Egypt, the papyrus, which had been unearthed from an ancient tomb, was a major find.

Westcar acquired the scroll in Egypt in 1823 — it had been unearthed shortly before that date — and immediately he began to pore over the ancient writings, hoping to uncover new insights into the glorious civilization of ancient Egypt. What he uncovered when he completed his translation was the tale of a dazzling feat of magic performed around forty-five hundred years before by the conjurer Dedi at the royal court of Khufu, pharaoh of Egypt and builder of the Great Pyramid at Gizeh.

Westcar's papyrus turned out to be all that he had hoped. It shed new light on the kind of entertainment that had awed and delighted the mighty pharaoh. Even more, it clearly conveyed the unique and special status of the art of deception and of the conjurers who had practiced it.

According to the text, Dedi was something of a legend among men. He was said to be 110 years old and to have appetites rivaling those of the gods.

It was rumored that every day he ate five hundred loaves of bread and a shoulder of beef and drank a hundred flagons of beer. His very presence inspired fear among ordinary men. Even the mighty pharaoh requested — rather than commanded — the conjurer to appear before him.

It was in response to such a request, according to the text of the Westcar papyrus, that Dedi had come to the royal court to perform his magic for the pharaoh.

The place is the great stone palace at Memphis, residence of Khufu, King of All Egypt and Lord of the Three Worlds; the time, nearly five thousand years ago.

The man walks slowly but with great dignity past the motionless guards standing on either side of the entrance to the throne room. He is old, but he walks with a firm step, and there is something about him that seems to command immediate respect.

As he approaches the throne, the man sitting there leans forward almost unconsciously, as if drawn by the power that seems to emanate from the old man's eyes.

The old man is Dedi the wizard; the man on the throne is Khufu, pharaoh of Egypt.

"It has been told that you have the power to restore a severed head to its body," speaks the pharaoh to the magician.

"That I can do," nods Dedi.

"Then I will order a prisoner brought before us so that you may perform this wonder."

"My power does not extend to men," Dedi answers. "I only resurrect animals."

With a wave of his hand the pharaoh orders a goose brought to the conjurer. Dedi takes the goose and strokes it gently, as if calming it before the ordeal. Then he snatches a knife from under his robe, severs the bird's head, and places it in his open palm for the pharaoh to see.

As the pharaoh watches intently, Dedi appears to place the severed head back against the neck of the goose. He mutters a magic chant, shakes the goose lightly, and sets the bird on the floor.

The pharaoh's eyes widen in amazement as the goose stands up, settles its feathers, and slowly waddles away.

Yet, Dedi has still more wizardry to present to the astonished pharaoh. He repeats the same illusion with several other birds and, finally and spectacularly, with a live calf.

His command performance completed, Dedi bows to the pharaoh and takes his leave, knowing full well that his dazzling display of magic had been well received and that his fame would grow a thousandfold.

What the Westcar papyrus did not reveal was that the illusion which had amazed the great Khufu was an easy enough trick to perform if the conjurer came prepared with a duplicate of the "decapitated" head hidden under his robes. Nor did it tell of the honors and rewards that the pharaoh most probably showered on Dedi—not even a mighty king would dare to do less for such a powerful conjurer.

Yet, Dedi never pretended to be more than he was—a master conjurer who claimed no powers beyond his own highly developed skills of misdirection and

Khufu, pharaoh of Egypt, watches in amazement while the legendary conjurer Dedi releases a goose whose head he has just decapitated and magically restored. Dedi's conjuring feats were recorded by an unknown scribe at least a thousand years after they were performed; their spectacular effect was probably further enhanced by the scribe's wonderment at such marvels.

sleight of hand. Although their names are lost to history, there were some court conjurers who, like Dedi, practiced the art of honest deception.

There were others, however, who were not quite so honest, who turned their conjuring skills to devious ends. They were the high priests, temple soothsayers, and oracles of the great ancient civilizations.

These wonder-workers shunned the name — but not the techniques — of the conjurer. Like Dedi, they played on the superstitions of the people. Unlike Dedi, they claimed to possess supernatural powers.

They were, they told their gullible followers, agents of the gods. In order to prove it, they combined their jealously guarded knowledge of scientific phenomena with a generous helping of hocus-pocus to create dazzling illusions.

Their aim was to gain profit, prestige, and power for themselves. Their theater was the temple itself. Their illusions, to those who knew no better, seemed to be the inspiration, if not the work, of the gods themselves.

How else could the masses explain the mysterious doors of the great Egyptian Temple of Thunder, which sounded a great trumpet blast every time they opened although there was no trumpeter to be seen? Or the wonderful statue in the Temple of Isis, which actually poured wine on the altar fire as a libation to the gods? Or the marvelous temple vessels, which remained full no matter how much liquid was dipped from them?

The explanations came centuries later when the Greek scientist Hero of Alexander, around the first century A.D., detailed the laws of physics that made such awe-inspiring tricks possible.

The ancient world's closely guarded secret of the trumpeting doors was nothing more than a matter of simple mechanics, utilizing a chain and pulley device, a large trumpet, and a container of water.

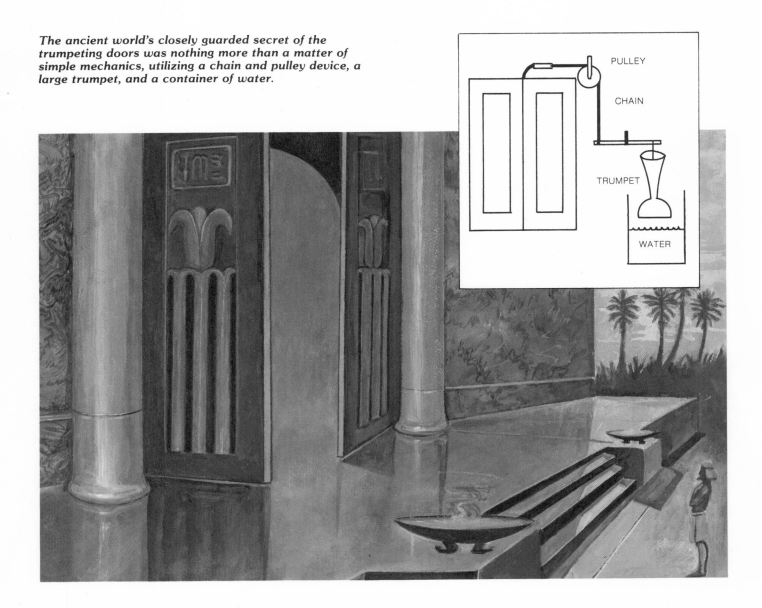

PULLEY

CHAIN

TRUMPET

WATER

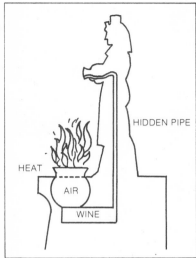

The wine-pouring statue in the ancient Egyptian Temple of Isis ingeniously applied a simple law of physics; that is, air when heated expands and then creates pressure.

The trumpeting temple doors, according to Hero, operated by means of a chain, which ran down a pulley connected to a lever, which, in turn, was attached to a trumpetlike device. When the temple door was opened, the chain triggered the lever, which dropped the trumpet into a container of water. The water then forced trapped air through the trumpet, creating an ear-splitting blast of sound.

The secret of the marvelous wine-pouring statue was a cleverly concealed pipe connected to a hidden wine reservoir. When the altar fire was lit, the heat from the fire expanded the air that was trapped in a special compartment just below the fire bowl. The resultant pressure from the expanded air forced the wine up through the hidden pipe until it miraculously poured onto the altar fire, although not enough to extinguish it.

When the temple priests extinguished the fire, the air cooled, the pressure was reduced, and the flow of wine automatically stopped. When another audience of devout worshipers entered the temple, the fire was relit and the wine flowed freely again.

The ever-full temple vessels, according to Hero's account, were based on the hydrostatic principle that water seeks its own level. A simple reservoir and plumbing system was all that was needed to create this temple "miracle."

While court conjurers like Dedi beguiled mighty kings and temple wonder-workers awed the masses, another kind of conjurer presented simpler entertainments to whatever audiences he could find. He was the wandering street conjurer, and his most popular trick, the cup and balls, was an ancient one even in Dedi's day. The origin of this oldest of all conjuring sleight of hand has been lost somewhere in the mists of history, but the trick has never lost its ability to delight and amaze the viewer.

The plot of the cups-and-balls trick is simplicity itself. Three empty cups are positioned facedown, and a small ball is put under one of them. The conjurer lifts the cup under which the ball was placed, and amazingly the ball is gone. He turns over another cup and discloses the missing ball. But when he turns the same cup over a second time, the ball has disappeared and reappears under the third cup.

Back and forth the little ball goes from cup to cup. Sometimes it pops out of the conjurer's mouth or even, to the delight of the audience, out of the ear or the nose of a bewildered spectator.

By the beginning of the first century A.D., the cups-and-balls routine was performed almost everywhere in the civilized world. Except for minor variations—for example, Egyptian and Hindu conjurers placed their cups on the ground, while those of Greece and Rome worked from a small table—the spectator saw the same trick.

Meanwhile, native American Indian conjurers in the New World had gone far beyond the simple cups-and-balls routines and were performing feats of magic that

The ageless fascination of the ancient cups-and-balls routine is captured in Bosch's painting L'Escamoteur. As a medieval spectator gasps in astonishment at the conjurer's deceptions, several of the conjurer's accomplices are pulling off a clever deception of their own.

rivaled and often surpassed those being presented in Europe and the Near East.

The place is the dry, rugged American Southwest; the time, over a thousand years ago.

The Navaho kiva—the special place set aside for tribal ceremonies—seems almost too small to hold all the braves who have gathered inside its earthen walls.

The fortunate ones have found room to squat near the front of the kiva; the others good-naturedly jostle for position near the back. All of them, from the oldest warrior to the youngest, lean forward in anticipation, waiting to see if the tribal magician can once again perform his wondrous feat of making an arrow dance.

The magician, resplendent in his ceremonial robes, arrives at last, and an expectant hush cuts off the last whispered sound.

Slowly the magician looks around. The flickering torchlight reveals an eager audience ready to accept whatever wonders he is about to present.

When all attention is focused on him, the magician nods his head almost imperceptibly, and two tall warriors, one on each side of the kiva, rise silently and move into predetermined positions along the side walls.

The magician spreads his arms wide and begins to intone a mysterious chant. He is calling on the spirits to aid him in the ritual. When the chant is ended, he picks up a small woven basket and places an arrow, tip down,

into it. He carefully positions the arrow so that the tip rests on one side of the bottom and the shaft rests against the top of the opposite side.

The magician sets the basket on the ground in front of him and casts his eyes over the audience once again.

With a sudden, dramatic gesture he points his finger at a young warrior sitting directly in front of the basket.

"Rise," he commands, "and dance!"

The warrior comes to his feet and begins to dance very slowly.

As the warrior takes his first few steps, the arrow seems to come alive. It rises on end in the basket and stands suspended before the wide-eyed dancer.

Hesitatingly the dancer sways to the left. The arrow instantly sways with him. The dancer sways to the right. Again the arrow sways with him.

The dancer picks up the tempo of his rhythmic swaying; so does the arrow. Grinning now, the dancer seems almost to be daring the arrow to follow his movements. He moves to the left twice and quickly sways back to the right. The arrow follows each move precisely—twice to the left and once to the right.

The contest between dancer and arrow continues while the warriors smile in appreciation. When both dancer and arrow stop, there are murmurs of disappointment—not in the performance, certainly, but because it has come to an end for another year.

The magician smiles in satisfaction; the two warriors

return unobtrusively to their seats. Only they and the magician know the work that went into knotting together a dozen or so individual strands of human hair to form the long, invisible wire that was attached to the top of the arrow and that made it dance each time it was pulled.

The dancing arrow was only one of many clever conjuring tricks developed by the Navaho tribal magicians. Other magicians from other tribes—there were almost a hundred distinct tribes scattered across the Western Hemisphere—developed their own repertoire of tricks and performed them exclusively for members of their own tribes.

Now and then an outsider was permitted to watch an Indian conjurer at work. Inevitably tales of the amazing magical abilities of native conjurers began to spread.

They were tales to challenge the imagination: unbelievable bullet-catching feats by Algonquin conjurers; magical vanishings by Apache conjurers of their young assistants from small woven baskets; corn and bean seeds that miraculously turned into full-grown plants in minutes in the hands of Hopi conjurers; marvelous doll-like figures that danced on the command of Toltecan conjurers; gory decapitations and miraculous restorations by Kwakiutl conjurers; and especially the astonishing ability of conjurers of many tribes to escape from all kinds of bindings.

Although the secrets of these conjuring feats and countless others like them were closely guarded by Indian conjurers, these illusions and tricks somehow managed to appear—in slightly different versions—in the repertoires of later conjurers in almost every part of the world.

As Christianity began to spread out from its birthplace in the Near East into Europe during the early Middle Ages, so did the practice and performance of magic. There were three distinctive forms, which followed the pattern already established in the ancient world: elegant court conjuring, simple street conjuring, and black magic, which, like temple magic, claimed supernatural powers.

An example of American Indian conjuring at its finest as a lithe young warrior challenges an arrow to duplicate his movements. Unseen is the tribal magician. Unseen by the rapt audience is a fine strand of knotted hair held by the magician's two assistants and used by them to make the arrow "dance."

Black magic, in particular, represented a major threat to the growth of Christianity. Therefore, pious churchmen of the Middle Ages launched ruthless campaigns against the practitioners of witchcraft, devil worship, and sorcery. Often, in their zeal to wipe out black magic, they punished and imprisoned conjurers who claimed no power beyond their own skills of legerdemain.

The ancient lure of magic, however, could not be erased quite so easily. Practitioners of the black arts and their followers continued to observe their esoteric rituals in secret, although in fewer numbers than before. Street conjurers continued to travel from one European city to the next, still presenting their theatrical amusements and sleight of hand wherever they could manage to attract an audience — without also attracting the stern disapproval of the authorities. The most skilled conjurers continued to perform in the royal courts, amusing their patrons and audiences with deft tricks and dazzling illusions.

One of the most spectacular of these medieval illusions was directly descended from the ancient decapitations that Dedi the Egyptian had performed; this time the victim was a young boy instead of a goose.

The boy was placed facedown on a large, boxlike table, and his head was covered with a large cloth. The conjurer dramatically drew a sharp knife and under cover of the cloth appeared to hack off the boy's head. He lifted the severed head, still hidden by the cloth, and placed it on the other end of the table.

With a flourish the conjurer lifted the cloth, exposing what seemed to be a living, breathing, moving head. With a second flourish he drew the attention of the audience to the headless body of the boy, lying still as death on the table.

There was, of course, a plausible explanation for this

An early eighteenth century magic-maker with some of his conjuring apparatus: the heavy draped table, the eerie skeleton and skull, the juggling monkey, the clown-faced assistant, and the inevitable magic wand.

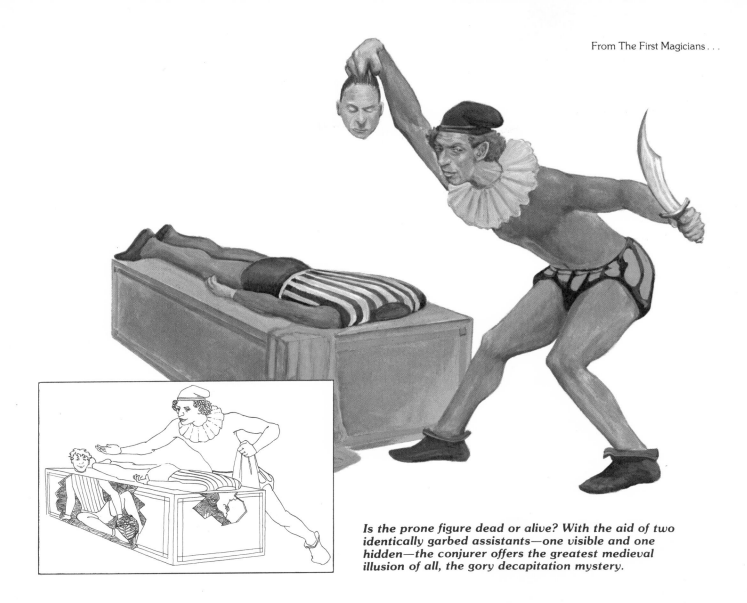

Is the prone figure dead or alive? With the aid of two identically garbed assistants—one visible and one hidden—the conjurer offers the greatest medieval illusion of all, the gory decapitation mystery.

glorious and gory illusion. The "decapitated" head *was* a living, breathing, moving one because it was attached to a second boy concealed beneath the table.

Although the actual operation of the illusion has never been fully detailed, it can be assumed that a series of cleverly concealed trapdoors, unseen by the audience, played a prominent part in its presentation.

The most likely explanation seems to be the following. While the conjurer was sawing away, the first boy ducked his head under the table through a well-concealed trapdoor, leaving only his headless body visible to the audience. When the conjurer placed the "severed" head—most probably a well-shaped cabbage—at the other end of the table, up popped the head of the second boy through another concealed trapdoor.

After the "disembodied" head amused the audience by talking, laughing, or rolling its eyes, the conjurer simply reversed the procedure. Down went the second

boy's head as cloth and cabbage were carried back to the first boy's prone body. The first boy pulled his head back up from another trapdoor, and after the conjurer pulled away the cloth for the last time, the boy rose from the table, miraculously restored to life.

Because illusions like the decapitation mystery required a certain amount of elaborate mechanical equipment in order to be presented successfully, they were generally limited to the repertoires of prominent court conjurers. Wandering street conjurers, not to be outdone, offered their own simpler—but equally gory—illusions.

Most of their torture tricks were based on the use of a double set of knifelike instruments called bodkins, one real and the other cleverly designed to look real.

After a magician announced to a half-believing audience that he was immune to all harm, he would then appear to thrust the fake bodkin into his forehead or arm or tongue or straight into his heart. Then, after

43

The frontispiece (right) *of a later edition of Reginald Scot's exposé* The Discoverie of Witchcraft, *originally published in 1584. Scot's book, a first attempt to separate the conjurer's craft from the wiles of black magic, was highly successful and was reprinted many times.*

A medieval conjurer (below) obviously successful—wears the elegant robes and high-pointed hat of a wizard.

THE
Difcovery of Witchcraft:
PROVING,
That the Compacts and Contracts of WITCHES with *Devils* and all *Infernal Spirits* or *Familiars*, are but Erroneous Novelties and Imaginary Conceptions.

Alfo difcovering, How far their Power extendeth in Killing, Tormenting, Confuming, or Curing the bodies of Men, Women, Children, or Animals, by Charms, Philtres, Periapts, Pentacles, Curfes, and Conjurations.

WHEREIN LIKEWISE
The Unchriftian Practices and Inhumane Dealings of *Searchers* and *Witch-tryers* upon *Aged, Melancholly,* and *Superftitious* people, in extorting Confeffions by Terrors and Tortures, and in devifing falfe Marks and Symptoms, are notably Detected.

And the Knavery of *Juglers, Conjurers, Charmers, Soothfayers, Figure-Cafters, Dreamers, Alchymifts* and *Philterers*; with many other things that have long lain hidden, fully Opened and Deciphered.

ALL WHICH
Are very neceffary to be known for the undeceiving of *Judges, Juftices,* and *Jurors,* before they pafs Sentence upon Poor, Miferable and Ignorant People; who are frequently Arraigned, Condemned, and Executed for *Witches* and *Wizards.*

IN SIXTEEN BOOKS.

By R E G I N A L D S C O T *Efquire.*

Whereunto is added
An excellent Difcourfe of the *Nature* and *Subftance*
O F
DEVILS, and SPIRITS,
IN TWO BOOKS:
The *Firft* by the aforefaid *Author:* The *Second* now added in this *Third Edition,* as Succedaneous to the *former,* and conducing to the compleating of the *Whole Work:* With *Nine Chapters* at the beginning of the *Fifteenth Book* of the *DISCOVERY.*

LONDON:
Printed for *Andrew Clark,* and are to be fold at Mris. *Cotes's* near the *Golden-Ball* in *Alderfgateftreet,* 1 6 6 5.

releasing the requisite amount of blood from a concealed sponge, the fake bodkin was withdrawn, leaving no trace of a wound.

The real bodkin was offered to the crowd for examination, and its deadly sharp point made believers of any who had doubted the conjurer's boast.

There were other tricks performed by street conjurers and court conjurers alike which amused medieval audiences throughout Europe. Sleight of hand with coins and cards was always popular; so was the ancient cups-and-balls routine and the cut-and-restored-rope trick, which featured a rope cut into several pieces and then magically made whole again.

The belief persisted that these conjuring tricks could not be performed, no matter how skilled the conjurer, without help from the devil or his agents. It was to combat this deep-seated belief in black magic that in 1584 an English justice of the peace named Reginald Scot published a treatise on conjuring titled *The Discoverie of Witchcraft.*

Scot's intention was to reveal the "vertue and power of naturall magike" by accurately explaining some of the conjuring feats of the day and stripping them once and for all of any connection with black magic. His explanations were so successful that the book is still being used by magicians today, more than four hundred years after it was written.

The Discoverie of Witchcraft opened the way for a series of how-to books dealing with conjuring. *The Art of Juggling,* published in 1612, further explained the tricks already described by Scot.

Still another of these explanatory books, titled *The Anatomy of Legerdemain; or, The Art of Jugling,* was published in London in 1634 under the pseudonym Hocus Pocus Junior. It, too, detailed a number of popular conjuring tricks, many of which are still being used today to entertain modern audiences. Just as important, the unknown author set out a brief and insightful definition of the successful conjurer ("description of the Operator") which is as valid today as it was then.

> First, he must be one of an impudent and audacious spirit, so that he may set a good face upon the matter.
>
> Secondly, he must have a nimble and cleanly conveyance.
>
> Thirdly, he must have strange terms, and emphatical words, to grace and adorn his actions, and the more, to astonish the beholders.
>
> Fourthly and lastly, such gestures of body as may lead away the spectators' eyes from a strict and diligent beholding of his manner of conveyance.

These how-to books often helped the individual conjurer to elevate his skills, whether he was attempting to learn a new and mystifying illusion or simply trying to improve his standard repertoire of tricks.

However, not even the most flamboyant skills could make the ancient art of conjuring—or those who practiced it—entirely respectable. There was still a lingering suspicion among the masses that the conjurer was somehow connected with the evil forces of black magic. This suspicion was reinforced by the conjurer's choice of traveling companions—jugglers, fire-eaters, bear trainers, rope dancers, charlatans, quacks, and other tricksters whose unsavory reputations often brought them into conflict with the law.

As street conjurers went from town to town, seeking audiences wherever they could find them, they were often greeted with mixed emotions. They were admired as entertainers; at the same time, they were often suspected of many kinds of fraudulent behavior, ranging from stealing a local farmer's chickens to sneaking out of town without paying their bills. Consequently their welcome was usually short-lived; their departures were often hasty and not always of their own choice.

This somewhat contradictory view of the conjurer as part gifted entertainer and part charlatan persisted throughout the seventeenth century. Yet, the art in Europe was constantly improving and advancing, steadily if slowly.

The street magician's so-called bag of tricks—a large, apronlike garment with pockets roomy enough to hold whatever apparatus he needed—was beginning to be recognized as a symbol of entertainment. His tricks and illusions were mystifying, perhaps, but, thanks to the books explaining the conjurer's art, they were no longer considered a result of supernatural powers.

In fact, some conjurers—a very few—were beginning to make a breakthrough as respectable entertainers.

One of the first of these "acceptable" magic-makers was Isaac Fawkes, perhaps the most famous of the early eighteenth century English conjurers.

Unlike his fellow conjurers who appeared at country fairs, marketplaces, local taverns, and barns, Fawkes hired a London theater for his act. In addition, he shrewdly advertised his performances to gather a larger audience and therefore gain more profit.

Those who came to see a Fawkes performance were not disappointed. They witnessed a masterful demonstration of sleight of hand: Fawkes produced gold coins and eggs and even a live chicken from a small cloth bag, and he performed a number of dazzling card deceptions, including one in which, in his own words, he caused the "whole pack to stick up to the ceiling and called them down by their Names, one by one."

Another conjurer who sought out fashionable audiences was the adroit German Philip Breslaw. He, too, was a skilled sleight of hand performer who conjured with cards, watches, silver coins, dice, handkerchiefs, and rings.

Breslaw may have been the author of a magic book entitled *Breslaw's Last Legacy*—at least his name appeared on the title page—which described several of his tricks. One of them was the production from a small cloth bag of at least a dozen eggs—one by one. After

The famous English fairgrounds in Southwark offered eighteenth-century conjurers an ideal stage for their presentations of magic. In this Hogarth painting Isaac Fawkes, far right with bird in hand, is preparing to offer one of his deft deceptions.

the eggs were stacked neatly together, Breslaw shook the cloth bag again and out came a hen.

Still another conjurer who found acceptance among the wealthy and titled of Europe was the Prussian Gustavus Katterfelto. Somewhat of a charlatan, Katterfelto claimed to have a cat with supernatural powers, and he often began his performances with lectures on natural philosophy and secrets of the occult.

Affecting the dress of an academician and calling himself professor, Katterfelto nevertheless conjured with the same materials as his contemporaries—dice, cards, coins, rings, and handkerchiefs.

These notable eighteenth-century conjurers shared more in common than just their props. They advertised their skills to attract audiences. Since the only people who could afford to buy newspapers were wealthy, they attracted rich audiences. They were the first conjurers to charge admission to their performances—two shillings was the usual entrance fee in England—and therefore the first conjurers to elevate their art from the hubbub of the street scene.

They were the exceptions rather than the rule. It was another half-century before the ancient art achieved true respectability.

While the conjurers of Europe were struggling to elevate their craft into a respectable and legitimate profession, anyone who attempted to pursue the art of deception on the North American continent faced a different struggle.

Those who dared to display their conjuring skills in

Jacob Philadelphia (above), *the first native-born non-Indian conjurer to come from the American colonies, never performed there. Instead, under the aegis of the English Duke of Cumberland he made his reputation as a master conjurer by performing in Europe.*

the American colonies—at least during the first century of their founding—risked being lashed or clapped into stocks by the authorities.

The straitlaced early colonists were convinced that any diversion, whether presented by actors or conjurers or performers of any kind, was harmful to the human soul. The obsessive witch-hunting that took place in Massachusetts during the last decades of the seventeenth century showed how deeply ingrained the fear of black magic was. In such a climate the practitioner of the conjuring art stood little chance of finding a suitable place in which to perform, let alone an audience willing to watch his performance.

Somehow, against all odds, a non-Indian American conjurer did appear, although he made his appearances and reputation in Europe.

His name was Jacob Meyer; he was born in Philadelphia, Pennsylvania, of immigrant parents but later went to England. By the time he was a teenager he had developed the ability to perform mystifying sleight of hand tricks, and he had gained the patronage of the Duke of Cumberland.

By age twenty-one Meyer had taken the name of Jacob Philadelphia—he sometimes billed himself as Philadelphus Philadelphia—and was already gaining a

The obsessive witch-hunting of Massachusetts colonists was not centered exclusively on girls and women. The painting (below) by T. H. Mattison depicts the 1692 trial of accused warlock George Jacobs, far right, being restrained by a court man-at-arms.

reputation in England as a deft and amusing conjurer.

From England, Philadelphia traveled to the European continent and made a successful tour. He presented a number of clever card tricks, a series of adroit sleight of hand with eggs, and a dramatic illusion —with the help of a magic lantern—of ghostly figures that seemed to materialize mysteriously on the darkened stage.

Philadelphia's somewhat pompous and grandiloquent presentation of his repertoire won him a few detractors—in particular, Georg Christoph Lichtenberg, a physics professor at the University of Göttingen in Germany, whose brilliant parody of Philadelphia's performance announcements made him cancel his scheduled appearance. Yet, Philadelphia's unquestioned conjuring skills also won him the admiration of many of Europe's rich and famous.

For all his European fame, Philadelphia never returned to the land of his birth and never performed in his native country. As the stringent laws against conjuring began to be repealed in the American colonies, other European magicians made the long trip across the ocean to perform there, and they gained a fair amount of acclaim for their skills.

Yet, the Puritan ethic persisted. The ancient art of honest deception may have been permitted in the American colonies, but it was never welcomed. It was almost a full century before the American continent produced another native-born non-Indian conjurer.

While the seventeenth- and eighteenth-century conjurers of the Western world continued to polish their skills, develop their illusions, and gain a higher degree of acceptance as legitimate entertainers, the fabled conjurers and illusionists of India and the Orient had already made a place for themselves in their own societies.

The magic of the East, like that of the West, boasted a long and ancient history. For the most part, that history had been an honorable one and the oriental magic-maker was widely respected for his skills.

Tales of those extraordinary skills had already begun to filter to Europe through the writings of the thirteenth-century Venetian adventurer Marco Polo and the English author of the fourteenth century known as Sir John Mandeville.

Polo's accounts were based on his own personal experiences in the court of Kublai Khan, the great Mongol emperor of China; Mandeville's, which were purported to be the author's, were actually compiled from the highly exaggerated witnessings of travelers who had returned from the Orient.

Whether based on eyewitness reports or secondhand information, these accounts were so incredible—the tricks and illusions seemed so miraculous—that they convinced many Europeans that the only real wonder-workers of the universe were Eastern conjurers.

For hundreds of years this exaggerated standard was the yardstick against which Western conjurers were judged. It was an unfair judgment, of course, but it was not rectified until much later, at the beginning of the twentieth century, when Western conjurers began touring the Orient to entertain and at the same time seek out the secrets of these legendary illusions.

What these touring conjurers discovered was that the feats of the oriental magicians had been grossly exaggerated. What they also discovered were a number of performable tricks that were still mystifying enough to dazzle and delight audiences in the West.

It was inevitable that Eastern and Western magic would eventually influence each other. Eastern audiences would marvel at the conjuring of visiting occidental magicians; Western audiences would be dazzled by updated versions of ancient oriental tricks and illusions.

The time might be the distant past or the twentieth century; the place, the bustling city of Calcutta.

The dusty street, deserted only a few minutes previously, now teems with life as the jadoo wallah—the oriental counterpart of the medieval European conjurer—appears.

As he positions himself carefully on the ground, the jadoo wallah looks over the gathering crowd and smiles to himself. Some of the onlookers appear to be quite prosperous. If they are as generous with their annas as he hopes they will be, the jadoo wallah can expect a most profitable afternoon.

When the crowd seems at a point of keen anticipation, the jadoo wallah begins his performance. His first trick is a simple but effective one; it is enhanced by his clever line of patter as he goes about his work.

As he talks, he places a number of small bowls, each filled with a different color sand, on the ground in front of him. He scoops several handfuls of sand from each of the small bowls and places them in a large bowl filled with water. A swish of the water with a pointed stick blends the colored sand—red, blue, yellow, green—into a muddy, darkish-brown solution.

The jadoo wallah then turns to the audience.

"Speak the name of a color," he says.

"Blue," says a young man.

The jadoo wallah reaches into the muddy water and pulls out a fistful of wet sand. He closes his eyes, recites some mystic words, gives the wet blob in his fist a final

The Hindu fakirs of India were, like the jadoo wallahs, reputed to have uncanny magical powers. However, the traditional magic of the fakirs was much more dramatic and was highlighted by their purported ability to perform such tremendous feats as those pictured here (clockwise from top): the marvelous midair levitation; the spectacular human chimney; and the incredible Hindu eye-lift.

Metal rod cradles fakir's body
(rod disguised to look like cane)

Sides slant inward, holding disk
securely; air space below protects
fakir's head from heat

Metal eye cup fits under eyelid

Fine wire is attached to
the article to be lifted

squeeze; miraculously a trickle of dry blue sand slowly escapes from between his fingers.

Again and again he calls for a color from the audience. Each time the wet sand from the bowl is changed to sparkling, dry sand in the color requested.

The audience gasps and the jadoo wallah smiles. His morning activities — preparing wads of each color of sand, covering them with grease, and baking them until they become solid — will pay off handsomely. By surreptitiously slipping the hardened wads into the bowl of water in just the right places, he has made his trick a success once more.

The performance continues, with each trick appearing more difficult than the last. Finally the jadoo wallah is ready to present his finest illusion — a mango tree that will grow from a sprout to a full six feet while the audience looks on in amazement.

He sets up three poles to form a tripod and centers a large, earth-filled pot under the tripod. He plants a mango seed in the pot and spreads a large cloth over the tripod, forming a kind of tent.

Moments later he removes the cloth; a small sprout has already appeared where the seed was planted. The cloth is again placed around the tripod; it is removed, and the sprout is almost a foot tall. Again and again the cloth is placed and removed, and every time the cloth is taken away there is another startling leap in growth.

The jadoo wallah removes the cloth for the last time to reveal a fully grown mango tree laden with fruit. Not one person in the audience is aware that under cover of the cloth the jadoo wallah has substituted a series of mango branches, each one bigger than the last, to create his marvelous illusion.

The jadoo wallahs of India performed these and other simple street tricks in exactly the same way they had been performed generation after generation for centuries.

A more dramatic kind of traditional magic was also handed down from one generation to the next by the fakirs of India — members of an ancient Hindu caste with a centuries-old reputation as holy men.

Hindu fakirs were reputed to have uncanny powers, including the ability to withstand the most incredible self-inflicted tortures. These powers supposedly formed the basis of the spectacular illusions that foreign travelers described when they returned to the Western world.

If those reports were to be believed, Hindu fakirs could actually lift tremendous weights with their eyes; they could withstand the scorching heat from roaring fires in clay cylinders perched on top of their heads; they could make young boys placed within small woven baskets disappear and then make them suddenly appear again; they could float in midair at will, defying the laws of gravity; they could make a boy vanish from the top of a rope suspended, unbelievably, in the air.

Or could they?

A pair of metal eye cups, painted to resemble real eyes — as well as a set of hooks, invisible to the viewer, that are attached to the fakir's knees — may well have accounted for the astonishing eye lifts.

A clay disk, inserted in a specially designed clay cylinder, forced heat and flames up and away from the head of the fakir.

The deceptive design of the woven basket made it possible for the agile young boy to squirm into a certain position and appear to have vanished.

Spectacular as it was, the midair levitation was always presented with the fakir sitting in the same position — and for a good reason.

His hand, which was resting on what appeared to be a cane set in a small stool, was actually resting on a metal rod fitted firmly into the stool. The rod, in turn, was just as firmly connected to a concealed metal support, which easily cradled the fakir's suspended body.

What about the fabled Indian rope trick? What hidden secret made possible this most fabulous of illusions?

"Legend," claimed the Times of India, *which in 1934 offered a large cash reward for "an actual, genuine, and unchallengeable" performance of the fabled Indian rope trick. That sizable reward has gone uncollected to this day.*

A version of the ancient Japanese ritual of hi-watari—this one performed in modern-day India by devotees of the Hindu mother goddess Kali.

The trick is simple enough to describe. A Hindu fakir tosses one end of a long rope high into the sky. The rope rises slowly into the air, and the fakir orders a nimble young boy to climb it. The boy climbs steadily until he is far above the crowd. At the fakir's command the boy suddenly vanishes, and the rope crumples to the ground in a heap.

This ancient illusion was already legend long before the beginnings of India's written history. It was mentioned in Indian writings that date back at least thirty centuries. It was reported to Marco Polo during his travels through the Orient. It was supposedly witnessed in China sometime around 1350 A.D. by Abu-Abdullah Mohmed, a visiting Arab sheikh, and startled him so much that he nearly had a heart attack. It was illustrated in a German book published in 1684 and purportedly eyewitnessed by the father of the builder of the Taj Mahal.

Other versions of the ancient illusion—as they have been reported by men of unchallenged integrity—defy credibility even further. One in particular is especially gory.

According to this bloodcurdling version, the fakir becomes angry when the boy refuses to descend the rope on command. The fakir, knife between his teeth, decides to climb up after him. Eventually both man and boy disappear. Then, one by one, pieces of the boy's body come tumbling to the ground. They are soon followed by the fakir himself, who reassembles the severed parts of the boy's anatomy on the ground. He chants some mystical words, and miraculously the boy is restored to wholeness and life.

There have been countless explanations of the secret behind this fabulous illusion, although most of them are as unbelievable as the trick itself. Some claim that the fakir hypnotizes the entire audience before he begins his performance. Others claim that before performing the trick the fakir waits until the moment just before sunset, when brilliant light almost blinds the spectators. Others suggest the use of a thin, strong wire stretched to a point at least twenty feet above the ground or some kind of trick rope with a hollowed-out center to accommodate a long steel rod. Still others insist that the trick is nothing more than a popular myth, perpetuated through the centuries by witnesses whose imaginations have been stimulated by what they expected to see rather than by what they actually did see.

Either way—myth or marvel—every attempt to reproduce this fabulous trick as described in the ancient writings of India has ended in failure.

The fakirs of India may have been the greatest illusionists of the Eastern world, but they were not the only holy men reputed to be able to withstand incredible physical hardships. The Shinto priests of ancient Japan practiced a number of rituals that seemed to stretch human endurance to the breaking point.

One of the most famous of these—it later became the inspiration for a standard conjuring trick—was the ancient ritual of hi-watari, that is, striding barefoot across a bed of burning coals without so much as raising a single blister.

The priests used no preparations or salves on the soles of their feet, which were already well calloused. However, they waited until a thick layer of ashes covered the red-hot coals before they began their walk. Once they began, they walked steadily but swiftly.

Whether the ashes served as insulation or the fire itself was banked in such a way as to draw heat from

51

the middle, the priests completed their walk unharmed.

This kind of ritualistic magic, based on religious custom, remained unfathomable to the Western mind for centuries. Yet, many Western-style tricks were adapted from these startling rites and became crowd pleasers wherever they were performed.

The repertoire of Chinese conjurers was another source of inspiration for their Western counterparts. One ancient trick, a delightful deception called Linking Rings, was a fine example of the Chinese way with the conjuring art.

As presented by generations of skilled Chinese conjurers—and later by equally skilled Westerners—the trick features a set of ten specially designed hoops or rings. Four of the rings are entirely separate; one set of two rings is linked together; another set of three rings is also linked together; the tenth ring has a concealed opening which permits any of the other rings to be joined to it.

With great dexterity and amusing nonchalance the conjurer links and unlinks the rings, creating ingenious designs such as a globe, a lotus blossom, a waterfall, or whatever else his fertile imagination and nimble fingers can devise.

The delight of this simple deception is that four of the rings—not the linked sets or the ring with the concealed opening, of course—have already been inspected by the audience and found to be solid. Yet, there stands the conjurer, linking and unlinking the rings with ease.

While the conjuring of India and the Orient, for all its mystifying tricks and illusions, continued to be presented in the same centuries-old manner, something new was happening to the magic-maker's art in Europe.

The time was the beginning of the eighteenth century; the precipitating event was the Industrial Revolution. Rapid advances in science and technology had already produced such marvels as steam engines and power-driven spinning and weaving machines. This knowledge provided European conjurers with the technical know-how to create another kind of marvel—automata, which were mechanical figures skillfully contrived to perform various magical feats.

While some men invented locomotives and steam-powered shovels and the tools of an industrialized society, others built automatic ducks and chess players and mechanical fountains capable of spouting forth unending streams of liquid on command.

This partnership of science and conjuring was an ancient one, dating back to the days of the first temple magicians. In this new age of technology, however, the partnership reached even greater heights of creativity.

The Frenchman Jacques de Vaucanson, born in Grenoble on February 24, 1709, was one of the first of these ingenious tinkerers.

Vaucanson's automatic flute player, exhibited in Paris in 1738, was a phenomenon of mechanical perfection. It stood five and a half feet tall, moved its fingers and lips like a living musician, and was capable of playing twelve different tunes without being touched by human hands.

A second Vaucanson automaton, a duck, was so cleverly designed that it quacked, ate, drank, and even appeared to breathe. It was so lifelike that one viewer, a Scottish physicist, called it "the most wonderful piece of mechanism ever made."

Thirty years later a Hungarian nobleman named Baron Wolfgang von Kempelen built a chess-playing automaton which dazzled and amazed most of Europe and triggered more than fifty years of controversy.

Kempelen's chess player was designed in the form of a Turkish pasha seated on a bench behind a large table. The tabletop was marked with an inlaid chessboard, and the many-doored cabinet below presumably held the mechanism necessary to operate the automaton.

The whole operation appeared to be perfection itself as the automaton took on—and usually defeated—the leading chess players of Europe and America.

How could a mechanical contraption, no matter how ingeniously designed, manage to beat skilled human

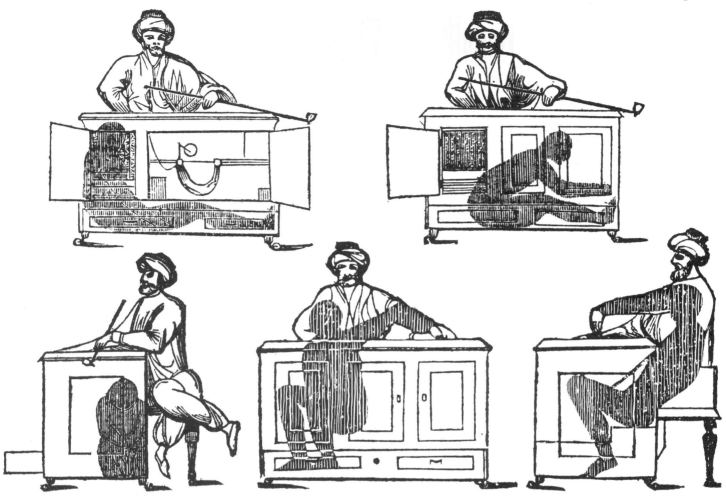

American writer Edgar Allan Poe was convinced that Baron von Kempelen's marvelous chess-playing automaton concealed a real chess player. Was he right? This series of sketches shows how a man could have been concealed inside the automaton.

players with such remarkable regularity? Perhaps there was an assistant concealed somewhere inside the cabinet or inside the figure itself?

The Turk was much smaller than life-size — certainly too small to hide a man. When the doors of the cabinet were opened for viewing — one by one in a set sequence — there appeared to be insufficient room for anyone to hide, except perhaps a midget. There was no midget traveling with the Turk and company or coincidentally appearing on the same bill.

For more than half a century the Turk and his owners toured throughout Europe and America. The owners amassed a considerable fortune, and, despite all speculation, not once did they disclose the secret of the amazing automaton's success.

Finally Edgar Allan Poe, the American writer, thought that he had definitely found the answer. There *was* a man concealed inside the cabinet — a superb chess player named Wilhelm Schlumberger — who positioned himself in such a way that he was never visible to the audience when the doors were opened.

What had given Poe his solution to the fifty-year-old mystery? He noticed that Schlumberger, supposedly an assistant, always disappeared during the Turk's performance. He also noticed that the times the Turk lost a chess match coincided with the times Schlumberger reappeared after the performance more than a little drunk. Had Poe actually solved the long-standing mystery of the Turk? Logic says he did.

Several years later, however, the amazing automaton was destroyed by a warehouse fire, and the answer to the mystery was buried somewhere in the ashes.

Although cleverly contrived automata like the chess-playing Turk added a new and spectacular dimension to conjuring, the art itself was still a long way from achieving respectability.

A few early eighteenth century conjurers won some

degree of fame and fortune by performing for the amusement of the nobility. A few sleight of hand experts, by advertising their skills in advance, were able to draw fair-sized crowds to the taverns and theaters where they were performing.

The majority of conjurers, however, were still itinerant wanderers, presenting their limited repertoires to whatever crowds they could muster, playing for the few coins that were thrown at their feet.

The street conjurer's inability to gain broad public acceptance as a performing artist traced directly to his stock-in-trade, deception. His skills were based on the same principles of deception that were used disreputably by charlatans, mountebanks, and practitioners of black magic. The only difference, which the general public had not yet perceived, was that conjurers deceived to entertain, and charlatans deceived for their own devious ends.

By the middle of the eighteenth century two dynamic men, by their dramatic actions, focused the attention of the public on the uses and abuses of deception. One was the Italian Giuseppe Balsamo, the last of the great charlatans. The other was also Italian, Giovanni Giuseppe Pinetti, the first of the great modern conjurers.

Giuseppe Balsamo, better known by his self-styled title, Alessandro, Conte di Cagliostro, was born into poverty in Palermo, Sicily, in 1743. He became a daring adventurer whose energy, intelligence, imagination, and charm would have made him a success in almost any endeavor. Unfortunately the practice he chose was charlatanry.

Early in life he was summarily dismissed from a monastery for incorrigibility. He ended his career deep in a dungeon under a sentence of life imprisonment. Between those two events he became perhaps the cleverest charlatan the world had known.

Under the title Conte di Cagliostro he roamed widely through Europe and Asia, posing as a physician, a writer, an alchemist, a mesmerist, or anything his fancy or the expediency of the moment demanded.

Cagliostro's victims were the wealthiest, the most powerful, and the noblest of Europe because, as he had learned early in his career, they were the only ones worth defrauding. Defraud them he did — by conjuring visions of the dead or appearing to synthesize gold and diamonds or predicting the future or magically curing the sick. Despite his deceptions, European aristocrats continued to lionize him, and mobs of common people fawned over him wherever he went.

For a time he wore the most elegant robes and lived in a magnificent house furnished for him by Cardinal de Rohan, who unfortunately became involved in one of his machinations. Cagliostro claimed to possess the secret of eternal youth and tried to prove it by citing the example of his beautiful wife. She was, according to Cagliostro, over sixty years of age; in actuality she was barely in her twenties.

He pulled off his amazing deceptions by means of a dramatic personality, a knowledge of psychology, an agile brain, skillful sleight of hand, and a total lack of conscience. Except for the matter of conscience, he was the personification of the perfect conjurer defined more than a century before by the author of *The Anatomy of Legerdemain.*

JOSEPH BALSAMO

Né a Palerme le 8 juin 1743 et Condamné à Rome en 1791.

During his life, which spanned just over a half century, Giuseppe Balsamo, the self-styled Count of Cagliostro, went from obscurity to fame to infamy as a master charlatan.

One of the highlights of Professor Pinetti's conjuring performances was the sensational feat of nailing a card to the wall by means of a pistol shot. Also evident is Pinetti's elegant costume and stage decor.

Inevitably Cagliostro's deceptions were uncovered. He was driven out of most of the capitals of Europe; finally charged with, and found guilty of, heresy and sorcery, he was sent to the prison where he died.

His blatant deceptions, along with the widespread publicity given to them, at last convinced the masses that the black arts—evoking dead spirits, turning base metal into gold, calling on supernatural powers to predict the future—were nothing more than clever frauds. In the hands of a master like Cagliostro, such frauds had deceived some of the most prominent, most sophisticated people in the world.

Cagliostro's dismal end, coming after such flamboyant successes, convinced most charlatans and mountebanks to develop new techniques of deception. They no longer dared to call themselves miracle-workers; that ruse had been discredited by Cagliostro. Thus, the stage was set for the conjurer—that creator of honest and entertaining deception—to take over.

The first conjurer to claim that role was Giovanni Giuseppe Pinetti, born in Orbitello, Tuscany, in 1750, seven years after the birth of Cagliostro.

Like his flamboyant countryman, Pinetti also possessed energy, intelligence, imagination, charm, and the same colossal ability to deceive. Fortunately, he chose to entertain people rather than fleece them.

The knack for entertaining first came to light in the Roman classroom where Pinetti taught physics and mathematics. Seeking a novel way to instruct his students, he devised a series of unusual physics demonstrations. When even his most reluctant students were amused by these strange and mystifying demonstrations, Pinetti began performing them for his friends. They were equally amused and urged him to present them publicly.

Pinetti's decision to do so may well have been influenced by accounts of a French conjurer named Comus, who had earned no less than five thousand pounds for a two-week performance in a rented room in London. Since five thousand pounds was far more than a Roman schoolteacher could hope to make even after years in a classroom, Pinetti decided to become a conjurer.

No more than fifteen years later Pinetti was able to claim extraordinary success. He had conjured before German nobility; he had created a sensation at the court of Louis XVI of France by deftly removing the shirt of a gentleman in the audience without so much as ruffling the man's coat.

Like Cagliostro, Pinetti glorified himself with a number of impressive titles, the fanciest of which was Chevalier M. Josêph Pinetti Willedale de Merci, Knight

A portrait of Pinetti's nemesis, Henri Decremps, author of **The Conjurer Unmasked.**

The frontispiece of the English edition of Pinetti's book, written to counter an exposé of his conjuring methods by Henri Decremps.

of the German Order of Merit of Saint Philip, Professor of Mathematics and Natural Philosophy, Pensioned by the Court of Prussia, Patronized by All the Royal Family of France, Aggregate of the Royal Academy of Sciences and Belles Lettres of Bordeaux, and so on. Although most of these titles were patently false, Pinetti's conjuring skills were quite real.

In December 1783, at the Theatre des Menus-Plaisirs du Roi in Paris, Pinetti opened a full-length show of conjuring which soon became the talk of the town. He presented a program of twenty-three tricks in a magnificent stage setting almost as impressive as the tricks themselves.

The stage was covered with an elegant carpet. The backdrop was hung with curtains of the finest silk; two enormous crystal chandeliers lighted the entire stage. A pair of massive tables, covered with scarlet cloths embroidered with silver and gold threads, were placed downstage. A long table at the rear of the stage held Pinetti's conjuring apparatus, which were beautifully crafted of silver and gold instead of the usual brass and tin.

After giving the audience enough time to admire the splendid setting, Pinetti—dressed elegantly in rich court costume—strode onstage to perform his wonders.

He ordered an assistant to tie his thumbs together with cord and conceal his hands under a hat. Instantly he slipped one hand free, reached out to drink a glass of water, then tossed the glass toward the ceiling where it miraculously changed into confetti.

He presented a bell-ringing automaton, called the Grand Sultan, which answered questions asked by the audience. He presented another automaton, a mechanical bird, which flapped its wings, blew out and relit a candle, and warbled any tune requested by the audience.

He appeared to make eggs hop from one hat to another, playing cards rise from the pack, knives suddenly leap out of ornate crystal goblets.

He showed a golden head which moved on his command, even though it was inside a crystal box covered with a silver lid.

He presented the illusion of an orange tree which uncannily bore fruit after he sprinkled it with a mysterious fluid.

He presented all twenty-three tricks with such elegance and flair his audiences did not realize that many of them were simply more stylish versions of feats presented by other conjurers.

Pinetti was complimented by King Louis XVI himself;

tickets to his performances were sold out weeks in advance; he was feted and lionized by the crème de la crème of Parisian society. He was, in short, a smashing success in Paris and for more than a year he reveled in it.

In March 1784 a French professor and amateur conjurer named Henri Decremps wrote a book that claimed to expose the secrets of an Italian magician called Pilferer, whose repertoire bore a remarkable resemblance to that of Pinetti.

In the book, entitled *La Magie blanche devoilee* (published in English as *The Conjurer Unmasked*), Decremps declared that Pilferer's bell-ringing sultan was controlled by wires operated by an offstage assistant; that the same assistant, using a concealed speaking trumpet, was responsible for the mechanical bird's warbling; and that both devices were copies of automata developed by other conjurers.

According to Decremps's exposé, invisible threads accounted for the hopping eggs and rising cards and leaping knives.

One by one, Decremps offered his own solutions for every one of Pinetti's twenty-three tricks. Some of his explanations were wrong, but that made little difference. Decremps's exposé effectively cut back

Pinetti's audiences and triggered a bitter feud between the two men.

In retaliation Pinetti hired a seedy-looking tramp to pass himself off as Decremps at every performance and serve as the butt of Pinetti's ridicule. Decremps countered by writing additional exposés of Pinetti's methods. Pinetti in turn wrote his own book exposing the mistakes in Decremps's exposé.

Finally Pinetti decided to end his Paris run. He retreated from the public eye to develop a new conjuring program and reopened his revised show several months later in London.

Surprisingly, the intense feud between the two men had several positive results. It helped Pinetti become the most influential conjurer of his time and led hundreds of other conjurers to copy his dramatic style. It aroused widespread public interest in the conjuring art. It especially stimulated the interest of scientists, whose knowledge helped refine and perfect new techniques of illusion.

In time these scientifically based illusions elevated the art of conjuring to the rank of superb entertainment, and the men who performed them became even more famous than kings.

BRESLAW'S New CAPITAL PERFORMANCES will be displayed,

AT the Great Room, PANTON STREET. HAY-MARKET, on MONDAYS, WEDNESDAYS, FRIDAYS, and SATURDAYS; and likewise at Mr. Loft's Great Room, late KING's ARMS TAVERN, CORNHILL, on TUESDAYS and THURSDAYS, in each place to begin precisely at seven o'clock.

Part I. Mr. Breslaw will exhibit his new invented Magical Card Deceptions, Letters, Numbers, Dice, Handkerchiefs, Rings, Pocket Pieces, &c. &c. and particularly he will communicate the thoughts from one person to another, without asking any questions.

Part II. Two Favourite Songs by a Young LADY, and several amazing DECEPTIONS by a Pupil of Mr. Breslaw's.

Part III. The celebrated Miss ROSOMOND, a Child about eleven years of age, will deliver a SATYRICAL LECTURE on HEADS, the particulars of which will be expressed in the bills.

Part IV. Mr. Breslaw will display a variety of new Deceptions, with six different Metals, Magical Watches, Gold Boxes, Silver Cup, Caskets, Glass and Silver Machinery, &c. &c. and particularly with a new grand Apparatus and Experiments, not to be equalled in Europe.

In each place the doors to be opened at six o'clock, and to begin at seven.

The Rooms will be kept warm, and elegantly illuminated.

Admittance Two Shillings each person.

Tickets and Places to be taken at the places of performance.

N.B. Any person inclinable to learn some Deceptions on reasonable terms, may apply to Mr. Breslaw, No. 57, Haymarket.

THis is to give Notice to all Gentlemen Ladies and others, that on Monday the 18 of March at the House of Charles Sleigh, in Duke-Street is to be seen the famous German Artist, who is to perform the Wonders of the World by Dexterity of Hand: The Things he performs are too many to be enumerated here. He here with invites all to be Spectators of his Ingenuity, 1 s. 9 d. & 6 d. is the Price for Admitance. He begins at 7 o' Clock in the Evening. To be continued every Night in the Week. Saturday Nights excepted. to be performed by. Joseph Broome.

Early eighteenth century newspaper announcements of conjuring performances. Above: from the New York Journal, *March 18, 1734, the first known record of a magician's appearance in New York. Left: a 1727 announcement in a London newspaper of a performance by the adroit Philip Breslaw.*

COLONIAL Theatre
TWO WEEKS BEGINNING MONDAY SEPT. 24
Matinees WEDNESDAY and SATURDAY
THURSTON'S
GREATEST MYSTERY
The
VANISHING WHIPPET
Willys-Overland
CAR
THE WONDER SHOW OF THE UNIVERSE
"MADE IN U.S.A."
THE OTIS LITHO. CO. CLEVELAND, OHIO — 0-1889

. . .TO THE MASTERS OF MAGIC

As the eighteenth century drew to a close, the art of conjuring began to take on a new look in Europe.

Conjurers were no longer automatically linked with black magic in the popular imagination. They were not as quickly suspected of being agents of the devil who cavorted with ghosts and witches, but they were not yet respectable either.

For the most part, the conjuring art remained in the somewhat grimy hands of itinerant practitioners, whose repertoires were usually limited to the simple sleight of hand and whatever else they could extract from their ample bag of tricks.

They still performed in the open air — on street corners, at local fairs, wherever they could gather an audience. More often than not, they still moved on to the next town barely one jump ahead of their creditors.

There were exceptions, of course, and at the end of the eighteenth century these more-professional conjurers began to increase in number.

There was the English sleight of hand expert Isaac Fawkes, whose illusion of a tree suddenly blooming and bearing fruit was staged many years before the brilliant Italian Giovanni Giuseppe Pinetti presented a similar illusion.

There was the extravagant Jacob Philadelphia, born Jacob Meyer in Pennsylvania in 1734, who won fame conjuring for European royalty.

There was the Prussian Gustavus Katterfelto, who performed tricks with dice, cards, and coins while giving "learned" lectures on the natural sciences.

There was Comus, the Frenchman Nicholas Philippe Ledru, whose conjuring earned him more than enough to open his own theater in Paris and whose moneymaking talents inspired Pinetti to take up the ancient art.

There was Pinetti himself, who became eighteenth-century Europe's leading conjurer by presenting updated versions of other conjurers' tricks in a fabulous stage setting.

These fashionable conjurers were the exception rather than the rule. In general, conjuring in the eighteenth century remained not so much an art as a flim-flam designed to beguile the masses in order to gain a handful of coins.

It was not until the middle of the nineteenth century that a French conjurer appeared who changed all that. With skill, intelligence, and exquisite taste he raised the performance of magic to a dramatic and sophisticated art and set the stage for a century-long golden age of magic.

Early eighteenth century etching (right) of Isaac Fawkes, who produced dozens of eggs and a live hen from a seemingly empty cloth bag.

The Innovator
Jean Eugène Robert-Houdin

The great innovator Jean Eugène Robert-Houdin in his favorite portrait.

The date was Thursday, July 3, 1845; the time, early evening; the place, an intimate, new two-hundred-seat theater of magic in the Palais Royal in Paris.

A less-than-capacity crowd, lured by the billboards that had been posted around the city, impatiently awaited the premiere performance of Jean Eugène Robert-Houdin, former law student, watchmaker, and tinkerer, and now, by his own declaration, a master of magic.

For forty-year-old Robert-Houdin (who was born Jean Eugène Robert but added his wife's surname upon marriage) this first public performance as a professional conjurer was to be the realization of a dream that had begun twenty years before when he received, quite by accident, two books on magic.

In those twenty years Robert-Houdin's fascination with magic had led him step by step to this night. Now,

rehearsed to perfection, he was ready to march onstage and present his first "Soirée Fantastique de Robert-Houdin."

Robert-Houdin had hoped to beguile his audience with his skill, his dexterity, his poise. Instead, trembling with stage fright, he fumbled and mumbled his way through his performance, as robotlike as the automata he had created especially for his act.

Even though his presentation lacked the flair and drama essential to the master performer, his magic had enough novelty to win a degree of approval from the audience.

Always the perfectionist, Robert-Houdin was deaf to the audience's applause. He left his little theater and returned to his rooms in a panic of dismay and self-doubt. How had he dared to pass himself off as a master of illusion? How had he dared hope to rival such celebrated conjurers as the great Italian Giovanni Bartolomeo Bosco or the Swiss-born Louis Comte or Robert-Houdin's fellow countryman, the spectacular Philippe?

Throughout the rest of that long and sleepless night, Robert-Houdin replayed his performance in his head, agonizing over every mistake, every imperfection. A thousand times he swore he would never again step onto a stage. A thousand times he cursed the fates which had led him twenty years ago into the little bookstore in his home town of Blois in central France and into the all-consuming study of magic.

Magic was the farthest thing from Jean Eugène Robert's mind when he entered the little bookstore that evening. But so was law, the career his watchmaker-father had hoped his son would follow.

The young Robert had tried hard to respect his father's wishes. He had gone willingly to school at Orléans, about thirty-five miles from Blois, to study the law. But his brilliant, inventive mind was stifled by his studies, and his deft hands were more comfortable holding the tools of a watchmaker than the pen of a law clerk.

During Houdin's early years he was particularly impressed by the famous cups-and-balls routine, whether it was performed by a celebrated conjurer such as the Italian Giovanni Bartolomeo Bosco (right), who performed in elegant theaters, or by an itinerant street conjurer (below).

At eighteen he finished his studies and returned to Blois, still undecided about a career. He wandered restlessly about town, knowing he must begin to put his life in order but not at all sure where or how to begin.

One evening he wandered into a small knot of spectators surrounding a street peddler-magician. As he watched in fascination, the peddler placed three gleaming goblets on a small table, then reached into a red bag of tricks tied around his waist and extracted three small balls.

With a few muttered incantations—and marvelously skilled hands—the peddler made the balls appear and disappear from under the goblets and then move magically from goblet to goblet.

Astounded, Robert watched the skillful performance with the cups and balls. For an instant he glanced down at his own hands. They were slender but strong and already skilled in the use of delicate watchmaking tools. Would they ever become so dexterous that they too could perform such marvelous manipulations?

With a flourish the peddler ended his presentation and began to hawk his wares. He was selling a book which he claimed he had written—a marvelous book that would divulge the secrets of magic.

Eagerly Robert pulled some coins from his pocket. He snatched the book and hurried home to delve into its secrets.

After reading only a few pages, he realized that he had been duped. The peddler had purposefully written a garbled, incomprehensible description of how he performed his tricks. Deeply disappointed, Robert tried to put aside all thoughts of ever duplicating the peddler's tricks with the cups and balls.

Soon after this Robert went to work as a copying clerk in an attorney's office. For the next two years he spent his days bending over his desk, copying dull legal documents; but at night, when he should have been studying the law, he pulled out his watchmaking tools and set himself to work devising all sorts of new and intricate mechanical gadgets.

Interior of a magic shop in the rue Richelieu in Paris. The shop became a meeting place for Robert-Houdin and his fellow magicians.

By now it was obvious that he would never become a lawyer. In fact, he was on the verge of being fired; so his father agreed, reluctantly, to let his son apprentice as a watchmaker.

Robert was delighted to be working full-time with his watchmaker's tools, though he found the routine shop repairs dull. Yet, no matter what the job, he always found a way to tinker, to improve, to innovate, to create something more novel than before.

To improve his knowledge of his new trade, he ordered a pair of volumes on clockmaking from the local bookstore. But when he went to pick them up, the bookseller mistakenly handed him two similarly bound volumes of "scientific amusements."

Robert did not notice the mistake until he got back to his rooms and glanced through the first book. Suddenly his eyes widened. Here, in his hands, were the magic secrets he had longed to know ever since he had watched the street peddler's performance. Here was information on how to guess a person's thoughts, how to perform card tricks, how to restore supposedly dead birds to life, how — at last — to manipulate the cups and balls.

The candle in the room flickered and died and night slowly turned into day. He could not tear his eyes away from the books, nor could he hold back the shock of realization that he had finally found the career for which he was destined.

Within a week he had memorized every trick in the two books. He spent every spare minute practicing sleight of hand with cards and coins until he could palm a coin or pass a card with either hand with smoothness and dexterity.

He even begged a local man with a modest reputation as a sometime entertainer to instruct him in the art of juggling. The man obliged — for ten francs — and soon the pupil became more skilled than the teacher.

Once again family pressure and the need to earn a living kept him from his chosen career. He was a watchmaker by trade, not a magician, as his father sternly reminded him. Thus, he had to be content giving an occasional magic performance at parties for the amusement of his friends.

One of those parties led Robert to a chance meeting with pretty Josèphe Cécile Eglantine Houdin, the daughter of a wealthy watchmaker. The meeting led to marriage, a job in his father-in-law's Paris shop, and, following the French custom, the addition of his wife's surname to his own.

Even with a new wife, a new name, and a new life in Paris, Robert-Houdin could not escape the lure of conjuring. He regularly attended the performances of all the leading magicians who played in Paris, not so much as a bedazzled spectator but as a shrewd evaluator of their methods and styles of presentation.

He was impressed with the marvelous cups-and-balls manipulations of the personable Italian conjurer

This small theater in the Palais Royal in Paris became the scene of Robert-Houdin's countless triumphs as well as his first and only failure.

Giovanni Bartolomeo Bosco, the Great Bosco — but not with his somewhat barbaric illusion of decapitating a pigeon and letting its blood flow freely into a saucer.

He was impressed with the theater of magic built to the specifications of the brilliant French conjurer Philippe and particularly with Philippe's dramatic opening trick.

The trick began when the curtain rose on a totally darkened stage. The dim figure of a man in evening clothes appeared suddenly. Apologizing for the darkness, the man declared he would light the stage with a small display of magic.

Then the man — Philippe himself — fired a pistol. Instantly hundreds of candles burst into flame before the gasping audience — which did not see a backstage assistant trigger a flow of hydrogen gas and send an electric current through thin wires spaced just far enough apart for a spark to jump at each turpentine-soaked candlewick, causing it to leap into flame.

Philippe's brilliant opening act—firing a pistol to light hundreds of footlight candles—became the talk of Paris. The secret of his conjuring marvel involved an early use of a scientific marvel, electricity.

As much as he admired the trick, Robert-Houdin was disturbed when it occasionally failed and swore that he would never present a trick if there was even the possibility of mechanical failure.

He also admired the deft presentations of the popular Louis Comte and, in particular, his clever stage use of flattery and humor; but he was just as impressed with Comte's great skill as a publicist and his ability to fill the theater for every performance.

Almost without realizing it, Robert-Houdin was cataloging the elements he did—and did not—like in each magician's performance and mentally re-creating them with his own unique embellishments. His fascination with the conjuring art went even further. He discovered a little magic shop in the rue Richelieu where he could examine firsthand the equipment that the performers used and where he could also exchange ideas with other magicians, both amateur and professional.

He was especially intrigued with the mechanical figures called automata. They were usually engineered with the precision of a fine watch, and the best of them were programmed to perform all sorts of amazing tricks.

He soon turned his watchmaking skills and his inventive mind to producing his own automata. One of the first of them, quite naturally, was a miniature conjurer performing a trick with the cups and balls; all of them were instant successes.

His growing fame as a maker of automata brought him a contract to produce a life-sized figure that could write and draw whatever was requested of it, but the complexity of the project almost brought him to a state of mental collapse.

Robert-Houdin isolated himself completely from his wife and family and put aside all other business to devote himself exclusively to the monumental project.

Then tragedy struck. His wife died, and he was left with the heavy responsibility of caring for his three young children. His funds were running low, but the challenge of completing his automaton was so great that he could not pull himself away from it.

Finally, after more than a year, the marvelous figure was completed and displayed, amid great admiration and acclaim, at the Paris Exposition of 1844.

Suddenly his life seemed to take a turn for the better. He remarried, and his new wife, Marguerite, helped him put his life in order. His automaton was awarded a silver medal by the exposition jury; this attracted several wealthy backers who were willing to build a theater of magic for him.

So, on that hot July evening in 1845, after twenty long years of patience and preparation, Robert-Houdin stepped onto the stage of his own theater to give his first professional performance—and stepped offstage a few hours later in humiliation and despair.

He might have ended his career then and there had it not been for the arrival early the next morning of a so-called friend. The friend could barely conceal a gloating smile when he asked how the performance had gone the evening before.

Robert-Houdin shook his head sadly, not wishing to speak of the disastrous performance. The friend persisted; had he not warned of the consequences of becoming involved with this business of conjuring?

Humiliation and pride battled within Robert-Houdin for an instant, but the battle was soon over. Pulling himself to his full height with as much dignity as he could muster, he coldly excused himself so that he could prepare for the evening's performance.

Once again Robert-Houdin walked onstage. But this time the terrible, clammy fear was gone, and the master of magic began to emerge.

Slowly, with each performance, Robert-Houdin began to put into practice all those precepts he had developed over the past twenty years.

He did away with the typical ruses that other magicians used—the heavily draped tables, the outlandish costumes, the confederates spotted in the audience. Instead, he designed elegant stage sets, streamlined magic appliances, and presented his tricks in the evening dress of a cultured Parisian.

He perfected the art of pacing, of varying each trick in speed or size or complexity in order to build to a strong and spectacular finish. He played to the audience as if he were an actor merely taking the role of a magician. He became master of the throwaway trick—in particular, the disappearing handkerchief—which seemed to surprise him almost as much as it delighted the audience.

Robert-Houdin begins his classic handkerchief vanish by casually mopping his brow between tricks.
While announcing his next trick, he holds the handkerchief nonchalantly in his hand.
When the handkerchief suddenly vanishes up his sleeve—with the aid of an unseen pull—the master magician appears somewhat startled.

Above all, he created an act which was elegant, tasteful, and witty and which appealed to intelligence rather than to base superstition.

Over the next few months his superb skills and his refreshingly new presentation of conjuring began to draw crowds to his little magic theater. But, despite his growing success, he was not satisfied. He wanted a smashing climax for his act, a deception so complete that it would leave his audience gasping.

Robert-Houdin's genius was so great that he developed not one but two such marvelous deceptions.

The first, which he called Second Sight, supposedly grew out of a game played by his two young sons, Emile and Eugène. One boy blindfolded the other and then walked around the room touching objects which the unseeing brother was miraculously able to name. Impressed—so he claimed—by his son's mystical powers, he brought young Emile into his act.

The secret of the trick, of course, was an elaborate code of key words memorized by father and son. Robert-Houdin would insert code words into seemingly innocent questions as he held up an object selected from a member of the audience. Onstage the blindfolded Emile instantly decoded the key words and correctly named the object.

The trick was not really a new one. It had been presented sixty years before by Giovanni Giuseppi Pinetti and his blindfolded wife. But with typical thoroughness and with months of practice Robert-Houdin elevated the trick to a dazzling new level of artistry.

He elaborated on his code so that his son could describe any object in staggering detail. When his audiences began to suspect that the questions to his son were not as innocent as they seemed, he developed an electrical device to transmit the necessary information silently.

Robert-Houdin's first season as a conjurer, which had begun in near disaster, ended in triumph. However, even after a successful summer tour of Europe, the great innovator was still not content to rest on his laurels.

A blindfolded Emile Robert-Houdin names objects held up by his famous father. The boy's gift of "second sight" depended on a secret code devised by Robert-Houdin.

**With the help of a concealed harness young Eugène
Robert-Houdin appears to defy the laws of gravity
in the dramatic Ethereal Suspension.**

He developed some intriguing new illusions—for
example, the Crystal Cash Box, in which coins vanished
and reappeared—and improved on others—such as
the Inexhaustible Bottle, which poured out any drink
requested by the audience.

When a new medical discovery, the anesthetic ether,
became the talk of Europe, he created a second
dazzling deception which won instant acclaim. The trick
was billed as Ethereal Suspension; it began with Robert-
Houdin's subtle suggestion to the audience that ether
was even more powerful than was believed.

He carefully stood his son, Eugène, on a stool, with
the boy's elbows resting on two upright rods embedded
in a platform.

He uncorked a bottle—supposedly of ether—and
asked Eugène to sniff deeply from it; at the same time
ether fumes, released from backstage, filled the theater.
Immediately the boy appeared to go rigid.

Robert-Houdin gently removed the stool, leaving his
son suspended by his elbows between the two rods. He
removed one of the rods, leaving the boy suspended
trancelike on the remaining rod.

Then, miracle of miracles, he gently swung Eugène's
feet to one side until his body was parallel to the floor,
suspended only by his elbow on the remaining rod.

As the audience looked on in shock, the father
backed away. Yet, he appeared to be watching closely
for the slightest sign that his son was coming out of his
trancelike state.

When the son showed such a sign, he immediately
lowered the boy's body back to its original position,
replaced the second rod under his other elbow, and set
the stool back under his feet.

At that instant the boy seemingly shook himself out
of his trance and went limp. The audience went wild.

Of course, there had been neither ether nor a trance.
Instead, there was an ingeniously designed metal

Poster announces Robert-Houdin's farewell performance at London's Saint James's Theater.

harness with a rigid frame that buckled around Eugène's body. Attached to the frame were two iron bars that ran from knee to armpit and from armpit to elbow. A clever pin-and-socket mechanism connected the rod attached to the elbow to the rod visible on stage, which enabled Robert-Houdin to swing the boy into any position he wished.

In fact, the entire ingenious contraption bore a strong resemblance to the metal arrangements that permitted the Hindu fakirs of India to perform their impressive levitations.

The illusion of floating in air never failed to astound and mystify Robert-Houdin's audiences and bring them cheering to their feet.

These masterful illusions—and others like them— delighted audiences all over Europe. Robert-Houdin's retirement after only seven years of performing

dismayed them, but he had other things to do.

He delved into the mysteries of electricity and other phenomena, not as a magician but as a true scientist. He wrote a series of textbooks which for the first time carefully explained how his tricks worked and documented his scientific approach to conjuring.

He wrote his autobiography, *Confidences d'un prestidigitateur*—a brilliant work which not only traced his career but set forth his revolutionary ideas about conjuring and crowd psychology. When he died in 1871, he left behind a legacy which reshaped the conjuring art and brought it to the threshold of a glorious golden age.

As Robert-Houdin's fame spread across Europe, magicians everywhere began copying his innovative style, his staging, and, if they were skilled enough, his tricks.

Most of them were poor copies of the original and gained, at best, an occasional success. But there were others who soon developed their own styles, their own masterful tricks and illusions, their own fame; and each added his own special quality to magic's golden age.

One of them, the English-born Joseph Michael Hartz, first appeared in London at the age of eighteen with a full-evening magic show closely resembling Robert-Houdin's *soirées fantastiques*. Within a few years, however, he had developed his own special apparatus, made entirely of glass, and had become known as the Crystal Illusionist.

Another Englishman, working under the improbable name of Signor Antonio Blitz, mixed wit and humor with his deceptions and considered a performance successful only when he amused his audience as much as he amazed them.

The climax of Blitz's presentation was guaranteed to amuse and amaze any audience. He placed five dinner plates on a long table and tried to start each of them spinning on end. By the time he reached the fifth plate and started it spinning, the first was wobbling crazily and threatening to fall off the table.

Blitz dashed back just in time to keep the first plate spinning and smiled at the audience in triumph. The triumph, however, was momentary, as another plate started to wobble and then another and another.

Like a madman, Blitz dashed up and down the length of the table, breathlessly trying to keep each plate spinning, and using such zany antics that the audience roared with laughter.

Still another English-born conjurer, Robert Heller, found his own special style by combining mimicry, sleight of hand, and skilled piano playing with his natural acting ability to become a success in both Europe and America.

But the conjurer whose fame came closest to rivaling that of the great French innovator was a Scotsman from Aberdeen named John Henry Anderson, the self-styled Wizard of the North.

Signor Blitz's comic plate-spinning routine became the inspiration for a waltz composed by J.A. Janke, Jr., which was published in Philadelphia in 1849. The cover of the sheet music for this waltz is pictured above.

Anderson, an actor turned conjurer, was a master at bringing the promotional techniques of the theater to the world of magic. His gaudy posters—pasted on every available wall in every city where he was scheduled to perform—announced the day of his arrival. As that date approached, handbills, advertisements—even pictures of himself impressed in butter molds—flooded the city.

Finally, on the day of the performance, a spectacular street parade with marchers, huge banners, and prancing horses wound noisily through the city's streets, urging one and all to see the master magician perform.

Although the ballyhoo drew the crowds, it was Anderson's spectacular tricks that brought them back again and again.

One trick, the Bullet Catch, was extremely dangerous and highly dramatic. It involved a member of the audience firing a marked bullet directly at the magician's heart.

The marked bullet was real and deadly, but Anderson deftly switched it with an identical-looking but harmless composition bullet before the marksman loaded his

Extensive repertoire of John Henry Anderson included (clockwise from top left) production of steaming puddings from a borrowed top hat, passing a handkerchief through an umbrella frame, catching a watch shot through the crown of a hat, and passing dice from one table to another.

gun. Yet, there was always the possibility that something might go wrong, that the real bullet might somehow be loaded into the gun before Anderson could discover the mistake.

In the few short years after Jean Eugène Robert-Houdin had brought conjuring to a new, exciting prominence, others were already adding their own special flair to the art: Signor Blitz with his sidesplitting humor; Hartz with his streamlined magic appliances; Anderson with his sensational publicity and high drama; Heller with his versatility and histrionic ability. The stage was now set for the Brothers Herrmann and their spectacular, breathtaking illusions.

The New World Reconquered
The Brothers Herrmann

It was almost inevitable that at least some of the Herrmann brothers of Hanover, Germany—there were eight of them—would find themselves attracted to the conjuring art. Their father, Samuel, who was a fine physician, was also an ardent magic hobbyist, and more than once he abandoned his pills and his medical practice to go touring through Europe as a professional conjurer.

Carl, the oldest son, grew up playing with his father's magic props much as other children grow up playing with toys. However, when Carl announced to his father that he, too, wanted to be a magician, his father put his foot down, insisting that no son of his would waste his time with such frivolities as conjuring. Instead, Carl was to become a physician.

Reluctantly Carl went off to the University of Paris. But the study of medicine paled beside the study of

The Brothers Herrmann, Carl (above) *and Alexander* (left), *deliberately cultivated similar mustaches and goatees to emphasize their almost satanic good looks.*

magic, and Carl, despite his father's vehement protests, dropped out of school to devote himself to the conjurer's art.

Disowned by his angry father, with barely enough money to keep alive, Carl began an apprenticeship that would last for ten long, hard years.

He joined a company of actors. While he was with them, he perfected a sleight of hand so quick and so deft that even up close it was impossible to detect his movements. He also developed an amazing skill as a ventriloquist and an uncanny ability to duplicate all kinds of bird calls.

"Will drop The GREAT HERRMANN in Your City shortly."

A pair of giant bats and a whimsical quarter-moon adorn Alex Herrmann's calling cards.

Dramatic poster (right) *shows the Herrmann version of the medieval decapitation mystery.*

Slowly and laboriously Carl mastered his art. He even began to build a modest reputation for himself. He was invited to perform—just as his father had once been—at the parties of wealthy French socialites. Finally he earned enough money to buy the equipment he needed to mount his own three-hour magic show.

The show itself bore a striking resemblance to the one being presented by his contemporary, Robert-Houdin, from whom he had "borrowed" a number of tricks. But Carl's masterful skills and his unique touches were usually enough to convince his audiences that he was what he billed himself—the First Professor of Magic in the World.

It took only two years after the 1848 London opening of his magic show for Carl to become the toast of Europe.

He appeared before kings, queens, sultans, czars, and emperors—in Germany, Austria, England, Belgium, Italy, Portugal, Turkey, and Russia. He received staggering rewards for his performances, from vast sums of money to priceless jewels to specially bestowed titles and high honors.

By now Carl's magic presentations were notably his own. He had discarded much of the complicated equipment that had highlighted his London show and specialized instead in starkly simple but perfectly executed sleight of hand.

As Carl's fame spread, he crisscrossed the Continent again and again. He even crossed the ocean to America, where he also won great acclaim and valuable rewards. He traveled throughout the United States and also performed in many South American countries.

Around this same time two things were happening in his father's house. Samuel Herrmann, finally accepting the fact that his oldest son was destined to be a magician, welcomed Carl back into the family; and Carl's baby brother, Alexander, twenty-seven years younger than Carl, decided to follow in his big brother's footsteps.

Once again the father protested vehemently; once again his arguments fell on deaf ears. Young Alex intended to become a conjurer, and that was that.

According to one version of the story, told many years later by Alex, Carl "kidnapped" his ten-year-old brother and brought him to Russia as his assistant.

According to another version, the younger Herrmann was really a runaway, who would not be denied the chance to travel with the big brother he idolized.

Alexander Herrmann and his bride, the former Adelaide Scarcez. The couple performed together until Alexander's death.

The Brothers Herrmann brought their marvelous magic to audiences all over the world — to the United States, where Alex was especially popular, and to Europe, where Carl had always drawn the warmest applause.

Surprisingly there was little jealousy — and even less competition — between the brothers. However, both were strong individualists, and their ideas on the practice of magic began to move in different directions.

As Carl discarded the complicated props which had dominated his earlier performances, Alex began to present gigantic stage illusions which often required much elaborate equipment to make them work.

The brothers therefore decided to separate, with Carl returning triumphantly to Europe and Alex, now billed as Herrmann the Great, staying on in the United States to capitalize on his great popularity.

That popularity was as great offstage as on because, no matter what the occasion, Alex always found a way to dazzle those around him with his amazing sleight of hand.

Routine visits to an open-air food market were enlivened when Alex "happened" to find a coin nestling inside a fresh apple or hiding behind the fruit seller's ear. Startling things also happened whenever Alex attended a dinner party. The wine glass he was holding might suddenly disappear from his hand only to reappear in another guest's pocket. With the aid of an accomplice the ring on his dining companion's finger might magically materialize on someone else's finger. Inevitably Alex would turn to those around him and say, "The closer you watch, the less you see."

By 1875 a new element had been added to Alex's act. Her name was Adelaide Scarcez; she was a beautiful London-born ballet dancer with a natural flair of her own for magic. She became Madame Herrmann in a wedding ceremony performed by the mayor of New York, and soon afterwards Adelaide joined her husband as his onstage assistant.

The act by this time was a skillful blend of smoothly executed conjuring tricks — for example, one billed as the Vanishing Birdcage, in which canary and cage suddenly disappeared — and spectacular full-stage illusions — like the somewhat diabolical Black Art illusion.

The dramatic Black Art illusion was not original with Alex. It had been invented a number of years before by the French magician Joseph Buatier de Kolta — a gifted creator of illusions whose presentations somehow never quite matched his creative genius. In Alex's hands, however, the illusion became an impressive spectacle.

Either way the result was the same. Alex, like his brother Carl, was preordained to become rich and famous as a conjurer. But Alex's fame would sweep across America, much as his brother's had swept across Europe.

That was yet to come. First, young Alex had to master the demanding skills of his trade. Fortunately there was no better teacher than his brother, and at the age of fifteen the youngest Herrmann was ready to make his solo debut before no less an audience than Queen Isabella II of Spain.

Three years later the brothers joined together in a partnership which made conjuring history. Both were tall, lean, and darkly handsome; they presented an almost satanic appearance in their elegant evening clothes. Both were professional, witty performers whose sheer force of personality could dominate an audience. Alex, especially, had such a natural talent as a performer — with such tremendously deft hands — that he could carry off the most audacious sleight of hand ever seen, onstage or off.

The illusion was presented on a completely darkened stage with brilliant lights shining into the audience. Black-garbed assistants, unseen by the audience, darted across the stage, covering and uncovering white objects with black cloths.

The effect was startling—and startlingly real—as ghostly figures appeared to rise into the air and suddenly disappear or come together in an eerie dance, only to break apart at the clap of Alex's hands.

Another classic illusion created by Buatier de Kolta and adapted by Alex was the mystifying Vanishing Lady, in which Madame Herrmann, seated on a chair, was completely covered by a thin cloth that clearly outlined her head and body. At the right moment Alex snatched away the cloth, exposing nothing but an empty chair.

How had Madame Herrmann vanished? By using another piece of equipment designed by Buatier de Kolta, an ordinary-looking chair with several extraordinary features.

There was a spring-hinged trapdoor built into the seat of the chair, which was always positioned so that it lined up directly over a concealed trapdoor built into the stage.

Attached to the top of the chair was a thin wire frame, which duplicated the shape of Madame Herrmann's head and shoulders. Another wire frame, attached to the chair seat, duplicated the shape of her knees. Since both forms were covered to match the backdrop, they were invisible to the audience.

The instant her movements were hidden by the cloth, Madame Herrmann slipped the first frame over her head, triggered open the stage trapdoor, released the seat and the second frame, and slipped below stage.

While Alex carefully positioned the cloth over what was now nothing more than the wire forms, Madame Herrmann closed the stage trapdoor and completed the vanish.

Seconds after Alexander Herrmann drapes a silk cloth over his lady to be vanished, she has already disappeared. The props that made the vanish possible include a wire fake attached to a chair and a trapdoor hidden in the stage floor.

Madame Adelaide Herrmann floats languidly through the air in this 1880s poster (above).

After Alex Herrmann's death in 1896, his widow and nephew, Leon Herrmann, took over the task of keeping the family name alive. Even though Alex was no longer alive, his picture always appeared on the company's posters (right).

Onstage Alex grandly removed the cloth—making sure to flip back the wire frames—and smilingly accepted the applause of the audience.

For a dozen exciting years Alex and his lovely Adelaide dominated the stages of America, while in Europe brother Carl continued to perform before admiring audiences.

In 1887 Carl died in Austria at the age of seventy-one. But the illustrious Herrmann name was not to die out either in Europe or in America. A young nephew, Leon Herrmann, took over Carl's show, while Alex and his wife continued to tour America for nine more years.

In 1896, while traveling by train from New York to Pennsylvania, Alex fell suddenly ill. Knowing he was about to die, he turned to his wife and begged her to take the company back to New York.

Sadly Adelaide buried her husband, but she followed his dying wishes. She took the company back to New York, where it continued to perform under her direction.

By the turn of the century the increasing popularity of vaudeville had begun to eclipse the large traveling magic show. Adelaide met the challenge head on. She condensed the show into a vaudeville headline attraction under the title "A Night in Japan."

For twenty-five years the graceful Adelaide, billed as the Queen of Magic, continued to beguile audiences with her clever sleight of hand and intriguing illusions.

Failing health eventually forced Adelaide into retirement, and when she died a few years later at age seventy-five, the illustrious name of Herrmann—a name which had dominated the conjuring art for almost a century—became a treasured memory.

The masterful skill of such great conjurers as Robert-Houdin and the Herrmanns brought the magician's art of honest deception into a spectacular golden age; at the same time it revived public interest in another deception which was not always honest, spiritualism.

The belief that the souls of the dead roamed the earth in ghostly form was an ancient one, and for centuries many charlatans exploited this superstition for their own ends.

The most masterful charlatan of them all, the Italian adventurer Count Alessandro di Cagliostro, claimed the ability to call upon and conjure up the denizens of the spirit world at will, an ability aided in no small part by the use of a hidden assistant and a clever bit of apparatus called a magic lantern.

The magic lantern was nothing more than a medieval version of the modern slide projector, but in the hands of a Cagliostro it became a potent instrument for deception.

The fabulous Pepper's Ghost illusion (left) as it appeared to the audience.

The secret behind the illusion (above). A picture of a ghost was projected onto a large, angled sheet of plate glass; the actor, standing behind the glass, pantomimed the action of a fighting duel with the ghost. The apparition disappeared when the projector was turned off.

By the middle of the eighteenth century, when its secret became more widely known, the magic lantern was used by professional conjurers to present "optical entertainments." Other techniques were also being developed to create similar ghostly materializations.

One such ruse—named Pepper's Ghost in honor of its inventor, English professor John Henry Pepper— utilized a large sheet of precisely angled plate glass onto which eerie apparitions could be reflected by an unseen projector.

The production of Pepper's Ghost, with its massive equipment, was generally limited to presentation at permanent theaters of magic like the renowned Kratky-Baschik's Zauber-Theater in Vienna. Wherever it was presented, it caused a kind of baffled delight and added greatly to the interest in spiritualism.

By the end of the nineteenth century that interest had reached a fever pitch. Spirit séances had become the new sensation, and fake mediums everywhere played on this intense interest by using their conjuring skills to create "manifestations" of the spirit world.

For a price they held séances which featured mysterious communications from the spirits. Their allies were concealed assistants. Their aids were mechanical table rappers to produce the eerie sound of ghostly knocks; concealed table lifters to produce the startling effect of the séance table rising slowly in air; hidden developing trays to produce mysterious "spirit"

photographs; cleverly rigged "spirit" trumpets to hover eerily in the room.

They transported themselves into trancelike states and pretended to speak with the voices of loved ones who had departed the earth. They played on the hopes and fears of those who believed and roused the suspicions of those who did not. Wherever they appeared, they became embroiled in controversy.

Two of the most controversial of these tricksters were the Americans Ira and William Davenport, the Davenport Brothers. Claiming to be true spiritualists, they toured Europe in 1865, and in the spring of that year they were playing the English town of Cheltenham.

At that time the Davenports were unmasked by a slender, twenty-six-year-old amateur conjurer named Maskelyne, who proved beyond a doubt that they were nothing more than clever manipulators.

Even more important, the experience convinced the young amateur magician to turn professional, and over the next sixty years his amazing magical entertainments enhanced the ancient art of conjuring and brought it to a new level of excellence.

Founder of a Dynasty

John Nevil Maskelyne

John Nevil Maskelyne, founder of a great English conjuring dynasty, at the beginning of his long career.

Like Robert-Houdin, John Nevil Maskelyne was a skilled watchmaker who often dabbled in magic as a hobby. Like the great French innovator, he too was captivated by the ancient art but was deeply disturbed by those who used it dishonestly.

When he first watched the performance of the notorious Davenport Brothers in his home town of Cheltenham, England, Maskelyne's good sense told him that what he was seeing was patently fake and that the brothers were charlatans.

Maskelyne voiced his suspicions to several members of his local conjuring club. Almost to a man they agreed with him, but proving their suspicions and exposing the Davenports was quite another matter. So Maskelyne and another amateur conjurer, fellow club member George Cooke, decided to attend the Davenports' next performance to see what they could uncover.

The show began, as usual, with a presentation of ghostly music from inside a so-called spirit cabinet placed squarely at center stage. Inside the cabinet, along with the "spirits," were the Davenports, hands and feet securely bound with ropes. They appeared to be just as securely bound when the cabinet doors were thrown open by an assistant a few minutes later—after the ghostly music had been heard.

Whether it was by accident—or deliberately set up by the two amateurs—a ray of light slipped through a draped window in the darkened hall and fell on the cabinet just as the eerie spirit music began.

It lit up the cabinet's partially open door, permitting Maskelyne to see one of the brothers deftly slip his hand free of its binding, pick up a tambourine, and create the music himself.

Angrily Maskelyne leaped to his feet, shouting to the stunned Davenports that they were frauds and warning the audience that they were witnessing a hoax.

The Davenports quickly regained their composure. They threw their own challenge back at the intense young Maskelyne by daring him to prove his claim.

Maskelyne responded by shouting that he would do just that by duplicating everything the Davenports had presented, and that he would do so without the help of so-called spirits.

The audience buzzed with excitement, and John

Maskelyne, still angry, set out to make good his boast.

Maskelyne and Cooke constructed a spirit cabinet of their own. They researched methods of slipping their hands in and out of tightly knotted ropes and practiced until they were as adroit and as skilled as the Davenports themselves.

Step by step they reconstructed and rehearsed each of the tricks on the Davenport program. Because they were gifted conjurers in their own right, they created additional tricks which were more baffling than anything the Davenport Brothers had ever presented.

One trick in particular made use of the same infamous spirit cabinet but with a spectacular new twist.

Somehow Maskelyne managed to squeeze his five-foot, eight-inch frame into a small box three feet long, two feet wide, and only nineteen inches deep. The box was locked, tied with a strong rope, then set on end inside the cabinet.

George Cooke then placed several bells on top of the sealed box and closed the cabinet doors. The drama began. Within seconds the bells began to ring. Then the bells came flying out of the slowly opening cabinet doors. After a few minutes the cabinet doors were flung wide open to reveal a smiling John Maskelyne sitting casually on top of the box, which was still bound and locked.

The trick depended, of course, on the special construction of the box itself, which Maskelyne, with his superior watchmaking skills, had devised. When it was presented onstage along with the other duplications of the original Davenport show—exactly three months and eleven days after Maskelyne had accepted their challenge—it flabbergasted and delighted the audience.

A few days later the Birmingham *Gazette* reported the event to its readers. The headline read, "The Davenport Brothers Outdone." It might as easily have read, "Sensational Debut of New Conjuring Duo."

The team of Maskelyne and Cooke, brought together by sheerest accident, embarked on a conjuring career which would culminate in the longest-running theatrical entertainment of all time—and which would establish in England a veritable dynasty of magic.

These two Englishmen from the West Country were an unlikely pair. Maskelyne, the younger of the two by fourteen years, was aggressive, dramatic, with the natural flair of a showman. Cooke, in contrast, was somewhat shy and retiring, a perfect foil for his more dynamic partner.

In 1873, only eight years after their sensational debut, Maskelyne and Cooke signed a temporary lease on a theater in London's famous Egyptian Hall. They featured a number of Maskelyne's ingeniously designed automata along with a clever show of magic. Not content to rest on the team's original success, Maskelyne continued to bring improvements and innovations to the show.

He was enchanted by the plate-juggling feat he had once seen Signor Antonio Blitz perform. So he perfected his own juggling technique until he could perform the feat with the same consummate skill as Blitz.

Like the rest of the world, he was greatly impressed with Robert-Houdin's marvelous illusion Ethereal Suspension. Consequently he developed his own levitation—he called it Levitation Extraordinary—in which he appeared to rise miraculously from the stage on which he was standing and float up to the dome of the theater, high above the heads of the audience. Once there he appeared to turn effortlessly in midair and then slowly, serenely, float back down.

This amazing illusion depended on split-second timing, a dummy wearing an exact replica of Maskelyne's clothes and face, and a clever rigging

Poster announcing the appearance in Nottingham, England, of the traveling Maskelyne and Cooke company. The company's managing partner, David Devant, eventually became Maskelyne's partner when George Cooke died.

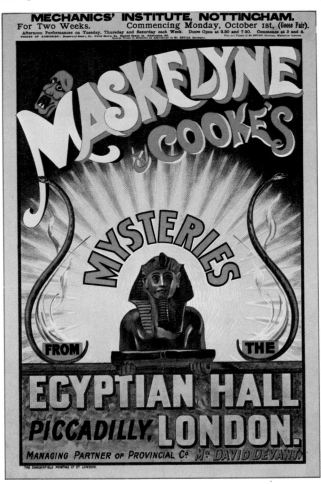

Maskelyne appeared to float high above the stage during his amazing Levitation Extraordinary. The floating figure was actually that of a dummy wearing an exact duplicate of Maskelyne's clothes and face.

made of blackened wires invisible to the audience, which hoisted the dummy into the air at the proper instant.

Maskelyne continued to add new tricks and illusions to the show, and every year the presentations of Maskelyne and Cooke drew thousands to Egyptian Hall to be amused and amazed.

For twenty-nine years the conjuring team of Maskelyne and Cooke played at Egyptian Hall. George Cooke retired in 1902 and almost without missing a beat, a one-time protégé, David Devant, became Maskelyne's new partner.

By 1905 Maskelyne and Devant were performing in their new show, "Maskelyne's New Home of Mystery." Among the members of the company were Maskelyne's four sons and his grandson Jasper.

During his long years of dazzling performances, John Maskelyne was as much a patron of the ancient art as he was a performer. He hired hundreds of young magicians to perform in his shows and over the years launched the successful careers of many of them.

He encouraged magicians everywhere to cooperate with each other to advance the conjuring art rather than compete so much with each other that they undermined the mystery and magic of the art. As a direct result of his advice, magicians began to form their own organizations and magic societies.

He never forgot the rage he felt when he first saw the Davenport Brothers try to pass themselves off as genuine spiritualists. So he devoted much of his time to explaining, through books and lectures, how such tricksters operated. He also explained how other kinds of swindlers operated; for instance, how they used trick apparatus to cheat at cards and dice.

He fought charlatans whenever he could, often through the courts and often at the risk of his own reputation.

Like another famous watchmaker-turned-conjurer, he tinkered constantly in his workshop, regularly creating conjuring devices based on the latest scientific principles. When he died at the age of eighty-eight in 1917, he left behind a legacy of creative conjuring which has never been surpassed.

Since the renaissance of conjuring was brought about almost entirely by European magicians, it was only natural that the art should soar to new heights in Europe and that master magicians should appear everywhere.

The French-born Buatier de Kolta—he was born Joseph Buatier but later changed his name in honor of his first impresario—used the simplest of tools to create ingenious, big-magic illusions which formed the basis for hundreds of adaptations by scores of other magicians.

Unfortunately for de Kolta, his stage presence and manner of presentation never quite matched the genius of his inventive mind. He never won the acclaim which was so willingly given to such dynamic performers as Alex Herrmann or David Devant, the English heir-apparent of the Maskelyne dynasty.

Yet, de Kolta's inventions—a vanishing birdcage, multiplying billiard balls, flowers from a paper cone, and the incomparable vanish of the lady from a chair—promised success to conjurers all over the world and are still being used today.

The technical level of the ancient art was further advanced by a staid English lawyer named Angelo Lewis, an amateur conjurer himself, who wrote a book that described in detail how the tricks of the day were performed.

Because proper English lawyers were not supposed to write about the art of deception, Lewis's book, *Modern Magic*, was written under the pen name of Professor Hoffmann. It quickly became a kind of how-to encyclopedia of conjuring, which is still widely used today.

As detailed knowledge about the latest techniques of conjuring spread around the world, it was inevitable that interest in the performance of magic would quicken everywhere and that gifted amateurs would seek to duplicate the feats of the masters.

It was, perhaps, just as inevitable that the United States, with its own long tradition of native magic, would produce a conjurer skilled enough to join the ranks of the great European masters. Yet, the clumsy, thick-fingered Pennsylvania youngster who was to become America's first great non-Indian magician was surely the most unlikely candidate for the title of master of magic.

Egyptian Hall, built in 1811 as a museum, became the temporary home of the Maskelyne and Cooke company for twenty-nine years.

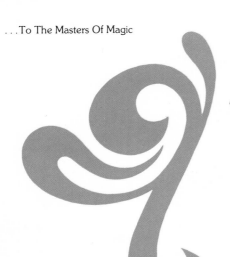

To the Far Corners of the World

Harry Kellar

The indomitable Harry Kellar conquered physical handicaps and economic disasters to become a master of magic.

The boy who later became Harry Kellar, master of magic, was born Heinrich Keller in Erie, Pennsylvania, in 1849. His was an unhappy childhood, even in an era when the well-being of children often ran a poor second to the economic needs of their families.

His mother died when he was barely four and his stern, domineering father remarried a woman whose concerns rarely centered on the son. He was apprenticed to a druggist as soon as he was old enough to earn a dollar, but a sudden explosion, caused by accidentally mixing together some volatile chemicals, dramatically ended his brief apprenticeship.

Rather than face the angry druggist—and knowing that his father's reaction would be even angrier—young Keller hopped the first freight train out of Erie and eventually ended up in the little upstate village of Canandaigua, New York.

The twelve-year-old runaway was taken in by the Reverend Robert Harcourt, who sheltered him, fed him, and even talked about adopting him and preparing him for a career in the church.

The young adventurer, however, was not quite ready to settle into such a life. When he saw a want ad in a Buffalo newspaper for an assistant to travel with a well-known magician, he went to try for the job.

The magician was English-born I.H. Hughes, who had built a rather substantial reputation for himself as the Fakir of Ava. Although he had interviewed hundreds of eager youngsters, he had not hired any of them because none of them seemed able to get along with his dog.

Keller was different. With a few pats on the head, he won over the magician's dog and, inevitably, the magician himself.

The association between Hughes and Keller lasted for six years, until Keller turned eighteen. During those six years he doggedly learned the tricks of the conjurer's trade.

Everything seemed to be against Keller's success as a magician. His fingers were thick and clumsy; his movements were jerky and uneven; he was barely educated and had a speech impediment, which made it difficult to understand him; he had none of the charm and flair of the debonair Alex Herrmann, none of the quick and easy wit of the elegant John Maskelyne.

What he did have was an iron-willed determination to become a magician in the face of all odds and a sense of perfection that kept him constantly at work improving himself and his routines.

When the eighteen-year-old Keller first set out on the road with his own magic show, he needed every bit of that determination.

In spite of a name change—from Keller to Kellar, to avoid confusion with the prominent English magician Robert Heller—and his self-styled billing as the World's Best Magician, Kellar's show was a flop.

By now he had all the skill he needed to pull off his tricks. The problem was simply that he never had enough money to buy a rabbit for his trick of pulling a rabbit out of a hat or enough silver dollars to attempt his best trick of snatching them out of the air.

Fortunately Kellar's travels brought him into contact with the more successful show of the Davenport Brothers. They needed an assistant and Kellar needed a job; so off they went together, traveling throughout the United States and Canada, across the ocean to Europe, and back to the United States.

The Davenport Brothers were already famous—or infamous—for their séance shows. But they were also extremely skilled magicians whose techniques and rope-tie escapes fascinated Kellar. These he mastered with the same determination he had used to master his other tricks. Then he decided to set out again with his own show.

Joining Kellar in partnership was another former traveler with the Davenport show, William Fay, known as Professor Fay. Together they traveled up and down the East Coast, from Canada to Key West, Florida, where their money ran out.

Another fortunate meeting, this time with a steamer captain, brought them to Havana, Cuba, just before Christmas of 1873; here they achieved their first real success.

Using a vanishing birdcage based on a de Kolta design—the cage was hinged in such a way that it could be made to collapse almost flat—Kellar delighted his audience by making the cage and the canary inside it suddenly disappear.

With a pull concealed under his coat and a Buatier de Kolta-designed collapsing birdcage, Harry Kellar effects an instant vanish of both bird and cage.

The secret of the trick, besides the specially constructed cage, was a cord with one end tied to the cage and the other to Kellar's left wrist. With a dramatic upward sweep of his arms, he directed the eyes of the audience toward the ceiling. As they looked up, the hidden cord was drawn taut, pulling the collapsed birdcage—with the bird still in it—up through his sleeve to a spot between his elbow and his shoulder.

The trick was a great success and so was the rest of the show. Suddenly bookings began flooding in for other appearances in Cuba and Latin America.

After his previous failures, Harry Kellar had every right to assume that he was finally on the road to fame and fortune. However, he would soon learn that the road ahead was a very dangerous one.

When Kellar and Fay completed their tour, they set out for Europe. They planned to sail from Brazil to Europe and then back home to the United States.

For Kellar it was a relaxing trip at first, with plenty of time to speculate on how far he had come and how much further still he intended to go. He owned his own magic equipment, stored safely in the hold of the ship. He had invested in Brazilian diamonds worth eight thousand dollars as a kind of nest egg. He was beginning to become accepted as a master conjurer, and he was convinced that if he worked harder than his rivals, there was no limit to how far he could go.

On a foggy Friday in 1875, the thirteenth of August, just as his ship neared the French coast, disaster struck.

The vessel ran aground and sank, along with all of Kellar's equipment, diamonds, and personal belongings—a total loss of almost twenty-five thousand dollars. Only the expeditious appearance of a French warship saved the passengers and most of the crew from drowning.

After this disaster, Fay left to join the Davenport Brothers and Kellar managed to get to London, where still another blow was awaiting him. He learned that the New York bank to which he had sent his remaining money had failed and that barely thirty-five hundred dollars of his funds had been saved.

Any ordinary man might have accepted the inevitability of his fate after two such financial disasters. But Harry Kellar was not an ordinary man.

With his skimpy funds, he managed to put together another show and soon after mounted one show after another, touring with them throughout the world.

His new company, the Royal Illusionists, traveled to Australia, Hong Kong, Singapore, and the rest of the Far East.

They moved on through Asia Minor, Africa, the countries of the Mediterranean, northern Europe, England, and then to the United States.

Harry Kellar was a consummate magician now. The clumsiness, the jerky movements, even the speech impediment were all behind him. Instead, when he walked onstage, he was perfection itself. Not a move—not even the blink of an eye—had been anything less than carefully planned and meticulously rehearsed in advance.

His conjuring style, unlike the laughing-devil approach of Herrmann the Great, was dramatic, mysterious, almost solemn. His tricks, spectacular to begin with, were made even more spectacular by the perfection of his presentations.

One good example of Kellar's quest for perfection was his execution of the classic growth-of-flowers illusion.

The illusion was basically a simple one. Two rosebushes in full bloom were produced from two empty flowerpots. Kellar placed the flowerpots onstage. He planted a seed in each pot, then covered each with a paper cone. After a few moments he uncovered the pots and revealed a sprouted seedling in each. He covered and uncovered the pots again, and the seedlings appeared to have grown. He did this repeatedly until he finally uncovered two flowering rosebushes.

In the hands of the masterful Kellar the roses were made to appear so slowly and so dramatically that his audiences insisted that the rosebushes had indeed grown and bloomed before their eyes.

To add to the illusion, Kellar, unlike other magicians, always used real roses—dozens of them—and often plucked them off and passed them out to the women in the audience.

The cost of the dozens of roses used in the illusion was often quite steep, especially during the winter months when they had to be shipped in daily from a considerable distance. However, such was Kellar's sense of perfection that he refused to perform the trick with imitation roses.

The world tours continued; Kellar and company crisscrossed the globe again and again. In most countries Kellar's performances drew sellout crowds and mounting acclaim. In the United States, however, a monumental rivalry developed between Herrmann the Great, the naturalized-American master, and Harry Kellar, the native-born master.

The advance men of one covered the posters and billboards of the other; each magician kept a sharp eye on the bookings of the other and more than once tried to arrange his own bookings so that his company would appear in the same cities ahead of his competitor.

There were undeniable benefits to the audiences of both great conjurers as the two fought to outdo each other with even more lavish presentations and even more spectacular illusions. Finally, realizing that the Western world was large enough for both of them, they became friends.

When Alex Herrmann died in 1896, the title of master American conjurer automatically went to Harry Kellar, and he, in turn, held it until he turned it over to the rising young Howard Thurston in 1908.

In 1922, fourteen years after his last professional performance, Harry Kellar died of pneumonia. He had reached the pinnacle of his chosen profession; he was acclaimed by millions in every part of the world; he had become, against all odds, a true master of magic.

The presence in the United States of two such marvelous masters of magic as Alex Herrmann and Harry Kellar may well have triggered an explosion of interest in magic in America.

Certainly there were a number of talented magicians performing for appreciative American audiences well before the turn of the century.

Most of them never quite managed to reach the same high levels of presentation and performance as Herrmann and Kellar. Nevertheless, by developing their own specialties, they were able to capture and entertain fair-sized followings of their own.

One of the best conjuring specialists was Thomas Nelson Downs, the self-styled King of Koins. A one-time railway ticket agent and telegrapher from Montour, Iowa, Downs developed an amazing ability to manipulate coins.

By combining his manipulative skills, his natural charm, and an updated version of the classic trick of snatching coins from the air—Downs called his version the Miser's Dream—he soon became a national sensation and one of the most imitated magicians of his day.

Another specialist was William Robinson, an American of Scottish descent, who found his greatest fame when he stepped into the character of an Oriental conjurer under the name of Chung Ling Soo.

Robinson was a kind of Renaissance man of magic, an all-around talent who worked as a designer of illusions, producer, stage manager, conjurer's assistant, and sometime conjurer himself.

One of Harry Kellar's greatest tricks—the slow, dramatic production of a fully-blooming rosebush from seed. Always the perfectionist, Kellar used real roses while other magicians used cheaper paper roses.

Poster announcement of "Page of Parlor Magic," a feature article that appeared in the New York World Sunday supplement on March 30, 1902. The article, describing some of Kellar's tricks, capitalized on widespread public interest in magic (right).

Bill announcing Harry Kellar's farewell tour. Accompanied by his hand-picked successor, Howard Thurston, Kellar began the tour in December 1907 and ended it in May 1908 with his final performance on the stage of Ford's Theater in Baltimore, Maryland (below).

Robinson was performing under the name of Achmed ben Ali when his Black Art illusion (inspired by Buatier de Kolta) caught the eye of Harry Kellar. Kellar was so impressed with the ingenious youngster's presentation that he hired him on the spot.

Kellar's confidence in Robinson's ability paid off handsomely. The young man designed and built a number of illusions that became highlights of the Kellar show. His insight into the deceptions used by mediums was invaluable when Kellar put together his own exposé of spiritualism. In addition, Robinson—under the name of Nana Sahib—turned out to be one of the finest onstage assistants in the business.

Several years and another name change later, Robinson—now Abdul Khan—was lured away from Kellar by his arch-rival, Alex Herrmann.

Working with Herrmann, Robinson continued to produce spectacular stage illusions, including one dramatic vanish based on an update of the classic Pepper's Ghost illusion.

The illusion involved the sudden disappearance of a girl from a chair that had been hoisted by ropes into the air. On a signal from the conjurer the girl vanished and the empty chair fell apart and crashed to the floor.

Robinson's clever illusion employed a sheet of plate glass built into the frame supporting the ropes. Once the girl was hoisted up behind the plate glass, the lighting was suddenly changed. The girl, supported by the ropes and hidden behind the glass, was now invisible to the audience. Simultaneously the breakaway chair in which she had been sitting—it was designed to fall apart the instant she was out of it—fell to the floor with a crash and added to the dramatic impact of the illusion.

In a somewhat different kind of vanish Alex Herrmann occasionally chose to take the day off from performing. On those days Robinson donned the costume and makeup of the master conjurer and did the entire show; the audience never discovered that it was not the Great Herrmann himself.

Eventually Robinson grew tired of being an unsung hero. He decided to go out on his own again, hoping to be recognized as a master conjurer in his own right. In spite of his acknowledged reputation among other conjurers as a genius, Robinson was notably unsuccessful until he adopted another name change and another change of character.

Robinson's inspiration for his Oriental-wizard character was a real Chinese conjurer named Ching Ling Foo, whose presentations of ancient Chinese magic had become an instant success in America.

Robinson, as Chung Ling Soo, hoped to duplicate that success—and did, until a tragic mishap during a presentation of his bullet-catching routine ended his life.

Meanwhile, out in what was still the Wild West, another young magician-to-be was practicing and perfecting a series of amazing card manipulations.

Those card tricks, along with a delightfully engaging personality, eventually brought the young conjurer to the attention of Harry Kellar and later to the attention of the whole world.

William Robinson as Chung Ling Soo performing the dangerous bullet-catching routine. During a March 1918 presentation, a gun misfired and sent a bullet into Robinson's right lung. He died the next day.

Magician
to
Millions

Howard Thurston

Thurston's long road to fame was marked with stops along the way as a newspaper boy, racetrack tout, budding missionary, and finally a master magician.

The young magician peered nervously around the room as he prepared to present his first trick — one that would ordinarily bring a generous round of applause.

But this was no ordinary audience eager to be dazzled and amused, and the young magician knew it. This was an audience of gamblers, of card sharps, of tough westerners who had learned to live by their wits as much as their brawn along this last American frontier.

Even the setting of the performance itself, a garish gambling hall typical of those which dotted the West in the 1890s, was a far cry from the elegant gas-lit theaters of the East.

The young magician took a deep breath. There was no turning back now. He bowed to the audience, smiled, and began the presentation of his trick Rising Card.

As he proceeded with the trick, he ordered the ten of diamonds to rise from the deck. Miraculously it did. Then he ordered the five of clubs to rise. Miraculously it did too. Then he ordered the queen of hearts to make her appearance. Nothing. Again he called, but this time

he used the flowery phrases of a cultured gentleman.

Suddenly the queen of hearts leaped out of the deck straight into the magician's hand, and the crowd roared its approval.

With a deck of cards carefully prepared in advance, a hidden silk thread, and a clever line of patter, the young magician Howard Thurston had won over one more tough audience. He had taken another step on the long road from newspaper boy to racetrack tout to budding missionary to master magician.

Thurston's interest in magic had actually begun in the summer of 1876 in the midwestern city of Columbus, Ohio. As a goggle-eyed seven-year-old boy, he peered down from the cheapest seats in the hall, watching a masterful performance of magic by Herrmann the Great, and swore that he too would become a magician.

There must have been thousands of youngsters across the country who saw the same show, made the same vow, and then went on to other things, and at first Howard Thurston appeared to be one of them.

Howard Thurston's famous Rising Card trick was first performed in a Wild West saloon.

He worked as a newspaper boy on the fast trains that ran from Columbus to other midwestern cities. He hoped to become a jockey and traveled from racetrack to racetrack, selling racing programs. He followed carnivals from town to town and began associating with an assortment of carnival folks, con men, and petty criminals.

Somewhere in his travels he stumbled across a used copy of Professor Hoffmann's encyclopedic *Modern Magic,* and his interest in magic was renewed. Using the book as a guide, Thurston began practicing sleight of hand every chance he could, and once again he vowed to become a magician.

During this time his mother was disturbed by the kind of life her son was leading. She was a deeply devout woman, and she was convinced that he should seek the comfort of religion as she had.

Her constant reminders, combined with a chance attendance at a revival meeting conducted by the famous evangelist Dwight Moody, convinced Thurston to become a medical missionary. He entered the Mount Hermon School in Massachusetts and earnestly began his studies. Yet, the lure of conjuring was not that easy to overcome. An occasional magic performance for his fellow students kept it alive, and even after graduation, as Thurston set out for Philadelphia with the full intention of enrolling as a medical student at the University of Pennsylvania, he could not shake the urge.

At a brief stopover in Albany he spotted a poster announcing a performance that evening by Herrmann the Great. Instantly a flood of memories filled Thurston's mind. He didn't hesitate. He could continue his journey to Philadelphia the next day; that evening he would watch the master magician once again.

The next morning both Thurston and the Herrmanns

happened to arrive at the Albany railroad station at the same time. Alex Herrmann and his wife were heading for Syracuse and another performance; Thurston was heading for Philadelphia and a career as a medical missionary.

Thurston walked up to the ticket agent and asked for a ticket to Philadelphia. The agent inadvertently punched out a ticket to Syracuse instead.

Thurston stared at the ticket just as the Syracuse train was being announced. For a second he paused. Then he caught a glimpse of the Herrmanns boarding the train and, almost without thinking, snatched up his bag and followed them aboard.

That evening in Syracuse Thurston watched Herrmann the Great perform, as he had the evening before in Albany, as he had seventeen years before in Columbus. While he was watching, he knew with certainty that he could never be anything but a magician.

Six months later, for the less-than-glorious sum of six dollars a week, Howard Thurston *was* a magician, performing with the Sells Brothers Circus in Nelsonville, Ohio.

From circus to dime museum to variety troupe, traveling through the Midwest and West, he performed before all kinds of audiences. Slowly but steadily he improved his conjuring skills, perfected his sleight of hand, and developed the sensational card tricks that were to become the highlights of his act.

The road to fame was a rough one, as Thurston's trips through the frontier West so often proved. However, an unexpected meeting in Denver, Colorado, seemed to offer a shortcut to success.

He was appearing at the Alcazar Theater at the same time as the Herrmann show was booked into the Tabor Grand Theater. This show was not the same one that had originally played such a decisive role in Thurston's life. Alex Herrmann had died and his wife and nephew Leon had taken over the company. Still, the Herrmann name was a great one and Thurston found himself irresistibly drawn to the lobby of their theater.

As he was admiring one of the Herrmann posters, a tall, sharp-eyed man walked over to him. The man asked if Thurston was the magician who had been appearing at the Alcazar. More than a little flattered, Thurston nodded. The man then told him that Leon Herrmann had expressed an interest in meeting the young conjurer, especially in discussing his Rising Card trick.

Stunned, Thurston watched the man walk away. Then he turned, went to the ticket office, and asked who the tall man was. When informed that he was Billy Robinson, stage manager for the Herrmann show, Thurston was beset by mixed emotions. The offer to meet Leon Herrmann seemed to be legitimate, and that pleased him. Yet, he certainly had no intention of disclosing to anyone—not even Leon Herrmann—how the Rising Card worked.

Thurston agreed to meet Leon Herrmann—it was an

The lovely young lady is about to become the subject of one of Harry Thurston's dazzling deceptions.

invitation he could not resist—but he politely refused to demonstrate the trick, claiming that it could not be shown in the confines of a hotel room. The quick-witted Thurston struck a deal with the curious Herrmann. He would show the trick to Herrmann and his company on their stage just before the curtain went up that evening for their regular performance.

As curtain time approached, Thurston dashed over to the office of the local newspaper, the Denver *Post,* and convinced the city editor to dispatch a reporter to the Tabor Grand Theater for a "mystifying" story. Then he rushed to the theater to set up the silk threads which were so essential to the success of the trick.

Thurston's presentation of the trick, ten minutes before curtain time, was as mystifying as he claimed it would be. It fooled the Herrmann company; it even fooled the sharp-eyed Leon Herrmann.

The next day the *Post* ran the story of the Rising Card, as presented at the Tabor, under the headline, "The Man Who Mystified Herrmann." Thurston gleefully sat back to wait for the offers he assumed would come flooding in.

After three weeks without a single offer Thurston was forced to face the fact that fame was still down the road, still waiting somewhere for him.

Somewhere turned out to be New York City and a brief engagement at the famous Tony Pastor's, which stretched into a solidly successful month of performances.

During that month Thurston gained a bright young assistant named George White, some money in his pocket at last, and a reputation as a rising headliner on the American vaudeville scene.

By 1900 Howard Thurston had arrived—as a vaudeville magician. He played the leading vaudeville houses in the United States and extended his fame to England, where he performed triumphantly at London's Palace Theater before cheering audiences, which now and again included the Prince of Wales himself.

Thurston certainly had every reason to be well pleased. But he was not—not yet. His fame so far had

In his Flowing Coconut illusion (below) Thurston appears to produce a continuous stream of water from an empty coconut shell. The water supply actually came from a series of pipes below stage.

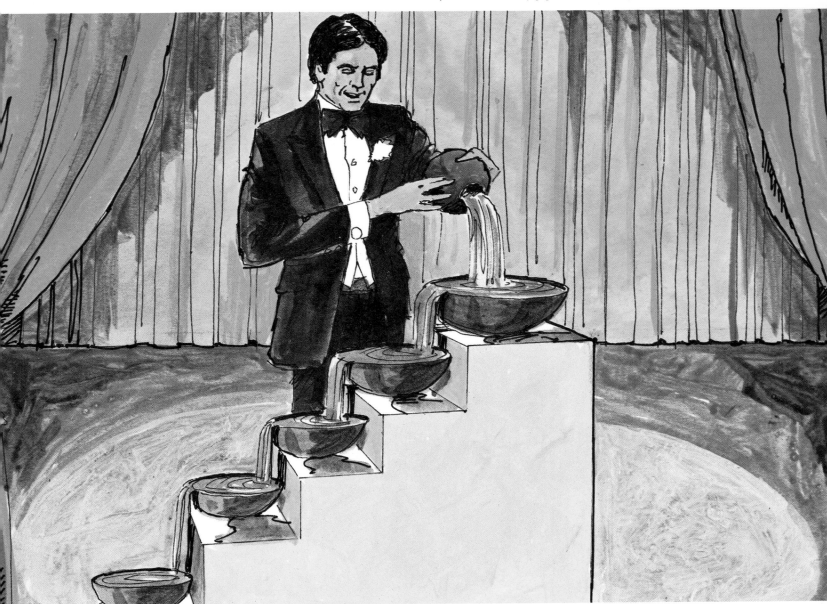

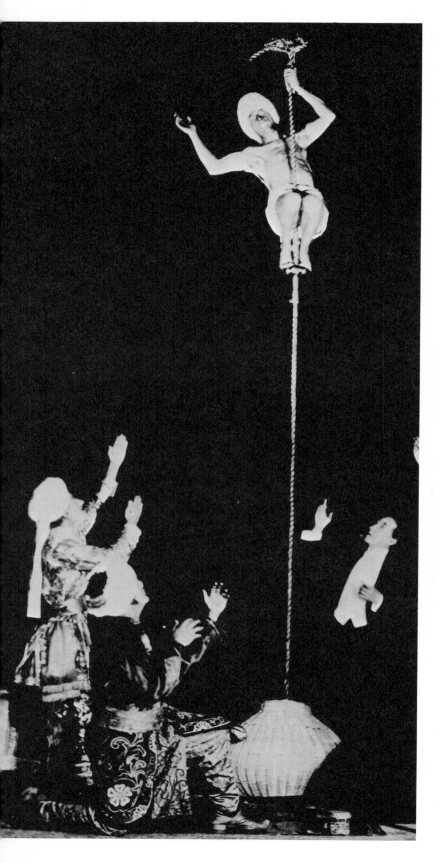

Thurston's version of the fabled Indian Rope trick, featuring a dramatic stage setting, several richly garbed assistants, and the vanish of the boy in a cloud of smoke.

been based on small magic—card manipulations and sleight of hand—amusing enough but in no way spectacular.

What he wanted to do was big magic—the same kinds of marvelous, mystical illusions that had dazzled a wide-eyed seven-year-old boy so many years before. With a courage rare among successful performers, he canceled his bookings, rented an apartment in London, and risked his total savings, some ten thousand dollars, to prepare a new big-magic show.

Working sixteen and eighteen hours a day with a hired crew of carpenters and costumers—and with the invaluable assistance of his new stage manager, George Townsend—Thurston put together his new show. Finally, when everything was ready—the exotic scenery, the beautiful girls in exquisite costumes, and, above all, the spectacular illusions—he invited several American booking agents to a special preview.

Impressed by what they had seen, the agents eagerly began bidding for his show. The winner was Paul Keith and the premiere American performance was scheduled for May 1902 in Keith's theater in Boston, Massachusetts.

According to the critics, the new Thurston magic show relied too heavily on elaborate scenery and special lighting effects. According to the audience, the show was nothing less than spectacular.

Thurston's illusions were incredible. He changed a marble statue into a beautiful woman and then made her disappear beneath a cloth of silk. He produced a cascade of inflated balloons from an empty opera hat. Instead of the customary fish bowls, he materialized a number of bowls which automatically burst into flame when they were raised to a certain position. He produced a marvelously staged illusion, called Flowing Coconut, which poured forth into a series of large tubs an unending supply of water. To further emphasize the fact that there was no connection between the water supply and the stage, he performed the illusion while standing on a glass stool.

The dazzled audience was so busy watching the water cascade down from the large coconut shell that they did not see the jet of water shoot up through a pipe concealed in the first of the tubs and splash into the shell before it splashed back down again. Once the hidden supply of water was turned off on cue below stage, Thurston could exhibit a perfectly dry coconut shell to the audience.

These astonishing illusions, along with the new ones he added each year, were surefire successes everywhere he played. However, they utilized large amounts of expensive heavy equipment, whose construction, shipping, and handling ate deeply into his profits.

The need to make more money and perhaps the desire to build a great name for himself abroad and return home like a conquering hero impelled Thurston to set out on a tour of the world.

He arrived in Australia in 1905 and did turnaway business for almost a year. He moved on through the Orient, where his audiences did not always appreciate his rapid presentation of one illusion after another. He continued on to India, where fear over a deadly plague severely reduced the size of his audiences, leaving him with a shortage of funds.

As he wondered where to turn next, he received a cable from Harry Kellar, inviting him to join Kellar's show in return for a part interest in it.

By 1907 Thurston was back in the United States, performing side by side with the master magician whose successor he would be.

For one full season they worked together. Then in May 1908 the old master, Kellar, stepped aside to make way for the new master, Thurston.

Thurston continued to travel from coast to coast for another twenty-seven years, bringing his big-magic show to millions. Every year he added a mystifying new illusion to his presentation or a dazzling new version of an old one.

One such update, a modern version of the classic Floating Lady, was one of the most spectacular illusions ever presented. In this adaptation, which Thurston called the Levitation of Princess Karnac, a shroud-covered figure seemed to rise slowly from a couch, hang effortlessly in midair, then suddenly disappear.

The secret involved several key pieces of equipment—a couch with a trapdoor through which the lady dropped; a wire fake, which duplicated her form under the shroud; and a backstage crank, which moved the shrouded form up and down on command.

Other magicians had presented levitations; but the greatness of Howard Thurston was such that when he presented his levitation, audiences were convinced that he was not merely a conjurer but a man who could actually create miracles.

When Thurston died at the age of sixty-six in 1936, he was mourned by millions who had been convinced that he was the greatest illusionist of them all.

Of all the great conjurers who enhanced and enlivened the golden age of magic, perhaps none captured the public's imagination as completely—nor won its adulation as totally—as the legendary Harry Houdini.

His fame was international; his daring escapes made newspaper headlines almost daily. His fees were the highest paid to any performer in his era. His appearances around the world shattered existing box office records and drew throngs of eager admirers who were willing to stand for hours just to catch a glimpse of him.

One of Thurston's finest illusions—the visible changing of a statue into a living woman.

Houdini's superb skills convinced millions that he possessed supernatural powers, that he could literally shrink his bones at will or make his body pass through any obstacle, from a metal box to a solid brick wall. How else could he make his miraculous escapes from the ropes and chains and steel coffins which so easily held mere mortals?

Throughout most of his career Houdini publicly denied that he possessed such supernatural powers and even went so far as to explain many of his tricks in detail. In spite of these denials, the legends grew and persisted, and even today, a full half century after his death, many people still believe them.

Unfortunately popular myth has almost totally eclipsed the man himself, obscuring the fact that he was, above all, a master showman whose physical stamina and raw courage could turn a series of ordinary tricks into extraordinary entertainment.

The Great Escape

Harry Houdini

The man who became a legend in his own lifetime was born Ehrich Weiss in Budapest, Hungary, in 1874 and was brought to the United States — to the small midwestern town of Appleton, Wisconsin — as a babe in arms.

Although he remembered nothing of his family's cultured and comfortable life in Budapest nor of their desperate flight from Hungary to escape persecution, Ehrich Weiss knew that he was different from the other boys in Appleton.

There was the inevitable struggle to learn the customs and culture of his new home land. There was the ritual practice of his religion under the firm guidance of his father, who had been a respected rabbi and teacher in Hungary. Also, there was the grinding poverty, which seemed even harder to bear since the family had been prosperous in Hungary.

By accident — or perhaps because there was never enough money to buy toys — the young boy developed an early fascination for piles of junk and, in particular, for discarded locks, which were intriguing playthings.

His interest in discovering how locks worked was surpassed only by his delight with the traveling circuses which often played in Appleton.

Whenever a circus arrived in town, Ehrich and the other boys followed along to share some of the glamour and excitement. While the others were content to stand back and watch the commotion, he was not. He begged the rehearsing performers to teach him some of their tricks. Impressed by the youngster's eagerness — or eager to get rid of him — some of them did just that.

Soon he had mastered a few tricks that he had learned from a sideshow magician and a few stunts copied from the routine of a circus acrobat. With these new skills he was able to entertain and amuse the other boys and gain for himself the kind of acceptance among his peers that, as a Jewish immigrant, he had never known before.

His tricks may have hastened his social acceptance but they did little to help his family solve the problem of economic survival. He therefore took all sorts of odd jobs to increase the family's limited finances.

One job, as apprentice to a local locksmith, deepened his already-keen interest in the manipulation and picking of locks. Another job, a brief stint as a boy

Hypnotic-eyed Harry Houdini became a legend in his own time with death-defying escapes.

Early poster (right) billing Houdini as the King of Cards during his stint with the Welsh Brothers' traveling show.

acrobat and contortionist with a traveling circus, helped to set a lifetime pattern of keeping himself in perfect physical condition.

The money that Ehrich and the other Weiss children brought in was added to the meager seven hundred fifty dollars that their father, Samuel Weiss, earned in a year as Appleton's first rabbi: the family just about managed to get by. When Samuel Weiss was replaced by a younger man, the family was forced to move—first to Milwaukee and then to New York City—in search of financial security.

In New York Ehrich put aside his interest in conjuring, at least temporarily, to take a steady job as an assistant tie-lining cutter in a necktie factory on lower Broadway. In his spare time, he continued to stay in top physical condition by running for a neighborhood track team and swimming in the East River near the Weiss home.

His interest in conjuring, however, could not be subdued for long. When he came across a copy of the memoirs of Robert-Houdin, he read it eagerly. The story of the great French conjurer inspired and

fascinated him and set him dreaming about becoming a master magician himself, "just like Robert-Houdin."

Ehrich dared not reveal his ambitions to his dignified father, but he did confide them to Jack Hayman, one of his co-workers at the necktie factory.

Jack could easily understand Ehrich's dreams because he too was an amateur magician with his own dream of breaking into show business. In fact, it was Hayman who suggested that Ehrich adopt the famous French conjurer's name—with an "i" added—to indicate that he was indeed comparable to the great Robert-Houdin.

So seventeen-year-old Ehrich Weiss—necktie maker, acrobat, apprentice locksmith, and dreamer—became Houdini the magician, partner of Hayman the magician.

The partnership, with Ehrich—now known as Harry Houdini—playing the conjurer and Jack Hayman

Young Houdini performs Metamorphosis, an early trunk escape, with his brother Theodore. Houdini used the same escape, under the title Substitution Trunk, in a later full-length magic show.

Snapshot taken in the late 1890s of the Harry Houdinis and the Harry Kellars (above).

Although he made his reputation as an escape artist, Houdini (left) conjured with cards at every opportunity.

acting as his foil, sputtered along with occasional one-night stands at fraternal meetings and social clubs. However, Hayman, understandably, was displeased with the arrangements and with the lack of bookings. He soon dropped out of the act and was replaced by his brother, Joe Hayman, who, in turn, was replaced by Ehrich's brother Theodore Weiss.

For all its changing personnel, the act—billed as the Houdini Brothers—never became successful, although one trick showed promise of the brilliance which would come later.

The trick, which Harry Houdini called Metamorphosis, came directly from the repertoire of John Nevil Maskelyne. Houdini, however, improved on it, added a few twists of his own, and eventually made it one of the highlights of his show.

In Houdini's version he had himself tied inside a cloth sack and lifted by Theodore into a trunk, which had been thoroughly inspected by several members of the audience. Next the trunk was roped and padlocked, and then it was concealed behind a cloth-sided cabinet, which Theodore pushed into position.

Within a matter of seconds Houdini pulled aside the cloth and revealed himself—free of the trunks, the sack, and the ropes which had bound him. But now, miraculously, Theodore was inside the trunk, bound precisely as Harry had been only a few seconds before.

A trick sack and a trunk with a secret panel accounted for most of the mystery. Skillful execution of the classic Kellar rope-tie escape, based on months of practice, accounted for the rest.

Not even the deft and dramatic Metamorphosis, however, could lift the Houdini Brothers out of their obscurity. Houdini therefore wangled a booking with a sideshow at the Chicago World's Fair of 1893 and set out once again for the Midwest.

Houdini's sideshow act leaned heavily on a series of escapes from ropes, handcuffs, and other bindings. This was a time when so-called escape artists were appearing in circuses and sideshows everywhere.

Most of them were not conjurers so much as skilled lock pickers, and audiences were already assuming, quite accurately, that their escapes were usually made from rigged or fake bindings.

Houdini's escapes, on the contrary, were legitimate. They were based on his encyclopedic knowledge of locks and his specially designed collection of master keys and wire lock picks. They were also based on his physical ability to make all of the muscles in his superbly conditioned body respond to the demands he put on them.

He had an additional ability which set him far above the others who called themselves escape artists. He was able to force his mind to focus on a single problem to

97

German poster features Houdini's famous Chinese Water Torture Cell. Houdini offers 5,000 marks to anyone who can uncover the secret.

the exclusion of everything else—even to the exclusion of natural, almost instinctive human fears.

These extraordinary abilities, together with his keen sense of publicity and drama, eventually made Harry Houdini an international sensation.

However, at this time, before he became famous, few people recognized the hypnotic-eyed, nineteen-year-old conjurer's vast potential. One who did was a pretty, young New York schoolgirl named Beatrice ("Bessie") Rahner.

Houdini met her soon after he returned from Chicago. Eager to accept any booking, he was performing at a school in Brooklyn; she and her mother were members of the audience.

The performance went badly, probably because Houdini could not take his eyes off the pretty girl in the first row. During one trick, he accidentally spilled some liquid on her dress. This led to their meeting; and ten

days later, over her mother's vehement protests, the two were married.

Once again the name of the act was changed, to the Houdinis, Harry and Bessie. Once again bookings were scarce and the newlyweds struggled to survive.

For the next half-dozen years Harry and Bessie Houdini fought to gain a foothold in the glittering world of show business. They traveled through the United States and Canada, playing second-rate engagements in half-empty halls. When their tours broke down for want of money, as they often did, they moved to circuses and traveling medicine shows. They tried developing a musical comedy act. They tried acting with a traveling repertory company. Houdini even tried opening a school for magic, which failed because of lack of students.

For all their failures, Houdini would not, could not, give up the magic he loved. He did not doubt for an instant that he could conquer any challenge, whether it was the escape from a seemingly inescapable confinement or the escape from his dismal failure to attain success.

After six heartbreaking years Houdini's first real success came early in 1899 in Saint Paul, Minnesota. His appearance at a small local hall—and his boast that he could escape from any restraint made by man— attracted the attention of Martin Beck, booking agent for the Orpheum vaudeville circuit.

Beck went up to Houdini, dangled a formidable looking pair of handcuffs in front of him and asked, somewhat skeptically, if he thought he could escape from them.

Houdini nodded emphatically—and he did. Impressed, Beck offered Houdini a chance to appear on the Orpheum circuit if he eliminated his magic presentations and redesigned his act to feature escapes from any shackles offered by the audience.

To publicize his new act, Houdini visited local police stations in the cities where he was to perform and dared the officials to prevent his escaping their shackles and their jails.

In Omaha he escaped from five pairs of handcuffs and a set of regulation leg irons. In San Francisco he escaped from ten pairs of handcuffs and a regulation straitjacket used for uncontrollable prisoners. In Kansas City, after being searched and stripped naked, he escaped from five sets of wrist and ankle shackles—and a locked jail cell—in just under eight minutes.

Local newspaper accounts of Houdini's miraculous escapes helped to guarantee a successful western tour. Yet, they did not convince the managers of the major vaudeville theaters in the East that his act deserved to be booked.

An ordinary man might well have savored even a regional success, coming as it did after many years of abject failure. But Harry Houdini was not an ordinary man. He was determined to prove that he was, as he claimed, the greatest escape artist who ever lived. The place to prove it, he decided, was London, England, home of the famed Scotland Yard.

In London he found himself in the same precarious position as before. He was running short of money; London theater managers were not eager to book the brash young American; even Superintendent Melville of Scotland Yard scoffed at his claims, until an almost instantaneous escape by Houdini from a pair of the Yard's finest handcuffs changed his mind.

Once again newspaper headlines told of the man who could not be held by handcuffs, and the bookings

Houdini (above) being shackled by police officials in Washington, D.C.

Artist's version (right) of Houdini's escape from an Amsterdam jail includes confirming statement by Dutch police officials.

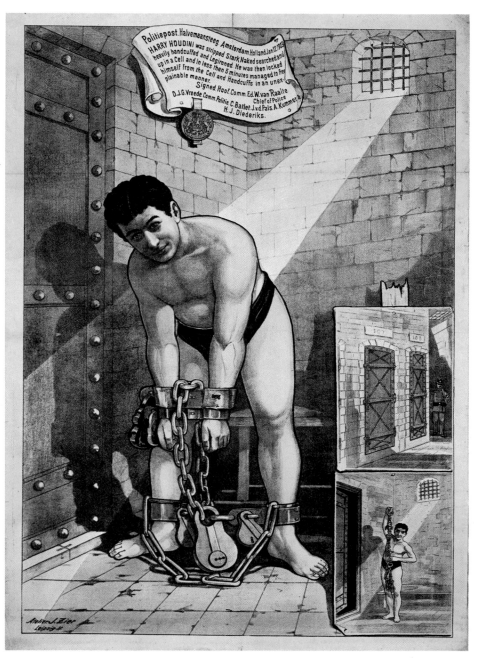

began coming in. Once again he dared the manufacturers of all kinds of restraints—handcuffs, leg irons, straitjackets, cages, packing boxes—to keep him from escaping. Once again he was able to free himself from all of them.

With each new escape Houdini's fame on both sides of the Atlantic Ocean increased, and so did his desire to undertake even more dangerous escapes.

In the winter of 1906, during one of his American tours, Houdini, shackled by two pairs of handcuffs, jumped off the Belle Isle bridge in Detroit, Michigan, into the icy waters below. He managed to free himself from the handcuffs seconds before his fingers became too numb to move.

He performed a similar escape from the bottom of New York's East River; this time his hands were shackled and he was nailed into a heavy wooden packing box weighted with two hundred pounds of lead.

Still another miraculous river escape took place

before twenty thousand gaping spectators in Melbourne, Australia, when he jumped off Queen's Bridge into the Yarra River.

As the legend of the great escape artist continued to grow, so did the number of imitators who sought to outdo the master. Houdini topped them all by the simple expedient of doing what they would not dare try.

He permitted himself to be lashed to the muzzle of a fully loaded cannon to which a twenty-minute fuse had been lit. In full view of a breathless audience of thousands he managed to free himself in thirteen minutes.

On another occasion he permitted himself to be tied to a railroad track just fifteen minutes before a speeding express train was due to reach the spot. He had freed his hands and was still struggling with the ropes binding his feet when the train came roaring down the track.

With every ounce of his strength he managed to fling his body over the side of the track and pull his feet, still bound, to the outside of the rail. A second later the train screamed past, slicing through the rope and missing his feet by inches.

On still another occasion he permitted himself to be locked inside a large milk churn, confident that he could pry off the clamped top with a concealed metal wedge.

Houdini's assistants casually placed a cloth-sided screen around the milk churn, assuming, as Houdini had assumed, that the escape would be a routine one. But because it was made of rough-hewn wood, the churn appeared bigger on the outside than it actually was. Houdini discovered to his horror that his own cramped body was blocking off most of the air holes which had been drilled into the churn in preparation for the escape attempt.

Houdini realized that his only chance would be to attract the attention of his assistants, who would instantly pry off the top.

Fighting for breath, he managed to topple over the churn. When it hit the floor, it landed by pure luck on the clamp, snapping it open.

Free of the churn, Houdini took a deep breath. He righted the churn, reclamped the lid, pushed aside the screen, and strolled casually to center stage to accept the cheers of the audience.

The most dramatic of Houdini's escapes was made from a large glass-front cabinet filled with water, the so-called Chinese Water Torture Cell.

Suspended upside down from iron ankle stocks, Houdini was lowered into the water-filled cabinet,

Houdini about to be sealed into a weighted box before attempting his escape from the waters of New York harbor in 1914.

Houdini struggles to free himself moments before an oncoming train slices through the rope still binding his feet to the outside of the railroad track. The crowd was convinced that Houdini had been killed—until the master escape artist reappeared unharmed.

which was then covered and locked. A curtained cabinet was then positioned around the cell so that the audience could not watch the escape.

It has been theorized that once inside the cell, Houdini doubled himself up, keeping his head above water. He quickly released his ankles from the stocks, righted himself, slid open the specially designed top to make his escape, replaced the top, and relocked it. Dripping wet, he waved away the curtained cabinet and permitted the awed audience to examine the sealed and locked torture cell.

With each new escape Houdini added to his legend. His name on a theater marquee guaranteed a standing-room-only audience. His appearances anywhere in public drew crowds of many thousands, eager for a glimpse of the superman who challenged death—and won.

Yet, Houdini was not satisfied. The daring escapes, which had brought him fame and fortune, were to him only stepping stones to his real goal, a full-length magic show of his own.

Finally, in 1925 he set out to prove to the world that he was a master conjurer and not just an escape artist.

He put together a three-hour show of magic, which opened with a series of standard conjuring tricks made outstanding by his skillful presentation. Next on the program was an old favorite—Metamorphosis—and an exciting new illusion in which he appeared to swallow a very long piece of thread and a dozen packages of needles and then pull them from his mouth fully threaded.

No Houdini show would be complete without at least one escape; so he offered the now-classic Chinese Water Torture Cell.

The second half of Houdini's show reflected his long-

standing interest in exposing fraudulent spiritualist mediums; it featured a series of dramatic exposés of their methods.

Houdini's interest in the techniques used by fraudulent spiritualists had begun as a professional one; he had used some of their ruses himself during the lean years when he traveled with circuses and medicine shows.

Later, following the death of his mother, he sought out spiritualists in the dim hope that he had been wrong, that somehow through them he might actually be able to communicate with her.

It was a vain hope, and when he gave it up at last, he was more determined than ever to expose their methods.

Houdini's show was an immediate success. But the burden of producing it, rehearsing it, and booking it into theaters around the country fell entirely on his shoulders and left him physically exhausted.

A brief summer vacation, taken before the start of the 1926 season, should have given Houdini, now fifty-two years old, an opportunity to rest and regain his strength. Instead, it became a continuing round of planning and publicity sessions for his upcoming tour.

When the tour began in the fall of 1926, his physical strength and stamina were still below par, which may have led indirectly to a broken ankle sustained during the presentation of an escape from his Chinese Water Torture Cell.

Against the advice of his doctors, he went on with the tour. A second accident occurred, and the fates, which had smiled on Harry Houdini for a long time, seemed suddenly to desert him.

He was resting in his dressing room when several young university students came to visit him. They talked briefly about the show and about his reported ability to withstand severe physical punishment.

One of the students asked Houdini if the stories were true; absentmindedly, Houdini nodded.

Taking Houdini's response as an invitation, the boy aimed a hard blow at the magician's abdomen. Unprepared, Houdini took the full force of the blow. He waved the boy off, but the damage had already been done.

The next day Houdini felt increasing pain in the area where he had received the blow. Still, he refused to call off his scheduled performance. He struggled through the first act, fighting off waves of pain. The pain intensified during the second act and only sheer willpower got him through it.

When the final curtain fell, he was rushed to the nearest hospital. A ruptured appendix, the cause of his intense pain, was removed by emergency surgery but it was too late. Peritonitis had set in as a result of the rupture, and the poison had spread throughout his body.

For seven days and nights he hovered between life and death. On the seventh night, October 31, 1926, the extraordinary Harry Houdini was dead.

Harry Houdini was by far the most famous conjurer to have appeared on the vaudeville stage, but he was not the only one.

By the turn of the century vaudeville had replaced the magic theater of Robert-Houdin's day. Rather than dim the glory of the conjurer's art, vaudeville served to broaden its appeal and its audiences. No vaudeville bill was complete without at least one magic act. The more unusual the act, the better.

Thousands of magicians developed novelty acts and were successful enough to be gainfully employed fifty-two weeks a year, even though they never quite gained the status or the salary of a headliner.

Others, however, by combining consummate skill and

Artist's rendition of Horace Goldin's version of the spectacular illusion of sawing a woman in half. Goldin claimed the illusion as his own, although it was originally created by P.T. Selbit.

unique presentation, headed the bill wherever they appeared and deserved consideration as masters of magic in their own right.

P.T. Selbit, a tall, thin Englishman, seemed much too polite and genteel to torture ladies. Yet, he built an entire act around a series of clever illusions presenting female assistants walking through walls or being crushed by weighted boxes or being stretched almost to the breaking point.

Selbit's most sensational conjuring trick was the now-classic illusion of sawing a woman in half, and the magician played his role to the hilt.

After locking his "victim" in a box, thrusting three panes of glass and two steel blades through several parts of her anatomy, and dramatically slicing the box in half with a crosscut saw, Selbit ordered his assistants to open the locks and raise the lid.

He peeked inside the box and immediately turned to the audience with a look of horror etched across his face. Almost instinctively the audience responded by leaning forward in anticipation of the worst.

When the tension became almost unbearable, Selbit's frown turned into a wide grin. He reached out to help his assistant, still in one piece, rise to her feet; the audience exploded in cheers of relief.

Selbit's sensational illusion was a smash hit on the vaudeville circuits and, incidentally, triggered an immediate reaction from his rival, Horace Goldin, who claimed that the illusion was his invention.

Goldin, born of Polish parents in Lithuania and brought to the United States when he was sixteen, had become a headliner himself; he presented as many illusions in a single act as most magicians present in an entire career. In keeping with his rapid-fire delivery of one illusion after another, Goldin, to save time, presented his version of sawing a woman in half using a power-driven circular saw.

Vaudeville's top illusionists, like Selbit and Goldin, dealt in spectacle and high drama. Specialists of small magic, who utilized sleight of hand and small props in their stage acts—like Nate Leipzig, Joseph Michael Hartz, Gus Fowler, and Richard Pitchford (better known as Cardini)—presented adroit manipulations which were finely honed gems of skill and style.

The successful presentation on a large stage of sleight of hand manipulations owed much to the trailblazing of a pair of earlier geniuses. One, the Viennese card manipulator Johann Nepomuk Hofzinser, invented dozens of methods of conjuring with cards. The other, German-born Wiljalba Frikell, turned to sleight of hand in desperation when his conjuring equipment was destroyed in a fire. His sleight of hand astounded his audience and he never returned to the use of elaborate equipment.

With their own lightning-fast sleight of hand, the inheritors of the small-magic school of conjuring amazed vaudeville audiences just as Hofzinser and Frikell had dazzled theirs.

Nate Leipzig, born Nathan Leipzinger in Stockholm, Sweden, won international fame by performing marvelous tricks with a deck of cards.

Joseph Michael Hartz, England's one-time Crystal Illusionist, capped a long conjuring career by creating an eighteen-minute vaudeville act titled "The Devil of a Hat."

On a bare stage, with only several thin-topped tables in front of him, Hartz would pull from a seemingly empty hat a hundred yards of ribbon, seven cigar boxes, seven lighted lamps, a canary in a cage, twenty silver and eighteen glass goblets, a wig, a skull, a dozen champagne bottles, thousands of playing cards, twelve large silk scarves, a doll, a handsome porcelain bowl, and a glass fish bowl complete with water and goldfish. He did it all with such natural movements that the effect seemed truly magical.

Gus Fowler, a former British librarian, worked swiftly and silently through a seventeen-minute act, producing and vanishing hundreds of watches and clocks with such skill that his audiences gasped in amazement.

Of all the sleight of hand magic specialists, perhaps the greatest was the Welsh conjurer Richard Valentine Pitchford.

Unsuccessful under the names of Valentine, Professor Thomas, and Val Raymond, Pitchford continued to polish his act and his stage personality until he became Cardini (so named because he was adept with cards), the slightly tipsy English gentleman who was bemused and somewhat victimized by his own dazzling sleight of hand.

A favorite portrait (far left) of the master sleight of hand expert Cardini in characteristic garb. Monocle and cigarette holder were standard Cardini props.

A bemused Cardini (center), holding a fan of cards which had materialized in his hand. After dropping the cards into a newspaper held by his assistant, Cardini (near left) is bewildered to discover another fan of cards beginning to materialize.

As Cardini, he appeared as bewildered as the audience when a fan of playing cards suddenly blossomed in his hand.

Dropping the cards into a newspaper held by an obliging assistant, Cardini was startled to see another fan of cards materialize in his other hand. Even as he struggled to pull off his gloves, perfectly formed fans of cards kept popping up to plague him.

Shaken, he removed his cape and top hat and struggled to light a cigarette, using a match which appeared from nowhere. As he reached out to light his cigarette, the match flew out of his hand and sailed in a high arc across the stage. The next match did the same; as did the next.

If the cards had plagued him before, the materialization out of thin air of billiard balls and what seemed to be dozens of lighted cigarettes plagued him even more.

As his audience gasped in astonished admiration, the performance continued without a word being spoken. No words were necessary. Cardini's slightly lurching walk, his bewildered expression, the comic drop of his monocle from his widened eye, and the final appearance of a lit pipe from nowhere enchanted his audiences, who responded with waves of applause.

Illusionists and sleight of hand experts may have been preeminent on the vaudeville scene, but there were also specialists in mental magic, and one of the greatest of them was New York-born Joseph Dunninger.

Like Houdini and Kellar, the sheer force of Dunninger's personality was a tacit challenge to his audiences. He could not read their minds, of course, but such was his skill and his dominating stage presence that he convinced audiences everywhere he was, as he billed himself, the Master Mind of Mental Mystery.

No matter what props they used, each of these successful conjurers, like the great past masters of magic, had the ability to control and direct and dominate his audience.

That ability to command an audience was never more evident nor more crucial than during a performance by Harry Blackstone, the last great illusionist of the golden age of magic.

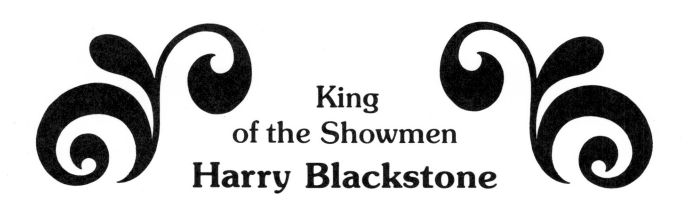

King
of the Showmen
Harry Blackstone

It was early September 1942. The Lincoln Theater in Decatur, Illinois, was packed with three thousand spectators, most of them children, eagerly awaiting the appearance of the great Harry Blackstone.

Blackstone finally appeared, smilingly acknowledged the audience's enthusiastic greeting, and began performing.

Like most magicians, Blackstone was aware that playing before an audience of children was difficult, if only because they were not as easily distracted as their elders and therefore not as readily fooled by the bits of misdirection which are so crucial to an illusionist's success.

Blackstone, the master conjurer, soon had his young audience agog with amazement and delight.

Master showman Harry Blackstone in a rare serious pose.

Blackstone appears on the sidewalk after having prevented a near-disaster by calmly leading the audience out of burning Lincoln Theater (right).

While he was performing, Blackstone heard a commotion going on backstage. An instant later one of his assistants whispered to him that some of the buildings next to the theater were on fire.

Blackstone cast a quick glance toward the wings and saw the agitated figure of a fireman gesturing to him to stop the show.

With barely a raised eyebrow to show his concern, Blackstone calmly strode to the front of the stage and raised his arms.

He announced to his audience that his next trick was so vast and so marvelous that it could not be presented on an ordinary stage; instead, it would have to be presented outside the theater.

At that point, willing to believe anything the master conjurer told them, the audience obediently followed Blackstone's instructions. They marched out of the theater calmly and quietly row by row exactly as he told them—and just barely in time.

Within seconds the theater was filled with the acrid smell of smoke and the sound of fire sirens cut through the air.

With the theater safely emptied and with the knowledge that his assistants were salvaging his magic equipment from backstage, Blackstone went out on the sidewalk. He was greeted by a rousing cheer as the audience suddenly realized how Blackstone's composure had averted a panic and had very likely saved their lives.

It was this kind of quick thinking that marked the career of the man who was born Henri Bouton in Chicago, Illinois, in 1885.

A chance visit to a performance by Harry Kellar convinced young Harry—he had already Anglicized his given name—to become a conjurer.

Before long Harry and his brother Peter had put together their own magic act as Harry Bouton and Company. When the act fell on hard days, Harry set out on his own as an illusionist, using equipment he had purchased cut-rate from another midwestern magician named Albini.

With another name change—to Blackstone—he enlarged and augmented his act until it became a full-length magic show. With almost a dozen assistants he set out on a tour of the United States just as it entered World War I.

Harry Blackstone's big-magic show was an immediate success. It featured spectacular illusions, a stage full of beautiful girls in elaborate costumes, and his own verve, flair, and impish sense of humor.

Although the big illusions—like sawing girls in half or levitating them or materializing them from empty cabinets—attracted audiences to the theater to be awed and amazed, it was actually Blackstone's small-magic tricks that captivated them night after night.

One such trick began with a handkerchief borrowed from a member of the audience. After tying a knot in its corner and attaching an invisible thread to it, he announced that he would "show you all a real live spook."

He placed the handkerchief in a cabinet, backed away, and watched as the handkerchief, to the

While two pretty assistants watch, Harry Blackstone prepares to vanish the bird and cage in his hands.

While an amazed spectator watches (left), Blackstone pulls his assistant's head from a magical tube. It's Blackstone's turn to be amazed (right) as he pulls a rabbit from an "empty" box.

accompaniment of the orchestra, began to stir.

A corner of the handkerchief first appeared out of the cabinet, as if to see what was going on. Then the handkerchief climbed out of the cabinet and began to follow Blackstone around the stage. It danced with him, although it insisted on leading rather than following. It squirmed and wriggled even as it was being returned to its owner, but back in its owner's hand it became once again a limp bit of cloth.

Blackstone's ability to make audiences accept a "dancing" handkerchief was an indication of his conjuring greatness. His ability to tailor his magic to the changing entertainment tastes of the times was an indication of his superb showmanship.

When large traveling magic shows lost their popularity to vaudeville, he condensed his show and played the circuits. When vaudeville began losing its audiences to the motion picture houses, he repackaged his tricks and illusions and performed in civic auditoriums and legitimate theaters throughout the United States and Canada. When the entertainment needs of World War II servicemen and women demanded a traveling show, he repackaged once again and was ready to go.

The Blackstone unit—sponsored by the United Service Organizations (USO) under the nonmagical designation of Camp Show 53—was made up of twenty-six performers and assistants and seventy tons of equipment, all under the direction of the white-haired master of magic.

The troupe performed at 165 military installations, traveled over thirty-six thousand miles, and faced the most horrendous logistics problems in moving its equipment. The troupe played in bare auditoriums or on makeshift stages when nothing else was available and still managed to become one of the most popular of all USO shows.

Blackstone and his company played through cyclones and tornadoes. They often played without sleep, without adequate preparation, without backdrops or curtains. They played as they fought off a horde of rats or exposed themselves to polio, risking the dangers of an epidemic.

No matter what obstacles the troupe encountered, Blackstone presented his magic with the verve and style and dashing instincts of a born showman.

Blackstone was the last of the great masters of magic,

BIGGEST NECROMANTIC EXPOSITION ON EARTH

BLACKSTONE

GREATEST MAGICIAN WORLD HAS EVER KNOWN

ORIENTAL NIGHTS — BLACKSTONE'S TENFOLD PAGEANT OF THE EAST — A STAGE SPECTACLE SUCH AS RIVALS THE REGAL SPLENDOR OF SOLOMON'S COURT AND IN KALEIDOSCOPIC METAMORPHOSES OUTBIDS THE AURORA BOREALIS—CORPS OF BEWILDERING, BEAUTIFUL NAUTCH GIRLS THE ENCHANTED CAMEL—THE PHANTOM STALLION—ALL AND MORE IN THIS COLORFUL EXTRAVAGANZA.

Poster inspired by Blackstone's "Oriental Nights" presentation features so-called oriental dancing girls, a levitating camel, and the legendary Indian Rope trick.

the last of a line of illustrious conjurers whose talent, taste, creativity, personality, endurance, and passionate love of conjuring had brought the magician's art of deception into its finest era.

When Harry Blackstone died on November 17, 1965, there was the distinct impression that one was witnessing the final curtain on a spectacular, century-long golden age of magic.

As the fabulous golden age was drawing to a close, a new breed of conjurers was appearing on the magic scene. They were superb showmen, just as the old-timers had been. They skillfully combined technological know-how with the flair of the ancient street performer and presented their magic mixed with a solid helping of practical modern psychology.

Unlike the old-timers, these modern conjurers had to compete with the marvels of twentieth-century technology. It was two of those marvels, motion pictures and television, that were instrumental in

shutting down vaudeville and forcing magicians, whose names had once been featured on vaudeville bills all over the world, to seek other arenas in which to practice their art.

However, the ancient art of conjuring is indestructible and so is its universal appeal; the vaudeville conjurer soon found new settings and new audiences.

One of the first of these new settings was the nightclub stage; one of the most successful of the nightclub conjurers was the American Jack Gwynne, a former vaudevillian.

Gwynne carefully engineered his illusions so that they were effective even within the restrictive confines of a nightclub floor. Since he had to work in the round, with the audience able to spy on him from many angles, he cleverly used his assistants to conceal his deceptions.

Gwynne's masterful new techniques helped to make possible the presentation of nightclub illusions and opened the way for illusionists to entertain successfully in the middle of a dance floor.

Although it seemed almost impossible for the sleight of hand conjurer to conquer the problems of performing in the round, by altering their methods slightly, master manipulators like Cardini, Nate Leipzig, and the Americans John Scarne, Fred Keating, and John Mulholland were able to dazzle, delight, and mystify their audiences.

The purveyors of mental magic, like the dynamic Joseph Dunninger, did not need to change their methods as the manipulators did. But with an increased public interest in the broad field of extrasensory perception (ESP), many of them tossed out their now-obsolete spirit cabinets and concentrated instead on telepathy, thought transference, and other displays of extrasensory perception, which intrigued modern audiences just as ghostly presences had once amazed earlier audiences.

Although the death of vaudeville forced many conjurers to develop new techniques and seek new audiences, it did not signal the end of the big-magic show, which specialized in classic illusion.

Packing a massive forty-six tons of equipment and transporting it by any method he could find, the

American illusionist Virgil the Great traveled to the far corners of the earth with his spectacular show of magic.

Another brilliant illusionist who came to prominence following World War II was the young Bengali Protul Chandra Sorcar. Sorcar had already built a reputation for himself as the greatest magician in the East. By 1955 he was ready to duplicate his success in the Western World and challenge all who laid claim to the title of World's Greatest Magician.

A single performance, aided by the electronic magic of television, made Sorcar a household word overnight and may well have guaranteed his success in Europe.

The performance took place on April 9, 1956, on England's BBC-TV "Panorama" telecast. It featured Sorcar's version of the classic illusion of sawing a woman in half.

Blackstone presents his version of the classic levitating lady in a splendid setting.

As the television cameras closed in, Sorcar began his presentation. He ran a power-driven saw through the prone form of his assistant, apparently slicing neatly through her waist. Then with a dramatic thrust he slammed a meat cleaver through the incision, looked straight into the television camera, and paused so that the viewing audience could get the full effect of the illusion.

At the right moment Sorcar removed the meat cleaver, rubbed the girl's hands, and ordered her to wake up. But the prone figure lay motionless, and in thousands of English homes viewers gasped in shock.

An instant later, because the scheduled telecasting time had run out, the television camera cut away from the limp form and focused on the host of "Panorama" bidding the audience goodnight.

Within minutes the switchboard at the television station was buzzing with calls from viewers who were convinced that Sorcar's assistant was dead.

The girl, of course, was not dead. She had been "restored" to life seconds after the telecast had ended. The classic illusion had clearly confirmed two things: the power of the conjurer to grip an audience and the potential of television to provide an audience of millions for a single conjuring performance.

American-born Milbourne Christopher, recognizing the potency of the electronic medium, became television's foremost conjurer by constantly changing the material he presented.

An amazingly versatile performer, Christopher began his career specializing in rope tricks. Over the years, however, he expanded his repertoire to include mental magic, sleight of hand, full-scale illusions, and practically every other kind of conjuring.

When television gained a reputation for squandering performers by exposing their material to vast audiences, Christopher was able to remain fresh and exciting by presenting new material with each television appearance.

The conjurers who have made a place for themselves on the small screen have become the twentieth century's pied pipers of the ancient art of conjuring. As they themselves were once lured into the practice of magic by the masters of the golden age, so they are initiating millions of others into the joys and triumphs of magic-making.

Millions of young people have become enthusiastic conjuring hobbyists because of them. Others have turned their conjuring skills to solid practical use in a variety of business, commercial, and social applications. Others—the very best of them—have carved out exciting careers for themselves as professional conjurers.

The new breed of modern miracle-makers comes from anywhere and everywhere magic retains its ancient appeal—like Sid Lorraine and Doug Henning of Canada; Mark Wilson and Harry Blackstone, Jr., of the United States; the skilled Scandinavians, Fin Jon of Norway and Topper Martyn of Sweden; William Strickland of England; and the brilliant Europeans, Claude Rix of France, Fred Kaps of Holland, Mickey Delf of Switzerland, Ernst Lechner of West Germany, the German-born team of Siegfried and Roy, Vito Maggi of Italy, and Antonio Navas Sanchez of Spain.

Panoply of old-time conjuring greats includes:

1. Count Alessandro di Cagliostro
2. Carl Herrmann
3. Antonio Blitz
4. Ludwig Doebler
5. John Henry Anderson
6. Bartolomeo Bosco
7. Robert Heller
8. Rudolph Becker
9. Chevalier Agoston
10. Henry Hiam
11. Bellachini
12. Wiljalba Frikell
13. Baron Seeman
14. Andrew Macallister
15. Alexander Herrmann
16. Harry Kellar
17. Bellini
18. Jacoby Harms
19. Monsieur Guibal
20. Signor Patrizio

21. H. Mellini
22. Buatier de Kolta
23. Professor Roberth
24. Professor Liebholz
25. William Basch
26. George Heubeck
27. St. Roman
28. Dr. Nix
29. John Nevil Maskelyne
30. David Devant
31. D'Alvini
32. Charles Bertram
33. Herr Alexander
34. Dr. Holden
35. Harry Rouclere
36. Joseph Michael Hartz
37. Max Rossner
38. Charles Thompson
39. Patrick Walsh
40. William Robinson

41. J. Hinricks
42. De Thorn
43. T. Nelson Downs
44. Frederick Eugene Powell
45. Servais Le Roy
46. Imro Fox
47. Soto Sunetaro
48. Robert Ankele
49. Stevenson
50. Bancroft
51. Adrien Plate
52. Horace Goldin
53. Leon Herrman
54. Albert E. Smith
55. E. Maro
56. F.J. Werner
57. J. William Elliot
58. Robert-Houdin

The Zig-Zag Woman illusion is considered to be one, if not the greatest trick to be introduced by today's masters of magic.

Today the modern magician is equally at home performing on the stage or in a fashionable nightclub or before the television camera.

He is, like his predecessors, an innovator and inventor of illusions; his modern-day presentations, like the amazing Zig Zag Woman illusion — in which a deceptively built box makes it appear that the woman inside has been cut apart at her torso — will probably become conjuring classics of the future, just as the gory medieval decapitation trick and the shocking sawing of a woman in half became classics of the past.

As long as magic, the most universal of all performing arts, continues to beguile the imagination — as it has done for thousands of years — magicians will continue to dazzle, delight, enchant, amuse, and amaze willing audiences everywhere.

114

Introduction to
150 Mystifying Tricks You Can Perform

When as a teenager I became engrossed in the study of the art of magic, my great-uncle George, a veteran of many years in show business, counseled me, "Young fellow, as a magician there are a couple of things you're supposed to do in front of an audience. Number one: Entertain them. Number two: Fool them. But remember which comes first!" Since the day my great-uncle spoke those words, I have become a professional magician, participated in countless discussions with fellow conjurers, and attended lectures and read books on magic and magic presentation. If I had to condense into a few words my own description of the role of a magician, I probably could not improve on my great-uncle's succinct advice. If you can truly entertain your audience and at the same time baffle them with your magic, you have done very well indeed.

Most people read a book on magic to learn a few simple tricks with which to amuse their relatives and friends. The novice does not want to be deluged with numerous and lengthy theories about routining, staging, pacing, lighting, and other topics which would better be directed to one pursuing magic as a livelihood. However, a few suggestions for the beginner might be helpful. Read through the descriptions of the tricks in this section of the book, and select those that you think would be most suitable for you. Sufficient rehearsal is important. Keep practicing until you have mastered an effect and can perform it smoothly.

You must also determine what you are going to say along with the execution of the trick. The patter you use can simply be a straight description of what you want the audience to think you are doing. It could also be a fanciful tale made up to go with the conjuring. Perhaps a comedy approach would be more to your liking. Your own personality will help determine what you will say and how you will present each magic effect. Some effects can be done without patter because they do not need any explanation; they have to be seen to be appreciated. In these cases a little musical accompaniment can be effective. The best guide in magic is to be yourself and work out a presentation that seems natural for you.

You might next do your trick for a relative to get constructive criticism. Follow that with more practice. Do not perform for an audience until you think you are definitely ready.

There are some practitioners of magic who insist that the sequence of tricks should allow one effect to blend into the next. For example, a handkerchief that is produced turns into an egg; the egg, broken into a pan, turns into a pair of doves; and then the doves and the cage into which they are placed disappear. That sort of routining can be impressive, but it is not absolutely necessary to the success of a performance. It is just as effective to perform individual, unrelated magic tricks one after another.

Some prestidigitation is best performed close to your audience in a living room. Other magic must be done at some distance, perhaps on a platform or stage. Naturally you should perform tricks appropriate for the room in which you find yourself.

When starting out in magic, the number of effects that you do at one time should be kept to a minimum. Two, three, or four at most will suffice. At social gatherings a few tricks would be a delight for your friends, but one too many might begin to pall. You will soon learn how long a performance you can do and still sustain the audience's interest. Some of the finest magicians have entertained throughout their long careers with a repertoire of less than a half-dozen tricks.

It is difficult to judge the potential effectiveness of a trick until you have performed it. Sometimes the simplest magic can be tremendously impressive to an audience. Years ago I saw Jack Gwynne perform at the Loews State Theater in New York. During the show Gwynne surprised the magicians in the audience by doing a very simple glass-suspension trick, which most local conjurers would have considered only a child's magic-set effect and not worthy of inclusion in a professional stage show. But Gwynne performed the trick with polish and made it a delightful mystery. Do not dismiss what may seem at first to be an elementary effect. In magic, as in other phases of life, it is often not what you do but rather the performance that counts.

The legendary Cardini became famous by performing primarily with cards, billiard balls, and cigarettes. Costumed impeccably in full dress with top hat, evening cape, cane, and monocle, he brought dignity and style to the conjuring profession with a beautifully conceived twelve-minute act. Every moment of the pantomime performance was precisely timed and choreographed. He manipulated billiard balls and originated the continuous production of playing cards. The appearance out of the air of what seemed to be an endless number of lit cigarettes and pipes and a cigar never failed to captivate his audiences. He performed with only a few simple props, and yet the millions of people throughout the world who were fortunate enough to see him work witnessed a presentation of the art of magic that has never been surpassed.

Even though you will be bombarded by your friends with the eternal request, "Do it again!" and the question, "How is it done?" never repeat a trick or tell how you accomplish the effect. The charm of magic for an audience is in *not* knowing how it is done. Once the secret of a trick is divulged, the sense of wonder that made the effect fascinating is lost along with interest in the trick.

I hope you enjoy doing the magic in this book. You may choose to perform close-up or stage tricks, serious or comedy magic, with patter or without, one trick or fifteen. Whatever you do, "Entertain them and fool them, but remember which comes first!"

George Gilbert

Card Magic

When playing cards were first introduced into Europe—probably sometime in the middle of the fourteenth century—they quickly became the exclusive property of European royalty.

The reason for this exclusivity had more to do with the cost of producing each deck by hand than with the pleasure of playing with them.

A century later a newly developed block-printing process had made the price of card decks far more reasonable and consequently available to every conjurer skilled enough to manipulate them. By the sixteenth century card manipulations were popular with conjurers and audiences alike. That popularity has continued unabated.

The reasons for this long-lasting fascination are simple: cards are now inexpensive; their design of identical backs and different faces seems to invite manipulation and trickery; and they are easily carried in one's pocket. Thus, card tricks have found a place in the repertoires of countless magicians for many generations.

Johann Hofzinser, the nineteenth-century Viennese conjurer, was one of the first great card manipulators. His inventiveness with a deck of playing cards made him a legend among other magicians, who then set out to duplicate his routines.

By the early twentieth century thousands of magicians had developed their own clever card tricks. Many of them, like Howard Thurston and Harry Houdini, went on to master other phases of the art of conjuring, on which they were able to build towering reputations.

Others, like the Belgian-born vaudevillian Servais Le Roy, made conjuring with cards a major part of their repertoires. Still others, by the very perfection of their execution, were to design their entire acts around card manipulations.

One of the best of these card virtuosos was Nate Leipzig, who enchanted audiences by performing the simplest of card tricks more deftly and brilliantly than they had been presented before.

Another was Richard Pitchford, who, under the name Cardini, presented card fans and manipulations that have rarely been equaled—and certainly never surpassed—by any other card conjurer.

John Scarne, the clever conjurer-turned-card-detective, has won international fame as an expert on gambling and an exposer of the dishonest trickery of some gamblers.

Although successful card manipulation usually takes great dexterity and years of practice, the following card tricks capture much of the flair of the masters' presentations without demanding the same degree of skill.

Card in an Orange

Although the innovative **Jean Henri Servais Le Roy** was particularly noted for his amazing illusions, he was a complete conjurer in every respect. He was as skilled in executing close-up magic as he was in presenting dramatic full-stage illusions.

Le Roy's masterful card conjuring was a sure fire crowd pleaser, and this modern version of a card deception retains all the inventiveness of the master himself.

THE EFFECT:

At the magician's request an audience volunteer selects a playing card, tears it into four quarters, and retains one of the torn quarters. The magician then makes the remaining pieces of the torn card disappear, to reappear again—magically restored except for the one missing quarter—inside an orange selected by another audience volunteer. The missing piece? It is in the first volunteer's hand, and it fits the restored card perfectly.

YOU WILL NEED:

Two identical decks of playing cards; a plastic pill container, about two and one-eighth inches high and one and one-eighth inch in diameter, with a snap-on plastic cap; two feet of round black sewing elastic; a safety pin; a kitchen knife; a skewer; two four-inch-square pieces of plastic food wrap; three oranges; a dinner plate; and glue.

(continued)

TO PREPARE THE TRICK:

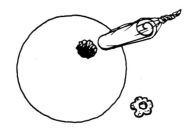

Select a card from the first deck of cards. (Assume you have selected the eight of hearts.) Tear off one quarter of the eight of hearts, making sure that the suit and number are included on the torn quarter. Slip this torn piece into your right jacket pocket.

Starting at one end of the card, roll the remainder of the eight of hearts into a tight, thin tube, and wrap it snugly in one of the pieces of plastic food wrap. Using the kitchen knife, carefully remove the stem from one of the oranges. Insert the skewer through the cut

stem opening, and ream out a hole just large enough to hold the wrapped eight of hearts. (Be careful not to push the skewer through the other end of the orange.)

Slip the plastic-wrapped eight of hearts into the hole in the orange, and glue the stem back in place. The prepared orange must look completely natural.

Place the prepared orange along with the other two oranges on the dinner plate, and carefully note its position.

Make a small hole in the center of the plastic cap of the pill container. Thread one end of the black sewing elastic through the hole, tying a knot in the elastic on the inside of the cap. Thread the remaining end of the elastic through the hole at the end of the safety pin and tie it. (The length of the elastic may need to be adjusted later.)

Attach the safety pin to the lining of your jacket at a point just to the left of your right shoulder blade. Stretch the elastic, and tuck the plastic cap under your belt at your right hip.

If necessary, readjust the length of the elastic so that it is taut enough to pull the plastic cap, with the pill container attached,

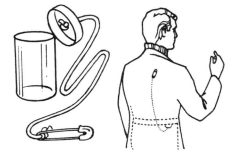

instantly out of sight under your jacket when it is released from your hand held in front of your body.

Place the empty pill container in your right trousers pocket.

Prepare the second deck of cards in the following way. Locate the eight of hearts, place it on top of the deck, and place the deck facedown on a table.

Place the knife, the dinner plate with the three oranges, and the remaining piece of plastic food wrap on the table.

TO PERFORM THE TRICK:

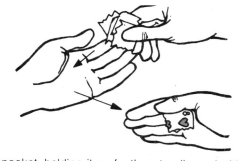

Pick up the deck of cards from the table, fan it out—with the card faces toward the audience—so that the spectator can see that it is an ordinary deck of cards. Square up the cards and place the deck facedown on the table.

Ask an audience volunteer to cut off about half the deck and to place the top half of the deck on the table next to the lower half.

You then pick up the lower half of the deck and place it at a right angle on top of the other half of the deck.

In order to misdirect the audience, remove the plastic pill container from your pocket, and ask an audience member to examine it.

Pick up the right-angled packet of cards, and ask the volunteer to remove the top card from the half deck remaining on the table. (It will be the eight of hearts, but the audience will assume that the card was selected from the place where the deck was originally cut.) Ask

the volunteer to show the card to the audience; then ask him to tear the card into quarters.

As the volunteer does this, put your right hand into your right jacket pocket, and conceal the torn corner of the prepared eight of hearts in your palm. Remove your hand from your

pocket, holding it perfectly naturally, and with your left hand take the four torn card pieces from the volunteer. Smoothly place the volunteer's torn card pieces in your right hand on top of the torn corner of the eight of hearts already concealed there.

Ask the volunteer who was examining the pill container to return it to you. Take it with your left hand, and begin to bend the card

pieces with your right hand and to push them into the container.

Stop suddenly, as if you have just remembered something. Remove the card pieces from the container, and shift the container in your left hand so that you are holding it with

your third and fourth fingers.

Grasp all the torn card pieces with your left thumb and first and second fingers of your left hand. The torn quarter of the eight of hearts, which fits the card in the orange, is still at the bottom of the pile of card pieces. Remove it, and give it to the volunteer to hold. Push the remaining card pieces into the pill container along with the remaining piece of plastic food wrap from the table.

Turn slightly to your right, still holding the pill container in your left hand, and reach with your

right hand toward your right trousers pocket. As your right hand moves under your jacket, it pulls the plastic cap out from under your belt and holds it securely as your hand continues into your pocket. Turn back to your left, and face the audience squarely.

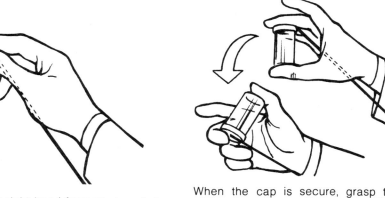

Remove your right hand from your pocket immediately, giving the audience the impression that you have taken the plastic cap out of your pocket.

Hold the plastic cap between the thumb and the first finger with the elastic hidden under the palm. Bring it directly in front of your body, and snap it onto the pill container.

When the cap is secure, grasp the pill container in such a way that your right thumb is holding its bottom and your right second finger is holding the cap.

Pivot the pill container by turning your right thumb and second finger in a clockwise direction. (The pill container is now upside down and positioned directly in front of the right edge of your jacket.)

Bring your left hand in front of your right hand and pretend to take the pill container into your left hand. However, as soon as your left hand shields the pill container from sight, your right thumb and finger release it, and the taut elastic instantly pulls the pill container out of sight under your jacket.

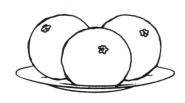

As you move your cupped left hand away from your right hand, make a slight throwing motion with your left hand, and open your fingers. Show your empty left hand to the audience; then open your empty right hand to show the audience that the pill container with the playing card pieces has disappeared.

Pick up the dinner plate, and pass the three oranges on it among the audience members for their inspection, making sure to remember which orange holds the concealed eight of hearts.

When the oranges have been collected and returned to the plate, force the selection of the prepared orange in the following way. Ask an audience volunteer to pick up two of the three

oranges. If the prepared orange is one of those selected, ask the volunteer to return one orange to you. If he returns the prepared one, you are ready to continue. If he keeps the prepared orange, place the orange he has given you on the plate. Take the prepared orange from him, and say that you will use the

orange he has selected. If the prepared orange is not selected and remains on the plate, say that two oranges have been eliminated and you are left with this orange to use in the trick.

After you have forced the selection of the prepared orange, pick it up in one hand, holding it with your fingertips. With the other hand take the knife from the table and cut all

around the orange at a right angle to the rolled-up card inside, but do not cut through the card. Slowly twist the two cut halves apart, leaving the rolled-up card in one of the halves.

Ask for a volunteer to remove the card from the orange half, unwrap it, unroll it, and show it to the audience. It will be the eight of hearts magically restored except for the missing

quarter. Ask the volunteer who originally selected and tore the card to confirm that the eight of hearts is the card he chose. Ask him to make perfectly sure by checking the piece of card he is still holding against the card found in the orange. It will, of course, fit exactly, to everyone's amazement but yours.

Do As I Do

Three times a week **Johann Hofzinser** rushed home from his office in the Austrian Ministry of Finance, hurriedly ate supper, and quickly prepared himself to entertain a houseful of guests.

Hofzinser entertained his guests not with the usual small talk of a host but with the thing he loved best of all, conjuring. Using his home as a stage, he presented all sorts of dazzling deceptions, but the ones he called the poetry of magic were his beloved card tricks.

This modern version of a Hofzinser card trick is simplicity itself to perform yet leaves the audience in puzzled amazement.

THE EFFECT:

The magician and a volunteer both think of a playing card. Two decks of cards are shuffled. The magician extracts the card he thought of from one deck and places it facedown on the table. The volunteer does the same from the other deck. When the volunteer turns over both cards, the audience is amazed to see that they are identical.

YOU WILL NEED:

Two decks of bridge or poker cards.

TO PERFORM THE TRICK:

Both decks are placed on the table, and the volunteer selects one of them (deck A). You pick up the other deck (deck B), and both you and the volunteer shuffle the decks you are holding. As you are shuffling deck B, note the bottom card. Assuming it is the ace of spades, it now becomes your key card.

You and the volunteer place each deck side by side facedown on the table.

Ask the volunteer to think of any card in the deck, and tell him that you will also think of a card. Pick up deck A—the deck shuffled by the volunteer—and ask him to pick up the other deck—deck B—which you have shuffled.

Tell the volunteer to hold his deck facing toward him and fan it out so that he can find the card he had selected mentally. When he finds it, ask him to pull it halfway out of the deck, close the fan, and leave the selected card protruding from the end of the deck. While the volunteer is doing this, you appear to be doing the same thing. However, you randomly select any card, pull it up, and close your deck.

Both decks are now placed on the table. You turn to the audience and tell them that total concentration is necessary and there must be complete silence. Ask the volunteer to pull his card completely out of the deck and, without allowing anyone to see which card it is, study it with total concentration. As the volunteer stares at his card, pretend to do the same with your card.

Tell the volunteer to place his card facedown on top of the deck (deck B, the one you originally shuffled). Meanwhile you do the same with your card and deck A.

Ask the volunteer to pick up half of the cards from the top of his deck and place them on the table next to the bottom half of the deck. Then instruct him to pick up the bottom half of his deck and place it on the top half of the deck. He has given the pack of cards a complete cut. Follow the same procedure with your deck. Now exchange decks. You will be holding deck B; the volunteer will be holding deck A.

Warn the audience once again of the need for complete silence so that you can concentrate on the selected card. Then each of you make two more complete cuts with your decks. Have the volunteer pick up his deck (deck A) and fan through it to locate his selected card, withdraw it from the deck, and lay it facedown on the table.

As he is doing this, you appear to be doing the same with deck B. Instead, you are really looking for your key card, the ace of spades. When you find it, pull out the card just below it—it will be the volunteer's card—and place it facedown on the table next to the volunteer's facedown card.

Have the volunteer turn over his card first and then the magician's card, and enjoy your triumph when the volunteer and the audience see that both cards are identical and they react as though both the magician and the volunteer *thought* of the same card.

Aces High

Although **Nate Leipzig,** one of the most adept of all sleight of hand experts, was equally adroit conjuring with thimbles, coins, and cards, it was his speciality of card tricks that made him famous.

His card tricks were always flawlessly presented—with the same flair and dramatic impact that other conjurers used to present their grandest illusions. One of the features of his act was a sleight of hand with the four aces in a deck of cards. The following trick is an easy-to-perform version of the classic four-aces effect.

THE EFFECT:

The magician extracts the four aces from a deck of playing cards. He places them in four different places on a table and then covers each ace with three other cards from the deck. A volunteer chooses one of the four piles. The magician snaps his fingers three times. When the cards in the other piles are examined, the aces have miraculously vanished and are discovered together in the pile selected by the volunteer.

YOU WILL NEED:

A deck of bridge or poker cards with a standard white border on the back.

TO PREPARE THE TRICK:

 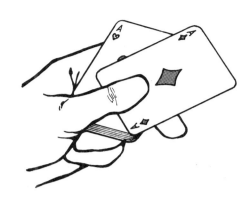

Remove the four aces from the deck along with three randomly selected cards. Place the three random cards face down in your hand. Place the four aces faceup on top of the random cards. You are now holding seven cards in your hand, three down, four up.

Square up the cards in your hand. Hold them the way you would if you were getting ready to deal them out. Make sure to keep them squared so that the audience will be convinced that you are holding only the four aces.

TO PERFORM THE TRICK:

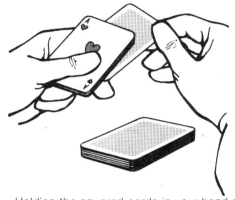 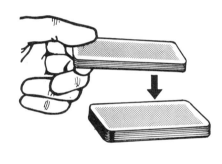 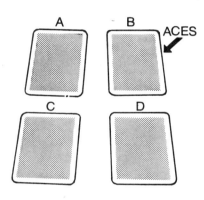

Holding the squared cards in your hand as described—with the rest of the deck facedown on the table—show the audience the first ace, which is faceup. Remove it from the group of cards in your hand, turn it facedown, and place it on the bottom of the cards in your hand.

The second ace is now visible to the audience. Show it to them, and follow the same procedure as with the first ace.

Continue until all four aces have been shown to the audience and each has been turned over and placed facedown at the bottom of the cards in your hand. All seven cards should now be facedown and positioned as follows: from the top, three random cards followed by the four aces.

Place these seven cards on top of the deck.

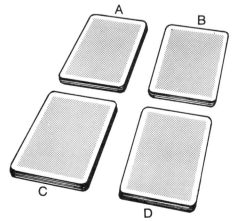 

Then deal the top four cards, one at a time, onto the table to form a square. The last card you deal will be an ace.

Deal the next three cards—all aces—onto the ace on the table. (Make sure that you remember where the pile of aces is positioned.) Deal three cards each on the other cards on the table, and place the remainder of the deck aside.

Ask a volunteer to choose any number from one to four. With the location of the pile of aces in mind, begin counting the piles so that the number chosen by the volunteer falls on the pile of aces. If, for example, the volunteer chooses the number three and the pile of aces is at the upper-right corner (marked B in the figure), begin counting with pile C. Since you have not told the audience in advance how you will count the piles, they will suspect nothing.

After your counting brings you to the pile of aces, snap your fingers three times.

Turn over the cards in pile A, showing the audience that the ace has vanished. Continue by turning over the cards in piles C and D, also showing the audience that the aces have vanished.

Then dramatically turn over the four aces in pile B, and show them to the audience.

Card Stabbing

Although he was barely out of his teens—a struggling conjurer trying to survive on the twelve dollars a week he earned performing twenty shows a day in dime museums—**Harry Houdini** dared to bill himself as the King of Cards. Even after Houdini's daring won him international fame as an escape artist, he never gave up his love for card conjuring.

This dramatic card trick has all the boldness of a Houdini performance and enough suspense to keep a contemporary audience on the edge of its seats.

THE EFFECT:

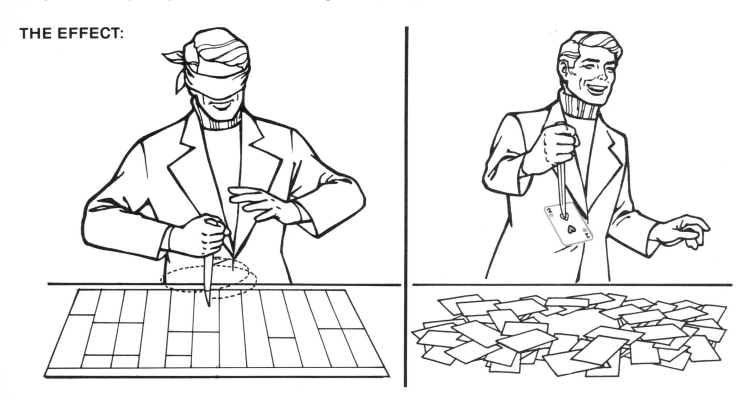

The magician asks a volunteer to select a card from a deck of cards. He is asked to remember the card and to return it to the deck. Another volunteer is asked to shuffle the deck and to spread out all the cards facedown on a large board. The cards are then covered by a sheet of newspaper. The magician blindfolds himself and then takes a penknife out of his pocket. He slowly circles the open penknife over the newspaper. Suddenly he stabs the penknife into the newspaper. When the newspaper is torn away, the audience sees that one card has been stabbed. It turns out to be the very same card the volunteer had selected from the deck.

YOU WILL NEED:

One complete deck of playing cards plus one card—for example, the two of hearts—from another deck with an exactly matching back design; a large wooden board about the size of an artist's drawing board; two sheets of newspaper; rubber cement; a penknife; and a man's handkerchief large enough to be used as a blindfold.

TO PREPARE THE TRICK:

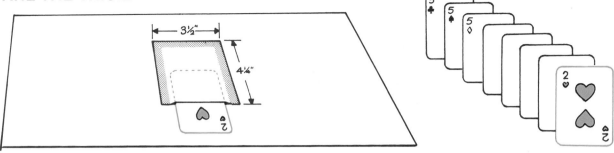

From one of the sheets of newspaper cut out of the center a piece measuring three and one-half inches by four and one-quarter inches. Apply rubber cement to three edges of the cut piece—leaving uncemented one three and one-half inch edge—and paste down the piece to the center of the second sheet of newspaper. This forms a card-sized pocket.

Slide one extra card, the two of hearts, into the pocket with its face toward the pocket. Turn the newspaper sheet over, with the pocket underneath, and note carefully the printing or illustrations that appear on the newspaper directly over the pocket. This will be your key to locating the exact position of the hidden pocket.

Arrange the deck of cards in the following order from the top down; three fives from any of the four suits, any other four cards, and then the two of hearts. The deck is now ready for forcing, with the two of hearts as the eighth card from the top.

Place the handkerchief and penknife in your pocket.

TO PERFORM THE TRICK:

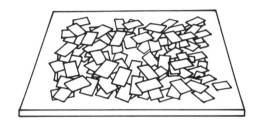

Shuffle the cards, using a riffle-shuffle, but be careful not to disturb the top eight cards. Casually deal one by one the top three cards—all three are fives—placing them face-down onto a table.

Ask a volunteer to turn up any one of the cards. He will, naturally, turn up a five. Tell the volunteer that the card value—five—indicates the position of the card that should be looked at by the next volunteer.

The deck is handed to the second volunteer, who deals down to the fifth card—the two of hearts. Ask the volunteer to memorize the card, show it to the audience, and return it to the deck. As he does, pick up the three fives, and slide them back into the deck.

Ask the volunteer to thoroughly shuffle the cards and to return them to the first volunteer.

The first volunteer is asked to spread all the cards in the deck facedown on the wooden board. Help the volunteer spread them out, and while you do, unobtrusively leave a small space in the center of the board.

Pick up the sheet of newspaper, and place it so that the hidden pocket is underneath with the opening facing toward the audience. Position the newspaper sheet carefully over

the spread-out cards so that the hidden pocket with the two of hearts in it is placed on the small space you created as you helped to arrange the cards.

Fold the handkerchief into a triangle, and flip up the triangle point to form a blindfold. Blindfold yourself as shown above. You will still be able to see if you look down along the line of your nose.

Reach into your pocket, and, fumbling a bit,

take out the penknife and open it. Hold it in you hand with the point facing down, and move it in a large circle over the newspaper. Gradually decrease the size of the circle you are making with your hand while you find the spot that locates the hidden pocket. Stab dramatically into the newspaper directly over the pocket with the knife edge facing in the same direction as the pocket opening. (The knife will pierce both the newspaper and the card in the pocket.)

Remove your blindfold. Hold the knife—with the hidden two of hearts impaled on it—with one hand. With the other hand pull the newspaper off the board in the direction away from the audience. This will permit the hidden pocket to slide easily off the card. Ask the volunteer who selected the card to call out its name. As he does, raise the knife with the two of hearts impaled on the blade.

Deck of Many Tricks

Johann Hofzinser, the Austrian official who became a master card conjurer, spent many hours designing specially prepared card decks to use in his ingenious card deceptions. Another master magician and designer of trick decks was the American Theodore DeLand.

Although both men intended their trick cards to be used by conjurers for entertainment, it is easy to see why card sharps began using them for less honest purposes.

This clever card trick is inspired by a deck of specially prepared cards, but here it is being used to create an honest—and amusing—deception.

THE EFFECT:

The magician asks a volunteer to select a card from a deck of cards and to show it to the audience. The card is returned to the deck and the deck is shuffled. A second volunteer cuts the cards and places them in a hat. After the magician is blindfolded, a third volunteer calls out any number from one to fifty-two. Still blindfolded, the magician one at a time pulls out of the hat the exact number of cards corresponding to the number called out. The last card is the one selected by the first volunteer and shown to the audience.

YOU WILL NEED:

A deck of bridge or poker cards; a ruler; a hat; a knife or other instrument with a sharp cutting edge; and a handkerchief.

TO PREPARE THE TRICK:

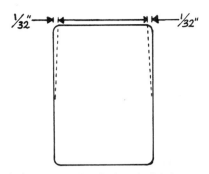

With a ruler and knife (or similar instrument with a sharp cutting edge), measure and cut off one thirty-second of an inch from both sides at one end of every card in the deck. After you have tapered every card, the deck will be one-sixteenth of an inch narrower at one end.

To get the feel of this fractional difference, pull out one card, turn the deck around, end for end, and replace the card in the same way that it was pulled out. Run your fingers along the sides of the deck, from the wider end to the narrower end, and you will be able to find the selected card easily. Because the wider end of the returned card will now be protruding slightly from the sides of the narrower end of the

deck, your fingers can automatically slide the card out of the narrow end of the deck. Make sure that all cards are positioned in the same direction in order to accomplish the trick.

Place a hat, with its crown down, on a table, and place the handkerchief next to it.

TO PERFORM THE TRICK:

Ask a volunteer to remove a card from the deck, and have him show it to the audience but keep it concealed from you. While the volunteer is doing this and the audience is looking at

the card, turn the deck around in your hands so that the volunteer's card, when returned, will

be reversed (end for end) in the deck.

Shuffle the cards, using an overhand shuffle. Ask a second volunteer to cut the deck and place it in the upturned hat. Ask the same

volunteer to use the handkerchief to blindfold your eyes and lead you to the hat. The volunteer is then asked to return to his seat.

Still blindfolded, ask a third volunteer from the audience to call out any number from one to fifty-two. (Assume, for instance, that the volunteer calls out the number fifteen.)

Reach into the hat with both hands and feel along the side edges of the deck. The selected card will immediately be evident because it will be wider where the rest of the deck is narrower.

Slip the selected card out of the deck and position it on one side of the hat interior.

Start removing cards from the deck one by one, and place them on the table. When you

reach the number fifteen, pull out the selected card, and ask the volunteer to confirm the fact that this is indeed the card he chose.

127

Rising Cards

One of the greatest of all card manipulators was **Howard Thurston**, and one of his earliest and best tricks was his famous Rising Card trick.

Thurston's trick required the services of backstage assistants, who controlled a thread that was stretched across the stage and camouflaged by a special backdrop. This updated version of the classic trick does not require assistants. It can be performed anywhere yet is spectacular enough to leave the audience in amazement.

THE EFFECT:

Three playing cards selected at random by members of the audience are shuffled back into the deck. The entire deck is placed in a glass resting on a nearby table. On command of the magician the selected cards rise mysteriously out of the deck, even though no one touches the cards or the glass. As a dramatic finale the last selected card jumps out of the glass and flies into the air.

YOU WILL NEED:

A man's handkerchief; fine black sewing thread; a standard playing card box; two decks of bridge or poker cards with identical white-bordered designs on their backs (these decks will be designated deck A and deck B); and two glasses—the ten-ounce size usually works best—that have flat bottoms and straight sides and are large enough to hold a full deck of cards which, when resting on the bottom of the glass, extends slightly above the rim.

TO PREPARE THE TRICK:

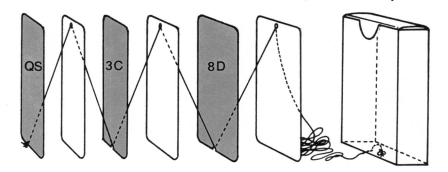

Remove any three cards from deck A; for example, the queen of spades, the three of clubs, and the eight of diamonds. On the first card, the queen of spades, measure to the exact center of one end, and make a one-six-teenth-inch cut at that spot. At the exact spot where the first cut was made, cut a small half circle on the three of clubs and the eight of diamonds. The half circle should be one-eighth inch in diameter.

Randomly select three other cards from deck A. In each card, at the exact center of one end and one-sixteenth inch from the edge, put a hole one-eighth inch in diameter.

Tie a small knot in the end of a piece of black thread and slip the thread—with the knot end on the face side of the card—into the slit cut in the queen of spades. Thread the remaining cards, all facing the same way as the queen, as follows: from the queen of spades up through the hole in the first random card; down under the half circle cut into the three of clubs; up through the hole in the next random card; down

under the half circle cut into the eight of diamonds; up through the hole in the third random card. Allow an additional fifteen inches of thread before inserting it—now threaded through a needle—into the bottom of the card box. Next to the first hole push the threaded needle down out of the box. Remove the needle from the box, and tie the end of the thread securely to the box.

Place the remaining cards from deck A inside the box and close the flap.

Remove the queen of spades, the three of clubs, and the eight of diamonds from deck B

and place them on top of deck B. In addition, remove five cards from deck B so that it will not appear to contain too many cards when the prepared packet from deck A is added later.

Prepare for presentation in the following way. Place the two glasses side by side on a table. Place the prepared packet faceup three or four inches behind the glasses, with the card box lying alongside and the loose thread tucked under the box. Bunch the man's handkerchief in front of the packet to hide it from the audience.

TO PERFORM THE TRICK:

In the performance of this trick you must force the spectators to select the queen of spades, the eight of diamonds, and the three of clubs from deck B because the duplicates of those cards will later rise out of the glass.

With the queen of spades, the eight of diamonds, and the three of clubs on top of deck B, shuffle carefully, using a riffle-shuffle, so that these three cards remain in place. Place the deck on the table, and ask a member of the audience to pick up about half of the cards and place them next to the bottom half of the deck. You pick up the bottom half of the deck and place it at a right angle on top of the cards cut by the audience member.

Distract the audience from the cut deck on the table by telling them you will need three people to assist you in this trick.

As the volunteers come up, pick up the top half of the deck and ask the first volunteer to pick up the top card of the half deck resting on the table. The next two people are asked to take the second and third cards. Keep track of which spectator selected each card. Each volunteer will have taken one of the three cards originally placed on the top of deck B, but all will believe they have selected random cards from the cut part of the deck. Ask each volunteer to memorize his card, show it to the audience, and return it to the deck. Then ask another volunteer to shuffle the entire deck.

When the shuffled deck is returned to you, make sure that none of the forced cards are on the bottom. If one should be there, cut the deck.

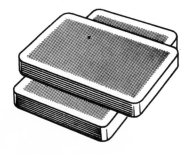

Walk to the table. As you bring the deck behind the bunched-up handkerchief and place it faceup on top of the prepared packet, simultaneously pick up the handkerchief. With a flourish wipe both glasses with the handkerchief. Then return the glasses to the table.

Stand directly behind the table. Pick up the prepared packet of the threaded cards and the deck as one. Place this combined deck into one of the glasses with the deck facing the audience and with the end of the prepared packet from which the thread emerges uppermost. Be sure to place the deck with the

holes of the randomly selected cards facing up so that your selected cards will rise. Pick up the card box with your right hand, and put it into your right jacket pocket. Pick up the handkerchief, and put it in your left breast pocket. The loose thread will now extend from the back of the packet in the glass up to the opening of your jacket pocket. If you wear a dark suit, the thread will not be visible to the audience in normal light. The proper length of the thread will vary with the individual. By experimenting with different lengths you will find the suitable length.

(continued)

Ask the volunteer who took the eight of diamonds to command his card to rise out of the deck. As he is speaking, slowly move backward by shifting your weight from one foot to the other. The thread becomes taut as you move. As you continue to move, the eight of diamonds will begin to rise from the deck. When the card is about three-quarters of the way out of the deck, remove it, making sure to hide the half circle on its bottom edge with your fingers.

Now pick up the empty glass, and turn it upside down. Place it on top of the first glass so that the deck is enclosed within the two glasses. (Enclosing the deck between the glasses is to give the impression that no outside assistance is causing the cards to rise.) The thread, however, will still move easily between the glasses, and the three of clubs will rise inside the glasses when the second spectator requests it. (It might be necessary to steady the top glass with your hand if the movement of the thread causes it to slide.) When the second card has risen, remove the glass and the card. Do not cause the third card to rise, even when commanded to do so. Because the card is slow to rise, ask the volunteer to name it. He, of course, will say,

"The queen of spades." Turn to the deck and say politely, "Please rise, Your Majesty." Let it rise until only the index shows.

Pretend impatience with this slow-moving card and say, "When I clap my hands, I want you to jump." Raise your hands, clap them together, and say, "Jump!"

As you clap, make sure your left hand comes down sharply on the thread. The sudden pressure will cause the queen to jump entirely out of the glass for a fine climax to the Rising Cards trick.

Mental Magic

In the world of modern conjuring there is no trick quite so marvelous as the one which seems to divine human thought and no conjurer more awe-inspiring than the one who performs such mind-reading miracles.

Mental magic as a branch of the conjurer's art dates back to the ancient oracles of Greece and Rome. Some of its techniques were revealed and explained as early as 1584 in Reginald Scot's classic exposé, *The Discoverie of Witchcraft.* Other exposés have appeared over the centuries. Yet, even the most knowledgeable audiences have been eager to believe that the conjurer really does possess a sixth sense.

In the early eighteenth century the flamboyant Italian conjurer Giuseppe Pinetti capitalized on the credulity of an audience by presenting his stunningly effective "second sight" act with his wife. Some years later Jean Eugène Robert-Houdin and his young son performed a similar act, which became the talk of Europe.

In more recent times, particularly with the aid of modern technology, hundreds of conjurers have incorporated some form of mental magic into their acts.

Robert Heller used a telegraph apparatus concealed in the couch on which his assistant reclined to present his "second sight" act. Karl Germain's mind-reading feats were aided in no small part by the use of a thread and the Morse code system to communicate with his assistant.

A clever English couple, Sidney and Lesley Piddington, brought their mind-reading act to British radio in 1949 and became an overnight sensation.

The contemporary performer who really brought mental magic to its highest level was the dynamic Joseph Dunninger, the self-proclaimed Master Mind of Mental Mystery.

Dunninger capitalized on the resurgent interest and scientific experiments in extrasensory perception, as well as on his own dominating personality, to convince millions of radio listeners and television viewers that he could actually read minds. He became an international celebrity, all the while insisting that his presentations were based on thought reading rather than conjuring trickery. Later, a young American named George Kresge, Jr.—Kreskin—gradually took over Dunninger's preeminent position as America's master mentalist.

Today, as in the past, mental magic is fascinating to behold and even the most skeptical audience is entertained by a clever mind-reading presentation.

The mental magic tricks that follow have no basis in the scientific study of extrasensory perception. They are modernized versions of conjuring tricks that have amazed audiences for years and will continue to amaze them for years to come.

Book Telepathy Experiment

When audiences came to see "Heller's Wonder Theater"—the name **Robert Heller** gave to his magic presentations—they could expect the unexpected. The versatile Heller might amuse them with clever sleight of hand or entertain them with an impromptu piano recital or dazzle them with one of a number of second sight routines.

One of Heller's most popular mental magic routines was a mind-reading act using some of the popular novels of the day.

This update of Heller's mind-reading trick is designed to mystify a modern audience as effectively as the versatile conjurer dazzled his nineteenth-century audiences.

THE EFFECT:

A volunteer from the audience, at the request of the magician, selects one word by chance from the thousands of words printed on the pages of five books and concentrates on that one word. Miraculously the magician is able to read the volunteer's mind and discover the exact word chosen by the volunteer.

YOU WILL NEED:

Five books; a deck of playing cards; and a note pad and pencil.

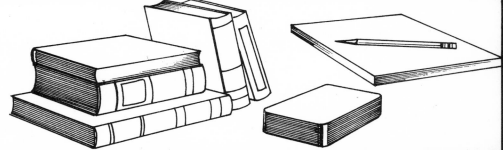

TO PREPARE THE TRICK:

On the second page of the note pad write down the names of each of the five books. Next to each name write the words that appear in the following positions in each book: the fourth, fifth, and sixth words on page 14; the fifth, sixth, and seventh words on page 15. Make sure to begin counting with the first word on the top line of the page.

On the pad underline the following words from each book: the fifth word on page 14 and the sixth word on page 15. These are your key words, the ones that you will be forcing the volunteer to select when you perform the trick. The illustration shows the best format to use when writing down book titles and selected words.

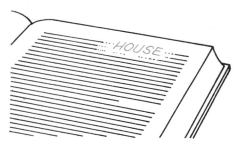

TITLE OF   PG. 14: 4TH, 5TH & 6TH WORDS... HE ASKED FOR....
BOOK A   PG. 15: 5TH, 6TH, & 7TH WORDS... THE FORCES GAVE...

TITLE OF   PG. 14: 4TH, 5TH & 6TH WORDS... THOMAS TOLD THEM...
BOOK B   .PG. 15: 5TH, 6TH & 7TH WORDS... MY HOUSE WAS...

TITLE OF   PG. 14: 4TH, 5TH & 6TH WORDS... IMPOSSIBLE TO SEE..,
BOOK C   PG. 15: 5TH, 6TH & 7TH WORDS... COUNTY FAIR ENDED...

TITLE OF   PG. 14: 4TH, 5TH & 6TH WORDS... SAW YALE UNIVERSITY
BOOK D   PG. 15: 5TH, 6TH & 7TH WORDS... MY COUSIN IS...

TITLE OF   PG. 14: 4TH, 5TH & 6TH WORDS... GIVE HEATHER ANY..?
BOOK E   PG. 15: 5TH, 6TH & 7TH WORDS... RABBIT HUTCH TO...

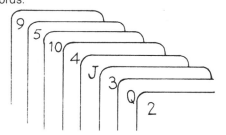

9
5
10
4
J
3
Q
2

Remove two of the aces from the deck of cards and set them aside. They will not be used. Arrange the remaining fifty cards so that the number value of any two adjacent cards adds up to either fourteen or fifteen. To do this, give the jack the value of eleven, the queen the value of twelve, and the king the value of thirteen. All other cards retain the number value printed on their face.

The following order of cards will give you the proper two-card values (suits are unimportant and should be thoroughly mixed throughout the deck): 9, 5, 10, 4, jack, 3, queen, 2, king, ace, king, 2, queen, 3, jack, 4, 10, 5, 9, 6, 8, 7, 7, 8, 6, 9, 5, 10, 4, jack, 3, queen, 2, king, ace, king, 2, queen, 3, jack, 4, 10, 5, 9, 6, 8, 7, 7, 8, 6. At a glance you can see that the addition of the number values of any two adjacent cards will give a total of either fourteen or fifteen:

TO PERFORM THE TRICK:

Place the five books on a table. Ask a volunteer to select any one of the books. Spread out the prepared deck of cards faceup on the table. Be careful not to disturb their prearranged order. To the audience the deck will appear to be completely mixed.

Assemble the deck once more; turn it facedown, and cut the deck by picking up the top half and placing it next to the bottom half. Pick up the bottom half and place it on top of the top half. Repeat this cut in the identical manner twice. Walk away from the table as far as possible. As you are walking away, explain to the audience that you wish to leave the entire experiment to chance, and therefore you want the volunteer to cut the deck anywhere and pick up the top two cards from the top of the bottom half of the deck.

Ask the volunteer to add together the number values of the two cards. Ask him to pick up the book he selected and turn to the page with that number on it. When the volunteer has located the page, ask him to add together the digits of the page number. Then tell the volunteer to begin counting the words horizontally from the first word of the top line until he reaches the word corresponding to the number of the sum of the two digits. (This will be either five or six, depending on whether the volunteer has chosen page 14 or 15.) When he reaches that number, he is to stop and commit to memory that word.

It may be helpful to explain by an example precisely what the volunteer is to do: "If you turn to page 19, add together one and nine, and starting from the first word on the top line, count to the tenth word on the page."

After the volunteer has followed your instructions and arrived at his word, ask him to concentrate on the word as hard as he can.

4
J   = 15
     1+5 = 6

Take out your pad and pencil, casually letting the audience see that the top sheet of the pad is blank, and also make a show of heavy concentration.

Pretending deep concentration, begin to write on the top sheet of the pad. Then shake your head, make a comment about not getting a clear picture, and rip off and crumple the top sheet of the pad. Throw it away, leaving the second page exposed. Holding the pad in such a way that the audience cannot see the writing on the page, begin questioning the volunteer. Assuming that book B was selected, you know that the volunteer would have selected the word *told* if his cards totaled fourteen or the word *house* if his cards totaled fifteen.

As if in great concentration, ask if the letter *s* appears in the volunteer's word. If he says yes, you know that the word is *house*; if not, the word must be *told*.

Assume that the word is *house*. Before revealing the word, it is a good idea to say that you seem to be telepathically receiving other words. One is *was* and the other *my*. You can say, "Perhaps you are letting other words on the page into your thoughts, and they are causing interference." Encourage him to make a great effort to concentrate on the one word selected at random. Then reveal the key word, and ask the confounded volunteer to confirm that it is the word he selected.

The fact that you have been able to identify other words on the page, as well as the selected word, is a very effective part of the trick. The word should be revealed slowly, letter by letter. Since this is supposed to be an experiment in telepathy and not a magic trick, at first get a letter of the word out of place. Too smooth and fast a demonstration of telepathy can arouse suspicions in the minds of the audience.

Clairvoyance Extraordinaire

One of the most impressive feats of the mental magic of **Joseph Dunninger** was the divination of a handful of messages that had been written out in advance by members of his studio audience and placed in an envelope.

This update of the classic Dunninger clairvoyance trick involves the divination of ten audience questions; it guarantees ten accurate answers and a thoroughly amazed audience.

THE EFFECT:

Members of the audience are asked to write their names and questions on small slips of paper. The papers are folded, collected, and placed inside a sealed dated envelope, which is then placed on a table in view of the audience. Yet, an assistant to the conjurer —blindfolded and completely covered with a bedsheet—is able to divine the information on each slip of paper and answer every question.

YOU WILL NEED:

Three large envelopes, approximately four by nine inches; a pad of note paper, approximately three by five inches; ten pencils; a folded bedsheet; a large man's handkerchief; a clear plastic double-faced tape; a chair with a solid back; a table; and a glass tumbler.

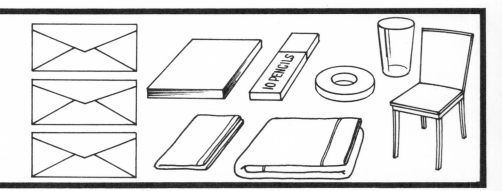

TO PERFORM THE TRICK:

Remove ten sheets of paper from the pad, and fold each sheet separately as if it had been folded by a member of the audience. Vary your folding technique so that the ten sheets of paper would appear to have been folded by ten different people. Insert these folded papers into one of the envelopes—envelope A. Seal the envelope and write the date of the performance on the envelope flap.

Place the chair at center stage, about three-quarters of the way back from the front of the stage; position it so that it faces the audience.

Attach a one-inch strip of double-face tape to the center back of the chair.

Tuck envelope A inside the upper folds of the folded bedsheet, and place the bedsheet—with the hidden envelope—on the seat of the chair.

Place the table to your right as you stand onstage facing the audience. On the table place the second envelope (envelope B), the pad of paper, the ten pencils, and, toward the back of the table, the glass tumbler with the mouth down.

Meanwhile your assistant is backstage with the third envelope (envelope C)—with the same date written in the same place as on envelope A—unsealed and concealed in his inside breast pocket.

Place the handkerchief in your pocket for use as a blindfold later in the trick.

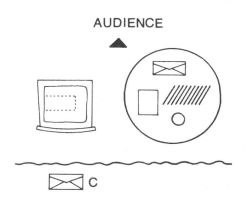

TO PERFORM THE TRICK:

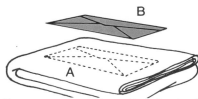

Pass out ten pencils and ten sheets of paper from the pad to ten members of the audience. Ask each member to write on the sheet of paper his or her name and any question (or information such as his telephone number or address) the person wants answered. Then instruct the ten audience members to fold the sheets of paper.

Ask a volunteer to collect the folded papers, place them in envelope B, seal the envelope, and bring it to you.

As this is being done, casually pick up the folded bedsheet—with envelope A hidden inside—and move toward your left onstage.

When the volunteer hands you envelope B, place it on top of the folded bedsheet, still holding it in your hand, and with the other hand write the performance date on the flap of envelope B exactly as you had written it on the flap of hidden envelope A.

Leave envelope B on top of the bedsheet, holding it there with your left thumb, and walk to the table. As you move toward your assistant, introduce your assistant, who enters and proceeds to sit in the chair, facing the audience.

When you reach the table, turn the glass right side up with your left hand slightly away from the audience, keeping it close to the upturned glass.

Pretend to slide envelope B, which is on top of the bedsheet, into your right hand. Instead, maintain the pressure of your left thumb on envelope B, holding it securely against the bedsheet, place your right thumb on top of the bedsheet, and with your right fingers slip into the fold to extract hidden envelope A.

After you have grasped envelope A with your first and second fingers, pull it out of the bedsheet, and with a smoothly executed motion stand it up against the glass tumbler so that the date on the flap faces the audience.

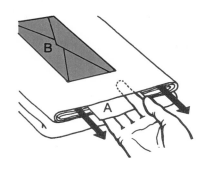

This entire action should be so matter-of-fact and so well practiced that the audience assumes without a shadow of a doubt that the envelope you place against the tumbler is the envelope with their questions. Keeping envelope B on the side of the folded bedsheet away from the audience, walk toward your assistant, taking the handkerchief out of your pocket at the same time. Tell your audience that you will blindfold your assistant.

Place the bedsheet on your assistant's lap, with envelope B underneath the bedsheet.

This frees your hands to fold the handkerchief into a triangle and to flip over the point once to form a blindfold.

Tie the blindfold around your assistant's head over the eyes. (Your assistant will still be able to see by looking down along the sides of his nose.)

Stand directly in front of your blindfolded assistant, and begin unfolding the bedsheet on his lap. As you bring one edge of the sheet up over your assistant's head, he grasps envelope B so that it does not fall to the floor. (Your back to the audience covers this action.) You continue adjusting the bedsheet until your assistant is fully covered.

The instant that your assistant is covered by the bedsheet, he quietly opens envelope B and unfolds the messages written by the audience.

Slowly and hesitatingly he begins to call out bits of information written on the papers. A skilled assistant might say: "I seem to be getting a question from someone whose initials are TJW,—no, wait, uh, TWJ. Yes, that's right, TWJ."

The magician asks if anyone in the audience has those initials. When an audience member acknowledges these initials, the assistant continues. "I am getting the impression of some letters—uh, wait, the letters of a name. Tom. Thomas seems to be very clear."

With each statement from the assistant, the magician turns to the writer of the note for confirmation.

The information divulged by the assistant should be given hesitatingly, almost unsurely, and should not include all facts written down by the writer. This kind of presentation is far more convincing than a straight reading of each message. Not all of the questions have to be answered. Use only those that seem most interesting or humorous. Perhaps five or six would be enough.

While the last message is being divined, the assistant refolds the slips of paper, slides them into envelope C, which had been concealed in his pocket, and seals the flap. He places the now-empty envelope B into his pocket.

As you lift up the sheet from the back to uncover your assistant, he reaches behind the chair and sticks envelope C to the tape. As the audience applauds him, gather up the bedsheet, and secretly remove envelope C from the back of the chair. It is carried to the table under cover of the bunched-up bedsheet and placed in front of the glass.

With your right hand slide envelope A under the bedsheet, and set envelope C in its place against the glass. (If someone wishes to examine the envelope afterwards, envelope C may be given out for examination.)

ESP Mail Prediction

Theodore Anneman, a many-faceted master of magic, was an expert card conjurer, a successful performer of the dangerous bullet-catching routine, and for many years the owner of a magazine for conjurers entitled *The Jinx.* Of all his connections with magic, he was probably best known as a master of mental conjuring.

This clever mail prediction best demonstrates the kind of mental magic Anneman presented and is guaranteed to amaze even the most sophisticated audience.

THE EFFECT:

The magician shows the audience a series of cards bearing symbols, some of which are traditionally used in experiments of extrasensory perception. One member of the audience is asked to concentrate on one of the symbols, and after some effort at concentration, he or she shows it to the audience. Then another member of the audience, to whom the magician has mailed a sealed envelope a week before, is asked to open the envelope and display its contents to the rest of the audience. Can it be a coincidence that the contents of the envelope reveal the identical symbol selected by the audience member and that the magician predicted that selection a full week before? No, it must be the amazing power of extrasensory perception.

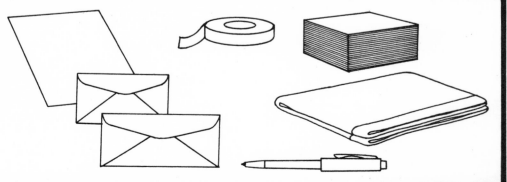

YOU WILL NEED:

A sheet of unlined paper, approximately eight and one-half by eleven inches; two envelopes, one standard and the other legal size; clear plastic tape; a packet of forty-eight blank three-by-three-inch cards (easily available three-by-five-inch index cards can be cut down to size); a black felt marker; and a heavy cloth dinner napkin.

TO PREPARE THE TRICK:

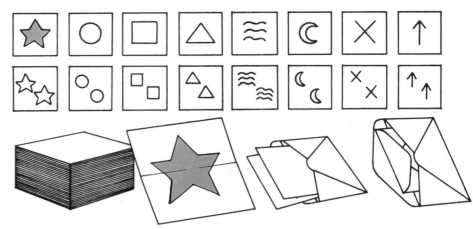

Using a black felt marker, draw the sixteen symbols and combinations of symbols on sixteen of the cards, one symbol to a card. Repeat the process twice on the remaining cards. (You will have three complete sets of symbols on a total of forty-eight cards.)

Select randomly any one of the sixteen symbols, and draw it in broad outline on the sheet of blank paper. (Assume that you have chosen the star.) Fold the star drawing, and put it inside the standard-size envelope, seal the envelope; then seal the flap with tape.

Slip the sealed, taped envelope inside the legal-size envelope, and seal and tape it as you did the first envelope.

A week before the trick is to be performed, tell someone who will be a member of the audience that you intend to send a letter to him, and ask him to bring that letter, unopened, to the performance.

Immediately before the performance select one of the cards with a star symbol on it, remove it from the pack, and place it faceup on a table with the cloth napkin casually crumpled in front of it.

TO PERFORM THE TRICK:

Shuffle the prepared symbol cards so that they appear in a random order as you fan them out and show them to the audience. Explain that symbols like these are routinely used in ESP experiments and that you hope to conduct such an experiment of your own. Ask a volunteer from the audience to shuffle the symbol cards and return them to you.

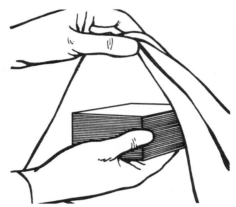

Turn all of the cards faceup in your hand as you walk toward the table; the instant before you pick up the cloth napkin, place the deck directly on top of the star card already on the table.

Shake out the napkin and place it over your left hand with the palm facing up.

Pick up the symbol cards in your right hand. (They must be turned facedown in your hand.)

With your left hand bring the napkin up over the symbol cards, but just as the pack is covered from view by the napkin, flip the entire deck over with your right hand so that the cards are faceup in your hand.

Ask for the help of a volunteer and explain that ESP works best when only one symbol enters the mind; for that reason you have covered over all of the cards. Ask the volunteer

to cut off some cards by picking them up through the napkin. As soon as the cards are cut, flip over the remaining cards in your right hand—they are now facedown—and withdraw them from under the napkin.

Ask the volunteer to look at the top card of those remaining in your hand and to show it to the audience. (Without his knowing it, you have forced the volunteer to take the star card that

you had secretly added to the deck.)

Explain to the audience that one week previously you had mailed your prediction to someone who is in the audience. Ask that person to stand up and to hand the sealed envelope containing the prediction to another audience member.

Ask that person to open the envelope and remove its contents.

To build the suspense, ask still another volunteer to open the second sealed envelope, remove the paper, and show it to the audience.

At the same time ask the first volunteer to name the symbol that he had selected. He will say, "Star," and the paper being shown to the audience will show the symbol of a star, miraculously predicted a full week in advance.

Dice Divination

The 1949 radio broadcasts of the English mentalists **Sidney and Lesley Piddington** caused a modern sensation. Half of England was convinced that the brilliant husband-and-wife conjuring team could actually read minds. The other half was convinced they were nothing but clever frauds.

Either way, divination has always had great appeal to audiences, both ancient and modern; this divination routine continues that long tradition of audience appeal.

THE EFFECT:

An audience volunteer places a pair of dice in a box and covers the box. He then draws on a pad of paper the exact number of dots that appeared on the top of the dice after they had been placed in the box, and he turns the pad facedown. Even though the box is covered, the magician—by finger impulses—is able to miraculously divine the precise number of dots on the top of the dice and confirm his divination with the volunteer's sketch.

YOU WILL NEED:

A pair of dice; a small, lidded cardboard box in which the dice will fit snugly; a small rubber band; a pad of paper; and a black crayon or felt-tipped marker.

TO PREPARE THE TRICK:

In advance slip the rubber band into your pocket. Draw two squares—to represent the tops of the dice—on the pad.

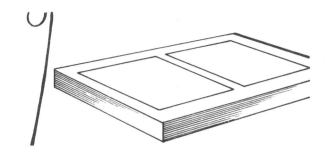

TO PERFORM THE TRICK:

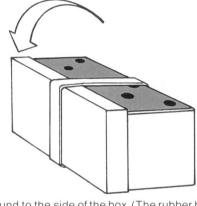

Set out the pad, dice, box and cover, and marker on any convenient surface. Ask for an audience volunteer, and give him or her the following instructions. After you leave the room, the volunteer is to place the dice in the cardboard box—remembering the number of dots that appear on their tops—and cover the box. He is to draw the same number of dots in the corresponding squares on the pad. Then he is to turn the pad facedown so that the drawing cannot be seen.

After you have been called back to the room, turn your back to the audience, place your hands behind your back, and tell the volunteer to place the covered box in your hands. Take the rubber band out of your pocket, and slip it around the box.

Keeping the box behind your back, turn and face the audience. When you are facing the audience, lift off the box cover, and slide it

around to the side of the box. (The rubber band will expand enough to let the cover move freely and yet prevent the dice from falling out of the box.)

With the box still behind your back, ask the volunteer to pick up the pad, and concentrate on the spots he has drawn. As he does, close your eyes, and appear to be concentrating on receiving his thoughts. Ask the volunteer to show the audience the drawing on the pad

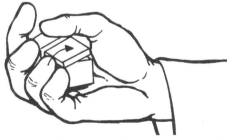

without letting you see it; suggest that it would be helpful if the rest of the audience also sent their thought waves to you.

As you make this request, casually bring the box in front of you, being careful to keep the open side of the box positioned away from the audience.

Put the box down on the table, and with your hands now free demonstrate how you want the volunteer to hold the pad so that you cannot see the drawing when he shows it to the audience.

As the volunteer follows your directions and draws the attention of the audience to the pad, pick up the box and glance quickly at the

exposed dice, mentally making note of the number of dots on each die.

Casually put the box behind your back, and move the lid back so that it covers the dice.

Pretend to be struggling to receive the thought waves of the audience, and then slowly turn your back to the audience so that they can see that the box in your hands is still covered.

Now tell the audience the number of dots that you have divined on each die, and ask the volunteer to confirm your answer with his drawing.

Magic Photography

The gifted American conjurer **Karl Germain** was noted for the artistry of his magic presentations. He devised and constructed his own illusions with great skill and presented them with consummate grace.

Superb artistry was also evident in Germain's presentation of mental magic and, in particular, in his use of paintings to divine the thoughts of his audience.

In this modern version of a Germain divination, a photograph substitutes for a painting, but the end result is just as startling.

THE EFFECT:

The magician shows the audience an eight-by-ten-inch photograph of himself holding an empty picture frame. The photograph is wrapped in newspaper and placed on a table. The audience is also shown a number of folded slips of paper, each one bearing the name of a famous individual. A volunteer selects one of the slips of paper and reads out the name written on it. When the photograph of the magician is unwrapped, the face of that famous individual, along with the date of this performance, is miraculously visible in the empty picture frame.

YOU WILL NEED:

An eight-by-ten-inch picture frame without glass; an eight-by-ten-inch photograph of you holding the empty picture frame; a second eight-by-ten photograph of you with the picture of a famous person in the same frame and with the date of your performance written across the picture; enough thin cardboard to mount the two photographs; two hundred two-by-three-inch slips of paper; a pen; several sheets of newspaper; two paper bags; rubber cement; scissors; a large soup bowl; and a saucer.

TO PREPARE THE TRICK:

Select the name of a famous person in advance. (Assume that you have chosen Thomas A. Edison.) Have two eight-by-ten-inch photographs of yourself prepared as follows: photo A with you holding an empty picture frame; photo B with you holding a picture of Edison, with the performance date written across it, inside the same frame.

Mount the two photographs on cardboard. Cut a sheet of newspaper to fit the cardboard that backs photo A, and cement it to the cardboard, trimming away excess newspaper.

Place the mounted photo B in the empty frame.

Trim the edges of photo A so that it fits easily into the picture frame from the front.

With the pen write the name of a famous person on one hundred of the two-by-three-inch slips of paper; write only one name on each slip, for example, Shakespeare, Queen Elizabeth, George Washington, Elizabeth Tay-

lor, and so forth. Fold each slip of paper in half, and then fold the slip in half again in the other direction.

On the remaining one hundred slips write the name of Thomas A. Edison. Fold these slips in the same way that you have folded the first hundred slips, and set them aside separately for the time being.

Prepare a paper bag with a secret pocket in the following way. From the side of one paper bag cut out a section large enough to form a hidden pocket inside the second paper bag. Cement down the edges of three sides of the hidden pocket.

Place the one hundred slips with Edison written on them inside the main section of the prepared paper bag.

Place the one hundred slips with various famous names on them in the soup bowl. Place the soup bowl, saucer, and several sheets of newspaper on a table.

TO PERFORM THE TRICK:

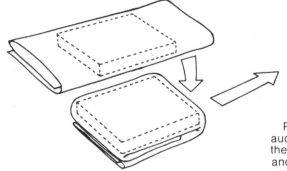

Show the framed photo A to the audience, being careful to tilt the frame back slightly to prevent the photograph from falling out. Photo B is placed into the frame in the usual way (from the back).

Lay the frame faceup on the table, and cover it with a sheet of newspaper. Wrap the newspaper around the frame as illustrated. After you have wrapped the newspaper around the frame—securing the loose photo A—lift the whole package, and turn it facedown on the table. With one hand holding the newspaper wrapping, reach with the other hand for the saucer. Place the saucer on top of

the wrapping to hold it closed while you proceed with the trick.

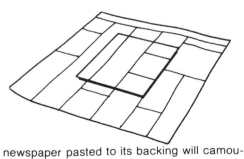

Pick up the soup bowl, and walk into the audience. Ask several volunteers to reach into the soup bowl, extract a slip of paper, unfold it, and read the name written on it to the rest of the audience. Then tell the volunteers to refold the slips of paper and to place them back in the bowl.

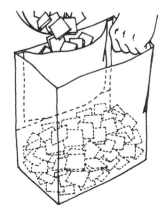

Return to the table, and giving the impression that you are putting the slips of paper into the main part of the paper bag, casually dump the slips into the hidden pocket of the bag.

Close the top of the bag, including the hidden pocket, and with one hand holding the top closed, shake the bag vigorously, as if the slips of paper are being mixed.

Open the bag, keeping your fingers over the opening of the hidden pocket, and have a volunteer reach into the bag and select one of the folded slips of paper at random. (The volunteer will be reaching into the main part of the bag, where all of the slips bear the name of Thomas A. Edison.)

Ask the volunteer to read the audience the name on the slip of paper. As the volunteer does this, walk to the table and begin unwrapping the framed picture, keeping it flat on the table as you unwrap it. When you unwrap the frame, photo A will remain facedown on the newspaper wrapping. It will be unnoticed by the audience because the

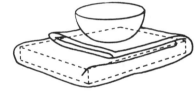

newspaper pasted to its backing will camouflage it.

Raise the picture frame, with photo B now exposed, and show it to the audience. Point out to the audience the picture of Edison that is now visible in the frame that you are holding in the photograph and the mysterious appearance of the date of this particular performance.

Telephone Telepathy

Those marvelous magic-makers who reach the pinnacle of success in their profession have usually traveled a long and hard road, and the acclaim they win is both fitting and welcome. But there is often another not-so-welcome aspect of their success—the stream of requests from well-meaning friends to do a little trick at a social function that is unconnected with magic.

The **Zancigs,** a famous husband-and-wife team of vaudeville mentalists, were constantly beset—like so many other conjurers—with requests to perform for friends. This clever update of a Zancig feat of mental magic is a delightful way to amuse friends, even those who are miles away.

THE EFFECT:

The magician telephones a friend, and although the two may be thousands of miles apart, the magician miraculously identifies a card his friend has just selected from his own deck of cards.

YOU WILL NEED:

Pencil and paper; and a willing friend with a telephone and a deck of cards.

TO PREPARE THE TRICK:

Ask a friend to have a deck of cards and a pencil and paper at hand near his or her telephone; have paper and pencil at hand near your own telephone.

TO PERFORM THE TRICK:

Telephone your friend, and ask him to thoroughly shuffle his deck of cards. Ask him to spread out the cards faceup on a table, and select any card from the deck. Tell him to place the selected card faceup apart from the rest of the deck.

Ask him to jot down the name of the card for future reference. Then instruct him to gather the spread-out cards into a deck once again and hold the deck faceup in his hand.

Ask him to deal on top of the selected card the same number of cards as the value of the selected card. Assuming that the nine of clubs has been selected, nine cards are to be dealt out faceup. (Tell your friend that a jack has a value of eleven, a queen has a value of twelve, and a king has a value of thirteen.)

Ask him to gather all of the cards on the table as a group—in this example, the nine of clubs and the nine other dealt-out cards—and place them faceup on top of the rest of the deck, which he is holding faceup in his hand.

Finally ask him to turn the entire deck facedown in his hand.

After the deck is positioned facedown in his hand, ask your friend to deal the top card onto the table faceup and name it for you. (Assume that the card is the king of hearts.)

The instant the card is identified—it now becomes your key card—ask your friend to stop, explaining that you forgot to tell him something. Ask him to return the card just dealt to the top of the deck facedown. Remember, or jot down, the name of the key card.

Then ask him to take about two-thirds of the cards off the top of the deck and place them facedown on the table and take the remaining cards and place them on top of the pile on the table.

Ask your friend to pick up the deck and to deal one card at a time from the top of the deck and place it faceup on the table, calling out the name of each card as he deals it. As he begins calling out the cards, record them on your paper. (Use abbreviations—2H, 2S, 3D, and so forth—for speed and accuracy.)

Keeping in mind the key card identified before the deck was cut—in this case, the king of hearts (KH)—record the cards as they are called out: for example, 2H, 2S, 3D, 6H, 6D, 8D, 9C, 10S, AH, JH, 4C, QD, 2C, 9S, 10H, 8H, KH.

When you hear the key card called out—KH—stop recording but permit your friend to

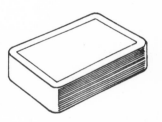

keep on calling out the cards until he deals out and names the entire deck. Since the key card was the top card of the deck before it was cut, you eliminate that card and the one called out just before it, and begin counting backward—in this case, the ten of hearts (10H). When the number of your count corresponds in value to the card you are counting, you will have found your friend's selected card.

Referring back to the assumed list above as an example, your count will read as follows: card number 1 = 10H; 2 = 9S; 3 = 2C; 4 = QD; 5 = 4C; 6 = JH; 7 = AH; 8 = 10S; 9 = 9C; 10 = 8D; 11 = 6D; 12 = 6H; 13 = 3D. In this example, the only number with a matching card value is number 9 and 9C (the nine of clubs), which is your friend's selected card.

In a rare case two cards may happen to have values equaling the number of their count. If that should occur, a bit of clever questioning on your part—Is it a red card? Does it have a high value?—will eliminate one of the cards and give you the right one, while your answer leaves your friend dazzled at your long-distance powers of telepathy.

Rope Magic

Since that distant time in prerecorded history when the legendary Hindu rope trick was supposedly first performed, the rope has been one of the magic-maker's favorite props—and for good reason. In the hands of a skilled conjurer it can be a marvel of versatility.

A simple length of rope can seem to be stretched out to many times its original length; it can be the focal point of a variety of dazzling escapes; it can appear to be cut and then magically restored.

No accomplished medieval street conjurer ever traveled about without a length of string in his bag of tricks—that apron tied around his waist and filled with his magic devices. In fact, the cut-and-restored-rope trick was a classic deception well before 1584 when Reginald Scot described it in his book *The Discoverie of Witchcraft.*

It was not until the nineteenth century that the rope escape became a conjuring standard and the deception on which countless other deceptions were based.

The Davenport Brothers, by using an ingenious rope escape and return, were able to pull off their clever spirit cabinet ruse.

Houdini, Blackstone, and Kellar, among others, featured their own dramatic versions of an instant rope escape in which they slipped their wrists out of seemingly secure bindings with lightning speed.

Japan's most famous vaudeville conjurer, Ten Ichi, bewildered audiences by being able to pass solid rings up and down an arm even though his thumbs appeared to be tied together securely.

An American named Harlan Tarbell—a doctor, author, lecturer, and magician—revived the ancient cut-and-restored-rope trick by retaining its basic principle but giving it an exciting new treatment. That new treatment made magicians everywhere realize the appeal of rope magic and set them working out their own rope tricks.

One up-and-coming magician, Milbourne Christopher, was so taken by this revival in rope magic that he decided to specialize in rope tricks. Those tricks helped him launch a long and brilliant career in conjuring, which eventually included all categories of magic.

Today rope tricks are routinely included in the repertoires of amateur and professional conjurers alike. Even in modern dress the rope tricks that follow are guaranteed to keep an audience amused and amazed.

One-Two-One Rope

The classic cut-and-restored-rope trick dates back in time to the days of the medieval street conjurer; yet, this ancient deception has never failed to charm an audience.

In more recent times such leading conjurers as Harry Kellar, Karl Germain, and **John Mulholland** have delighted their audiences with their own versions of the medieval classic.

This rope trick ends with a catchy midair restoration.

THE EFFECT:

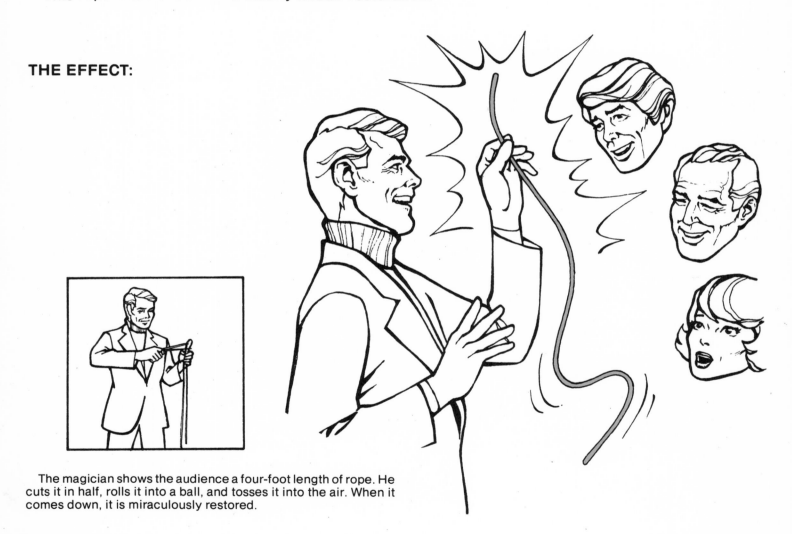

The magician shows the audience a four-foot length of rope. He cuts it in half, rolls it into a ball, and tosses it into the air. When it comes down, it is miraculously restored.

YOU WILL NEED:

A four-foot length of cotton clothesline; a separate five-inch length of clothesline; two feet of round, black sewing elastic; a safety pin at least one inch long; a standard sewing needle; black thread; and a pair of scissors.

TO PREPARE THE TRICK:

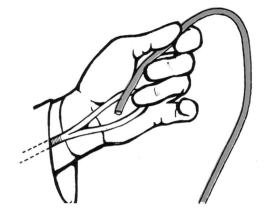

A hidden pull is prepared in advance in the following way. Fold the five-inch length of clothesline in half, and sew the ends together securely with black thread to form a rope loop. Thread the black sewing elastic through the hole in the closed end of the safety pin and then through the rope loop. Secure the elastic temporarily—the length must be adjusted later—by tying together the ends of the elastic.

Pin the safety pin—with elastic and loop attached—to the armpit inside your left jacket at the underseam.

Draw the rope loop down through the sleeve until it comes out at the cuff.

Adjust the length of the elastic so that when it is stretched taut, the rope loop can be held in the palm of the left hand by the tip of the third finger. It is important for the elastic to be pulled as taut as possible so that when the rope loop is released, it flies out of sight well up inside the jacket sleeve.

TO PERFORM THE TRICK:

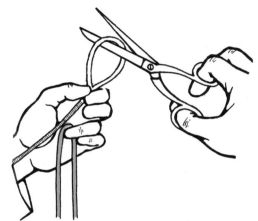

Make sure that the rope pull is properly positioned in your sleeve. Pull the rope loop down to your left palm where it is held by your third left fingertip.

Holding the four-foot clothesline rope near the end with the thumb and first and second fingers of your left hand, turn slightly to your right as you face the audience. With your right hand grasp the rope just as it emerges from the top of your left fist. Slide your right hand along the rope until it reaches the center.

Pull the rope until the end falls free of your left hand, leaving both ends dangling.

Bring your right hand—with the rope in it—under your left hand and pretend to draw the center of the rope up through your left fist.

Actually your left fingers take hold of the rope's center as your right hand picks up the palmed rope loop, the one attached to the pull and hidden in the left palm. Your right hand draws the palmed loop up through the top of your left fist. From the audience it will look as though the center of the four-foot clothesline rope has been brought up into your left hand and the

center of that rope is protruding from the top of your left fist.

Pick up the scissors with your right hand and cut through the loop, making it appear that the four-foot rope has been cut in two.

With the right hand pick up the dangling rope ends and coil them loosely around the left fist,

making sure to tuck the cut ends of the loop back into your fist.

With a continuous, sweeping motion drop your left hand down almost to your side—simultaneously releasing the cut loop which now shoots up your sleeve—and without hesitation move your left hand up and throw the rope into the air.

As the rope drops, catch it, and immediately stretch it out to its full length, showing that the cut has been magically restored and the rope is in one piece. While the audience registers surprise, toss the rope to a viewer for closer inspection of the miraculous restoration.

Bracelet Knot

When the beautiful Adelaide Scarcez married Alexander Herrmann, she became more than just his wife. As his onstage assistant, **Adelaide Herrmann** developed her own considerable conjuring skills and eventually took over the show when Alex died.

This modern update of one of Adelaide Herrmann's own deceptions presents to the audience a most diverting bit of entertainment.

THE EFFECT:

The magician threads a solid bangle bracelet onto a length of rope, grasps a rope end in each hand, and without letting go of the rope ends manages to capture the bracelet in a knot at the center of the rope. To prove to a doubting audience that the rope ends were never released, the magician repeats the knotting procedure, this time with the rope ends tied to his forefingers. Yet, the magician is still able to capture the bracelet in a knot at the center of the rope.

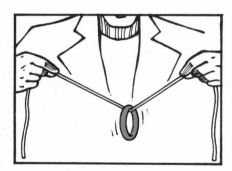

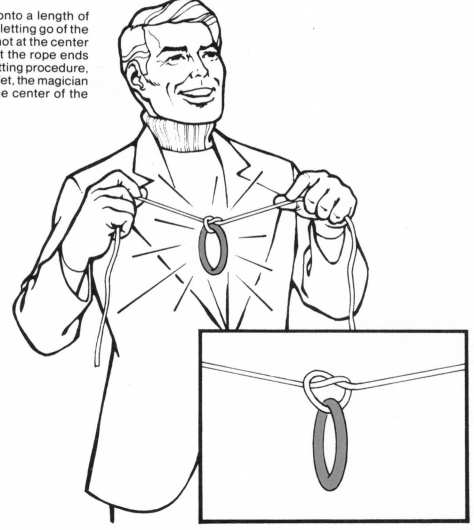

YOU WILL NEED:

A four-foot length of rope; two eight-inch pieces of household string; and a bangle bracelet.

TO PREPARE THE TRICK:

Sufficient practice with rope and bracelet in hand is the only preparation necessary.

TO PERFORM THE TRICK:

Thread the bracelet on the length of rope. Tell your audience that you intend to make a knot securing the bracelet to the center of the rope and that you will do it magically, without letting go of the rope ends.

Grasp an end of the rope in each hand. Letting the bracelet hang about in the center of the rope, move the left hand up over the right arm just above the wrist, carrying the rope around to the other side and back under the part of the rope that is hanging down from the right hand. (These directions will be clear if you follow the arrows in the illustrations.)

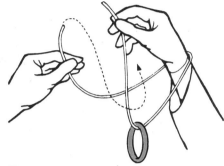

After you have brought your hands to the position indicated by the arrow, spread your hands apart.

When you have arrived at this point in the rope arrangement, hold your hands with their palms down, and bend your wrists downward. This will cause the rope to fall off your wrists and hands and will focus the audience's attention on the movement of the rope.

At this very moment of distraction release the rope end from your left hand, and regrasp it immediately at the point marked by the arrow in the illustration. (This release and regrasping maneuver should be made as smoothly as possible and will be obscured by the downward motion of your wrists.)

Still grasping the rope ends, move your hands apart, and show the audience that the bracelet is now securely knotted by the rope.

Untie the knot, leaving the bracelet threaded on the rope.

Ask the audience volunteers to tie your forefingers securely to the rope ends with the short lengths of household string as further proof that the rope ends are never released.

Repeat the first three hand moves exactly as before.

At this point—the knot has already been made—ask the volunteers to examine your tied forefingers to confirm the fact that the strings binding them are undisturbed.

Ask the two volunteers to untie your fingers and hold the rope ends themselves.

As they do and you withdraw your hands, the audience will realize that the bracelet has been mysteriously tied to the rope a second time.

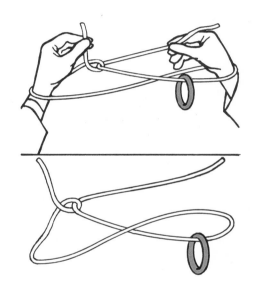

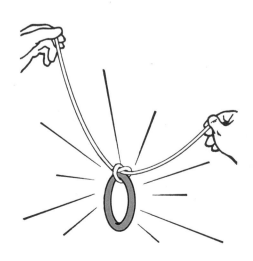

Rope Penetration

When Harlan Tarbell decided to turn his magic hobby into a full-time profession, he had no idea that his rope tricks would fool even the great magicians of his era. As a result, many magicians began incorporating rope tricks into their own repertoires.

One master magician, the marvelous **Dante**, presented a mysterious rope-penetration trick. In this updated version it is given a modern twist while still retaining its ability to fool an audience.

THE EFFECT:

Two ten-foot lengths of rope are held taut by a pair of audience volunteers. Large solid rings are threaded on the ropes; handkerchiefs are tied around the ropes. Yet, miraculously the magician is able to remove all the objects from the center of the ropes even as his assistants hold the rope ends tightly.

YOU WILL NEED:
Two ten-foot lengths of clothesline; a short piece of thin, monofilament fishline; four large embroidery hoops; five brightly colored handkerchiefs.

TO PREPARE THE TRICK:

With the fishline make a loop just large enough to fit snugly around the two ropes at their centers. Tie the loop ends together securely.

TO PERFORM THE TRICK:

Ask two audience volunteers to assist you onstage. Stretch the two ropes between them, and have each volunteer grasp his two rope ends in one hand. Ask the volunteers to test the strength of the ropes by tugging hard on their ends. As they do this, grasp both ropes in the center at the point where the loop has been tied.

Ask the volunteers to drop the rope ends they were holding and to examine the embroidery hoops and handkerchiefs, which you hand them.

While the attention of the audience is misdirected, place your thumb between the two ropes on one side of the loop and your second finger between the two ropes on the other side of the loop, and reposition the ropes by pressing your thumb and fingers together.

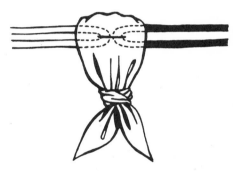

Keeping the loop hidden by your hand, ask the volunteers to pick up the rope ends again. (Each volunteer will now be holding both ends of the same rope.)

Take one of the handkerchiefs, and tie it around the ropes at their center, making sure to conceal the loop.

Ask the volunteers to thread two of the embroidery hoops on the ropes, positioning them on either side of the handkerchief. Then tie on the remaining handkerchiefs, and slip the remaining embroidery hoops on the ropes, alternating them as illustrated.

Slide all the handkerchiefs and hoops toward the center of the ropes.

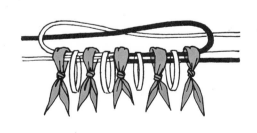

Take one rope end from each of the two volunteers, bring the two rope ends back toward the center, and tie them snugly over the hoops and handkerchiefs. (In making this knot, you reverse the rope ends so that each volunteer, as at the very start of the trick, is now holding one end of each of the two ropes.)

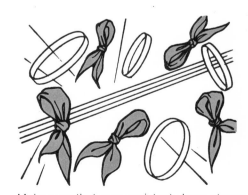

Make sure that your assistants have strong grips on the rope ends. Ask them to pull on the ropes. Their pulling will snap the monofilament loop, and then you may pull the knotted handkerchiefs and hoops free.

The part of each rope within the hoops and handkerchiefs will slip out, and it will appear that you have caused the articles to penetrate the two ropes.

Rope-Tie Escape

A marvelous rope-tie escape was handed down, so the legend goes, from an American Indian shaman to the Davenport Brothers, who, in turn, taught it to **Harry Kellar,** whose brilliant presentation of it marked it forever with his name.

Whatever the origin of this magical machination, this version of a rope-tie escape adds a touch of larceny and many laughs to a magical performance.

THE EFFECT:

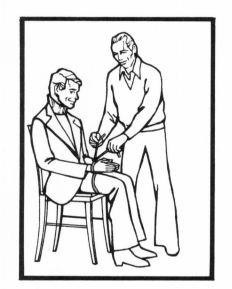

The magician's wrists are tied with rope by a volunteer from the audience, and his securely bound hands are covered by the volunteer's coat. Several times during the routine the amused audience sees the magician free himself from the rope without letting his assistant know it. Yet, whenever the volunteer is asked to reinspect the rope bindings to make sure that they are secure, the magician's hands are tightly bound. When the trick ends, the volunteer retrieves his coat, and the magician smilingly returns the items that he has picked from the pockets of the borrowed jacket (such as the volunteer's wallet, eye glasses, pen, and so forth).

YOU WILL NEED:

Two four-foot lengths of clothesline; and a pair of scissors.

TO PERFORM THE TRICK:

A volunteer from the audience examines both lengths of rope. The volunteer is asked to stand next to you as you seat yourself in a chair facing the audience.

Place one rope under your thighs near your knees, and then pull the rope ends up over your lap, lining them up parallel to each other with the right end closest to your knees.

Position your hands together—with the thumbs and the heels of the palms touching—and rest them on your knees over the rope. Tell the volunteer to tie the rope with a very tight knot above your wrists. (There should be just enough rope to tie one square knot. A four-foot rope will be the proper size for most people. The girth of your legs and wrists could require either a longer or shorter rope.)

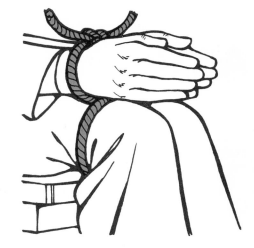

Finally, ask the volunteer to cover your hands and lower arms with his jacket.

The actual escape is executed in the following way. To slacken the rope and release your hands after they have been tied, bend both wrists to the right, and rotate the right hand clockwise under the left hand. This permits the right hand to slip free easily. To retie your hands, simply reverse the maneuver; on examination the rope will appear to be tightly tied on your wrists. Slight pressure of your knees outward to the side will make the rope even more taut when the tie is examined by your assistant.

At your request the volunteer brings the other rope to be examined by the members of the audience who are to the left side of the room. As the volunteer moves to the left, his back will be toward you. Quickly release your right hand, and raise your index finger to your lips as a warning to the audience to be quiet and not to let the volunteer know that you can release your hands. Quickly return your hand under the jacket and into the tied position in the rope. Your audience will chuckle as soon as they realize that you can instantly free your hand without the assistant's being aware of it.

When the volunteer returns, ask him to check the knot to be sure that it is tightly tied. When he affirms that your wrists are firmly tied, the audience will be further amused. The jacket is again used to cover your hands.

Ask the assistant to tie your ankles with the other rope—but position him to the left of your legs and facing the audience, ostensibly so that they can see what he is doing. (The reason for having him move to the side is to force him to face more toward the audience so that he will be unable to glimpse what you will be doing with your free hand.) You now go to work using your free hand to extract whatever you find in the inside breast pockets of the jacket on your lap, secreting each item in your own pockets. Then bring your free hand above the jacket and pull the jacket higher on your lap, again showing the audience that your hand is free.

As the audience watches with increasing amusement, ask the volunteer to double-check your wrist bindings. He, of course, will verify that your hands are securely bound and will not understand why the audience is now laughing out loud. Your hands are covered over once more. After he has finished tying your ankles, thank your assistant, and spend a

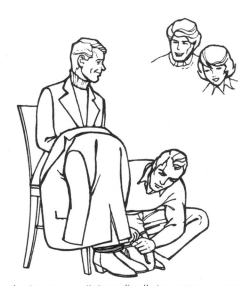

minute or so "struggling" to release your hands. In embarrassment tell the volunteer you cannot get free, and ask him to take the scissors from a nearby table and cut your ropes, beginning with your ankles.

As he cuts the ankle rope, stand up, and extend your hand in thanks. (The loose rope will fall down your legs to the floor.) As the bewildered volunteer begins to return to his seat, call him back, and return to him one by one the items you have picked from his coat pocket.

All Thumbs

Japan's great vaudeville conjurer **Ten Ichi** introduced many oriental feats of magic to Western audiences during his long career. One of the best, a clever thumb-tie escape and return, became one of the highlights of his unusual repertoire of tricks.

This version of a thumb-tie emphasizes its escape-and-return feature by the use of hoops, a broom, and an unsuspecting member of the audience.

THE EFFECT:

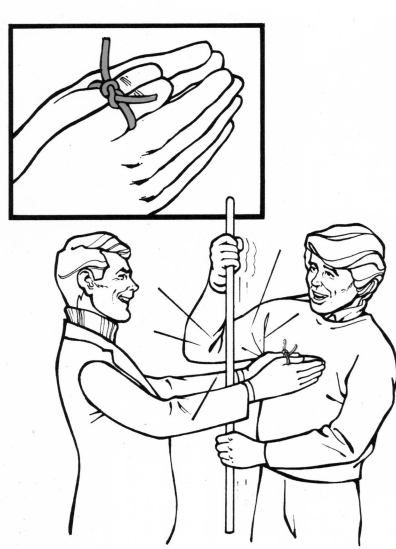

A volunteer from the audience securely ties together the magician's thumbs with heavy cord. Even with his thumbs tied, the magician manages to pass solid hoops up one arm. He links arms with a member of the audience who is securely holding his own hands clasped tightly together. He also has a spectator hold a broomstick at both ends, and still the magician, with his thumbs tied, is able to encircle the broomstick with his arms. The trick ends when the volunteer cuts the cord and releases the magician's thumbs.

YOU WILL NEED:

A twelve-inch length of heavy-duty twine approximately one-eighth inch thick; three or four large embroidery hoops; a broom; and a pair of scissors.

TO PERFORM THE TRICK:

Request a volunteer from the audience to stand at your left side and examine the cord. As he does, place your palms together with your fingers extended and thumbs raised straight up. Ask the volunteer to drape the cord well up across the forks of your thumbs. Close your thumbs over the cord and raise your hands, still palm to palm, until your fingers point straight up. With your thumbs still together, open your palms so that the audience can see the cord lying across the base of both thumbs.

Bring both palms together again, swing your hands to face the volunteer, and interlace your fingers as illustrated. Your bent right second finger slides on top of the part of the cord under the thumbs. (Not even a close examination will reveal the fact that one finger is concealed.)

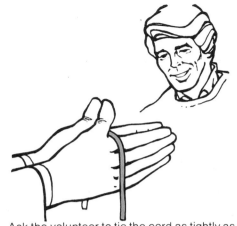

Ask the volunteer to tie the cord as tightly as possible around your thumbs. As he is tying the cord—he does not realize that the hidden finger is also being tied—push down slightly

with the concealed right second finger to create some slack in the cord, which will enable you later to release and return your left thumb easily.

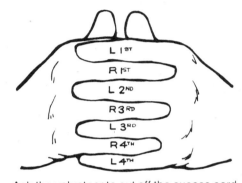

Ask the volunteer to cut off the excess cord. After he does, the fingers can be unclasped. (When it is necessary for audience inspection of the thumb binding, the fingers are reclasped in the same way, with the hidden finger pulling down on any slack in the cord.) Standing with your right side toward the audience, you can slip the left thumb in and out of the binding without being detected. Be careful to keep the

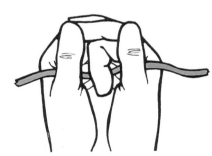

right thumb pressed tightly against the side of the right hand at all times to prevent the slack cord from slipping. Ask the volunteer to take the embroidery hoops, walk about a dozen feet away, and toss them one at a time as vertically as possible toward your tied hands. As each hoop comes through the air, release the left thumb from the cord—still holding it close to

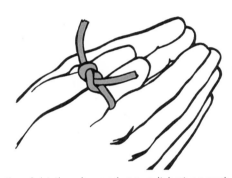

the right thumb—and move it just enough to permit the hoop to slip over your left hand and up your left arm. By swinging your hands to the left for a moment—away from the audience—you will be able to quickly reinsert your thumb into the tie without being observed. (Always keep both hands in motion whenever your left thumb is free.)

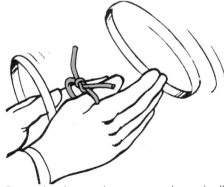

Once the hoops have passed magically through the thumb-tie, have the volunteer examine the knotted cord to prove that it is still tightly tied.

Position the volunteer with his right side facing the audience. Ask the volunteer to clasp his hands together and bend his right arm slightly away from his body.

Step up to the volunteer's right side from the rear. Quickly release your left thumb, swing

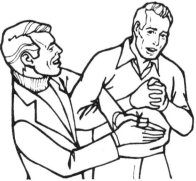

your left arm through the volunteer's right one, and instantly replace your left thumb in the binding, leaving the volunteer stunned and the audience buzzing with amazement.

To remove your arm, simply reverse the procedure.

To add to the mystery, ask the volunteer, still standing with his right side to the audience, to grasp the broomstick with both hands and hold it vertically. Follow the same procedure you

used when linking your arm through his, except in this case you will link your tied hands around the broomstick.

As a climax to the trick, return your hands to the clasped position, pull the cord taut with your hidden finger, and ask the volunteer to cut through the binding with the scissors, proving once and for all that the cord was intact all the time.

Money Magic

Money manipulations—the kind performed by conjurers—are almost as old as the coining of money itself. Once the Greeks began minting coins—around 600 B.C.—magicians soon realized that they had another perfect prop for their sleight of hand routines.

By the sixteenth century magicians were making coins hop magically from one hand to another, disappear and reappear, rise mysteriously into the air, and even pass through solid objects such as boxes and table tops. They were able to perform these wonders because they had developed many methods of palming, gripping, manipulating, and sleeving coins. If the magician was thoroughly skilled, not even the quickest eye could detect the deception.

Coin manipulations of all kinds quickly won a place in the repertoires of wandering street conjurers and elegant theater conjurers alike.

The great French innovator Jean Eugène Robert-Houdin featured a series of coin tricks in his trend-setting shows of magic; the man who "borrowed" his name many years later, Harry Houdini, often presented a deception called the Shower of Money, in which he transformed silver coins into gold and filled a top hat with bank notes.

One of the greatest of all coin manipulators was the American T. Nelson Downs, the King of Koins; his most famous coin trick was the Miser's Dream, in which he materialized a seemingly endless stream of silver dollars at his fingertips.

Although the illustrious Carl Herrmann—in contrast to Downs—chose not to specialize in conjuring with coins, he was a gifted sleight of hand expert, and his traveling-coin trick soon became a conjuring classic.

Marriage to a well-known conjurer—and a desire to enhance her onstage role—helped to produce still another marvelous manipulator of coins. Her name was Mercedes Talma; her husband was the clever Jean Servais Le Roy; her manipulative skill, developed in spite of tiny hands, earned her the title of Queen of Coins on the vaudeville circuits at the turn of the century.

The comic talents of another superb conjurer, the American Al Flosso, are never more evident than when he performs his own version of the Miser's Dream. Using the services of a young audience volunteer, Flosso pulls coins out of the most improbable places on and around the unsuspecting youngster and often convulses the audience with helpless laughter in minutes.

The same kind of amazement and delight which has characterized money manipulations over the years has been captured in the following deceptions; the simple directions should turn even an amateur into an adept money manipulator.

Currency Caper

Much of the charm of money manipulations comes from the sudden, unexpected appearance of the money from a place where it is least expected. This was a major part of the comic coin routines of **Al Flosso** and is a key ingredient of this clever currency deception.

In this somewhat inflated version of a Flosso deception—the coins have become dollar bills—the element of surprise is retained with a dazzling money disappearance and reappearance in a most unlikely place.

THE EFFECT:

The magician borrows a dollar bill from an audience volunteer, who notes its serial number. The bill then magically disappears and then, just as magically, reappears inside the cigarette the magician is smoking. A check of the serial number proves that it is the same dollar bill borrowed from the volunteer.

YOU WILL NEED:

One soft pack of filter-tipped cigarettes; two identical, dark-colored men's handkerchiefs; three one-dollar bills—one brand-new, one slightly used, and one very old; a large ashtray; a pad and pencil; a needle; and thread that matches the color of the handkerchiefs.

TO PREPARE THE TRICK:

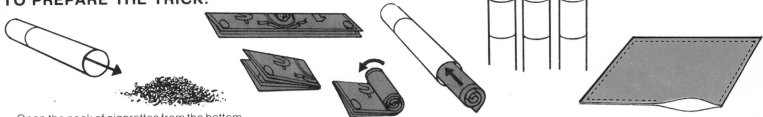

Open the pack of cigarettes from the bottom. (Do so carefully because the pack must be resealed later.) Remove three cigarettes, and, as carefully as possible, roll each cigarette between your fingers to loosen the tobacco. Pull out the loose tobacco bit by bit until most of it is removed, leaving the cigarette paper undamaged and as free of wrinkles as possible.

Record the serial numbers of each of the three bills on a small piece of paper, indicating which number represents the new, used, and old bills, respectively.

Tuck the paper behind the ashtray that you will be using during the performance of the trick.

Fold and roll each of the bills into tight little rolls. As carefully as possible, slide them into the tobaccoless cigarettes. Mark the top of each cigarette with pencil dots to indicate the condition of the bill inside; one dot for the new bill; two dots for the used bill; three dots for the old bill. Replace as much loose tobacco as you can so that each cigarette appears to be normal.

Return the cigarettes to the package—marked filter tips up—and reseal the package. Place it on the table near the ashtray.

Place the two identical handkerchiefs one on top of the other, aligning the edges. With needle and matching thread sew the edges together as invisibly as possible, leaving a small opening in one corner. The two handkerchiefs now appear as one, with a hidden opening just large enough to insert a dollar bill. Fold the handkerchief and slip it into your pocket.

TO PERFORM THE TRICK:

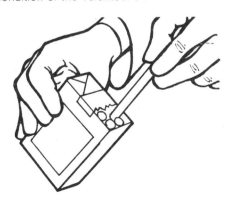

Ask an audience volunteer to lend you a dollar bill for use in the trick, and at the same time hand the volunteer the pad and pencil. As you take the bill, notice its condition—new, used, or old.

Return to the table and ask the volunteer to write down the serial number of his dollar bill as you dictate it to him. Pretend to read from his bill; instead, glance down at the slip of paper hidden behind the ashtray, and read off the serial number of the bill that best matches the condition of the volunteer's bill.

Reach into your pocket, and remove the prepared handkerchief. Fold the volunteer's bill in half and then in half again. Open the prepared handkerchief, and hold it by its corners, making sure that the pocket opening faces you.

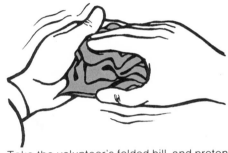

Take the volunteer's folded bill, and pretend to place it in the middle of the handkerchief. (You actually slip it through the opening into the hidden pocket.)

Roll the handkerchief into a ball, making sure to keep the pocket opening on the outside of the handkerchief. Hand the rolled-up handkerchief to another volunteer, and return to the table.

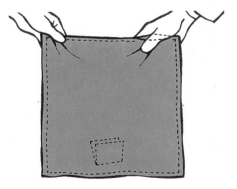

Back onstage tear open the top of the cigarette pack, and select the filter-tipped cigarette with the concealed bill's serial number that you have dictated to the volunteer (the dots key the three cigarettes).

Casually light the cigarette, and tell the audience that you will now try to make the bill disappear from the handkerchief, which the volunteer is holding.

Walk to the volunteer. Take hold of the handkerchief by the edge with the opening in it, and, keeping that edge at the top, ask the volunteer to release the handkerchief.

Shake the handkerchief, and show both sides to the audience to prove that the bill has disappeared. (It has actually slipped down into the concealed pocket.)

Put the handkerchief into your pocket, and

complain to the audience that your cigarette has a strange taste. Holding it at your fingertips, break open the cigarette, and remove the bill inside.

Unroll the bill; return it with thanks to the volunteer; and ask him to confirm that it is his by checking its serial number against the one written on the pad. He will, as you smile in triumph.

Traveling Coin

Master Magician **Carl Herrmann** decided early in his career to stop performing with elaborate conjuring equipment. Many of his small-magic tricks were coin manipulations. With a handful of coins and his own marvelous sleight of hand he was able to charm his audiences as much as he ever did with a whole trunkful of complicated magic appliances.

This version of Carl Herrmann's traveling coin trick uses a new presentation but still has the same appeal to modern audiences.

THE EFFECT:

The magician borrows a coin from a volunteer in the audience. He marks it for identification, wraps it in a handkerchief, and returns it to the volunteer to hold. He places a glass bowl containing a large ball of knitting yarn in full view of the audience. After a few mystical passes over the bowl the coin travels from the handkerchief into the ball of yarn. The volunteer discovers the coin in the center of the yarn ball when he unwinds the yarn.

YOU WILL NEED:

Any coin (for purposes of illustration, assume that you use a quarter); a large cotton bandana-type handkerchief and a small piece of matching fabric; a sewing needle; thread; a ball of brightly colored knitting yarn about four inches in diameter; a clear glass bowl large enough to hold the yarn ball; a three-inch strip of adhesive tape; a flat metal tube, three inches long and made of aluminum (the metal in an aluminum can may be used); a chair; and a square or rectangular table covered with a tablecloth.

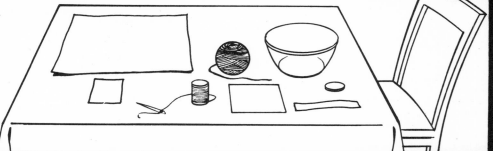

TO PREPARE THE TRICK:

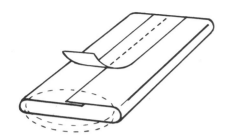

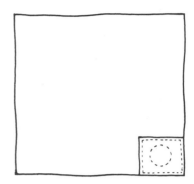

Using a flat sheet of aluminum, fold it into a flat three-inch-long tube. Use the strip of adhesive tape to hold the tube closed after you have checked to make sure that the tube is wide enough for the quarter to slide through it easily.

Beginning at one end of the tube, wrap the yarn loosely around the tube, and wind it into the shape of a ball. Allow one inch of the tube to protrude from the top of the yarn ball.

Place the yarn ball, with tube pointing up, into the glass bowl, and place the bowl on a chair behind the table covered with the tablecloth.

With needle and thread sew a small pocket of the matching fabric into a corner of the handkerchief, allowing enough room to hold the quarter snugly. Insert the quarter into the pocket and then sew the pocket closed.

TO PERFORM THE TRICK:

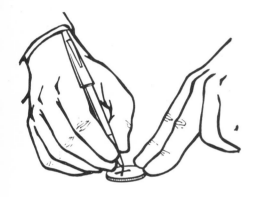

Make a show of wrapping the quarter into the handkerchief, and ask the volunteer to feel the handkerchief to verify that the quarter is wrapped inside. (He will feel the quarter that is already sewn into the handkerchief.) Then ask him to walk to the far side of the room with the handkerchief in his hand.

As he is walking away from the table, reach down to the ball of yarn in the glass bowl, and quickly drop the marked quarter into the tube. It will immediately slide down the tube into the center of the yarn ball. As quickly as possible, remove the tube, and place it quietly on the chair. Squeeze the yarn ball gently with your fingers to close up the small opening left by the extracted tube.

Invite a volunteer from the audience to assist you in performing the trick. Ask the volunteer to make an identifying mark on one of his own quarters.

Take the marked quarter from the volunteer. Pretend to wrap the marked quarter in the handkerchief, but, instead, hide it in your slightly bent right fingers.

Lift the bowl with the yarn ball in it onto the table. Walk over to the volunteer, who is still holding the handkerchief, and ask him if the coin is still inside. When he confirms that it is, tell the audience that you will now attempt a

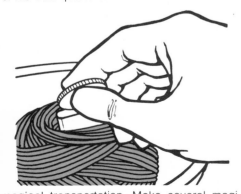

magical transportation. Make several magician like passes with your hands over the handkerchief.

Take one edge of the handkerchief, count to three, and tell the volunteer to release the handkerchief. Shake out the handkerchief with a flourish and show both sides of it. The coin has vanished! Casually pocket the handker-

chief while you ask another volunteer from the audience to go to the table and unwind the ball of yarn in the glass bowl by pulling on the loose end of the yarn.

As the second volunteer unrolls the yarn ball, it will roll around in the bowl. The marked quarter will become dislodged and fall with a clink to the bottom of the bowl.

Ask the first volunteer to check the quarter in the bowl for the marking that he originally placed on it. Enjoy his surprise when he discovers that it is his quarter and that his coin was transported magically from the handkerchief to the bowl, in full view of the audience, while you were standing far away from the bowl.

Quadruple Your Money

Although the Egyptian conjurer **Gali Gali** was well known for his clever production of live chicks from the most unusual places—from small cups as well as from the trouser legs of amazed audience volunteers—he was also skilled in performing sleight of hand with paper money.

This clever adaptation of a Gali Gali money manipulation offers a magic way to deal with inflation and is guaranteed to amuse and impress the audience.

THE EFFECT:

The magician shows the audience a five-dollar bill. He folds it up, snaps his fingers, and when he unfolds the bill, it has magically turned into two ten-dollar bills.

YOU WILL NEED:

One five-dollar bill; two ten-dollar bills; and rubber cement.

TO PREPARE THE TRICK:

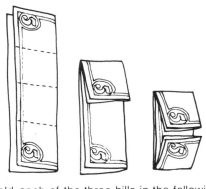

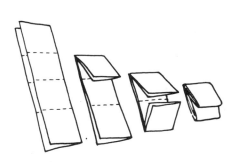

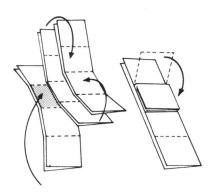

Fold each of the three bills in the following manner. Fold the bill in half lengthwise and then in half crosswise.

Unfold the last fold, and then fold both ends toward the center crease. Fold at the middle

crease, leaving each bill folded into a small, compact square.

Unfold the bills until there is simply the one fold lengthwise, and using rubber cement, glue one of the ten-dollar bills to the five-dollar bill as illustrated.

Place the second ten-dollar bill, folded lengthwise, on top of the glued ten-dollar bill. Following the creases you made previously, fold the two ten-dollar bills together.

TO PERFORM THE TRICK:

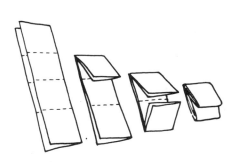

Hold the five-dollar bill in your left hand with the folded ten-dollar bills underneath the shaded area.

Fold the five-dollar bill lengthwise. Then fold in the end farthest from you. Fold in the end nearest you. Using the center crease, fold the

end farthest from you *over* the end nearest you.

With your right hand take hold of the far end of the whole packet by placing your thumb on top and your fingers underneath. Straighten

your right wrist, and turn your left hand with the palm facing down. Rub the packet in a circle on the back of your left hand, and then turn your left hand palm up. Open your left hand, and place the packet—now turned over—in the left hand in the same position it was before the

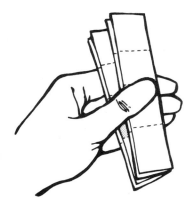

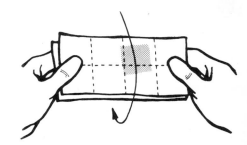

right hand picked it up.

Immediately unfold the portion of the two ten-dollar bills farthest away from you, and then open the other fold toward you.

Push the top ten-dollar bill slightly off the lower ten-dollar bill. Unfold the top ten-dollar

bill completely, and then unfold the other ten.

Slip the lower ten-dollar bill—now opened and with the folded five-dollar bill attached underneath—on top of the other unfolded ten-dollar bill, and hold them both by their ends with both hands.

Turn both ten-dollar bills over together to show the reverse side. Turn them over again, align them evenly, fold them once across the middle and put them into your pocket, leaving your audience amazed and mystified.

Migrating Coins

T. Nelson Downs, one of the most skilled of all coin manipulators in the history of conjuring, was able to make a stream of silver dollars materialize magically from thin air.

In this amazing coin trick the coins have already appeared. But with the same wizardry that marked every Downs manipulation, they now mysteriously migrate from one place to another as the baffled audience watches.

THE EFFECT:

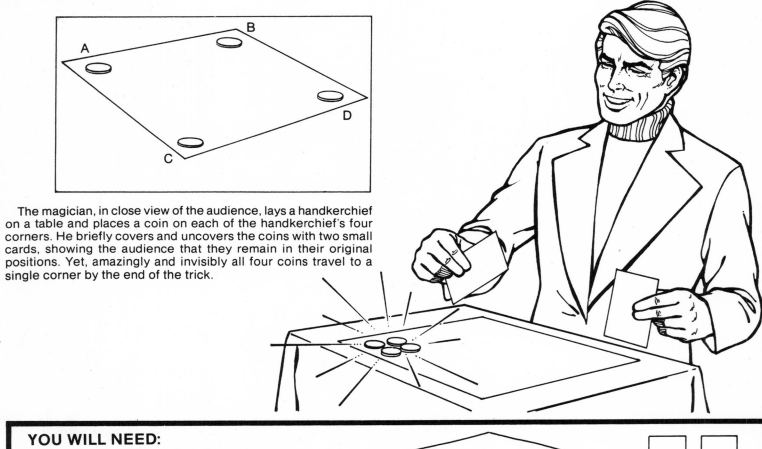

The magician, in close view of the audience, lays a handkerchief on a table and places a coin on each of the handkerchief's four corners. He briefly covers and uncovers the coins with two small cards, showing the audience that they remain in their original positions. Yet, amazingly and invisibly all four coins travel to a single corner by the end of the trick.

YOU WILL NEED:

A large handkerchief; a soft, resilient surface slightly larger than the handkerchief on which to work—for example, a folded blanket, a large placemat, or a one-quarter-inch foam rubber pad; four nickels; and two three-by-four-inch cards cut from standard three-by-five-inch index cards.

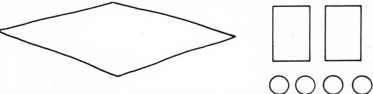

TO PREPARE THE TRICK:

Place the foam rubber pad—or any suitably resilient substitute—on a table. If you wish, the pad may be covered with a tablecloth for a neater presentation.

Lay the handkerchief flat on top of the pad. Place a nickel on each corner of the handkerchief. In order to follow the instructions precisely, designate each of the coins with a letter of the alphabet: coin A, coin B, coin C, and coin D. (Note: Although this trick requires some dexterity, it can be mastered in a short time if you follow the instructions with cards and coins in hand.)

TO PERFORM THE TRICK:

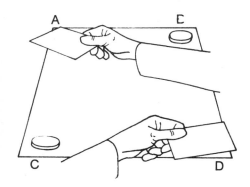

Explain to the audience that there are many ways to cover the exposed coins with the cards. As you are saying this, demonstrate by picking up one card in each hand, placing your thumb on top and your fingers underneath the cards. Hold the cards horizontally to the table. (The cards will be moved around close to and across the handkerchief surface.)

Briefly cover coin A with the right-hand card and cover coin D with the left-hand card. Hold the cards in these positions for an instant. (Your hands must move deliberately and unhurriedly during the following moves.)

Move the left-hand card to cover coin A and the right-hand card to cover coin C. Under cover of the card concealing coin C press down on the edge of coin C, which is nearest

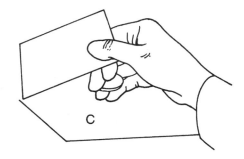

you, with the back of the third right finger. This will cause the far edge of Coin C to tilt upward. Secretly grasp the raised coin between your second and third fingers. At the same time, start moving the left-hand card toward the coin C position.

When the leading edge of the left-hand card

is above and covering the front edge of the right-hand card, move the right-hand card under the left-hand card—with coin C held between your fingers—over to cover coin A. Meanwhile, the left-hand card continues to move to and remains over the corner from which coin C was taken. (When these moves are timed well, the audience will not see that coin C has been removed.)

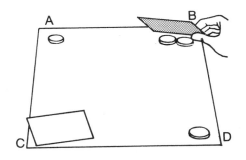

Let the right-hand card pause briefly over coin A and then move it to cover coin B.

Once over coin B, release coin C from between your fingers, and lay it next to coin B. (Both coins are under the card.)

Lay the left-hand card—already positioned at corner C—on the handkerchief so that it conceals the now-empty corner. At the same time lay the right-hand card on corner B to conceal the two coins now positioned there.

Move the left hand to—and openly pick up—coin D. At the same time, with the right hand pick up corner D of the handkerchief with your thumb on top and your fingers well underneath the corner.

Lift corner D about three inches off the pad, and at the same time with the left hand bring coin D under the lifted corner. As your left hand

passes your right hand, grasp coin D between the second and third fingers of your right hand. (The move is concealed by the handkerchief corner.)

Continue moving your left hand—still under the handkerchief—to a position approximately two inches to the right of the exact center of the handkerchief. (The movement just completed by the left hand should be executed in an unhurried manner, but without stopping. The coin must be taken by the right fingers quickly so that there is no hesitation in the movement of the left hand. To the audience it should look as though the left hand merely picked up coin D and brought it under the handkerchief.)

The left second finger lightly jabs up against the under side of the handkerchief to give the audience the impression that coin D is

brushing against the cloth. Withdraw your left hand immediately from underneath the handkerchief to show that coin D has, in fact, disappeared.

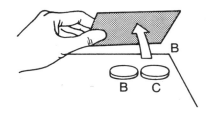

With your left hand lift the card at corner B, exposing the two coins and suggesting that one of them penetrated the handkerchief to join the other.

Immediately slide the card in your left hand under your right thumb. The right hand is withdrawn from the corner of the handkerchief holding the card with the fingers (and the hidden coin D) underneath and the thumb on top.

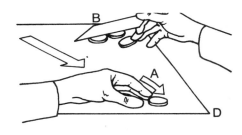

With the left hand pick up coin A, and place it on corner D. Then bring the right hand to corner B, cover the two coins lying there, and

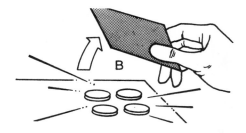

leave coin D next to them hidden under the card. (There are now three coins on corner B.)

Pick up coin A openly with your left hand. Follow the same penetration moves as with coin D.

Once coin A is concealed in the right hand, again slide the card from your left hand to your right hand—held again by the right thumb on top and the right fingers underneath—and move your right hand to corner B. Place the card along with coin A down on top of the three visible coins on corner B.

With your left fingers tap the card that has been covering corner C. Lift the card to show that the coin on that corner has vanished. Then with a flourish pick up the card at corner B, revealing all four coins.

Paper Magic

Many centuries ago the ancient Chinese realized that a thin, wet layer of tiny interlocking fibers dried into a sheet of paper. That important invention reached a high state of development in China before it spread to the Arabs. The Arabs gave it to the Europeans, and eventually it extended to the rest of the world.

It was many centuries before paper came into widespread usage. When it did, it became —like coins and lengths of rope—an ideal prop for the conjurer.

Today the uses of paper—for the layman and magician alike—are myriad. Where would the conjurer be without his confetti, his paper cones, his magically blooming paper flowers, his playing cards, his nests of cardboard boxes, his paper fans, his conjuring currency? Where, too, would he be without posters, billboards, programs, tickets, newspaper advertisements?

Not surprisingly a number of magicians have presented tricks using paper in one form or another as a prop. Horace Goldin produced flags from a paper drum; Cecil Lyle and the Great Raymond did paper hat tricks; Frank Ducrot featured a torn-and-restored-paper trick and Theodore Bamberg—also known as Okito—amazed his audiences with a strip of paper which he tore and magically restored.

The following modernized versions of several of these masterful tricks combine ordinary paper with some extraordinary wizardry; the simple and explicit instructions make it easy for a modern magician to perform these versions of the masters' paper tricks.

Newspaper Plus

Being born into the famous Dutch Bamberg family was almost a guarantee that the new arrival sooner or later would become a conjurer. Six generations of Bambergs—from Eliaser, founder of the dynasty, to David, present-day scion—have performed their magic in almost every part of the world.

Each of the conjuring Bambergs had his own favorite trick; at least two of them chose to perform in Chinese costume and bill themselves under Chinese names. Theodore Bamberg—as Okito—played in vaudeville theaters around the world. His son, David, won conjuring fame as Fu Manchu.

A favorite trick of **Okito** was a deft deception involving a torn and restored strip of paper. That clever ruse is the inspiration for this particular bit of paper wizardry.

THE EFFECT:

The magician shows the audience a column cut from a daily newspaper. He tears the column into pieces and rolls the pieces into a ball. Then he waves his hand over the ball, opens it up, and shows the column completely restored. But something goes wrong: a small bundle of paper slips out of his hand and falls to the floor. Hastily the magician tries to cover the exposed bundle with his foot but only convinces the audience that he has attempted a clumsy switch. The embarrassed magician picks up the bundle of papers from the floor, says some magic words, and miraculously the bundle of papers, too, is restored into one long strip of paper.

YOU WILL NEED:

Three identical copies of a full-sized newspaper; and scissors.

TO PREPARE THE TRICK:

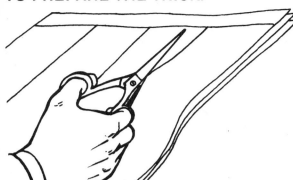

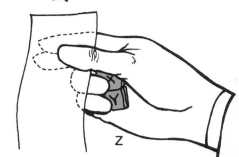

With scissors cut out the same long column from each of the three newspapers.

Accordion-pleat two of the columns (column X and column Y) with your fingers.

Fold both accordion-pleated columns into small, compact bundles. Conceal both bundles under the fourth and fifth fingers of your right hand.

Grasp the remaining unfolded column—column Z—in your right hand with your thumb and forefinger.

TO PERFORM THE TRICK:

Show column Z—it is held in your right hand—to the audience. Then tear it into four or five pieces. Crumple the torn pieces of column Z into a ball, and place column Z on top of

column X in your right hand. (In actuality you will be switching column Z with column X.)

Clench your right hand into a fist and wave your left hand magically over your right fist.

Open your right fingers slightly, reach into your right hand with the fingers of your left hand; remove column X, and unfold it with your left hand and the thumb and first finger of your right hand.

As you begin to unfold column X, allow column Y—the second accordion-pleated column—to drop to the floor in view of the audience. Cover column Y with your foot immediately.

When column X is completely unfolded, show it to the audience. Then crumple it into your right hand and place it, along with column Z—the torn column—into your right coat pocket.

Tell the audience that you have made a clumsy mistake, and pick up column Y from the floor. Somewhat abashed, tell the audience that you have suddenly remembered some special magic words to cover this kind of embarrassing situation. Say those magic words, and then unfold column Y, showing the audience that it has been restored into one long, untorn strip of paper. Supposedly you have restored the original torn-up column of paper, which the audience thought had dropped on the floor.

Magic Hat

England's **Cecil Lyle**, like so many vaudeville performers, built his conjuring reputation on a specialty act. In Lyle's case it was the onstage production and manufacture of ladies' hats from odd bits of trimmings or out of seemingly empty hat boxes. Quite naturally this clever act earned Lyle the reputation and billing of the Magical Milliner.

One of Lyle's delightful deceptions turned paper into an elegant chapeau. With a bow to the Magical Milliner, this modern adaptation also changes paper into a hat, while winning lots of audience applause.

THE EFFECT:

The magician shows the audience two sheets of tissue paper, one red and one black. He tears up the sheets of tissue paper and rolls the pieces into a ball. Then the magician unrolls the paper ball and transforms the paper into a hat.

YOU WILL NEED:

One twenty-by-thirty-inch sheet of black tissue paper; two twenty-by-twenty-inch sheets of brightly colored red tissue paper; black masking tape (also known as photographers tape); rubber cement; scissors; and a Styrofoam wig form.

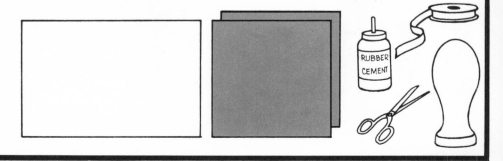

TO PREPARE THE TRICK:

Prepare the hat in the following way. Drape one sheet of red tissue paper over the wig form, gathering it in with your hands to conform to the shape of the wig form. Wrap a strip of black tape around the gathered-in tissue paper to make a hatband. Trim the edge of the tissue paper to create a brim.

Fold the hat as compactly as possible, as illustrated.

Cut a ten-by-fourteen-inch rectangle from the sheet of black tissue paper.

Apply a dab of rubber cement to the masking tape hatband, keeping the hat folded up, and glue the folded hat to one side of the tissue paper rectangle, positioning it in the center of that side.

Cut a rectangle six and three-fourths by nine and three-fourths inches from the remains of the black tissue paper and glue it, along its edges, over one side of the larger ten-by-fourteen-inch rectangle—in order to conceal the folded hat.

Cut a ten-by-fourteen-inch rectangle from the second sheet of red tissue paper.

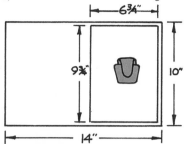

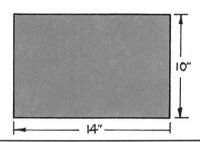

TO PERFORM THE TRICK:

Show the audience the red and the prepared black tissue paper rectangles, with the red rectangle facing the audience and the black rectangle facing you.

Without giving the audience time to notice that the black one is prepared, momentarily separate the rectangles so that the audience can see the two of them.

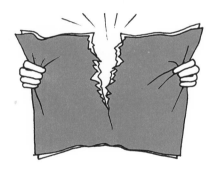

Hold the two rectangles with their edges lined up, and tear them in half a little to the left of center so that the prepared half of the black tissue paper stays intact.

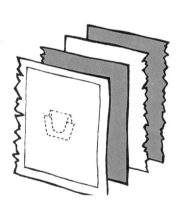

Place the four torn pieces of tissue paper together, alternating the colored tissue paper and ending up with the prepared black tissue paper—and the concealed hat—facing you.

Slowly crumple the four pieces of tissue paper by rolling all edges toward the audience. At the same time tear a hole in the black sheet facing you to expose the folded hat.

Cover the crumpled ball with your hands, and turn the ball over so that the hat now faces the audience. Unfold the hat, and place your hand inside the hat and spread it out. The hand

inside the hat takes hold of the crumpled ball of torn paper through the side of the hat. With the aid of the other hand on the outside of the hat, crush the torn pieces firmly into a very tight ball to form a flower on the side of the hat, which is now suitable for wearing by a member of the audience.

Liquid Magic

The early seventeenth century performers who conjured with liquids were called human fountains or water spouters. Their feat: swallowing huge amounts of liquid and spewing it back as a kind of anatomical miracle.

One of the first of these water spouters was a Maltese named Blaise Manfre; two others were Frenchmen, Floram Marchand of Tours and Jean Royer of Lyons.

As conjuring techniques developed, the human fountain gave way to the mechanical fountain, a device that was engineered to spout forth several streams of different liquids at the same time.

Eventually even this marvelous mechanism began to lose its audience appeal, and conjurers began using liquids in other ways.

The masterful Giuseppe Pinetti featured a trick in which he tossed a glass of wine toward the ceiling and the glass and wine magically turned into confetti; nearly a century later Alex Herrmann delighted in performing a similar trick at dinner parties.

Frederick Eugene Powell, an American vaudeville performer, presented several illusions in which liquids were changed into flowers. The spectacular showman Howard Thurston used a series of hidden pipes to supply water for his famous Flowing Coconut illusion.

Yet, the seventeenth-century water spouter was not completely forgotten. One conjurer, the American Charles Hoffman, designed an entire act around liquids. He billed himself as Think a Drink Hoffman, and with a bit of conjuring hocus-pocus he offered to pour from a cocktail shaker any kind of drink—tea, coffee, beer, milk, cocktail, highball—that his audience requested.

Today, as ever, audiences enjoy watching a conjurer make magic things happen to liquids. The following tricks are designed to quicken that enjoyment.

Rainbow Liquids

When **Charles Hoffman** performed, he claimed that he was the highest-paid bartender in the world and that his customers—the audience—need only think of a drink and he would produce it magically for them.

Hoffman's act was clever enough to bring him headline billing on the vaudeville stage. This modern version of the Hoffman deception should bring a hearty round of applause from any audience that views it.

THE EFFECT:

The magician shows the audience four glasses of water and four empty paper cylinders. He covers the glasses with the cylinders. He then asks a spectator to select four cards from a specially prepared packet of cards with each card naming a different color. Each of the four selected cards is placed against one of the cylinders. When the cylinders are removed, the water in each of the glasses has turned magically into the color indicated on the card propped in front of it.

YOU WILL NEED:

Four glass tumblers; heavy paper—about the weight of two-ply bristol board—to make four cylinders that will fit over the tumblers; a sheet of good-quality drawing paper; a package of assorted liquid food colorings; a package of three-by-five index cards; a pitcher of warm water; scissors; and rubber cement.

TO PREPARE THE TRICK:

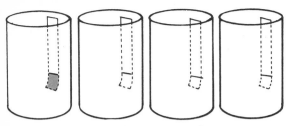

With scissors and glue cut out and prepare four paper cylinders from the heavy paper to fit over the four glass tumblers. Make sure that each cylinder is two inches taller than the tumblers.

Cut four half-inch-wide strips from the drawing paper. Each strip should be one inch shorter than the height of the paper cylinders.

Using the food coloring, saturate the ends of each of the strips with a different color: red, blue, green, and yellow. The food coloring

should be applied only to the inner side of each strip. Cement one of these strips inside each of the paper cylinders as illustrated.

Prepare the special packet of cards in the following way. On twenty-seven of the three-by-five index cards write the name of one color: red, blue, green, yellow, orange, violet, brown, black, and white. The name of each color should appear three times in the packet.

Place one card each naming red, blue,

green, and yellow on top of the packet of mixed cards.

Turn to the trick of Rising Cards in the card trick section of this book, and review the card force method described there. This same card force will be used later to force your audience volunteer to select the top four cards in the packet. In actual performance you will use a riffle-shuffle when shuffling the packet of cards. As you shuffle, be careful to leave the four prearranged cards on top of the packet.

TO PERFORM THE TRICK:

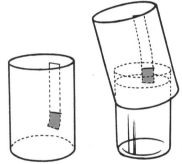
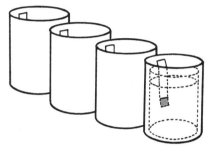

Pour enough warm water from the pitcher to fill the four tumblers. Pick up the paper cylinders one at a time, and look at the audience through each of them to show that they are empty. As you do this, hold the cylinders horizontally with the paper strips on the bottom so that the strips cannot be seen by the audience.

Place a cylinder over each of the tumblers,

tilting the cylinder just enough so that the unglued end of the hidden strip goes into the water. As soon as the strip enters the water, the food coloring previously applied to it will begin to color the water.

Be sure to place the cylinders over the tumblers keyed according to the cards that you will force the volunteer to take. If, for

example, the order of the color cards reads *red, blue, green,* and *yellow* from the top of the deck down, place the cylinder with the red strip over the tumbler to the audience's far left; the cylinder with the blue strip over the tumbler second from the left; the cylinder with the green strip over the next tumbler; and the cylinder with the yellow strip over the tumbler to the audience's far right.

Show the packet of cards to the audience. Shuffle them carefully so as not to disturb the top four cards. Using the card force method as described in the Rising Cards trick, ask the volunteer to take the top card from the packet and show it to the audience. The audience will be able to read the word *red* written on it.

Take the card from the volunteer and stand that card up against the cylinder to the far left

with the word *red* facing the audience. Ask the volunteer to pick up each of the next three cards, which will have the words *blue, green,* and *yellow* in that order. Stand the cards in front of the other three cylinders.

Tell the audience that these colors, picked by chance, are magical colors.

Wave each of the four cards over their respective cylinders. Than grasp each of the

cylinders—one after the other — turning them with a circular motion in order to mix the color from the hidden strip thoroughly through the water. Remove each of the cylinders, and your audience will be amazed to see that the water in each tumbler has turned into exactly the color called for by what appeared to be a card randomly selected by the volunteer.

Milk to Flowers

During the glorious days of vaudeville the most successful vaudeville conjurers were the ones who designed their acts around some form of novelty, like a highly specialized routine or a spectacular trick.

This quest for something different led three masterful magicians to combine their acts into a single show. The magicians were the Belgian Servais Le Roy, the German-born comic Imre Fox, and the American Frederick Powell; their show was billed as "The Triple Alliance."

Each conjurer presented his own favorite tricks, and vaudeville audiences were able to see a wider range of magical marvels than would be possible in a single conjurer's performance.

One of the best of this vast repertoire of tricks was the production of flowers from a paper cone presented by **Frederick Powell.** In this updated version of that vaudeville classic, milk is poured into the empty paper cone, but miraculously the paper flowers still appear.

THE EFFECT:

The magician makes a cone out of newspaper and pours milk from a pitcher into the cone. He waves his hand; the milk has vanished and the cone is filled with flowers.

YOU WILL NEED:

A tall, fluted, transparent glass pitcher; a sheet of .020 or .030 weight clear acetate, available in an art supply store; acetate cement; several double sheets of a full-size newspaper; scissors; enough small flowers—real or artificial—to fill a cone made from the sheets of newspaper; a short headless nail; milk; a large mixing bowl; a lead fishing weight, or similar metal weight, to be placed inside an acetate container you will make (the weight must be heavy enough to hold the acetate container on the bottom of the glass pitcher); a small funnel; and a solid-back wooden chair or a chair with a cover that fits over the back.

TO PREPARE THE TRICK:

From the acetate make a cylinder that is two inches shorter than the height of the pitcher and smaller than the circumference of the inside of the pitcher. When the cylinder is placed inside the pitcher, there should be a one-quarter-inch space between the inside walls of the pitcher and the outside walls of the cylinder. After assuring a proper fit, use the cylinder as a pattern to cut a circle out of acetate.

Close off one end of the cylinder by cementing the circle to the cylinder rim.

Place this acetate container—with the closed end at the bottom—inside the pitcher. Put the lead weight into the container.

Using the funnel, carefully pour milk into the one-quarter-inch space between the inner side of the pitcher and the acetate container so that the pitcher appears to be full of milk.

Place the pitcher on the seat of the chair, and place the mixing bowl on the floor six feet to the right of the chair.

Make a cone out of two double-page sheets of newspaper folded in half.

Make a second cone out of a single sheet of newspaper. Tape the second cone so that it will not slip open; then, with the scissors trim the second cone so that it cannot be seen when it is nested inside the first cone.

Unroll the first newspaper cone, and place the sheets of newspaper on the chair next to the pitcher.

Drive the short headless nail into the back of the chair at a point two inches below the top and centered across the back.

Fill the smaller, taped cone with flowers, and hang the cone on the nail.

TO PERFORM THE TRICK:

Stand facing the audience with the chair to your left. Pick up the sheets of newspaper from the chair, and show them to the audience. Then fold the sheets, and roll them into a cone.

Holding the cone in your left hand, walk back to the chair. Bend down over the chair, and pick up the pitcher of milk. As you are bending down, pass your left hand behind the chair until

the empty cone is positioned directly below the suspended flower-filled cone. As you pick up the pitcher in your right hand, scoop up the flower-filled cone so that it rests inside the empty cone. Since the flower-filled cone is shorter than the empty cone, the audience still thinks the cone in your hand is empty.

Pretend to pour milk from the pitcher into the cone as follows: hold the pouring spout of the pitcher directly against the cone, and slowly tilt the pitcher toward the cone. As you do this, the

milk in the outer compartment flows down into the acetate inner compartment, and does not leave the pitcher. But the audience sees the level of milk in the pitcher begin to drop as you make the motion of pouring, and they are convinced the milk has gone into the cone.

Continue pouring until the level of milk in the outer compartment of the pitcher has dropped to about one-half or one-third full.

Now place the pitcher back on the chair seat.

Carrying the cone carefully as if it is full of milk, walk toward the bowl you had previously

placed on the floor. Wave your hand magically over the cone, and tell your audience that you have just turned the milk into flowers. The instant you say *flowers*, pour them out of the cone and into the bowl with a flourish. Crush the now-empty cone into a ball, and bow to the applause of the audience.

Vintage Magic

The many thousands who saw **Alexander Herrmann** perform were usually convinced that he was a conjurer beyond compare. Those fortunate enough to see him perform in more impromptu situations—a dinner party or a private entertainment—were just as convinced that they were in the company of a true conjuring genius.

One of Alex Herrmann's most delightful after-dinner deceptions was the startling appearance, seemingly out of nowhere, of a goblet filled with vintage wine.

This streamlined update of Herrmann's after-dinner wizardry can be performed with the same magical effect.

THE EFFECT:

The magician shows the audience that his hands are empty. He then shows a handkerchief on both sides and drapes it over his hand. He waves a coin over the handkerchief, removes the handkerchief that was draped over his hand, and there, appearing magically in his fingers, is a glass full of wine.

YOU WILL NEED:

A man's large handkerchief, about sixteen inches square; a stemmed wine glass, about five inches tall with a mouth approximately two and one-quarter inches in diameter; a piece of plastic food wrap; a small amount of red wine or, if you prefer, the same amount of water with red food coloring added; a large safety pin at least an inch long; a pair of pliers; a large, strong paper clip, about two inches long; and a large coin (a half dollar works well).

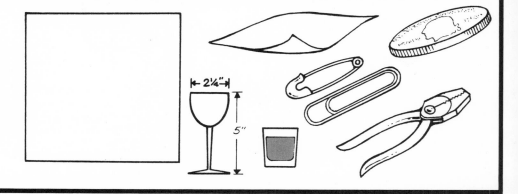

TO PREPARE THE TRICK:

Fill the wine glass about three-quarters full with wine or colored water. Stretch the piece of plastic food wrap over the mouth of the glass, and pull it down securely against the sides of the glass. Twist the ends of the food wrap around the upper part of the stem, making sure that the seal—even when the glass is turned upside down—is completely watertight.

Straighten out the wire paper clip, and thread one end of the wire through the eye of the safety pin.

With the pliers bend the wire until it forms a clip tight enough to securely hold the stem of the wine glass.

Pin the safety pin—with the clip attached—

to your shirt or to the waistband over your left hip.

Insert the stem of the wine glass upside down into the clip so that it is held in the inner opening formed by the clip. (Make sure that the stem of the glass is positioned waist high and

that the entire glass is concealed under your jacket.)

Slip the half dollar into the left outer pocket of your jacket.

TO PERFORM THE TRICK:

Show the audience that your hands are empty; then show both sides of the handkerchief. Hold out your left hand palm up in front of you, and drape the handkerchief over your hand so that most of it hangs down from the thumb side—the side away from your body—

with only a small corner hanging over the fourth finger of your left hand; with the palm facing up, this is the side closest to your body. (The handkerchief arranged this way should cover the wine glass when you remove it from under your jacket.)

Tell the audience that you will use a coin to

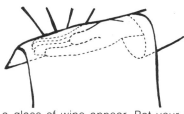

make a glass of wine appear. Pat your right jacket and trousers pockets as if looking for a coin, and show some annoyance when you cannot find one.

While you are doing this, hold your left hand at waist level directly in front of you but slightly away from your body.

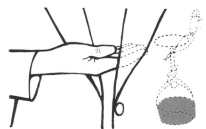

As if continuing your search for a coin, reach under the left side of your coat with your right hand palm up.

Grasp the wine glass—it is still upside down—with your first and second fingers on either side of the stem, and place your thumb over its base.

Immediately pull the glass to your right, and release it from the clip. Continue moving your right hand, still grasping the glass, out from under your jacket and forward under your left hand where both right hand and glass are completely hidden by the handkerchief. In the same continuous movement, sweep under

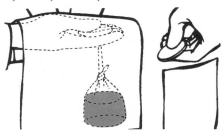

your left hand and take the handkerchief away on your right hand. The handkerchief now conceals the glass you are holding in your right hand.

With your left hand now free, reach into your left jacket pocket, and take out the half dollar

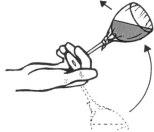

Wave the coin over the handkerchief like a magic wand; then return it to your jacket pocket.

With your left hand, raise the handkerchief a few inches off your right palm. At the same instant curl your right fingers inward to raise

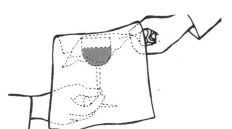

the glass into an upright position.

Let the handkerchief rest on the rim of the glass, and with your left hand feel through the handkerchief for the twisted ends of the plastic wrap.

Quickly untwist the plastic wrapped around the stem of the glass, and then with one motion

lift both the handkerchief and the plastic wrap hidden under it away from the glass. Show the audience the glass of wine which had materialized under the handkerchief; if the glass contains real wine, you could offer it to a member of the amazed audience.

Handkerchief Magic

A silk handkerchief, when manipulated by a master conjurer, can be an endlessly fascinating magic prop. It can be made to vanish suddenly or to change into a rainbow of colors, or it can mask the deft vanish of another prop.

The great French innovator Robert-Houdin discovered over a century ago that his audiences enjoyed a simple vanishing-handkerchief trick as much as any of his more elaborate deceptions.

Some years later the innovative Buatier de Kolta—whose father happened to be a silk importer—discovered that the lustrous fabric made an ideal prop for all kinds of marvelous manipulations. He created numerous deceptions with silk handkerchiefs, and some of the remarkable things he did with them became classics of magic which are still being performed today.

In time just about every magician who merited the name conjured with silk handkerchiefs. Some of them, like the American vaudevillian Ade Duval, built an entire act around the manipulation of silk handkerchiefs and scarves.

Duval presented a stage-filling spectacle called "Rhapsody in Silk," which climaxed with the production of seemingly endless yards of billowing silk from a small tube sealed with tissue paper.

David Devant, successor to the great John Nevil Maskelyne, charmed his audiences with a series of handkerchief tricks capped by the vanish of one handkerchief and its startling reappearance tied between two other handkerchiefs.

Another Devant handkerchief deception, dyeing white handkerchiefs by passing them through a small tube, started conjurers everywhere devising their own methods of dyeing handkerchiefs by magical means.

One of the most captivating handkerchief routines ever presented was Harry Blackstone's creation of a spooky handkerchief which seemed to come to life at his command.

Although Blackstone built his reputation as one of the greatest illusionists of all time, his simple—and simply delightful—handkerchief routine may well be remembered long after his spectacular illusions have been forgotten.

In the brief century since Robert-Houdin discovered the delight of a simple handkerchief vanish, hundreds of handkerchief tricks—each with countless variations—have been developed and presented by conjurers.

The handkerchief tricks that follow are modernized versions of several of the classic deceptions of the masters. Although they feature a bit of twentieth-century pizzazz, they retain the same old-fashioned charm which has captivated audiences of all ages for more than a hundred years.

Vanishing Handkerchief

This is a modern version of a handkerchief vanish. It has all the startling suddenness of the Vanishing Handkerchief trick performed by **Jean Eugène Robert-Houdin** and is guaranteed to produce instant audience appreciation.

THE EFFECT:

The magician places a silk handkerchief into a tall drinking glass, covers the mouth of the glass with one hand, and holds the bottom of the glass with the other. He announces that he is going to make the handkerchief disappear. As soon as he says the words, the handkerchief suddenly vanishes, leaving the audience staring at the empty glass.

YOU WILL NEED:

A tall ten-ounce glass; a brightly colored, lightweight silk handkerchief about sixteen inches square; approximately six feet of strong cord; and eight inches of nylon fishline.

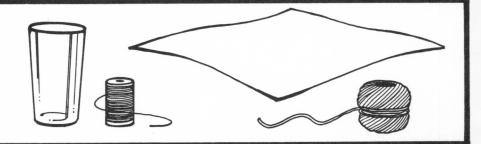

TO PREPARE THE TRICK:

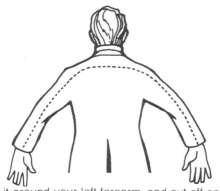

Form a loop by tying together the ends of a fishline. Attach the loop knot to one end of the cord. Slide the loop and attached cord up the left sleeve of your jacket, across the inside of the back of the jacket at the shoulders, and down the right sleeve until the end of the loop emerges from the right sleeve under the wrist.

Holding the loop with the fingers of your right hand, bend both arms and bring your hands up close to your chest. Pull the cord out of your left sleeve as far as it will go. When the cord is taut,

tie it around your left forearm, and cut off any excess cord. Prepared this way, the loop will travel up your right sleeve whenever you release it from your right hand and straighten

out your arms.

Pull the loop down out of your right sleeve and run the silk handkerchief through it, corner first. The nylon loop will be invisible to the audience; they will see only the handkerchief itself.

TO PERFORM THE TRICK:

Hold the bottom of the glass firmly in your left hand. Hold the glass horizontally, and stuff the handkerchief into it. When the handkerchief is in place, clamp your right hand over the rim of the glass.

Warn the audience that since this is the fastest trick they will ever see, they must watch the handkerchief closely.

When you feel certain that everyone's eyes are riveted on the handkerchief, with your right fingers resting on the top of the glass move your right palm slightly away from the rim of the glass to allow just enough room for the handkerchief to slip out.

Quickly thrust your hands—and the glass—toward the audience and straighten your arms. As you do this, the handkerchief will fly out of the glass and up your sleeve. (With a bit of practice you will be able to judge the exact distance necessary to move your hands and arms forward so that the handkerchief disappears entirely.) If you move quickly enough, it is impossible for the audience to detect the handkerchief going up your sleeve. After the handkerchief has vanished, push up your jacket sleeves, bringing the cuffs to just below the elbows so that the audience will not think that the handkerchief disappeared up your sleeve. When you push up your right sleeve, the handkerchief will continue to slide far enough up your arm so that it remains out of sight.

To cap the trick, pass the glass to the audience so that they can examine it for themselves.

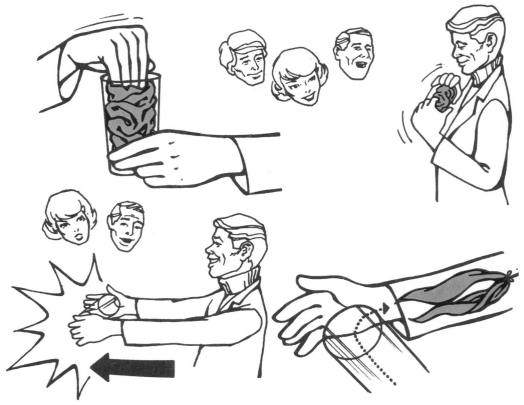

Traveling Knots

Ade Duval (born Ade Amrein), the masterful specialist with silk, often filled the stage with yards and yards of brightly colored, billowing silk when he presented his full-stage magic act. He was just as adept at producing small tricks with nothing more than a handful of silk squares.

This scarf trick was inspired by one of Duval's most delightful handkerchief deceptions.

THE EFFECT:

The magician shows the audience six separate scarves. Three of the scarves are placed on a table to the magician's left; the other three scarves, knotted together, are placed on a table to his right. After a series of mystical passes, the scarves on the right-hand table have become unknotted. Magically the knots have traveled to the left-hand table, and the three unknotted handkerchiefs are now shown to be knotted.

YOU WILL NEED:

Six identical scarves, each eighteen inches square; and two small tables.

TO PREPARE THE TRICK:

In advance tie together three of the scarves at diagonal ends.

TO PERFORM THE TRICK:

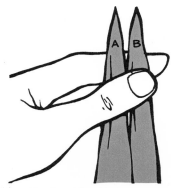

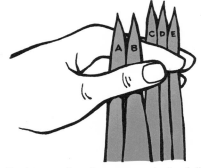

Pick up the three knotted scarves so that the knots are concealed within the folds.

Hold them by the corners designated C, D, and E between the first and second fingers of your hand. Place the corners of the other three scarves so that one scarf is held far into the fork of the thumb and the other two scarves are held between the thumb and first finger (these corners are designated A, B, and F).

Begin counting the scarves in the following way to give the audience the impression that all scarves are separate. With the left hand take the corner of scarf A and move the scarf to the left. Swing the left hand back, retaining corner A, and take the corner of scarf B. Again swing the left hand away and as you swing it back, grasp the corners A and B between the left thumb and first finger.

When you swing the left hand back, take corners A and B by the right thumb and first finger. At the same time take hold of corners C, D, and E with the left first finger and second finger and move off to the left with them.

Return the left hand to take corner A, and on the next swing back take corner B. Finally remove corner F from the right hand.

Each time the left hand swings to the left, a single count is given, which will make the

audience believe that you have counted six separate scarves.

Place scarves C, D, and E—the three preknotted scarves—on the table to your left in a loosely folded pile.

Drape one of the three loose scarves over your shoulder while you tie the two remaining loose scarves together with a special knot. This knot will hold the weight of the

handkerchiefs if handled carefully. To make the dissolving knot, carefully follow the directions illustrated.

After the two loose scarves have been tied together, tie the third scarf to the other two with the same knot. When the three scarves are tied together, they should appear as illustrated.

Hold up the tied scarves, and place them on the table to your right.

Pretend that you are magically causing the knots made in the scarves on the right-hand table to cross over and tie themselves into the scarves on the left-hand table.

Reach out and pick up the scarves on the right-hand table one at a time. As you do, the knots will come apart easily. Reach out and pick up the end scarf on the left-hand table. Lift up the scarf, and show the audience that all three scarves are magically tied together.

Color-Changing Handkerchiefs

The color-changing handkerchief trick, originated by **David Devant,** has been performed in countless different ways. In this updated version the trick still remains one of the best—and easiest to perform—while retaining all of the magic and mystery of the original trick.

THE EFFECT:

The magician shows the audience a sheet of heavy paper. He rolls it into a tube, picks up three white handkerchiefs, and pushes them through the paper tube. When they emerge, they have become transformed into one red handkerchief, one blue handkerchief, and one green handkerchief, while the tube itself is shown to be empty.

YOU WILL NEED:

Six lightweight handkerchiefs—each approximately ten inches square—three of them white, one red, one blue, and one green; a large sheet of heavy black construction paper or lightweight black cardboard; black cloth tape, one inch wide; scissors; glue; a sewing needle; black sewing thread; and a magician's wand or a long, unsharpened pencil.

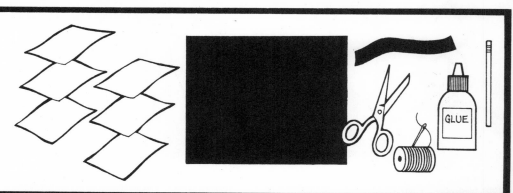

TO PREPARE THE TRICK:

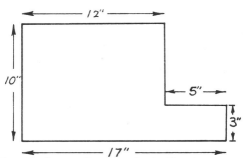
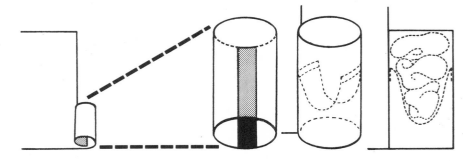

Measure the cardboard and cut with scissors according to the dimensions in the illustration. Roll the small three-by-five inch section and glue in place. This small tube should be able to fit comfortably in the left hand when the hand is partially cupped and remain com-

pletely invisible to the audience. If it feels too bulky, it may be rolled tighter, or it may be trimmed to fit more comfortably.

Once the small tube is adjusted to fit your hand, place the strip of black tape inside, and using needle and thread, sew the tape ends

firmly to the inner sides of the tube.

Roll the entire cardboard, with the small tube concealed inside. Keep the cardboard rolled so that it will automatically roll when released.

Push the three colored handkerchiefs one at a time into the top end of the small tube.

TO PERFORM THE TRICK:

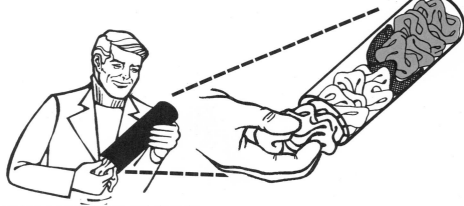

Hold the prerolled cardboard tube vertically with both hands, and unroll it so that the audience can see that it is empty. As it is unrolled, the left hand—partially cupped—hides the small inner tube that contains the concealed colored handkerchiefs. Reroll the

cardboard into a tube, pick up and show the audience the first white handkerchief; then push it carefully into the bottom of the hidden inner tube.

As you push, the colored handkerchiefs will be forced out of the small tube and into the

upper part of the large tube. You may use whatever pressure is necessary because the tape will prevent the white handkerchief from leaving the inner tube. As you do this, tilt the top of the large tube slightly toward the audience

so that they cannot see inside the bottom of the tube.

With the wand, or the unsharpened pencil used as a wand, reach into the large tube, and pull out the first colored handkerchief.

Show the audience the remaining two white handkerchiefs, and insert them in the hidden inner tube as you did the first white handkerchief.

Reach into the top of the large tube, and pull out the two remaining colored handkerchiefs.

While the audience is still buzzing, immediately unroll the tube, being careful to keep the inner tube concealed in your hand, and show the audience that it is completely empty, telling them that only magic could have turned three white handkerchiefs into three colored ones.

Hanky Panky

The inventive genius **Joseph Buatier de Kolta** devised countless ways to trick an audience with his handkerchief magic. In his clever hands handkerchiefs could shrink and grow larger, multiply and divide, appear and suddenly disappear.

In this whimsical update of a Buatier de Kolta deception, two handkerchiefs—one red, one white—are cut up by the magician. His magical formula somehow goes awry when he tries to restore them. All ends happily, however, when the handkerchiefs are eventually restored to their original condition.

THE EFFECT:

The magician, holding a red handkerchief, borrows a white one from a member of the audience. He cuts large holes out of both handkerchiefs; then he restores them only to find that the red handkerchief has a white center and the white one has a red center. The magician tries once again to restore the handkerchiefs to their original condition and does, returning the white one unharmed to its owner.

YOU WILL NEED:

Three white cotton men's handkerchiefs; three red cotton men's handkerchiefs; scissors; rubber cement; a sewing needle; two spools of thread, one red and one white; and two large paper bags, each one approximately thirteen and three-fourths inches tall, seven inches wide, and four and one-half inches deep.

TO PREPARE THE TRICK:

Cut off one side—thirteen and three-fourths by seven inches—of one of the paper bags. Apply rubber cement to the bottom edge and both side edges of the cut piece, and cement the piece to the corresponding side of the second bag to form a hidden pocket.

With scissors cut tiny slits along both vertical foldlines of the paper bag with the pocket on it. These tiny slits will enable you to easily rip apart the bag at the end of the trick.

Prepare the mismatched handkerchiefs in the following way. Pick up one of the white handkerchiefs by its center, and with scissors cut off the center. Pick up one of the red handkerchiefs and follow the same procedure, trying to cut the same amount of fabric from each.

Lay out both handkerchiefs, placing the white center under the red handkerchief and the red center under the white handkerchief. With a sewing needle and thread to match each handkerchief sew the white center to the

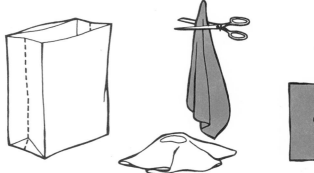

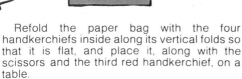

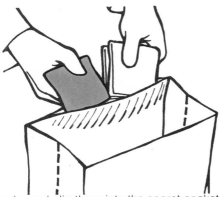

red handkerchief and the red center to the white handkerchief with tiny running stitches.

Fold each of the prepared handkerchiefs in half and in half again, and place them inside the paper bag. Similarly fold one unprepared white handkerchief and one unprepared red handkerchief, and put them also in the paper bag.

Refold the paper bag with the four handkerchiefs inside along its vertical folds so that it is flat, and place it, along with the scissors and the third red handkerchief, on a table.

Fold the remaining unprepared white handkerchief in the same way that the others were folded, and give it in advance to an accomplice in the audience.

TO PERFORM THE TRICK:

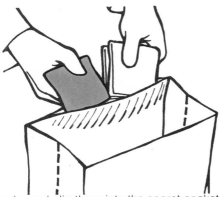

Ask to borrow a handkerchief from a member of the audience, making sure to accept the one offered by your accomplice. Pick up the red handkerchief from the table, and show both red and white handkerchiefs to the audience.

Taking each handkerchief in turn, hold them by the center, and cut out a piece as you did

before with the prepared handkerchiefs. Try to make both cuts identical in size to the cuts that you had made in the prepared handkerchiefs.

Pick up the paper bag from the table and snap it open, making sure to hold the side with the secret pocket away from the audience.

Pick up the cut handkerchiefs and their separate centers, fold each in half and in half

again, and slip them into the secret pocket of the paper bag.

Wave your hand dramatically over the paper bag, reach into the bag, and remove the two mismatched handkerchiefs. Show them to the audience, with your grin of triumph turning to dismay when you realize they are mismatched.

Refold them, and slip them into the secret pocket of the paper bag.

With a somewhat bemused expression, tell your audience that you will try the trick again. Wave your hand over the paper bag again, chant some new magic words, reach into the

bag, and pull out the remaining unprepared handkerchiefs from the bag.

Show each of the handkerchiefs to the audience, triumphantly but with an expression of relief. Place one hand over the opening of the secret pocket in the back of the paper bag and the other hand on the front top of the bag. Pull your hands apart so that the paper bag rips open. (It will rip easily along the slits you have

cut in advance.)

Show the ripped bag, front and back, to the audience to point out that it is empty.

Return the borrowed handkerchief to your accomplice.

Flying Handkerchief

One of the most popular of all handkerchief tricks is the magical disappearance of one handkerchief and its sudden reappearance tied between two other handkerchiefs.

This classic of handkerchief conjuring has been performed by many magicians in a variety of versions designed to suit their individual styles of presentation. Frank Ducrot's Twentieth-Century Silks and Theodore Bamberg's Oriental Silks (Bamberg performed under the name of Okito) were both based on an original Buatier de Kolta deception, but each man stamped the trick with his unique style.

Here is a version of **Ducrot**'s marvelous flying handkerchief—modernized and updated—needing only the special touch of a twentieth-century conjurer.

THE EFFECT:

After knotting together two solid-colored handkerchiefs in full view of the audience, the magician shows a third handkerchief, this one multicolored. He then makes it vanish only to suddenly reappear magically tied between the two solid-colored handkerchiefs.

YOU WILL NEED:

One fourteen-inch-square handkerchief of yellow silk or nylon (handkerchief A); one fourteen-inch-square handkerchief of blue silk or nylon (handkerchief B); two identical fourteen-inch-square handkerchiefs in a bright multicolored print with at least one solid-colored corner in a blue that matches handkerchief B; a full-size newspaper (tabloid size would be too small); a glass tumbler; scissors; and rubber cement.

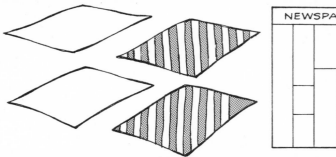

TO PREPARE THE TRICK:

With the scissors cut two pages from the newspaper. Place one page on a flat surface, apply cement along three edges, and cement down the second newspaper page. The fourth—open—side now becomes the opening of a newspaper "envelope." (The newspaper envelope should appear to be an ordinary, single newspaper page.)

Tuck this newspaper envelope inside the front page of the newspaper.

Grasp one of the multicolored handkerchiefs by the corner diagonally opposite its solid-blue corner, and tie it to one corner of handkerchief B (the solid-blue handkerchief). Fold the multicolored handkerchief in half, placing it on top of handkerchief B to which it was just knotted. Make sure that the blue corner of the multicolored handkerchief extends well over the handkerchief knot.

Roll up handkerchief B, making sure that the multicolored handkerchief is well concealed inside it.

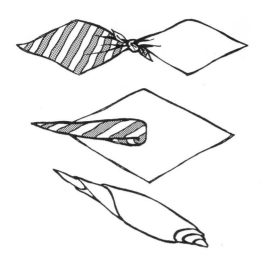

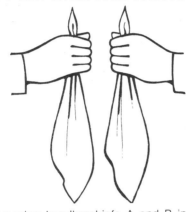

TO PERFORM THE TRICK:

Grasping handkerchiefs A and B in each hand so that the blue corner of the multicolored handkerchief appears to be part of handkerchief B, hold them up to show your audience. As the audience watches, give the appearance of tying handkerchief A and handkerchief B together. You actually tie handkerchief A and the exposed blue corner of the hidden multicolored handkerchief.

Roll the tied handkerchiefs into a ball, and stuff them into the glass tumbler.

Open the newspaper, and remove the page with the concealed envelope. Roll the newspaper page into the shape of a cone,

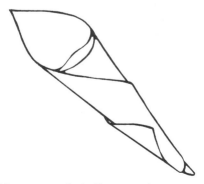

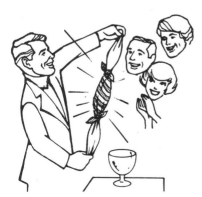

making sure that the envelope opening remains on top.

Show the audience the second multicolored handkerchief; then push it into the opening of the concealed envelope. Dramatically count to three, unroll the newspaper cone, and show that the multicolored handkerchief has vanished by displaying both sides of the newspaper page. As you do this, be sure to keep the envelope opening closed with your fingers.

Grasp one of the handkerchiefs (A or B) in the tumbler, and quickly pull the **handkerchief** ball out of the tumbler. It will immediately fall open, disclosing the multicolored handkerchief magically tied between handkerchiefs A and B.

189

Spooky Scarf

One of the most popular bits of magic ever performed by the masterful **Harry Blackstone** was a delightful routine with an ordinary handkerchief, in which it wiggled, squirmed, sat up, danced, and totally charmed the audience.

In this trick the scarf takes on some characteristics of Blackstone's dancing handkerchief in that enchanting routine.

THE EFFECT:

The magician ties a knot in the center of a large scarf and holds it by one corner. The audience watches in amazement as the scarf slowly, mysteriously unties itself without help from the magician.

YOU WILL NEED:

A colorful silk or nylon scarf, approximately twenty-two inches square; a standard sewing needle; and fine black thread or a very thin monofilament fishline, about three feet long.

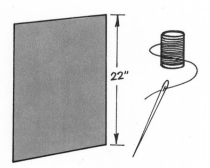

TO PREPARE THE TRICK:

Thread the needle with either the black thread or the monofilament fishline. Using several small sewing stitches, secure one end of the thread or line to one corner of the scarf.

Remove the needle and make a small knot in the opposite end of the thread. After practice, the length of the thread should be adjusted to suit your height and the length of the scarf when loosely knotted and held in front of you.

TO PERFORM THE TRICK:

This trick is best performed standing in subdued light or far enough away from the audience so that they cannot see the thread. Grip the scarf in both hands by the corners, and show both sides to the audience.

Grasp the threaded corner of the scarf in one hand, and with the other hand grasp the corner diagonally opposite. Twirl the scarf with both hands until it is well furled.

Tie a single loose knot in the center of the furled scarf, making sure that the loose thread runs through the knot.

Grasp one end of the scarf in one hand, with the threaded end pointing to the floor. As casually and unobtrusively as possible, position yourself so that your foot is placed firmly on the knotted end of the loose thread.

With several magical gestures of your free hand and a series of mystical incantations, slowly and gently raise the hand holding the scarf. As you do, the pull of the thread will cause the scarf to spookily untie itself.

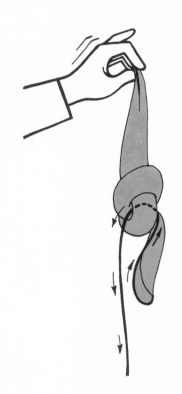

Production Magic

Think of a conjurer in action, and the first thought that comes to mind is the marvelous production of a rabbit out of a hat—a conjuring classic that dates back to the 1850s and the era of such master magicians as Antonio Blitz and John Henry Anderson.

Production magic—producing concealed objects from an innocent-looking hat or an empty box or other container—has been a major part of the conjurer's stock-in-trade since the days of Blitz and Anderson and even before that time.

In times past, the standard wizard's costume with its voluminous folds and deep sleeves offered ideal concealment for objects which would be produced later during a performance. But the use of formal evening clothes as a working costume—Wiljalba Frikell introduced the custom in the 1840s—made concealment more difficult until one conjurer's clever tailor built hidden loading pockets into his client's evening suit.

What was not secreted in the magician's loading pockets was often concealed in a servante—a hidden shelf or receptacle secretly attached to the back of a table or chair.

Over the years countless magicians have featured production tricks in their acts or have built complete acts around a single production trick.

One of the greatest of all production conjurers was Joseph Michael Hartz, the adroit English conjurer who appeared to pull unlimited numbers of items from a borrowed hat. Another amazing production conjurer was the Hungarian-born Tihanyi—his original name was Franz Czeiler—who pulled bowls of fire, bouquets of flowers, and flocks of birds from an innocent-looking box.

The famous Dante—Danish-born Harry Alvin Jansen—was noted for his spectacular illusions, but his spectacular production of a girl from a nest of trunks was always a showstopper.

Since not everyone has a convenient rabbit—or a girl—around the house, the following production tricks have been simplified and updated from the marvelous productions of the masters. Yet, they retain all of the drama and excitement that makes the rabbit-out-of-a-hat trick one of the conjurer's most popular feats.

Cylinder-Box Rabbit Production

Mention the word *magician*, and almost instantly the image of a conjurer pulling a rabbit out of a hat leaps to mind. Yet this particular production, which has come to epitomize the ancient art of conjuring, is a relatively new one.

It was less than a century and a half ago that **John Henry Anderson**, the self-styled Great Wizard of the North, became one of the first magicians to pull a rabbit from a hat. Anderson may have been the originator of this spectacular production; he certainly was not the last to perform it.

In this updated version of the Rabbit Production the hat becomes a cylinder and box nested together, and the rabbit can easily be a child's stuffed toy or any other simple object you have handy. But the enchantment of this classic production is as great today as it was when it was first presented.

THE EFFECT:

The magician shows the audience an empty box and an empty cylinder. He places the cylinder in the box, and out comes a rabbit.

YOU WILL NEED:

Two cardboard cylinders—one smaller in circumference and shorter than the other; a box that is open at both ends and has slots cut in one side; a square piece of plywood; enough black velvet to line the box and to cover both the outside of the smaller cylinder and the top of the piece of plywood; an all-purpose cement; a paint brush; a small amount of white paint; two bright-colored paints; and a rabbit—live or stuffed—or anything else you wish to produce, such as flowers, handkerchiefs, or candy.

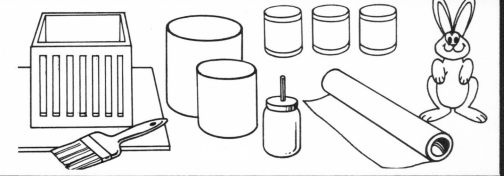

TO PREPARE THE TRICK:

Construct the two cylinders so that one is both smaller in circumference and shorter than the other. Make sure that the smaller cylinder nests easily within the larger one. The dimensions and proportions of the cylinders can be adjusted to fit whatever item you intend to produce.

Construct the box with slots cut in one side according to the pattern and proportions in the illustration.

Paint the outside of the slotted side of the box with white paint. Paint the other three sides in a bright color.

Line the inside of the three solid sides of the box with black velvet, leaving the slotted side unlined. Secure the lining with cement.

Paint the outside of the larger cylinder in one of the bright colors. Cover the outside of the smaller cylinder with black velvet, securing the velvet with cement.

Cover the top of the plywood base with black velvet. Place the box on the plywood base. Nest the smaller cylinder inside the larger one, and place the nested cylinders inside the box. Place the item to be produced inside the smaller cylinder.

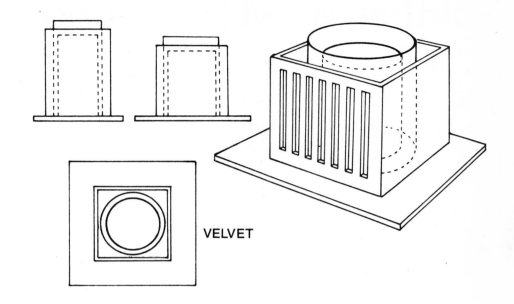

VELVET

TO PERFORM THE TRICK:

Pick up the box, and look at the audience through it to show that it is empty. Replace the box on the plywood base over the nested cylinders.

Lift the larger cylinder out of the box and show the audience that it, too, is empty. (Because the outside of the smaller cylinder and the inside of the box are both covered with black velvet, the audience will not be able to see the smaller cylinder through the slotted front of the box when the larger cylinder is removed.)

Replace the larger cylinder in the box over the smaller cylinder.

Carefully holding the edge of the smaller cylinder with your hand so that it remains within the large cylinder, lift out the rabbit with your other hand, and hold it up to show it to the audience.

If you are using a live rabbit for your production, please remember that no rabbit—not even a magical one—should be picked up by its ears. Instead, grasp the rabbit by the loose skin on its back and, as you lift it out of the cylinder, bring your other hand up under it to support its body.

Goldfish Bowl Production

The sudden magical production of everything from flowers and birds to lissome ladies has been for many years a standard feature of the conjuring presentations of the masterful **Tihanyi**—pseudonym of Hungarian-born Franz Czeiler.

This goldfish bowl production takes its inspiration from one of Tihanyi's spectacular presentations and is no less fabulous in this modern version.

THE EFFECT:

The magician shows the audience a large square of printed cloth on both sides. He drapes the cloth over his arm, and moments later a round shape mysteriously appears under the fabric. The magician whisks the fabric away and reveals a goldfish bowl, complete with goldfish.

YOU WILL NEED:

A small round table with a pedestal base; a somewhat flattened glass bowl whose rim is the same circumference as the tabletop; enough yardage of black velvet to make two table covers; gold tape to trim both table covers; a forty-eight-inch-square piece of heavy printed cloth and an additional four-inch square of the same cloth; a small sponge; a plastic bag; approximately twenty small lead weights (fishing sinkers or dressmakers' hem weights work effectively); five goldfish; scissors; a sewing needle; black thread; and gold thread.

TO PREPARE THE TRICK:

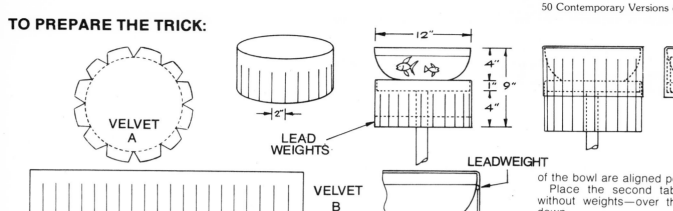

VELVET A

VELVET B

LEAD WEIGHTS

LEADWEIGHT

UNDERNEATH COVER
2 INCH SECT. WEDGED

With the scissors cut out from the black velvet a circle which is one-half inch larger than the circumference of the tabletop. Cut notches at two-inch intervals around the edge of the velvet circle.

Cut out a strip of velvet long enough to wrap around the table and wide enough to cover the fishbowl plus the thickness of the tabletop plus one additional inch. Along the bottom edge cut slits at two-inch intervals, and sew lead weights to the inside bottoms of each of the two-inch sections.

Fold the velvet circle (velvet A) at the dotted line—which is the same as the size of the tabletop—and sew the long, uncut edge of the strip of velvet (velvet B) to the folded edge of velvet A.

Trim the outside bottom edges of each two-inch section of velvet B with gold tape. This completes the first table cover.

Make a second velvet table cover following the instructions for the first, with two exceptions—first, cut the second velvet A slightly larger than the first, and, second, do not sew lead weights into the inside bottom of the second velvet B.

Place the table cover with the weights sewn into it on the table. Fill the glass bowl three-quarters full of water; place the goldfish in the bowl, and set the bowl on the table, making sure that the edges of the table and the edges

of the bowl are aligned perfectly.

Place the second table cover—the one without weights—over the bowl and pull it down.

Lift up the weighted ends of the underneath table cover, and tuck them up out of sight between the outside of the bowl and the side sections of the top table cover B. When tucked away, the weighted ends of the two-inch strips of the underneath table cover should be completely concealed under the top table cover. (They will stay wedged in place. During the performance when you remove the top table cover, the weighted strips of the underneath cover will drop down.)

Sew the small four-inch square of printed fabric to the center forty-eight-inch piece of fabric on three sides to form a pocket. Line the pocket with the plastic bag. Soak the sponge with water, and slip the wet sponge into the plastic-lined pocket.

Place the table with table covers and bowl on it toward the back of the stage.

TO PERFORM THE TRICK:

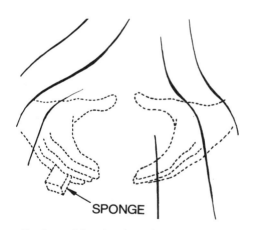

SPONGE

Stand near the edge of the stage. Hold up the large square of printed cloth, and show both sides of it to the audience. (Show the sides quickly so that the small pocket with the sponge in it will not be seen by the audience.)

Drape the cloth over your left hand, arm, and shoulder, making sure that the pocket side faces away from the audience.

Using the cloth to shield your movements, secretly slide the sponge out of the hidden pocket with your right hand. Place it between the third and fourth fingers of your right hand, and with both hands make a shape corresponding to the shape of the bowl. Bring your hands forward slightly, and make a bulge in the fabric, which suggests to the audience that you are actually carrying a bowl.

Begin walking backward toward the table. As you move toward the table, squeeze your third and fourth right fingers together, forcing water out of the sponge; this heightens the illusion that the bowl is filled with water. Further add to the illusion by walking gingerly, as if trying not to spill more water.

Approach the table from your right side and bring your left arm in front of and above the table, as if you are placing the bowl down carefully.

As soon as the tabletop is concealed from audience view by the cloth, remove the top tablecloth from the bowl, and place it together with the sponge in your left hand. (All of this is done under cover of the cloth.)

As you remove the top table cover, the weighted sections of the lower table cover will drop down into place.

With a dramatic flourish remove the cloth, keeping both the table cover you have just removed and the sponge concealed under the cloth. Reveal the fishbowl that you have magically produced from under the printed fabric.

Dip your right hand into the bowl, and flick a few drops of water up from the surface to show that there is nothing covering the top of the bowl and that it is indeed filled with water. As the audience applauds, you can be quite sure that none of them have noticed the fact that the table is slightly shorter than it was before the production of the fishbowl.

Newspaper–Handkerchief Production

Joseph Michael Hartz called his marvelous production routine "A Devil of a Hat." He began with a borrowed hat and a couple of tables placed in the center of a bare stage. When the routine was finished eighteen minutes later, the stage was crammed with enough items to stock a miniature department store, all seemingly extracted from that one borrowed hat. In fact, just about the only item missing was the daily newspaper.

In this condensed update of the famous Hartz production, a newspaper substitutes for the hat, and several handkerchiefs are miraculously produced from its pages.

THE EFFECT:

The magician shows both sides of a newspaper to the audience. Holding the sheet in the air, he punches a hole in it and miraculously pulls a handkerchief from the hole. He shows the newspaper on both sides again and then punches another hole and another and another and pulls out three more handkerchiefs to complete this amazing production trick.

YOU WILL NEED:

A large double sheet of newspaper; a small flat box about the size of a matchbox—it must be small enough to be completely concealed on the back of your outstretched hand; a one-quarter-inch strip of aluminum, which may be cut from a beverage can; a strip of double-faced adhesive tape; a strip of plastic tape; three small brightly colored silk handkerchiefs; one larger silk handkerchief (when folded together, all four handkerchiefs must fit inside the box); a small amount of flesh-colored paint; and a paintbrush.

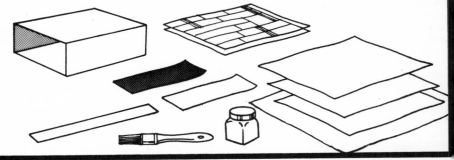

TO PREPARE THE TRICK:

After testing the box to make sure that it can be concealed by the hand, make a clip out of the one-quarter-inch aluminum strip in the following way. Shape the metal strip as illustrated, making sure that it fits between your first and second and your third and fourth right fingers. Cut two one-quarter-inch slits in the top of the box, slip the clip through the slits, and secure it on the inside of the box with a small piece of plastic tape.

Paint both the box and the clip with flesh-colored paint. Attach a piece of double-faced adhesive tape to the outside of the box (on the side opposite the clip).

Insert one corner of the larger handkerchief into the open end of the box; push the handkerchief into the box bit by bit until only one corner protrudes.

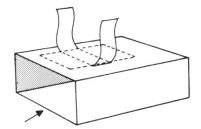

Loop that corner around a corner of one of the smaller handkerchiefs, and push the looped corners into the box. Continue pushing until all but a corner of the second handkerchief is in the box. Loop that corner around a corner of the next handkerchief. Continue until the third handkerchief is in the box. (The looped corners facilitate removal of the handkerchiefs pushed far inside the box.)

The final handkerchief does not need to be looped to the others. It is simply pushed into the box.

Place the sheet of newspaper on a table and keep the box clipped behind the right hand. (One part of the clip is held between the first and second fingers, and the other part of the clip is held between the third and fourth fingers.) When the trick is performed, the box is kept on the side away from the audience.

TO PERFORM THE TRICK:

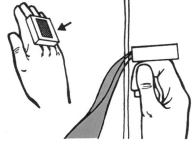

With the box positioned on the back of your right hand—the open end of the box facing toward your right finger tips—stand with your left side toward the audience.

Open the newspaper, and hold it vertically at the side edge with your right hand—between the palm and thumb—somewhat near the top, still with the box facing away from the audience.

With your left hand grasp the bottom edge of the newspaper. Show both sides of newspaper in the following way. Release the

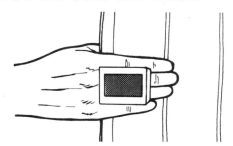

left hand places each "produced" handkerchief on the table.)

Reach through the punched hole with the left second finger and left thumb, and pull the first handkerchief out of the box through the newspaper hole. Drop the handkerchief on the table.

Hold the newspaper as you did before, with the right hand holding the side, and repeat the process of showing both sides of the newspaper to the audience.

Punch another hole in the newspaper in the

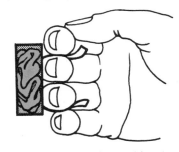

newspaper with your right hand. As you do, the top edge will fall behind your left hand—away from the audience. Still holding on to the lower edge of the newspaper with the left hand, bring that edge of the newspaper up to the right hand, which must remain in its original position so that the audience does not see the box.

Move your right hand to the center of the newspaper on the side away from the audience, and bring your left hand to the corresponding spot on the side of the

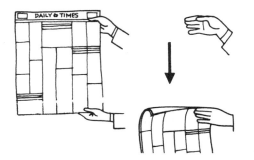

same manner as before—this time in a different place—and repeat the production procedure.

Follow the same routine—showing both sides of the newspaper, punching a hole in it, and producing another handkerchief—until all handkerchiefs have been produced and placed on the table.

After the final handkerchief has been produced, show the audience both sides of the newspaper once more. Then turn to your left and face the audience. As you are turning,

newspaper facing the audience.

Punch a hole in the newspaper with the second finger of your left hand. Curl your right fingers toward your right palm, bringing the opening of the box against the hole punched in the newspaper.

With your left thumb press the newspaper back against the right hand so that the right thumb and the side of the right first finger can grasp a small fold of newspaper. (This prevents the newspaper from falling while the

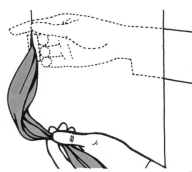

begin to fold the newspaper. Then bring the back of your right hand up against the folded newspaper on the side facing away from the audience. Press the box against the paper, causing the double-faced tape on the box to adhere to the newspaper.

Place the newspaper on the table, making sure that the box, which is now fastened to the newspaper, is concealed under the newspaper. With both hands free you can now accept the audience's applause.

Candy from Confetti

The masterful early nineteenth–century magic-maker **Antonio Blitz** never considered a performance successful unless he had made his audience laugh. To that end, he presented a number of tricks that combined conjuring skill with his own inimitable wit.

One of Blitz's most amusing deceptions was the production of gaily colored confetti from a glass of wine.

With a bow to the delightfully deceptive Signor Blitz, this up-to-date production trick, which is a tasty treat for the audience, turns confetti into candy.

THE EFFECT:

A tall drinking glass is filled with confetti. The magician covers the glass for an instant, and when he uncovers it, the confetti has miraculously changed into candy, which is then sampled by the delighted audience.

YOU WILL NEED:

A tall sixteen-ounce drinking glass with straight parallel sides, about five and one-half inches high; a cardboard box, approximately ten by ten by fourteen inches; enough confetti to fill half of the cardboard box; four sheets of lightweight cardboard, each approximately twelve inches square; a small envelope—about two inches square—from which the flap has been removed; adhesive tape; rubber cement; scissors; pencil; and a quantity of small individually wrapped candies.

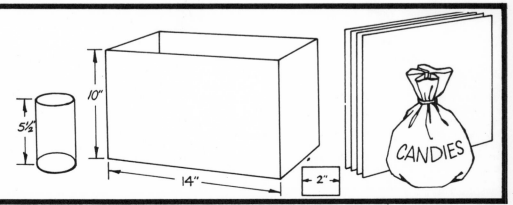

TO PREPARE THE TRICK:

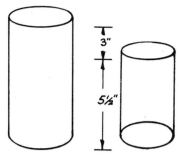

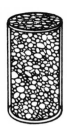

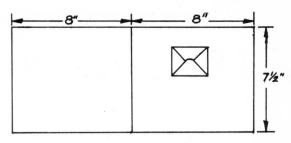

Roll a sheet of cardboard into a tube, and secure it with rubber cement and adhesive tape. The tube should fit loosely inside the drinking glass. Cut the length of the tube so that it extends approximately one-eighth inch above the rim of the glass.

Close one end of the tube in the following manner. Using the outer rim of the glass as a guide, cut out a circle of cardboard and glue and tape it into place. Coat the entire outside of the tube with rubber cement, and roll it in confetti until all sides and the closed end—which will be the top—are completely covered.

You have now made what magicians would call a "confetti fake," and it should fit easily inside the glass, with the circular top of the fake barely protruding all around the rim of the glass. When the fake is in the glass, the glass should look as though it is filled with confetti. If the fake is too tall for the glass, you can cut a little off the bottom.

With another piece of cardboard make a second tube that fits loosely over the glass. This second tube should be three inches taller than the glass.

Prepare a small folding screen by taping together two pieces of cardboard. The cardboard should be cut so that each side of the screen measures approximately two inches higher than the glass and eight inches wide.

Glue the small flapless envelope on the right panel near the top of the screen. Fill the envelope with confetti. If you wish, you may decorate both sides of the screen with brightly colored designs.

Fill the fake with the candy, and place it—open end up—inside the cardboard box. Fill the cardboard box halfway with confetti. (Be careful not to get confetti in the candy-filled fake.)

Arrange your props on the table; cardboard box with candy-filled fake and confetti farther away from the audience; the tube, the glass, and the cardboard screen closer to the audience.

TO PERFORM THE TRICK:

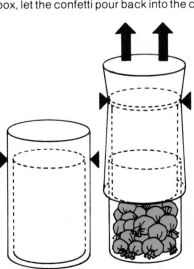

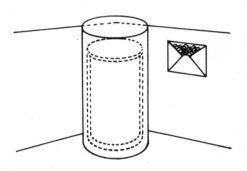

Pick up the glass from the table, and show that it is empty. Dip the glass into the cardboard box, and scoop out as much confetti as it will hold. Show the audience the full glass, and then holding the glass about a foot or so above the box, let the confetti pour back into the cardboard box.

Dip the glass back into the cardboard box as if you are about to fill it with confetti again. Instead, push the glass down over the fake. When the fake is in place, continue to make a scoop-ing motion with the glass as you did before. Lift out the glass—with the fake inside—and set it down on the table in front of the cardboard box. (The audience, of course, will assume that the glass is filled with confetti.)

Pick up the tube and show the audience that it is empty. Place it over the glass.

Pick up the folded screen from the table, open it—making sure that your fingers completely conceal the confetti-filled envelope—and show both sides of the screen to the audience.

Place the opened screen in front of the glass—which is covered by the tube—making sure to position it so that the confetti-filled envelope faces away from the audience.

Standing with the table to your left, grasp the tube with your left hand at a point just at the rim of the glass. Squeeze the tube slightly so that you can also grasp the top of the fake.

In one motion lift both the tube and the fake from the glass. (The candy, of course, remains inside the glass.) Carry the tube with the fake inside back over the top of the box. Show the audience your open right hand. Then lower it

down behind the screen, and take a pinch of confetti from the envelope. (Pretend to pick up the confetti from the top of the glass.)

While you are picking up the confetti with your right hand, lower the tube in your left hand until the bottom of it is slightly below the top of the box. Immediately let the fake slide out of the tube into the box.

Replace the empty tube over the glass, and with your right hand throw the confetti into the air with a flourish. Pick up the cardboard screen, again making sure that your fingers hide the envelope. Show both sides of the screen to the audience; then place the screen, folded flat, back on the table.

Lift the tube off the glass, and reveal its contents—candy. Confirm the fact that the tube is empty by looking at the audience through it.

Pick up the glass, and distribute pieces of candy to your marveling audience.

All Purpose Production

The **Great Raymond**—American-born Maurice Saunders—was an accomplished magic-maker who never quite managed to achieve a full degree of fame in his native land. Fortunately for Raymond the rest of the world was eager to see him perform and quite willing to shower him with acclaim.

Raymond's full-evening magic shows featured spectacular illusions, amazing escapes, and breathtaking productions. One of his best production tricks featured a virtual orchard of oranges magically produced from two bowls.

In this streamlined version of a Raymond production oranges and apples are used, but a variety of other items, such as a large number of silk scarves, can also be produced with great dramatic effect.

THE EFFECT:

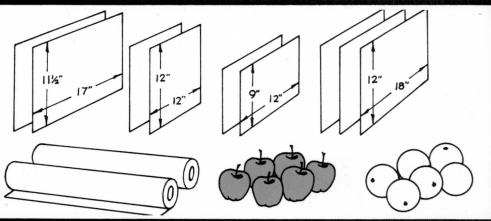

From a box, which is shown to be completely empty inside and out, the magician is able to produce a quantity of oranges and apples.

YOU WILL NEED:

Nine pieces of double-weight artist's illustration board in the following sizes: two sheets eleven and one-half by seventeen and one-half inches, two sheets twelve by twelve inches, two sheets nine by twelve inches, and three sheets twelve by eighteen inches; two rolls of decorative self-adhesive paper in two different designs—one to decorate the outside of the production box and the other to line its inside; approximately twenty-five feet of one-and-one-half-inch cloth-type adhesive tape in a color that blends with the decorative paper; a table; and a sufficient number of small oranges and apples to fill the small compartment which will be built into the production box.

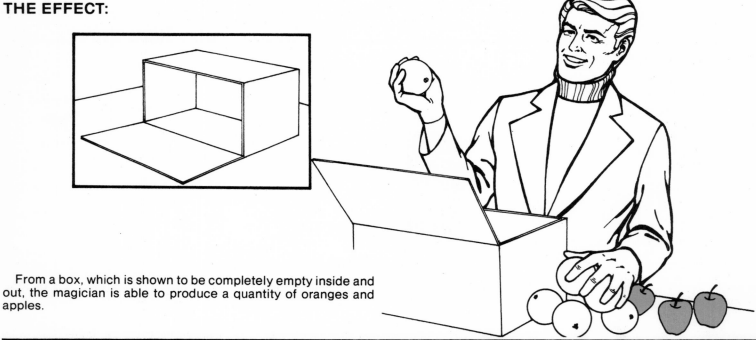

TO PREPARE THE TRICK:

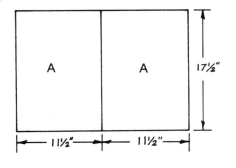

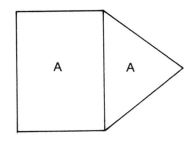

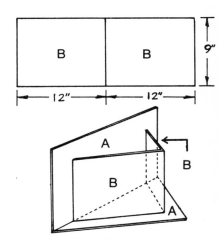

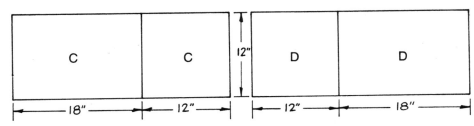

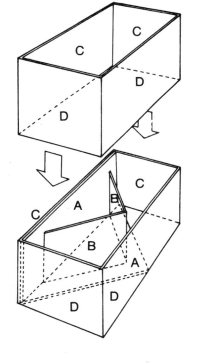

Prepare the all-purpose production box in the following way. Tape together the two pieces of eleven and one-half by seventeen and one-half illustration board—for purposes of description they are designated AA. (It is important to leave a slight gap between all joined boards to allow enough room for folding at the taped joints.) Cut one-half of AA to form a triangle.

Tape together the two nine-by-twelve pieces of illustration board (BB).

Tape together units AA and BB so that the triangle formed by BB rests on the triangle of AA and is taped against the rectangle of AA.

Tape together one twelve-by-twelve piece and one twelve-by-eighteen piece (CC).

Tape together the remaining twelve-by-twelve piece of illustration board and a second twelve-by-eighteen piece (DD).

Tape together sections CC and DD to form a rectangular box.

Place the CC-DD unit over the AA-BB unit. The AA-BB unit should fit loosely inside the CC-DD unit. If the fit is too tight, trim the edges of the AA unit to make it slightly smaller.

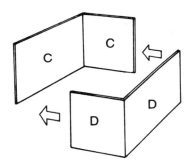

Tape the bottom of the AA unit, the triangular side, to one side of the CC-DD unit (side C)—that is, the side you will use as the front of the box.

Tape the remaining twelve-by-eighteen piece of illustration board (E) on top of the CC-DD unit.

The production box is now prepared so that when the CC-DD unit is tilted forward and pivoted on the front bottom edge, the AA-BB unit remains stationary. Check to make sure that the pivoting action is smooth and easy,

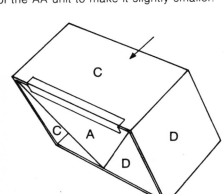

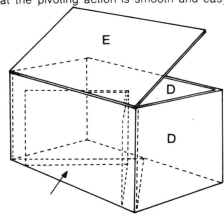

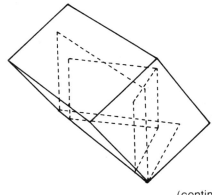

(continued)

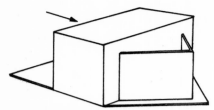

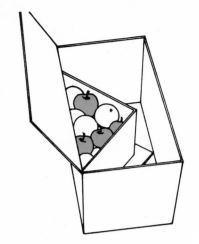

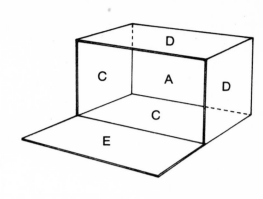

and then add additional tape to the joints to strengthen them.

Complete the production box by decorating its outside with paper from one of the rolls of self-adhesive decorative papers and its inside with paper from the other roll.

Fill the triangular BB compartment with oranges and apples.

Place the box on the table and position the table near the back of the stage.

TO PERFORM THE TRICK:

Show the audience that the production box is empty in the following way. With the box resting on the table slide it around so that the audience can see all of its outer sides.

Then slide the front of the box around to face the audience, and tilt the box (section CC-DD-E) forward so that side C now rests on the table. The instant the front side of the box touches the tabletop, open the lid (E) and let it drop flat on the table. Pause for a few seconds so that the audience can see that the box is empty. The rectangular side of unit AA—decorated to match the rest of the box's interior—will seem to the audience to be the bottom of the box.

Close the lid of the box and return the box to its upright position. Say some magic words, and wave your hand over the box.

Open the lid, and quickly remove the oranges and apples hidden inside triangular compartment (BB).

Casually toss the fruit into the audience for their inspection.

If you choose, this same production box may be used effectively to produce any number of things. One particularly effective production involves a large number of silk scarves tied together diagonally at their corners. After the scarves have been tied together, they should be accordian-pleated so that they are compact enough to fit into the secret compartment. The effect, when what appears to be an enormous quantity of silk is removed from the seemingly empty box, is highly dramatic and a surefire audience pleaser.

Occult Magic

The mysteries of the occult—the word itself evokes visions of ancient oracles, demons, and ghostlike apparitions—have plagued and fascinated men throughout history.

To solve these mysteries—or at least to try to understand them—men have invented the occult sciences: astrology, divination, sorcery, demonology, necromancy, wizardry, and countless others.

Those who delved into the mysteries of the occult claimed for themselves supernatural powers, and they usually based their findings on nothing more than the figments of their highly charged imaginations. The conjurer, on the other hand, rarely claimed powers he did not have and, instead, based his art in part on perception, crowd psychology, and long hours of practice. Yet, shrewd showman that he has always been, the master conjurer was not averse to borrowing the trappings of the occult to heighten his own presentations.

John Henry Anderson proudly billed himself as the Great Wizard of the North; the famous Philippe often appeared in the costume of an oriental wizard; even Robert-Houdin claimed that his young son was gifted with second sight, although the boy's occult powers could be traced directly to the use of a silent code.

Chung Ling Soo, the clever Bill Robinson, used his conjuring skills to expose the frauds perpetrated by spiritualists; so did John Maskelyne, Harry Kellar, and Harry Houdini.

Their targets were men like the Davenport Brothers, who claimed to be true spiritualists even though they were nothing more than skilled conjurers. They also worked diligently to expose the highly profitable business which fake mediums established around their so-called manifestations of the spirit world.

Yet, some of the most dramatic conjuring illusions ever presented on a stage—like the fabulous Pepper's Ghost and Buatier de Kolta's imaginative Black Art illusion—were inspired by eerie tales of the occult.

Even today the influences of the occult—the reciting of magical formulas, the devillike costume, the mysterious puff of smoke punctuating a mysterious vanish—can be seen in contemporary conjuring acts as practiced by the best of present-day conjurers.

The occult tricks that follow have nothing to do with the ancient black arts. They have been adapted from masterful conjuring tricks, but they retain the elements of occult mystery that have fascinated millions for many centuries.

Floating Ball

When his mother died, **Harry Houdini** became deeply interested in spiritualism and the occult. But he was far too expert in the art of deception to be easily fooled by fraudulent mediums. Instead he devoted much of his life to exposing their methods and often included a dramatic exposé of spiritualism in his performances.

Yet, Houdini was a master conjurer who always sought new ways to dazzle and delight his audiences. Adapting the spirit levitation of the medium, he presented a floating-ball trick which retained a bit of the mysterious occult but was offered as pure entertainment.

This updated version—using ordinary household items—makes the trick as impressive today as it was then.

THE EFFECT:

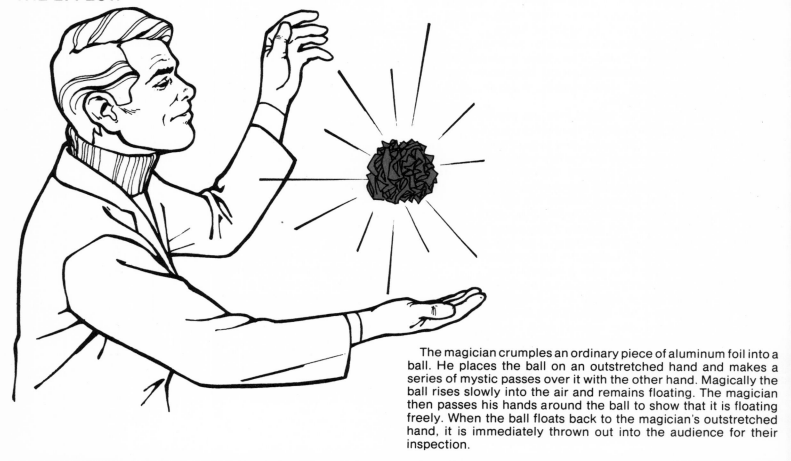

The magician crumples an ordinary piece of aluminum foil into a ball. He places the ball on an outstretched hand and makes a series of mystic passes over it with the other hand. Magically the ball rises slowly into the air and remains floating. The magician then passes his hands around the ball to show that it is floating freely. When the ball floats back to the magician's outstretched hand, it is immediately thrown out into the audience for their inspection.

YOU WILL NEED:

A roll of aluminum foil; a spool of very fine black thread; and a chair, such as a slat back chair, to which a thread can be tied.

TO PREPARE THE TRICK:

Break off approximately four feet of black thread. Tie one end of the thread to the top of the chair back. Tie a loop in the other end of the thread large enough to fit easily over your right ear. (The length of thread will have to be adjusted according to your height and the size of the chair.)

Place the roll of aluminum foil on the chair seat and place the chair off to your right. Do the trick far enough away from the audience so that the thread cannot be seen. (Dimming the room lights will also help to keep the thread invisible.)

Slip the prepared thread loop over your right ear.

TO PERFORM THE TRICK:

Pick up the roll of aluminum foil from the chair, and tear off a length of foil about twelve inches square. Turn to your right, facing the chair with one foot slightly in front of the other. Replace the roll of foil on the chair.

Reach out with both hands and shape the length of foil into a ball around the thread, which runs between your right ear and the back of the chair and is unseen by the audience. As you form the ball, casually make sure that it is shaped loosely around the thread so that it will move freely.

Hold the ball on the outstretched palm of your right hand.

Moving away from the chair, slowly shift your weight to your rear foot. This will cause the thread to become taut. As the ball begins to rise slowly into the air, make several mystical passes over the ball with your left hand.

Hold your head as steady as possible to avoid jiggling the thread—and the ball on it—and circle both hands around the ball, being very careful not to touch the thread itself. The audience will assume that your hands have actually circled the ball, proving that it is completely unsupported and floating freely.

Move your left hand under the ball, and bring your weight slowly back to the front foot, settling the ball back into your palm.

When the ball is settled on your left palm, grasp it firmly, and at the same instant casually raise your right hand and flip the thread loop off your right ear.

Immediately turn to the audience, and walk toward them with the ball extended in your left

hand. (As you move, the thread will slip through the loosely crumpled foil and drop unnoticed to the floor.)

Toss the ball to someone in the audience, and ask that it be passed around and inspected.

Genie Pencil

The multitalented William Robinson was deeply fascinated by two things: the mysterious Orient and the not-so-mysterious deceptions practiced in the name of the occult.

He combined both interests successfully during his conjuring career by appearing as the oriental **Chung Ling Soo** and presenting a variety of tricks with overtones of occult mystery. This updated version of the pencil-in-the-bottle trick assumes the help of an ancient genie hidden in a bottle while it presents to the audience a clever deception.

THE EFFECT:

After the audience has examined a pencil, a bottle, and a cork, the magician drops the pencil into the bottle and seals the bottle with the cork. Then the magician invokes a magic genie, who makes the pencil rise and fall inside the corked bottle and finally, when the cork is removed, makes the pencil rise out of the bottle. An audience reexamination of the pencil, bottle, and cork convinces them that it must be magic.

YOU WILL NEED:

A tall slim-necked bottle; two identical pencils with erasers; two corks; and several feet of fine black thread or very thin fishing leader or a long strand of hair; and a table.

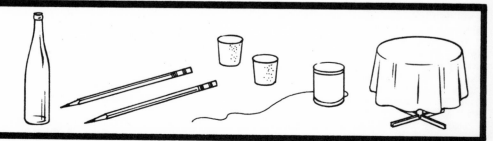

TO PREPARE THE TRICK:

Slit the tops of both erasers as shown.

Tie a tiny knot into one end of the length of thread—or hair or fishing leader—and slip it into the slit in one of the erasers.

Cut a small groove into the side of one of the corks from the bottom to about halfway up its side.

Attach the thread end to the button of your shirt, coat, vest, or sweater, and assume the position you will take behind the bottle when you perform the trick. Place the pencil, with the thread attached, into the bottle, eraser end down. Adjust the length of the thread so that it is long enough to move the pencil up and down

inside the bottle when you move your body backward or forward. Remove the threaded pencil from the bottle, and put it into your left

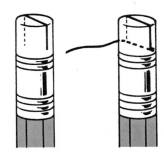

inside breast pocket. Place the two corks in your right pocket. Place the bottle and the other pencil on the table.

TO PERFORM THE TRICK:

It is important that this trick be performed in a dimly lit room or at enough distance from the audience that the thread remains invisible to them.

Bring the bottle and pencil, which are on the table to the audience for their inspection. At the same time remove the unprepared cork from your pocket for audience inspection. After the audience has checked out these items, place the cork back in your pocket. Pick up the pencil in your right hand and the bottle in your left hand, and turn to go back to the table.

As you are returning—with your back toward the audience—hold your elbows close to your sides so that no suspicious arm movement can be seen.

Slip the unprepared pencil into your left inside breast pocket, and remove the prepared one with the thread attached. Place the bottle on the table and drop the pencil, eraser end down, into the bottle.

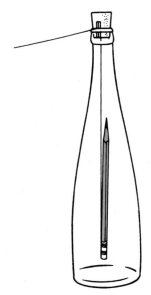

Remove the prepared cork from your right pocket, and slip it into the bottle, being careful to have the thread running freely through the groove in the cork. At the same time make sure

that the groove of the cork faces away from the audience.

Stand behind the table—with one foot slightly behind the other—and call on the genie of the bottle to appear and assist you.

As you do, slowly move your body backward by shifting your weight to your near foot. This will make the thread taut and cause the pencil in the bottle to rise. Continue shifting your weight forward, letting the pencil drop back to the bottom of the bottle.

Remove the cork with your right hand and place it back in your pocket next to the unprepared cork. Shift your weight backward so that the pencil rises three-quarters of its length out of the bottle. Pick up the pencil with one hand and the bottle with the other, and begin walking toward the audience. As you walk, remove the pencil entirely from the bottle, and disengage the thread from the eraser, letting the end of the thread drop unnoticed.

Allow the audience to examine the pencil and bottle once more to assure themselves that only a magic genie could have made such a marvel occur.

Séance Sorcery

The towering genius of **Joseph Buatier de Kolta** lay not so much in his performing ability but rather in his ability to create outstanding conjuring deceptions.

The list of de Kolta's creations seems almost endless: the Vanishing Birdcage, the Vanishing Lady, dozens of conjuring classics performed with lengths of silk, and the now-classic Black Art illusion. The list of conjurers who have built their own reputations on the performance of de Kolta's tricks and illusions is just as endless.

De Kolta's creative genius shines through this modernized version of the eerie Black Art illusion, which can be performed at home or onstage with dazzling effectiveness.

THE EFFECT:

The magician tells his audience that they are about to take part in a séance. He reveals the props to be used, all lying on a table—a candle in a candlestick, an empty candlestick, a tambourine, a horn, and a bell. The lights are turned off. Candles in two candelabras are lit. The séance begins. To the accompaniment of eerie music, magical things begin to happen. The candle floats through the air; the bell, horn, and tambourine rise into the air and seem to be played by invisible spirits. Suddenly the spirits become obstreperous. The bell drops to the floor. The candle dances across the table. The tambourine flies through the air and lands in a spectator's lap. The magician opens his eyes, and the amazing séance is ended.

YOU WILL NEED:

Enough black velvet to line a three-sided enclosure, to cover the floor within the enclosure, and to make a full-length hooded cape and mittens, which will be worn by a secret assistant; a card table; black flat paint; fluorescent paint; paint brushes; a candle; two candlesticks; a tambourine; a party horn; an old-fashioned dinner bell or school bell; two candelabra with candles or eight candles that are set in holders or attached to saucers; two small side tables; a chair; a tape or record player with a tape or record of eerie music; enough metal or wooden poles to create the frame of a three-sided screen; rope with which to lash the poles together; a hammer; and two small brads.

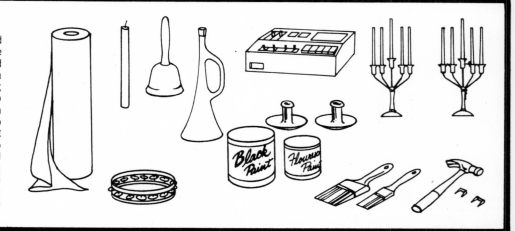

TO PREPARE THE TRICK:

Paint the "floating" props—candle, candlesticks, tambourine, horn, and bell—with fluorescent paint. Since each prop must be picked up undetected by the audience, paint a small section with the black flat paint for use as a gripping area.

With the hammer drive the two small brads into one side of the candle to be used as handgrips when the candle is made to float. (The brads are located on the side of the candle away from the audience.)

Make a simple floor-length cape, hood, and mittens from the black velvet. Cut very small slits in the hood for the eyes and mouth.

Prepare a three-sided screen as shown, by tying together the metal or wooden poles. (It must be two feet taller than your assistant.) Completely cover the frame with black velvet.

Arrange all props as shown in the floor plan. When placing the candelabra or individual candles on each of the side tables, make sure that they will throw light into the eyes of the audience, with only a small amount of light actually entering the screened area. (When the lights are properly placed, your assistant—dressed in his black velvet outfit—will be invisible against the black velvet screen.)

TO PERFORM THE TRICK:

Your assistant—in stocking feet—remains concealed in the next room until all of the lights have been extinguished. Turn on the séance music. The instant before the candles on the side tables are lit, your assistant quickly and silently enters the area inside the screen and stands in the back corner.

After lighting the candles on the two side tables, sit in your chair, and announce that the séance is about to begin. Close your eyes, and pretend to be in a trancelike state.

Your assistant then begins to move each of the props on the card table in an eerie manner, as though invisible spirits were at work. (The moves should be planned and rehearsed in advance.) Using the two brads as grips, he first makes the candle rise from the candlestick, float through the air, and settle into the second candlestick. He then makes the bell rise from the table and begin ringing in midair. Next the horn rises from the table and begins to blow in midair. The tambourine moves through the air and begins to shake. The props slowly settle back on the table.

Following this series of actions, your assistant moves the props so that they become more agitated. The candle in its candlestick slides around on the table. The bell dances around on the table and finally falls off the edge to the floor. The tambourine suddenly flies into the air in the direction of a spectator and lands in his or her lap. (Your assistant's movements with the props may be made in any order that gives the effect of a mysterious and capricious force at work.)

When all moves have been completed by your assistant, he returns to the back corner of the screen. At that moment you appear to come out of the trance, rise from your chair, and blow out all the candles on the side tables. As you do so, your assistant slips out of the room before the lights are turned on.

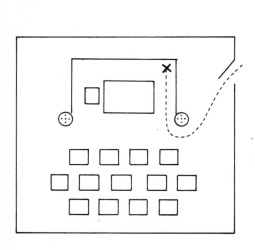

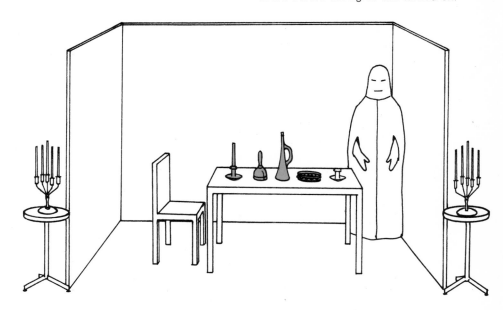

Devil's Black Mark

Of all the great masters of magic, none resembled a laughing devil quite as much as **Alexander Herrmann**. With mustache and goatee cultivated to enhance that resemblance, he played the onstage role of a friendly, laughing devil as he conjured.

Onstage or off Alex Herrmann performed his miracles at the drop of a conjurer's top hat. The trick that follows is typical of the type of impromptu magic that Alex would perform at a dinner or at any other occasion he happened to be attending.

THE EFFECT:

At the magician's request an audience volunteer tightly closes both fists. The magician places a bit of cigarette ash on a spoon, utters some mystical words, and blows the ash away. Yet, when the volunteer opens one of the fists—which he selects himself—a bit of black ash appears on the palm of the hand. It is the devil's black mark, and it has miraculously penetrated the closed fist.

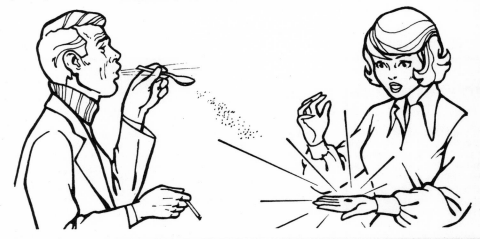

YOU WILL NEED:

A teaspoon; and an ashtray containing some cigarette ashes.

TO PREPARE THE TRICK:

In advance moisten the tip of the second finger of your right hand. Dip the moistened finger into the cigarette ashes, and then shake off any excess. Move the ashtray far enough away so that the audience assumes that you have had no access to it.

TO PERFORM THE TRICK:

Hold your right hand naturally at your side. Ask an audience volunteer—preferably a woman—to extend her palms to you. As she does, begin to tell the audience about the fine art of palmistry. At the same time stand in front of the volunteer, facing her, and pretend to read her palms—or merely discuss the lines in her palms.

Then ask her to turn over her outstretched hands so that you can examine the backs. After a few seconds bring your own hands up—palms down—and take hold of her hands separately in the following manner. Bring your right thumb to rest on the back of her left hand as your second right finger curls under her hand and lightly presses against her palm. Simultaneously your left hand follows the same procedure with her right hand. As you grasp her hands, your right finger leaves an ash mark on her left palm.

Still gripping both of her hands with yours, tell her you need her hands a little farther apart. As you speak, move her hands six inches farther apart. Release her hands, and drop your own hands to your sides.

Ask her to clench both his fists tightly. As she does, point your left index finger from one fist to the other, back and forth, asking her to say *stop* whenever she wishes. If she tells you to stop when your finger is pointing to her left fist, ask her to lower her right fist. If she tells you to stop when your finger is pointing at her right fist, ask her to lower that fist to her side. Remind her to keep her left fist tightly closed.

Ask an audience volunteer, who is smoking, to flick a small amount of ash onto your spoon.

If no one is smoking at the time, ask someone to get the ashtray and place a small pinch of ashes on your spoon. Step away from the volunteer, mutter some magic words, and blow the ashes off the spoon in the direction of your volunteer's clenched fist.

Tell her that the devil has been at work, and if she opens her left fist, she will see clear evidence of his presence. The surprised volunteer—and the audience—will see the ashes on her palm.

Classic Magic

The story of the ancient art of deception has been highlighted by the dominant personalities and dominating skills of the great masters of magic. But it has also been illuminated by certain tricks which, because of their universal appeal to audiences, have become classics of conjuring.

These marvelous deceptions have come from the creative minds of conjurers of every race; they have come from all over the world; they have appeared over the generations throughout the long history of the conjuring art.

Some of them, like the ancient cups-and-balls routine, have been handed down from one generation of performers to the next for centuries, while others, like Mini-Weighing Mystery, are comparatively new. Others, like the needle trick, come from magic's glorious golden age. Still others, like the Nest of Boxes, have their origins lost in history or, like the Vanishing Candle, are of uncertain origin.

Some of the following tricks have been based on classic deceptions; all of them have been modernized and, in some cases, adapted in order to avoid any risk to the conjurer or his audience. All of them require nothing more than ordinary household items for preparation and performance, and by following the explicit instructions, all of them can be performed simply and easily without losing one whit of the excitement and drama that made them the classics of the conjuring art.

Needle Trick

For all his international fame as an escape artist, **Harry Houdini** craved recognition as a full-fledged conjurer. He received it, finally, when he presented his own full-length magic show in 1925.

A highlight of that show was a brilliant trick in which Houdini appeared to swallow a packet of needles and a mouthful of thread and then drew them out of his mouth with the needles fully threaded.

This updated version of the classic Houdini needle trick is safer to perform—the needles never enter the magician's mouth—but its effect is just as startling as the original deception.

THE EFFECT:

The magician displays ten sewing needles and a spool of thread. He breaks off a piece of thread and then drops the needles and the thread into his cupped hand and seconds later starts to withdraw one end of the thread. As the thread emerges from the magician's fist, the needles appear one by one, each needle miraculously threaded and tied on the length of thread.

YOU WILL NEED:

Twenty sewing needles, each about one and one-half inches long; three five-ounce paper drinking cups; a spool of fine mercerized sewing thread; a saucer; a small file; scissors; clear plastic tape with a dull finish; a sheet of heavy white paper; rubber cement; and a box, approximately the size of a hat.

TO PREPARE THE TRICK:

Dull the points of all twenty needles with the file in order to prevent a mishap. Remove a length of thread from the spool. Thread ten needles on the length of thread, tying each needle in place—after it has been threaded—at a distance of about one and one-quarter inches apart from each other. Spread out the length of thread with the needles threaded and tied to it, leaving six inches of thread extending from each end.

At each end of the thread tie knot after knot until you have formed a small ball of knotted thread. Reposition the threaded needles close together so that the thread between each of them forms a downward loop.

Keeping the loops as formed, gather together the needles in one hand. With the other hand pick up one of the loose thread ends and wrap it securely around the needles near their points, and slip the very end of the thread between the needle points with the knot protruding from the side of the bundle. Wind the other thread end around the needles near the eyes, and wedge the end between the needles, allowing the knot to protrude out of the side of the bundle.

Take the first paper cup (cup A), and prepare it in the following manner. Cut off the

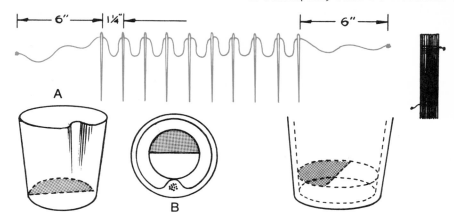

rim, and cut out half of the bottom. Make a small inward crease in the side of cup A.

Place cup A inside the second paper cup (cup B). Except at the point where cup A was creased, tape together cups A and B with clear plastic tape.

From the sheet of white paper cut out a circle large enough to fit the bottom of cup B. Cement the circle into place on the bottom to prevent the loose needles from showing through when they are in the false bottom and

the cup is tilted with the bottom facing the audience.

Drop the packet of wrapped threaded needles, eye ends first, into the gap created by the crease in cup A.

Place the ten remaining unthreaded needles into the third cup (cup C) and place that cup on a table in full view of the audience. Also place the saucer, the spool of thread, and the box on the table. Set the false-bottomed cup (cup AB) behind the box, out of sight of the audience.

TO PERFORM THE TRICK:

CUP C

Pick up cup C, and slowly pour the loose needles from the cup into the saucer. Place cup C behind the box, next to prepared cup AB. Place the spool of thread on the saucer.

Walk to the audience with the saucer in your hand so that they can view the needles and the spool of thread. Return to the table and place the saucer on it. Pick up cup AB from behind the box, holding the cup so that the creased side faces away from the audience.

Gather up the needles from the saucer, and drop them one at a time into cup AB, making sure that they all fall into the opening at the bottom of the cup. Place the cup back on the table next to the box, in full view of the audience.

Pick up the spool of thread, and break off a piece of thread approximately the same length as the one used to thread the first ten needles. Crumple the thread into a ball, and drop it into cup AB, making sure that it too falls through the opening into the false bottom.

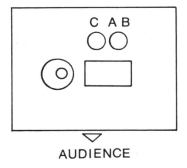

AUDIENCE

Turn to the audience, roll up your sleeves, and spread the fingers of both hands wide apart to show you have not concealed anything. Show both sides of your hands. Make a loose fist with your left hand.

With your right hand pick up cup AB, once again keeping the creased side away from the audience. Tilt the cup, and pretend to pour the loose needles and ball of thread into the opening in the top of your left fist. (The prepared bundle of prethreaded needles will slip out of the crease and into your fist while the loose needles and thread remain in the false bottom.) Return cup AB to the table *behind* the box and next to cup C.

Straighten out your left arm; and squeeze your left fist tightly several times, as if magically forcing the thread through the needle eyes.

Snap your right fingers. Bring your left fist close to the front of your body, and tilt it so that the opening at the top is inclined to your right. Reach into your fist with your right fingers, and grasp the thread knot at the eye end of the bundle of needles. Pull the thread slowly and dramatically out of your left fist, making the

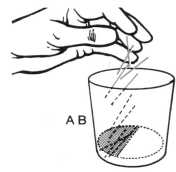

AB

needles emerge one at a time until all ten needles are displayed, fully threaded, between your two hands. Releasing the thread from your right hand, pick up cup C from the table,

and drop the threaded needles into the cup. You can, if you choose to, pass the cup to the audience and ask them to reexamine the miraculously threaded needles.

Belts of the Orient Magic Lesson

When Western magicians began performing in the Far East, they found eager audiences and a rich source of conjuring tricks in the classic Eastern repertoires.

Master magician **Harry Blackstone** took one classic trick, gave it his own special touch, and turned it into an amusing and delightful deception.

This version of the effect, with the added touch of a magic lesson, will entertain any audience.

THE EFFECT:

After inviting an audience volunteer to take a quick lesson in conjuring, the magician shows the audience two cloth belts. The volunteer selects one of the belts; the magician takes the other. The volunteer, following the magician's instructions, tries to duplicate his moves. They each tear their belts lengthwise and now have two belts each. They both say magic words and tear one of their two belts lengthwise again. The magician's belts are mysteriously linked together; the volunteer's belts are separate.

The magician suggests that the volunteer try it again with his remaining belt. He does and still ends with two separate belts. The magician offers his own belt to the volunteer and, using other magic words, tells him to tear it into one belt twice the size of the original. That, of course, is impossible—or is it? The volunteer does try, and to his own bewilderment and the delight of the audience he does the impossible and ends up with one large belt.

YOU WILL NEED:

A strip of cotton cloth eight inches wide and seventy-two inches long; scissors; and glue.

8″

72″

GLUE

TO PREPARE THE TRICK:

With the scissors make a four-inch slit at the center of one end of the strip of fabric. Make two additional four-inch slits, dividing the fabric on each side of the center slit in half, as shown in the illustration. (The four sections on this end of the fabric are numbered 1 to 4 in the illustration.)

Apply a thin line of glue to the edge of the opposite end—the unslit end 5 of the fabric. Twist section 1 two full turns, and press the twisted end onto the glued end. Twist section 2 one full turn, and press that end onto the glued end. Press sections 3 and 4 onto the glued end.

After the glue has dried and the ends are securely joined, cut small slits in the band as illustrated.

With your hands press down the twists in sections 1 and 2 as flat as possible so that they are not evident.

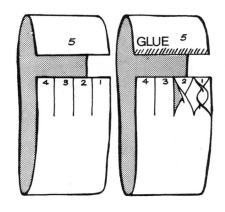

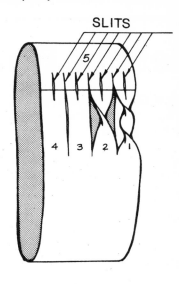

TO PERFORM THE TRICK:

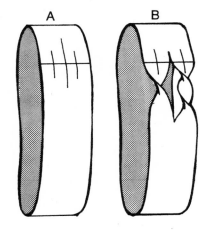

Ask for a volunteer who would like to learn something about magic. Show the audience the prepared fabric belt, keeping the twists in the belt concealed in your hand.

Tear the belt in half, and ask the volunteer to touch one of the halves. (The untwisted half is now belt A; the belt with the twisted strips is belt B.) If the volunteer moves his hand to touch belt A, simply hand it to him. If he reaches out to touch belt B, say "All right," and place it on a table, keeping the twists underneath and unseen.

Walk to him with belt A, and point out that there are small slits in the belt to aid him in tearing it in half. Ask him what will happen if he tears the belt in half. When he says that he would end up with two belts, agree with him, and then tell him to go ahead and tear his belt in half.

Pick up belt B, and tear it through the center. Place the one-twist section of belt B over your arm, and hold the two-twist section in your hands.

Instruct the volunteer to say the magic word *abracadabra*, tear one of his belts lengthwise, and turn it into two linked belts.

At the same time tear the two-twist section of your belt in half lengthwise. You will now be holding two linked belts; the volunteer will be holding two separate belts.

Suggest that perhaps the volunteer failed to say the magic word correctly, which caused his belts to become unlinked. Ask that he try again with his remaining belt, being very careful to say the magic word correctly. Once again the volunteer will be holding two separate belts.

Ask the volunteer to tell you his name. Say it, along with any magical words you wish to devise. Hand your one-twist belt to the volunteer, and tell him that with the help of your magic words he will now be able to tear the belt into one belt twice the size of the one he is holding.

He will begin to tear doubtfully but will be amazed to see that he has indeed torn the belt into another belt twice as large.

Thank him for being such a good—if bewildered—student of magic.

215

Nest of Boxes

The **Great Levante**—Australian-born Leslie George Cole—presented a number of classic feats of magic in his touring shows, including his own version of a locked trunk escape and a dramatic spirit cabinet.

One of his most beguiling presentations was still another conjuring classic—the nest of boxes, which one after another were opened to reveal a magical ring.

This is an update of the classic nest of boxes. Once prepared, it offers the audience great viewing enjoyment.

THE EFFECT:

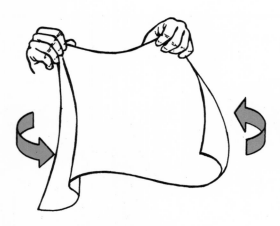

The magician borrows a ring, places it in a jeweler's box, and wraps the box in a scarf. While an audience volunteer holds the scarf, the magician points out a ribbon-tied box that has been sitting on a table in full view of the audience. When the magician retrieves the scarf from the volunteer, the jeweler's box with the ring inside has disappeared—but not for long. It is found inside a box which is inside a box which is inside the box that had been in full view of the audience throughout the trick.

YOU WILL NEED:

Two identical jeweler's ring boxes—box A and box B; two eighteen-inch square scarves made of a heavy print fabric; three white square cardboard boxes which easily nest together, with the smallest box measuring about four by four by three and one-half inches; red ribbon; a six by fifteen-inch sheet of thin white cardboard; a sheet of plain white paper; enough black velvet fabric to make a table cover; about four yards of gold trimming tape to decorate the table cover; gold fringe to trim the bottom of the table cover; a fifteen-inch-square piece of one-quarter-inch plywood; a pedestal suitable for use as a table base; a rubber band; thumb tacks; all-purpose cement; a needle; and black thread.

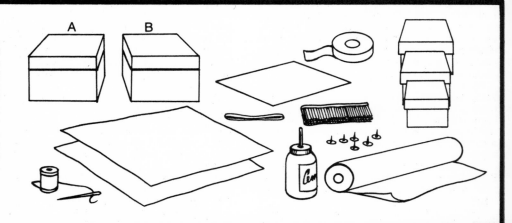

TO PREPARE THE TRICK:

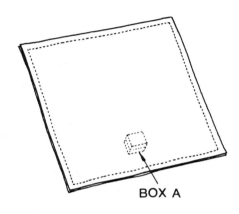

BOX A

With the needle and thread sew together the edges of the two scarves with jeweler's box A sewn between the two scarves.

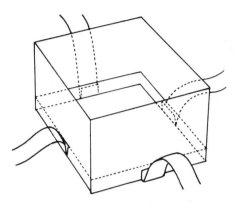

Cut out the bottom of the smallest of the three nesting cardboard boxes, and paste the ends of four pieces of the red ribbon inside the bottom of the box as illustrated. Paste a strip of white paper around the inside bottom of the box to conceal the ribbon ends.

Place the lid on the box, tie the ribbon ends into a bow on top, and place the box into the next-largest box. Place the lid on the second box, tie a ribbon around it, making a bow on top, and place that box into the largest box. Place the lid on the largest box, and tie a ribbon with bow around it, and place all three nested boxes on a side table.

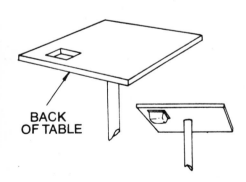

BACK OF TABLE

Prepare the special table in the following way. Cut a three-inch-square hole out of the sheet of plywood, near one corner. (See the illustration for the proper position.) Attach the sheet of plywood to the pedestal base to form a table.

Lay out the black velvet fabric on the table top, and cut two slits in the velvet directly over the hole in the plywood top.

According to the pattern and dimensions shown, cut a piece of velvet and sew it together to make a small three-by-three-inch bag.

Attach the velvet bag to the underside of the tabletop by tacking it around the hole in the plywood.

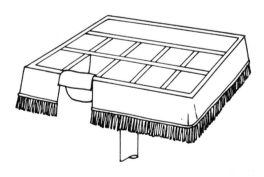

Sew the decorative gold tape to the top of the table cover and trim the lower edges with gold fringe.

Press the precut strip of the velvet table cover down through the hole in the plywood so that it forms a lining for the small velvet bag.

Cement a strip of thin white cardboard over the velvet table cover across the front of the table as shown in the illustration.

Place the rubber band on the right side of the table, and place the sewn-together scarves loosely bunched up—with jeweler's box A sewn inside—on top of the rubber band. Hold jeweler's box B in your hand.

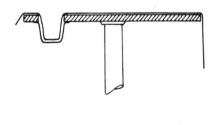

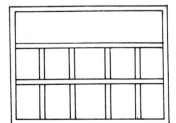

(continued)

TO PERFORM THE TRICK:

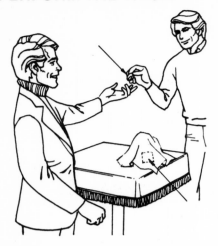

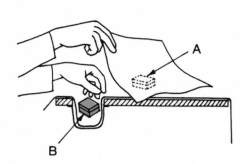

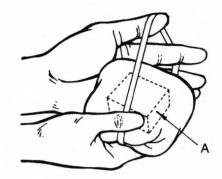

Borrow a ring from an audience member, and place it in jeweler's box B. Carry the box to the table in your left hand, and hold it three inches above the hole in the table.

With your right hand pick up the sewn-together scarves—they will appear to be a single scarf—and bring them in front of box B.
Pretend to wrap box B in the scarf. Instead, using the scarf as a shield, drop box B into the pocket in the table.

At the same instant grasp box A through the scarf, wrap the scarf around it, and secure the wrapping with the rubber band. Ask a volunteer to hold this wrapped box while you continue the trick.

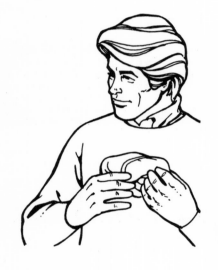

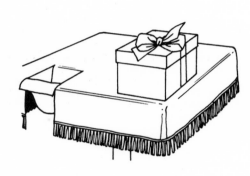

As you return to the stage, pick up the nest of boxes from the side table, and place it at the rear of the velvet-covered table away from the hole. Walk back to the volunteer holding the scarf-wrapped box, and ask him if he can feel the box inside the scarf.

When he says that he can, take the scarf from him, remove the rubber band, and shake out the scarf with a flourish. The box has vanished, and you show both sides of the scarf to the audience to prove it.

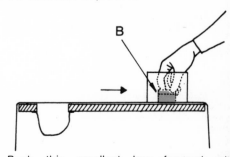

Go back to the velvet-covered table. Untie the ribbon around the largest of the nested boxes, and remove the lid. Take out the next nested box, and place it in front of the first box. Untie the ribbon of the second box, and remove the lid. Pick up the remaining box, tilting it slightly forward so that the audience cannot see its open bottom.

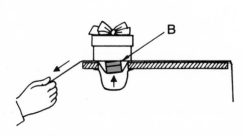

Place this smallest box directly over the hole in the table, and pull the loose strip of velvet that lines the hidden bag. As you pull, jeweler's box B—with the ring inside—will rise out of the hidden bag up to the level of the table and into the smallest of the nested boxes positioned directly over the hole.

Push this smallest box forward—with jeweler's box B inside it—until it is directly over the white cardboard strip glued to the front edge of the table. Remove the ribbon and take off the lid.
Ask the audience member who volunteered the ring to come up to the table and to reach in and remove the jeweler's box. Miraculously the borrowed ring is found inside.

Magic Paddle

Like many of the great masters of magic, **Harry Blackstone** was never far away from his props and never lacked an audience eager to see him perform one of his wonderful deceptions.

On those occasions when he was asked to perform informally, Blackstone slipped his hand into his pocket, took out the paddle he usually carried, and presented his version of the classic magic paddle trick.

This deception, in an updated version, remains a perfect trick to present in an informal setting.

THE EFFECT:

The magician shows the audience both sides of a small wooden paddle, which has four rubber bands wrapped around it. He shakes the paddle, and four pennies magically appear secured by the rubber bands. The rubber bands and the pennies are removed, and another shake of the paddle mysteriously produces the name of an audience member clearly written on the wood.

YOU WILL NEED:

A paddle made of thin wood (approximately one-sixteenth inch thick—a doctor's tongue depressor might be used); four pennies; four rubber bands; and a pen.

TO PREPARE THE TRICK:

Cut the thin piece of wood into a paddle as shown.

With the pen print the name of someone who will be in the audience—your host, perhaps—on one side of the paddle. Make sure that the printed letters will be covered by the four pennies when they are lined up side by side on that side of the paddle.

Set the four pennies in place and secure them with the four rubber bands.

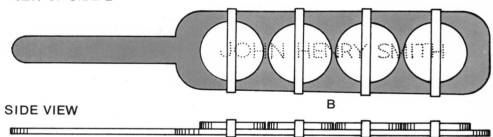

VIEW OF SIDE B

SIDE VIEW

TO PERFORM THE TRICK:

Gather your audience around you, making sure that they are looking *down* at the paddle, which you hold at waist height.

Hold the paddle in the fingers of your right hand, with the side holding the pennies—side B—facing downward. In proper position your palm is facing up, and the handle of the paddle is held with the right thumb on top and the first finger on the bottom.

You are now ready to make a special move with the paddle that will convince the audience that they are seeing side B of the paddle when they are actually being shown side A twice.

Make the paddle move in the following way. Rotate your wrist to the left so that the paddle turns over end for end, but at the same time flip the paddle over with your right thumb and first finger. (The arrows in the illustration indicate the direction the paddle is turned when the wrist is rotated.) The audience is aware, of course, of your wrist movement but unaware of your fingers flipping over the paddle.

Reverse the move by rotating your wrist to the right while flipping over the paddle again with your right thumb and first finger.

With your hand once again positioned so that the palm is facing up and the pennies are

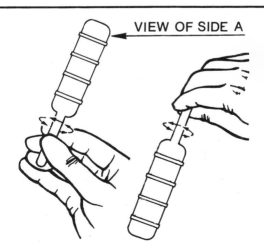

VIEW OF SIDE A

concealed underneath the paddle, produce the pennies by quickly shaking the paddle about twelve inches to the right and, as it is moving, flipping the paddle over with your fingers so that side B—the side with the pennies—is on top. It will appear to your audience that the pennies have suddenly materialized under the rubber bands.

Slowly turn the paddle over so that side A—without the pennies—is on top. Remove one

rubber band at a time, along with each penny secretly held by it to the underside of the paddle.

When all of the rubber bands and pennies are removed, execute the special paddle move to prove to the audience that the paddle is empty on both sides.

Hide the paddle for a fraction of a second by holding your left hand over it. At the same time flip it over to side B, remove your left hand from above the paddle, and the name (written in advance) has mysteriously appeared.

Mini–Weighing Mystery

The master magician has just presented another marvelous conjuring feat; his enthralled audience gasps in amazement and delight. After the performance is over, many of them will speculate on how such magic was accomplished.

More often than not, the magician is something of a scientist, and his scientific curiosity has led him to devise some of his most successful tricks.

John Nevil Maskelyne had that kind of scientific curiosity and a repertoire of tricks that sprang directly from his inquiring mind. This modern update of a simple trick is based on keen observation. It is guaranteed to leave any audience puzzled but pleased.

THE EFFECT:

The magician displays twenty-five matchbooks identical in size—the kind generally given away at cafés and restaurants. The magician instructs a volunteer to select nine of them, extract a single match from one and tuck it away in his pocket. The magician is then recalled and blindfolded. Even though he has been out of the room during the entire selection, he unerringly selects the matchbook from which the match was removed by lifting each matchbook in his hand and discovering which is lightest in weight.

YOU WILL NEED:

Twenty-five matchbooks—all the same size—from a variety of business establishments; a man's handkerchief; and a large bowl.

TO PREPARE THE TRICK:

In advance close the matchbook covers as tightly as possible by pushing them down as far as they will go into the lower flaps. Check to make sure that each cover is secure. Discard any that still appear to be loose, substituting others until you have the requisite number.

TO PERFORM THE TRICK:

Place all twenty-five matchbooks on any convenient surface. Place the large bowl nearby, and next to the bowl lay out the handkerchief folded in the form of a blindfold.

Ask for an audience volunteer, and give him the following instructions. After you leave the room, the volunteer is to select any nine matchbooks from the twenty-five, remove one match from one of the nine selected matchbooks, place the match in his pocket, and then close the matchbook and place it—along with the other eight—in the bowl. The volunteer is then to tell you to return to the room.

Once the instructions have been carried out and you are back in the room, ask the volunteer to blindfold you and lead you to the bowl.

Explain that you will weigh each of the matchbooks in your hand and select the one that weighs less than the others—the one with the missing match.

Reach into the bowl, and pick up the matchbooks one by one. As you do, try to slide the match cover slightly with your thumb as you remove the matchbook from the bowl. Do *not* try to open the cover. With your thumb simply try to feel whether the cover is loose as you lift out the matchbook in a steady movement.

As you take out each matchbook, pretend to weigh it momentarily in your hand. Then place it on the table. Continue feeling and weighing each matchbook until you discover the one with the loose cover. Place it aside from the others.

Continue until you have removed all nine matchbooks from the bowl. Then, still blindfolded, pick up the one matchbook you have placed apart from the others, and declare that you seem to detect a slight difference in weight and that therefore this must be the matchbook from which the volunteer removed the match. As you pull off your blindfold, the volunteer is asked to open the matchbook cover and verify that it is the one he chose.

Ring and String

Most of Europe's eighteenth-century conjurers were itinerant street performers, but there were a few exceptions—the more elegant stage magicians like Fawkes, Katterfelto, and Pinetti.

There was also the occasional magician who disdained street performing but was not quite famous enough to appear regularly in a theater. Such a conjurer was the German **Philip Breslaw,** who rented rooms in London for his performances.

A skilled magician, Breslaw often conjured with dice, handkerchiefs, cards, and finger rings. It has been said that one of his best tricks utilized a ring and a piece of string. The following trick, in modern dress, is a new and entertaining version of that classic deception.

THE EFFECT:

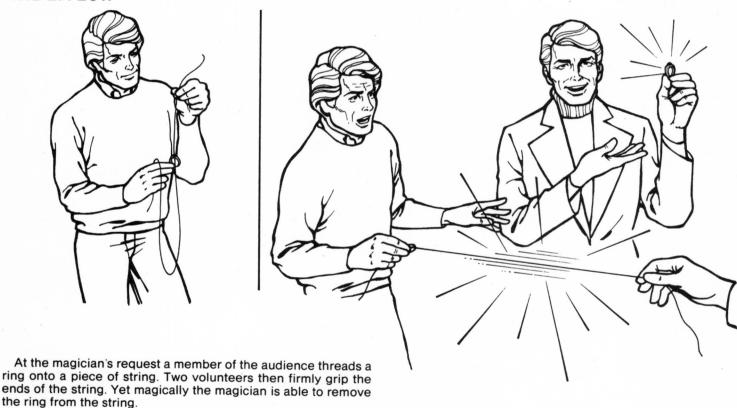

At the magician's request a member of the audience threads a ring onto a piece of string. Two volunteers then firmly grip the ends of the string. Yet magically the magician is able to remove the ring from the string.

YOU WILL NEED:

A cloth napkin, approximately sixteen inches square; two distinctive but identical finger rings; and a four-foot piece of ordinary household string.

TO PREPARE THE TRICK:

Tie a knot in each end of the piece of string. Place one of the rings (ring A) on your finger. Place the other ring (ring B) together with the napkin in the right pocket of your jacket.

TO PERFORM THE TRICK:

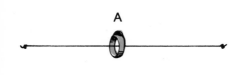

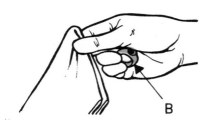

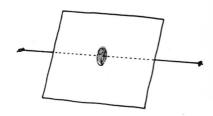

Lay the string straightened out on a convenient table. Remove ring A from your finger, and ask an audience volunteer to thread it on the string and to slide it toward the string's center.

While the volunteer is doing this, place your right hand into your pocket, and using the thumb and the first and second fingers, remove the napkin. At the same time lift out ring B, keeping it hidden behind the slightly bent third and fourth fingers of your right hand.

Unfold the napkin with both hands, shake it out with a flick of your wrists, and place it over threaded ring A on the table.

With both hands reach under the napkin, and immediately to the left of ring A draw a loop of the string through Ring B. Bring the loop up

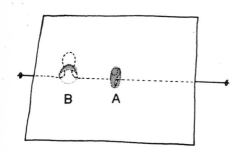

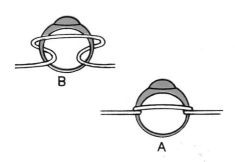

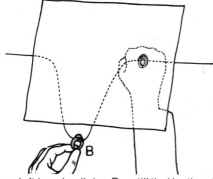

and over the edge of ring B, and holding the string against the ring to prevent it from slipping, pull on the string to tie ring B securely.

Explain to the audience that you are having some difficulty performing the trick with the

napkin covering your hand. Tell them you will have to proceed differently. Casually and unhurriedly make the following moves. Under the napkin encircle the string and ring A with your right hand, and grasp ring A by bending your third and fourth fingers around it. With

your left hand pull ring B—still tied by the string —out from under the napkin and into audience view.

At the same time ask a spectator to your left to pick up the end of the string nearest him. (Make sure that some slack is left in the string;

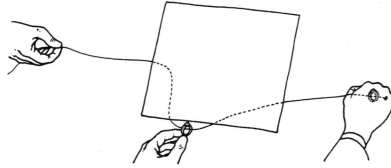

do not permit him to pull it taut.)

As the spectator grasps the string, slide your right hand—with ring A concealed in it—along the string to your right until it is out from under the napkin and reaches the knotted right end of the string. As you make this move, look at a

spectator on your right, and ask him to grasp that end of the string, making sure that he grasps it just to the left of your hand.

As soon as the spectator on your right has a firm grasp on the string, slip ring A—still hidden in your right hand—off the end of the string.

Keep your right hand moving smoothly to pick up the napkin. Slip the napkin—along with the hidden ring A—back into your right jacket pocket.

Cover ring B—still on the string—with your right hand, and under cover of both hands untie ring B by reversing the tying process you used before.

With ring B untied but still hidden in your hands, ask the two volunteers to tighten up on the string, and remove the slack. As they do, snap ring B up and away from the string with a dramatic flair. Show the ring to the audience even as the spectators are still holding the string taut.

Add to the mystery by passing the ring and the string to the audience for their inspection.

Cups and Balls

Throughout history probably no conjuring trick has been performed more often by more conjurers in more variations than the ancient deception of the cups and balls.

This classic of the conjurer's art dazzled the ancient Greeks and Romans; it helped to trigger the conjuring career of the great French master, Robert-Houdin; even in the modern technological age it still delights audiences of all ages.

Of all those who have conjured with the cups and balls, one of the most adroit was the dramatic eighteenth-century Italian magic master **Giovanni Bartolomeo Bosco.**

This modern version of the ancient conjuring classic manages to capture much of the impact of a Bosco presentation and proves again why the cups-and-balls routine has maintained its age-old popularity.

THE EFFECT:

The audience examines three standard paper cups and three small balls made out of tissue paper and finds them to be ordinary in every respect. Yet the magician manages to make the paper balls hop miraculously around and through the cups, then multiply into ten balls, and finally completely disappear when a lemon materializes to take their place.

YOU WILL NEED:

Three five-ounce paper cups with recessed bottoms; two sheets of tissue paper, each approximately ten inches square; a man's handkerchief; scissors; a pencil; a lemon small enough to fit easily into a five-ounce paper cup —or if you prefer, an equally small lime, potato, onion, or rubber ball; chairs; a table; and tablecloth.

TO PREPARE THE TRICK:

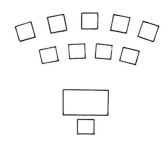

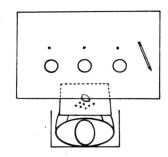

Set up viewers' chairs in a semicircle around a tablecloth-covered table, and place your chair behind the table. The viewers' chairs should be far enough away from the table so that when the paper cups are placed on the table right side up, the inside bottoms of the paper cups cannot be seen by the audience.

From one sheet of the tissue paper cut out seven squares, each two and one-half by two and one-half inches. Crush and roll each square in your fingers until if forms a small compact ball.

Place the second sheet of tissue paper, uncut, on the table along with the scissors, the pencil, and the three paper cups, designated cup X, cup Y, and cup Z.

Sit at the table, and spread the handkerchief across your lap. Place the lemon and the seven paper balls on the handkerchief in your lap. (The tablecloth will shield the contents of your lap from the audience.)

An Important Note. A turnover move is used to turn a cup upside down on the table and at the same time keep a ball that is secretly inside the cup from falling out. In the process you give the audience the impression that the cup is empty. Before attempting to perform the trick, you must be able to execute the turnover move smoothly and skillfully so that the proper amount of centrifugal force keeps the ball securely in the cup until the rim of the cup touches the table. The best way to learn this

move is to mark three practice cups with the letters X, Y, and Z and to follow the instructions and illustrations closely until you have mastered the move and the whole routine. Whenever you turn a cup upside down during this trick, even though it may be empty, you should do the same turnover move so that the viewers will not become suspicious about the move with a cup in which a ball is secretly hidden.

As you follow the instructions, swing the cup smoothly from the right-side-up position (RSU) to the upside-down positon (USD) and bring it down quickly directly to the surface of the table.

TO PERFORM THE TRICK:

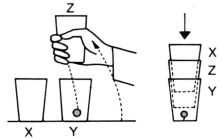

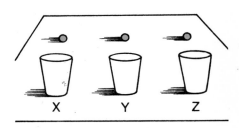

Hand out the three paper cups for audience examination. While they are being examined, cut out three squares—two and one-half by two and one-half inches—from the tissue paper of the table, and shape them into three paper balls. While the audience is examining the three paper balls, drop your hands into your lap, and secure one of the seven concealed

balls in your right hand between your third and fourth fingers. Bring your hands back to the table, holding your right fingers horizontally with the backs of your fingers on the table surface. This prevents the audience from seeing the ball concealed between your fingers. As you can see in the illustration, the ball

is clipped *behind* the fingers.

When the cups are returned, with your left hand line the three paper cups across the table, and ask a spectator to line up the three paper balls parallel to, and about four inches in front of, the three cups. Rest your left hand on the table behind cup Y and your right hand on the table behind cup Z.

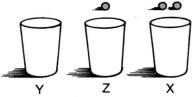

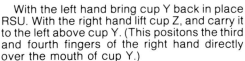

Grasp cup Y with the thumb and the first and second fingers of the left hand—keeping the third and fourth fingers resting on the table—and tilt the cup slightly toward the audience so that they can see inside the cup. Pick up cup Z in the identical manner with the right hand and tilt it toward the audience.

With the left hand bring cup Y back in place RSU. With the right hand lift cup Z, and carry it to the left above cup Y. (This positons the third and fourth fingers of the right hand directly over the mouth of cup Y.)

With the left hand pick up cup X, and tilt it toward the audience. Explain that you are using paper cups for this trick because they nest together easily. As you speak, push cup X into cup Z, and at the same instant separate your right third and fourth fingers just enough to drop the hidden ball into cup Y. Push the nested X and Z cups into cup Y, and slide the nested cups to the left of the table.

With the right hand pick up the pencil, and ask a spectator to select one of the three visible paper balls. The ball chosen by the spectator is kept in the center of the table as you push the other two balls to the right with the pencil.

Pull cup X out of the nest, and place it RSU to the right side. Pull out cup Z, and place it RSU in the center. Place the remaining cup—cup Y with the ball inside it—RSU on the left.

(continued)

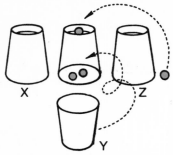

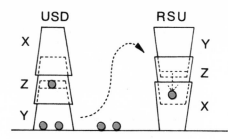

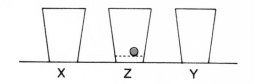

With the right hand pick up cup X, and turn it USD to the left of the paper ball at the center of the table. Using the turnover move, with the left hand put cup Y USD on top of the paper ball. (Cup Y now has two balls under it.) With the right hand turn cup Z USD to the right of cup Y.

Ask another audience volunteer to select one of the remaining two balls visible on the table. Place the ball chosen by the volunteer in the recessed bottom of cup Y. Then slide cup

Z, still USD, on top of cup Y, and slide cup X, also USD, on top of cup Z.

With the left hand slowly pick up the pencil, and tap the nested cups with it. At the same time let your right hand rest in your lap—to accustom the audience to seeing your hand in your lap. With your right hand lift up all three nested cups, revealing two balls, one of which apparently penetrated the cup to join the ball on the table. As you lift the nested cups, turn

them so that the mouth of cup Y—the bottom cup—faces the audience.

Transfer the nested cups to your left hand, turning them RSU as you make the transfer. Pull cup Y—now the top cup—out of the other cups with your right hand, and place it RSU to the right on the table. Remove cup Z—with the hidden ball—from cup X with your right hand, and place it in the center of the table RSU. Place cup X RSU to the left of the table.

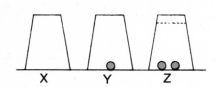

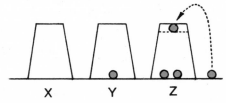

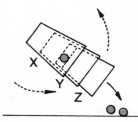

Using the pencil, separate the two balls just uncovered, and with the right hand pick up cup Y, and turn it USD covering the left-hand ball. With the left hand pick up cup Z—with the hidden ball—and, using the turnover move, place it USD over the ball on the table. With the right hand pick up cup X, and place it USD to the left of the other two cups.

Ask an audience volunteer to call out either number 1 or number 2. If number 1 is called

out, pick up the remaining ball on the right of the table, and place it in the recessed bottom of cup Z, which is USD and the first cup on the audience's left. If the volunteer has called out number 2, pick up cup Y, which is the second cup to the audience, and remove the ball from under it, and place it in the recessed bottom of cup Z. (In other words, no matter which number is chosen, you arrange to put a ball in the recessed area of cup Z. The audience gets the false impression that it has some choice in the conduct of the trick.)

Place cup Y on top of cup Z and cup X on top of cup Y, nesting them all USD. Once again pick up the pencil with your left hand, and tap the nested cups.

At the same time, rest your right hand in your lap, and secure one of the hidden balls between your first and second fingers.

With your left hand place the pencil back on the table, and, using the same hand, lift all three nested cups off the two balls on the table. As you do, casually show the inside of cup Z by tilting the nest of cups away from the audience.

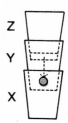

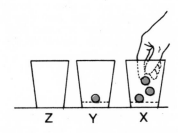

Turn the nested cups in your left hand RSU, but do not set them down on the table. Meanwhile move your right hand—with the ball concealed between your fingers—toward the nest of cups, and remove cup X from the bottom of the nest. Place cup X in the center of the table RSU.

With the right hand pull cup Y—with the ball hidden inside it—out of cup Z, and place both cups RSU on the left side of the table.

With the thumb and first finger of your right hand pick up one of the balls just uncovered, and drop the ball in cup X. As you do, move your hand down so that your fingers are just inside the rim of the cup, and also let the hidden ball slip into cup X. Then with the right hand pick up the second ball on the table and drop it into cup X.

With the left hand execute the turnover move with cup X, and with the right hand pick up the last ball on the table. Bring your right

hand—with the ball in it—down under the table, explaining to the audience that you intend to make the ball in your right hand penetrate up through the table and miraculously join the other two balls under cup X.

As you lean down with your arm under the table, push your elbow under the table edge, and bend in your arm toward your body so that your hand can rest in your lap.

(continued)

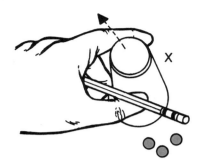

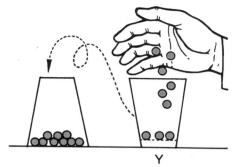

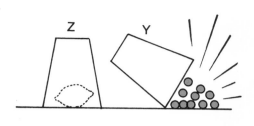

With your right hand pick up the five hidden balls remaining on your lap, and grasp them—along with the one already in your hand—with your second and third fingers.

While you are picking up the hidden balls with your right hand, pick up the pencil with your left hand, and tap on cup X—which is now USD—and, still holding the pencil sit up straight, pick up cup X, and show three balls under it. Immediately bring up your right hand, and grasp the pencil. (For the sake of the audience, this provides a good reason for your right hand to be partially closed, since they must not be aware that you are also holding the six hidden balls.)

Still holding cup X with your left hand, turn it RSU, and place it to the left on the table. With your left hand pick up cup Y—which has a ball in it—and place it in the middle of the table.

Let the pencil slip out of your right hand, and, with the same hand pick up one of the balls from the table, and drop it into cup Y. With the same hand pick up another ball from the table, and drop it into cup Y, and as you do, also let the six hidden balls fall into the cup. Using the right hand again, pick up the last of the balls on the table, and drop it into cup Y.

Inform your audience that this time you intend to make the three balls in cup Y pass down through the table instead of the other way around as before. As you speak, execute the turnover move with your left hand with cup Y, and then pick up cup Z with your right hand, and bring it under the table.

Move your left hand under the table, supposedly to aid in the catching of the balls that will penetrate the table. While you are leaning over, pick up the lemon in your left hand. With your right hand hit cup Z against the

bottom of the table, claiming difficulty in making the balls pass through the table.

Bring your right hand—holding cup Z—back on top of the table, positioning cup Z at the table edge in front of you. Tilt cup Z toward the audience to show them that it is empty. Then ask a spectator to lift cup Y and see what happened to the balls.

As the spectator lifts cup Y, turn the mouth of cup Z toward you, and slant it down over the edge of the table. At the same instant, the left hand lifts the lemon to the table edge and pushes it up into USD cup Z, and the right hand squeezes the sides of the cup slightly in to keep the lemon inside. The left hand takes the cup from the right hand and places it USD on the table to the left. While you are doing this with your left hand, the audience will be surprised at the spectator's discovery of ten—rather than three balls under cup Y, and they

will not notice you loading the lemon into cup Z.

Take cup Y from the spectator, and turn it RSU next to cup X on the left side of the table. Close your right hand into a loose fist near the edge of the table, and with your left hand pick up the paper balls, one or two at a time, and drop them into the top of your right fist.

With your left hand move cups X and Y to the center of the table, and place them on their sides with their mouths facing the audience. Ask a member of the audience to point to one of the cups. While you are asking the spectator to do this, slowly mover your right fist back to the edge of the table, and let all the balls drop into your lap by loosening your third and fourth fingers slightly. The instant the balls have dropped, slide your right fist slowly forward a little away from the edge of the table. (As you

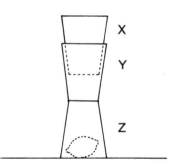

are doing this, keep your attention on the two cups that the spectator is deciding upon.) After the spectator has made his choice, pick up that cup in your left hand, slide it into the other cup, and tilt the two cups RSU. With the left

hand place the nested cups X and Y, which are RSU, on top of cup Z, which is USD.

Still holding the nested cups with your left hand, bring your right fist over them, and pretend to drop the ten balls into the top cup. As you do this, position your right fist so that it rests on the rim of the top cup, and slowly open the palm toward your body. Immediately turn your right hand palm down over the mouth of the top cup, and tap the side of the cup with your left fingers. Then pick up both cups X and Y, and pull them apart, showing the audience that they are empty.

Put the empty cups back on the table, and with a dramatic gesture pick up cup Z, revealing the lemon, which has magically appeared.

Disappearing Candle

Dash, surprise, excitement, and a touch of humor. So the critics described any performance by Danish-born Harry Jansen, the world-famous **Dante.**

As Dante, he presented a splendidly paced full-length show of magic, which combined dazzling large illusions with amusing smaller tricks. One of his most delightful tricks, a vanishing-candle routine, had been a conjuring standard for years. In his skilled hands it became a surefire audience pleaser.

This adaptation of the delightful vanishing-candle deception retains some of the elements that made Dante's show a masterful magic experience.

THE EFFECT:

The magician displays an ordinary white candle, wraps a sheet of newspaper around it, and asks an audience volunteer to hold it. Then the magician miraculously vanishes a red silk handkerchief. The vanished handkerchief is discovered inside the newspaper in the volunteer's hand, but now the candle has vanished—until the unsuspecting volunteer turns around and the audience sees the vanished candle hanging from the back of his jacket.

YOU WILL NEED:

Two identical twelve-inch-square red silk handkerchiefs; a tall, straight-sided white candle one inch thick; a candlestick; several large sheets of strong white paper with a glossy finish which resembles the wax candle; two sheets of newspaper; a small wire carpentry staple; rubber cement; and a man's hat.

TO PREPARE THE TRICK:

Cut three three-quarter-inch sections from the candle.

Trim off one-quarter inch of wax from two of the three candle sections, freeing the wick.

From one sheet of white paper prepare a tube, one inch by ten inches, which duplicates the shape of the candle. Insert one of the trimmed candle sections into one end of the rolled paper tube. (Make sure that the fit is secure and the wick protrudes from the end.)

From another sheet of paper prepare a second ten-inch tube narrow enough to nest easily inside the first one. Slightly shave the edges of the second half-inch candle section

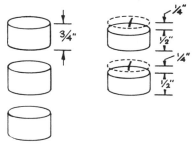

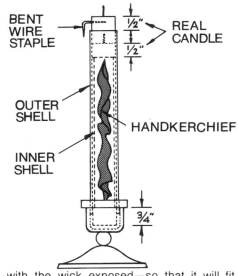

—with the wick exposed—so that it will fit securely into one end of the narrower tube. Again make sure that the wick protrudes.

Push one of the red handkerchiefs up into the narrower tube, and insert the remaining section of candle—the three-quarter-inch

piece—into the open end after trimming it to fit tightly.

Straighten one leg of the wire staple, and push it straight into the side of the outer tube, making certain that it is securely held in the wax candle section.

Slide the narrow candle tube into the larger tube, wick end first. Then place the nested candle tubes into the candlestick, with the wire staple facing away from the audience.

Prepare the newspaper envelope in the following manner. Cut two twelve-inch squares out of the sheets of newspaper, and cement them together on three sides. The fourth side becomes the envelope opening. The envelope should look like a single sheet of newspaper.

Place the newspaper envelope, a single sheet of newspaper, the man's hat—crown down—the remaining red handkerchief, and the prepared candle tubes in their holder on the table.

TO PERFORM THE TRICK:

Ask for an audience volunteer, and select one who is wearing a jacket. As he walks toward you, remove the nested candle tubes as one from the candlestick with your right hand, grasping them at the bottom in order to conceal the protruding inner tube. (Be sure to hold the side with the staple hook away from the audience.) Pick up the handkerchief with your left hand, and put it in your right hand along with the candle.

With your left hand pick up both the newspaper envelope and the sheet of newspaper, and as the volunteer faces the audience, approach him on his left side. Extend your left hand in front of him, and ask him to hold the two sheets of newspaper—one is actually the prepared envelope.

At the same instant bring your right hand inconspicuously behind the volunteer's back,

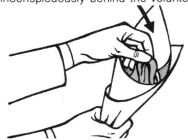

of newspaper, twist the ends, and ask the volunteer to hold it. At the same time take the prepared newspaper from him and roll it into a cone, making sure that the envelope opening is on top.

After showing the audience the handkerchief, pretend to push it into the newspaper cone, but instead stuff it into the hidden envelope.

Say some magic words, unroll the newspaper cone, holding the envelope opening

twisting the candle tube around so that the hook now faces his back. Holding the candle tube straight up, make a downward movement at the center of his upper back, and hook the tube onto his jacket. Continue moving your right hand straight down until the inner candle tube is free of the tube hooked on the jacket.

closed with your hand, and show it to the audience on both sides so that they can see the handkerchief has vanished. Casually crumple up the prepared newspaper, and drop it on the table.

Take the candle tube wrapped in newspaper from the volunteer, and tear it open at the center. Take both torn halves in your left hand, and with your right hand pull out the concealed handkerchief. (Hold the halves of the candle tube, which are wrapped in the newspaper, at

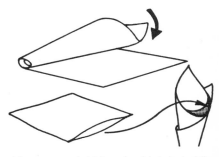

Move your right hand, which is holding the inner candle and the handkerchief around to the front, and take the red handkerchief from your right hand with your left hand.

Ask the volunteer to hold the handkerchief, and take back from him the unprepared sheet of newspaper. Roll the candle tube in the sheet

such an angle that the audience cannot see inside the halves of the tube.) After showing the handkerchief to the audience, drop it on the table, and with both hands tear halves of the candle tube through their centers, further proving to the audience that the candle has disappeared from the newspaper. Drop the torn newspaper pieces—with pieces of the candle inside—into the hat.

Suggest to the volunteer that the candle has somehow traveled to the back of the stage, and ask if he can see it. As he turns around, the audience will see the candle tube attached to his jacket.

When he turns back to you, explain that the candle only traveled as far as his back; remove the candle tube from his jacket, keeping your hand over the hollow end and turning the hook away from the audience, and thank him for his help in the mystery of the vanishing candle.

Knife through Handkerchief

The elegance and high drama that **Giovanni Giuseppe Pinetti** brought to the ancient art of conjuring are well represented by this classic of penetration wizardry.

Pinetti, of course, conjured with the finest of linen and the most elaborate silver cutlery, but many of his tricks were borrowed from the less elegant wandering conjurers who were his contemporaries.

A modern adaptation of this classic penetration trick can be performed with an ordinary handkerchief and a simple penknife, without losing its strong audience impact.

THE EFFECT:

Two audience volunteers hold the four corners of a borrowed handkerchief, stretching it out horizontally. An open penknife is placed under the handkerchief, and a small piece of paper is placed on top of it. The magician causes the penknife to penetrate the handkerchief and cut through the piece of paper. Miraculously the handkerchief itself is completely unharmed.

> ### YOU WILL NEED:
> A small penknife with its point and blade dulled for safety; and a piece of paper, about eight inches square.

TO PERFORM THE TRICK:

Borrow a standard-size man's handkerchief—about sixteen inches square—from a member of the audience.

Ask two volunteers to assist you. Have one volunteer stand to your left and the other to your right. Ask them to grasp the four corners of the handkerchief and stretch it out horizontally between them, tilting the front edge downward slightly. (This prevents the audience from seeing the underside of the handkerchief.)

Place the piece of paper on top of the handkerchief at its center.

Pick up the penknife and hold the knife in your right hand with the handle pointing up. Bring the knife under the handkerchief, and as soon as it is out of sight of the audience, flip the knife over, positioning it in your right hand as illustrated. Simultaneously press up on the underside of the handkerchief with your right thumb. This will create a bulge in the handkerchief, which the audience will assume is being made by the knife handle. At the same time it will lift the paper upward.

On the pretext of taking a closer look at the bulge in the handkerchief, grasp the paper at the edge nearest you with your left hand—thumb on top and fingers below—and slide the paper toward you. As your left hand passes over the edge of the handkerchief, stretch back your right-hand fingers—with the knife gripped between them—to meet your left-hand fingers.

Under cover of the handkerchief—with your right thumb still maintaining pressure on the underside of the handkerchief—reach out

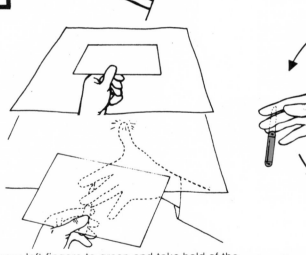

your left fingers to grasp and take hold of the knife by its handle.

Once the knife has changed hands, continue to move your left hand toward your body until the knife—concealed by the paper—clears the edge of the handkerchief. The knife is now on top of the handkerchief but unseen by the audience because it is concealed by the paper. Move the left hand back to its original position over the center of the handkerchief.

With the fingers of the right hand—still under the handkerchief—grasp the knife handle through the fabric, and tilt the point of the knife upward. With additional pressure from your left hand—on top of the newspaper—press the knife into the paper and pull it through. The paper is penetrated by the knife, and the

handkerchief is completely unharmed. The knife, paper, and handkerchief are passed to the spectators for their inspection.

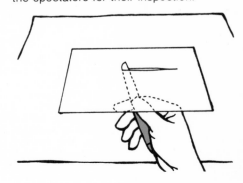

Another 100 Mystifying Tricks
You Can Perform

STRING THE BRACELET

Take out a bracelet and ask the audience to look it over very carefully. Tell them to examine it for any possible break or opening. They will find that the bracelet is completely solid.

Take out a piece of string about thirty inches long and ask someone to tie a circle around both your wrists, using the two ends of the string. This will leave a length of string about fifteen inches long between your tied hands (see diagram). As the person is tying the string around each of your wrists, tell your audience that you will have the bracelet dangling on the string between your hands right after your hands are tied.

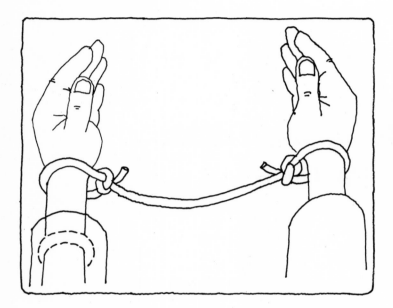

When both your wrists have been tied, ask someone to place the bracelet in your right hand. Holding the bracelet, turn your back to the audience for just a minute. When you turn around again, the bracelet will be threaded on the string between your hands, which are still tied exactly as they were before you turned around.

The trick calls for some simple preparation. Before putting on your jacket, push an exact twin of the bracelet high up on your left arm, high enough for it to be caught and held in place by your flesh. As soon as you turn your back, keep your elbows close to your sides so that the audience will not see excessive arm movement, and hide the first bracelet in your nearest pocket. Using the slack of the string, move your right hand up and quickly release the twin bracelet from your left arm. Guide it down your arm, over your left hand, and onto the string which still imprisons your locked hands. Turn back to the audience and watch their reaction as they see the bracelet dancing on the undisturbed string, just as you promised.

THE GRAB BAG

Bring out a large paper bag. Ask a volunteer to shuffle a deck of cards and divide the deck into two approximately equal parts, one that he keeps and the other that he gives to you. As you put your half of the deck into the bag, unseen by the audience, bend your

cards forcefully. If the trick is to succeed, the cards must remain curved until you are finished. Then pick up the bag, closing its top in your hand, and shake it vigorously. Hold the bag over your head, shake it several times again, establishing that the cards have been completely scrambled.

Ask the volunteer to drop several of his cards, which he has made a note of, in the bag, letting them fall one at a time and with their faces down. Once more shake the bag thoroughly, and then announce that your fingers are going to lead you to the volunteer's cards. Reaching in, you immediately single out the volunteer's unbent cards from among the rest. After you have shown them around, collect the cards remaining in the bag into a deck and quickly straighten them before you bring them into view, leaving no clues to their crooked career.

THE BOTTOMLESS CHANGE PURSE

Holding a small change purse with your right hand, place its left side into the palm of your left hand. Open the top of the change purse with your right hand, put your right thumb and index finger into the opening, and slowly bring out the end of a pencil. Continue to draw out a full-length brand new pencil from inside of this small purse.

There are several things you need to have done in preparation for this trick. One is to cut a small slit in one end of the change purse; you always keep this end covered so that the slit is never seen by the audience. You must also attach the pencil to the lower part of your inside left forearm with a rubber band. Position the lower part of the pencil slightly above your left sleeve edge, out of sight of the audience until you are ready to perform the trick. Then before you are about to do the effect, pull the pencil part way out of your left sleeve into your left palm.

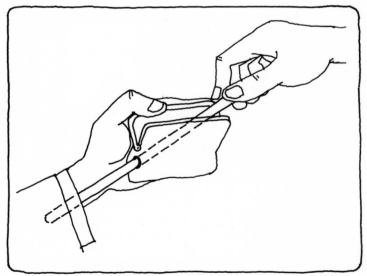

When you put the purse into the palm of your left hand, place the slit so that it faces the end of the pencil. When you put your right index finger and thumb into the opening of the change purse, reach through the slit at the end of the purse and take hold of the end of the pencil—and slowly withdraw it through the purse's open top.

THE BEWITCHED BOTTLE

How would you like to be able to put one end of a rope into the mouth of a bottle and have the bottle just dangle in midair as you hold up the other end of the rope? That's only for openers; you'll also be able to swing the bottle to and fro and in a circular motion as you continue to hold just the outside end of the rope in your hand.

After swinging the bottle around to the amazement of everyone watching, you can remove the rope from the bottle and offer to pass both rope and bottle around for inspection. Rest assured the audience will find no evidence of trickery.

A mystery? It will seem so to those watching. But you, having prepared for the trick beforehand, are aware of the very simple device that makes it all possible —a small rubber ball.

Yes, the rubber ball, which you have hidden inside the bottle before starting, does the trick. The bottle must be very opaque, black if possible. The thickness of the rope plus the width of the rubber ball should equal the approximate diameter of the bottle opening. When you first lower the rope into the bottle, you slowly turn the bottle over. This allows the ball to fall into the mouth of the bottle and rest against the rope. Then you pull the rope out toward you slightly; this action wedges the rope tightly against the ball. Now, with the rope and ball wedged tightly in the bottle's mouth, you can move the bottle to and fro.

Before relinquishing the bottle and the rope for inspection, simply pull the rope out gently, forcing the ball out along with the rope. Carefully palm the ball as it emerges and subtly pocket it as you offer the rope and bottle to the audience for their scrutiny.

X-RAY VISION

For this trick you need a partner who secretly cooperates with you while giving the impression that he has simply volunteered as a skeptical witness.

Ask your partner to collect from the audience four coins of different denominations: a penny, a nickel, a dime, and a quarter. Have him place a coffee cup upside down on the table, and then instruct him to place one of the coins under the cup while your back is turned. Claim that your X-ray vision will permit you to identify the concealed coin correctly.

Actually, you and your partner have agreed upon a system of signals that depends on the position of the cup's handle. If your partner positions the cup so that its handle points to nine o'clock on an imaginary clock face, the cup conceals the penny; if the handle points to twelve o'clock, the hidden coin is the nickel; three o'clock stands for the dime, and six o'clock for the quarter. Your partner's placement of the cup handle will go completely undetected, since he makes this maneuver in the act of covering the coin.

TRICKY DISKS

Take two identical, large, square scarves. From the four corners of one, cut away triangles of material whose sides measure about three inches in length, and sew these pieces over the corners of the other scarf to form pockets. Hidden from the eyes of your audience, these four pockets will help you to achieve a bewildering effect.

From three sheets of colored paper, each one a different color, cut out disks that are approximately an inch and a half in diameter. Make two disks in each color. In the center of each disk punch out a small hole through which a string may easily be passed. Take one set of colored disks and place one disk in each of three of the scarf pockets, leaving one of the scarf pockets vacant. Note the location of each color.

Now you are ready to perform. Show your audience the other set of disks, and run a three-feet-long piece of string through the three center holes. Have two volunteers take opposite ends of the string. Place the scarf over the string, covering the three disks. Ask a spectator to name one of the three colors.

Reach under the scarf, and, with your hands out of sight, quickly and unobtrusively tear the disk whose color was named away from the string, placing it in the scarf's vacant pocket. Bring the matching disk from the other set out of its secret pocket and display it before the audience—off the string but still intact.

PING-PONG ON A TIGHTROPE

A truly dazzling display of prestidigitation—and yet this trick can be mastered with a minimum of practice. What your audience observes—a Ping-Pong ball rolling along on top of a rope—will seem to them nothing short of miraculous, but your method of producing this effect is very simple indeed. The secret lies in an invisible length of thread equal to that of the rope and of the same color.

Before bringing out the rope, tie each end of the thread to each end of the rope. Both should be approximately two feet long, but there should be enough slack in the thread so that it can be moved slightly away from the rope along its entire length, forming a track to support the Ping-Pong ball.

Stand back a distance from your audience and hold the rope so that the thread faces you. The rope should be stretched out between your hands, and the ball held in your right hand. Turn both hands palms up, and insert your thumbs between the rope and the thread at both ends, creating a parallel track less than one-half-inch wide. Lower the rope in your left hand and release the ball from your right hand onto the track you have created.

Make the ball roll back and forth, alternately raising and then lowering each end of the rope to change the ball's direction. The audience will be astonished by your incredible tightrope act.

HIGH ROLLER

Announce to your audience that you can predict the outcome of a roll of the dice. Produce a pair of small dice and an empty container of the kind that holds wooden matches. Give the dice to a volunteer and pull out the drawer of the match box a short way; ask him to drop the dice into the drawer and then close it. Have him shake the match box vigorously.

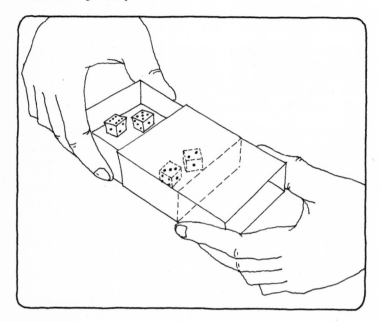

Take a piece of paper and write your prediction on it; fold the paper and give it to your volunteer, asking him to keep it in his pocket. Then pull the drawer about one-third of the way out of the box and show the dice to the audience. When the volunteer reads the written prediction, the audience sees that your prophecy was accurate.

The trick works because beforehand you glued an identical pair of dice to the inside bottom of the match box drawer, and this pair shows the number of spots you have named in your prediction. Glue the dice at one end of the drawer. Pull out the opposite end of the drawer when you ask your volunteer to insert his dice; this way the glued dice will be invisible to the audience.

After the box has been shaken by your volunteer, tip it so that the loose dice come to rest at the end of the drawer opposite the glued dice. Then pull out the drawer by the end where the glued dice rest and show this set to the audience.

CUT TO THE QUICK

Use an ordinary sheet of paper (a business letterhead, about 8½-by-11 inches, will do nicely) and a piece of thick string about 18 inches long. Offer both of them to your audience for inspection. Ask them to verify that there is nothing unusual or tricky about either the paper or the string.

Insist that they scrutinize both items very, very carefully. It is important that they all be completely satisfied. When the paper and string are given back to you with their vote of approval, inform

them that they are wrong. This string, you say, holding it up in the air dramatically, has a unique, mysterious quality—it can restore itself!

Take the sheet of paper and fold it lengthwise. Make the first fold a wide one, leaving a balance of only an inch of paper. Then fold that inch on top of the first fold. Now open the two folds and place the string in the center panel (see figure 1). Allow the ends of the string to hang down from both ends of the sheet of paper.

Then, holding the folds towards you, with the short fold at the bottom, fold down the wide section, letting the string fall into the

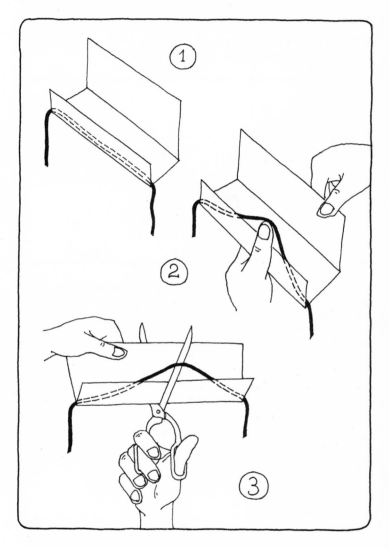

valley of the short fold. As you do this, use your thumb to inconspicuously lift the string by pushing it up and slightly above the top edge of the short fold (see figure 2).

Take out a pair of shears and cut the sheet in half, skillfully maneuvering the blade under the string (see figure 3) as you cut. Hold the cut paper and string together for a moment and after saying the magic words, "Restore the cut string to one piece," slide the cut paper off the string, and pass everything out to the audience for examination.

TO BE OR KNOT TO BE

Tie a knot in one corner of a handkerchief before you try this trick. That is the trick, in fact.

Tell the audience you are able to tie a knot in a corner of a handkerchief while it is in midair. Then produce the prepared handkerchief, carefully holding the corner with the knot in the palm of your right hand so it cannot be seen by the audience.

With your left hand, pick up the opposite corner of the handkerchief (the one now dangling toward the floor) and place it between the fingertips of your right thumb and right index finger. Lifting your right hand halfway up, bring it down fast and hard as if you were trying to snap a knot into the handkerchief as it moves through the air.

Look surprised when the knot hasn't appeared as promised. Try it again, placing the unknotted corner between the thumb and index finger of your right hand. This time bring your hand up even higher than before and come down faster.

Stare at the handkerchief with disbelief—once again the knot has not appeared! Try again, but this time as you bring up the bottom unknotted corner, place it in the palm of your right hand and hold on to it. As you bring your right hand down very quickly, release the knotted end you've been holding in your palm from the start.

Practice the switch several times before performing before an audience—it's well worth the effort.

A SURE SINKER

After a meal you can puzzle your companions with this clever disappearing act. When the coffee in your cup has cooled slightly, surreptitiously place a rectangular sugar lump on the bottom of the cup so that the lump stands on one end. Then take another cube and balance it horizontally on top of the one that is submerged under the coffee. At this point, show the group that a lump of sugar is mysteriously floating on the surface of your coffee, and then order the floating cube to submerge.

To everyone's surprise the cube slowly sinks out of sight in response to your instructions—and to the laws of gravity. As the cube on the bottom dissolves in the warm—not hot— coffee, the cube on top is bound to sink. Remember, if hot coffee is used the lower supporting cube dissolves too quickly. After practicing a few times you will get to know the approximate time it takes for the lower cube to dissolve. You can order the visible cube to submerge at the time you know from experience that the one underneath is dissolving.

COLOR VIBRATION

Tell the audience that you believe each and every color has its own specific vibration. Say that you've been studying this phenomenon and are already able to recognize the feel of several colors. You have learned the aura of three colors so far and are working on others.

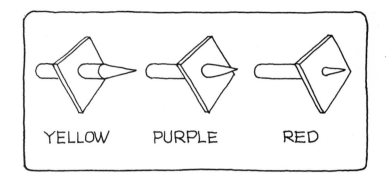

YELLOW   PURPLE   RED

At this point take out and pass around three pieces of cardboard: one red, another purple, and the third, yellow. Each piece is 1½ inches square and each has a hole in its center. Offer to prove your theory. Hand the squares to someone nearby and suggest they blindfold you. That done, ask them to hand you any square they wish. You will report its color strictly by its vibration.

Face the group. Take the first square handed to you and put it behind your back. Concentrate for a short while and call out its color, loud and strong. Give that one back and continue guessing the colors of the three squares.

The device that makes the trick work is a short, sharpened pencil concealed in your back pocket beforehand. Each time you bring a square behind your back, you take out the pencil and push it as far through the center hole as is possible. How far it goes tells you which color it is because the diameters of the holes in the centers of the squares vary. The hole in the red square is wide enough to allow only half of the sharpened front part of the pencil to enter. The purple hole is large enough for almost all of the front of the pencil to enter, and the yellow hole large enough to allow the whole pencil to slip through.

ANY NUMBER WILL PLAY

This is a simple trick that calls for a very stark, dramatic opening Suddenly point at someone in the audience and blurt out the command that he stop thinking, especially of numbers. Wipe away all and every number, you beg, because you've just received the answer to numbers that person hasn't even thought of yet!

Quickly find a scrap of paper and secretly write "1089" on it. Do it as if the answer had to be written down quickly, before it suddenly disappeared. Give a short sigh as you roll the scrap into a ball and place it on a nearby table.

Now you start: give the person in the audience a pencil and some paper and ask that he select any three-digit number, each digit different from the others. Wait until he has written it down and then ask him to reverse that number and subtract the smaller from the larger. Be sure to tell him to record all zeros, whenever they appear (even if the first digit), so that the result will always be a three-digit number. This done, you tell him that it is necessary now for that answer to be reversed. Have him add those two final figures together.

Stare above his head, walk to the table, retrieve your answer, unwrap it, and announce the number written there: "1089, am I right?"

Rest assured it will always be right. Yes, the answer will always be 1089, regardless of what numbers that person first selected.

Let's do one. Take the number 6 5 2. The reverse is 2 5 6. Subtract 256 from 652 and you get 396, which reverses to 693. The sum of 396 and 693 is indeed 1089. See?

Don't forget to do the trick only once or your audience may also discover that the answer is always 1089.

AMAZING COIN DROP

Hand a penny to a volunteer, and ask him to drop it into an envelope you are holding. Close the envelope, seal it, and fold it over twice. Then set the envelope on a china saucer and rest the saucer on top of a glass tumbler. With a single tap on the envelope you send the coin falling through the solid saucer to the bottom of the glass.

This trick requires the use of an envelope that opens at one of its narrow ends. Prepare the envelope beforehand by taking a razor blade and slicing through the end opposite the flap. With a daub of soft soap stick to the bottom of the saucer a penny bearing the same date as the one you give to your volunteer. Place the saucer on the table and the envelope and second penny in your pocket, and you are ready to begin.

Holding the envelope so as to conceal the slit end in your hand, extend the end with the flap in it to the volunteer and let his penny fall clear through the envelope into the hollow of your palm. While you fold the envelope, keep the coin well hidden between your palm and the paper folds. Deliver your tap to the folded envelope with the hand that is not concealing the penny; as you strike the envelope, drop this coin into one of your pockets. The tap knocks the other penny loose from the bottom surface of the saucer, and your audience thinks it sees a penny actually pass through the china to clink against the glass below. Quickly shred the envelope to destroy all evidence of deception.

HIS MASTER'S VOICE

Announce to your audience that you, and only you, can make a playing card actually rise on command. Hold up for inspection an empty drinking glass and a deck of cards. Challenge someone from the audience to try the trick. Have the volunteer take any card from the deck and hand it to you. As you push his card down into the glass, urge him to try to talk the card into rising. Regardless of what your volunteer says or how he says it, however, the card will not budge.

Suggest that someone else try his luck. Have him pick a different card and repeat the trick. Encourage him to try even harder than the first volunteer did. No matter, the card will stay stubbornly down in the glass.

When your turn comes to perform the trick, remove the card from the glass and mysteriously run it up and down your sleeve several times as you whisper your command, "Rise for me!" Insert the card into the glass and watch as, this time, it responds by slowly rising on your command.

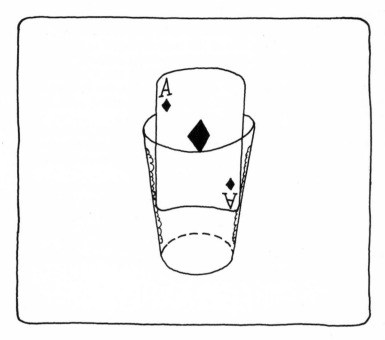

The reason you are successful is because you have specially prepared and used the glass. The glass must have tapered sides, narrower at the bottom. You rub a piece of dry soap along the inside of the glass on opposite sides, working from the top to the bottom of the glass and leaving two deposits of soap about half an inch wide.

When you insert your volunteers' cards into the glass, you are careful to push the cards down along the unsoaped sides so they will not move. When you take your turn, you push the card down along the soaped sides—and the card, aided by the soap, will indeed slowly rise (see diagram).

COMBINATION PUZZLE

In this trick, using both a pair of dice and a deck of cards, you make a prediction and then fulfill it in front of an amazed audience.

On a piece of paper write down the name of a card you predict, folding the paper to conceal your choice from the audience. Instruct someone to roll the dice and then add up the total number of spots showing on both the top and bottom sides. When he has his number, tell your volunteer to count down from the top of the deck of cards until he reaches the number matching the total he took from the pair of dice. Have him hold up this card; then unfold your paper and reveal, to the audience's surprise, your accurate prediction.

Since the combined spots from the top and bottom sides of a pair of dice will always number fourteen, you had only to note beforehand the fourteenth card from the top of the deck in order to make the trick work.

THE HANDKERCHIEF-PRISON BREAK

To perform this trick you will need a large men's handkerchief, a napkin, a ring with a one-inch diameter, and at least four assistants. Taking the handkerchief from your pocket, open it up and turn it so that the audience can see both sides. Have someone inspect it for any invisible holes. Once the audience is satisfied that the handkerchief is whole, retrieve it and inform them that there is, indeed, an invisible opening and that you will prove it by having an object escape from it.

Ask that someone in the audience pass you a small object, such as a matchbook. Place the object carefully in the center of the handkerchief, making sure that everyone can see it. Gather up the handkerchief by its four corners and slip the ring securely over them. To prevent your removing the ring, have four members of the audience each grasp a corner of the handkerchief and hold on to it tightly. This done, take out the napkin and drape it so it completely covers the handkerchief and the four hands holding its corners.

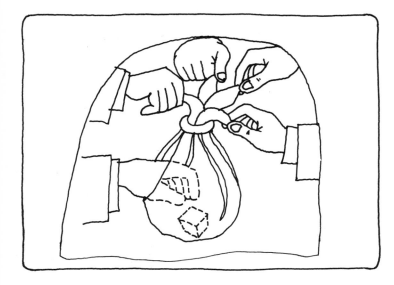

Roll up your right sleeve, show the audience your hand is empty, and then reach with it under the napkin. Have it emerge a few seconds later, holding the object that was wrapped inside the handkerchief. With your other hand pull off the napkin to show that the ring still encompasses the four corners of the handkerchief, preventing the very escape they've just seen accomplished.

The secret of the trick is that when you reach under the napkin, you simply put your hand into the opening between any two folds of the handkerchief and remove the object (see diagram). Any small object can be used, as long as it can be slipped out through the side of the handkerchief.

BURNT MATCH RELIGHTED

Here's a simple trick that's usually good for a double take from your unsuspecting friends.

Take out a cigarette, put it in your mouth, and pretend to search for a match. Pull out a small box of wooden matches and open it, only to discover it empty. Make a point of letting the others know that it's empty by noisily throwing it down on a nearby table, as you say in a frustrated tone something about always being out of a match when you need one. Search your other pockets without success. Then turn to your friends and ask if anyone has a match. Quickly, before anyone can offer one, look into a nearby ash tray and tell them not to bother; there are some burnt matches in the ash tray and you'll just use one of them.

Pick up one of the burnt wooden matches, saying that there's no reason to throw away a match after it's been used only once. If someone points out that a used match can't be lighted again, just smile and say that it can if one knows how. Pick up the empty box of matches you recently discarded and strike the used match on its striking edge. It will indeed burn. Bring up the flame to light the cigarette in your mouth.

You must prepare for this trick beforehand. Take five or six unused wooden matches from the match box and whittle off some of the wood from each match—about the center up to the bottom of the match head. Blacken the whittled part of the match and the head with a black felt marking pen so that they resemble burnt matches, and place them in the ash tray you are going to spot when you need a match. Pick up and light one of these burnt matches, and watch your friends do a double take.

THE FORTY-NINER

Have a volunteer shuffle a deck of cards thoroughly, and instruct him to deal seven cards to each of seven persons. Tell each person to look at his cards, to select one in his mind, and to remember its identity. Then ask each person to place his cards facedown in front of him in any order he wishes.

Collect the cards in a special way. Starting with the person on your immediate right, take one card from his pile and proceed around the table in order, picking up a single card from each of the seven piles and placing them facedown on top of each other in the order in which you take them. Repeat this procedure until all 49 cards are gathered into a single pile in front of you.

Pick up the top seven cards in the stack, one at a time, and arrange them in your hand so that the top card is on the left and the remaining six move in sequence to the right. In this way each group of seven cards that you pick up will not only contain one card from each person's pile but will also be arranged so that the order of the cards in your hand matches the order of the people at the table. The card at the right of your hand will belong to the person sitting on your right; the second card from the right will belong to whoever is on the first person's right, and so on. Show each group of seven cards and ask each time if anyone sees his card among them. When someone responds that he does, you hand the right card to him at once. If no one spots his choice, simply discard the group and take another.

Remember that not every set of seven cards will include someone's selection. Some sets may include more than one such card, but in this event, your sequences still give you the necessary clues.

WHICH IS MUTT AND WHICH IS JEFF?

Here is a convincing optical illusion. Take two pieces of cardboard, one red and one blue, and place one cardboard on top of the other; cut them together into identical curving strips approximately ten inches long and four inches in width. The top and bottom edges should fan outwards from the inside of the curve (see diagram 1).

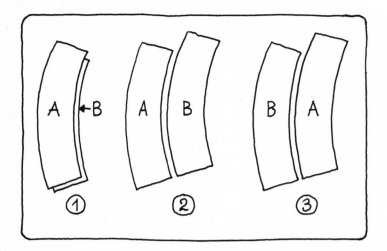

First show them on top of one another to prove they are exactly the same length (as in diagram 1). Then "stretch" one (B) to make it look longer by placing them together (see diagram 2). (B) looks longer.

Then "stretch" (A) by putting them together (see diagram 3). (A) will now look longer.

Finally "stretch" (B) a little to make it the same size as (A) and place them on top of one another as in diagram 1. They are now once again the same size.

A SWEET DECEIT

A dinner party would be the ideal occasion for this trick, and it is best done at a table covered with a white tablecloth. You can make your preparations during the meal itself, as it will not be difficult for you to conceal your simple maneuvers from the people dining around you.

See that the sugar bowl is filled with lump sugar. After the coffee has been served, you may go to work; your handling of the sugar cubes at this time is not likely to arouse anybody's close attention. Your goal is to set five or six cubes of sugar in front of you, each cube with a tiny, undetectable portion of salt lying on its top surface. When you have done this, introduce the trick by saying that you have developed the ability to receive mental vibrations from someone through an object that has touched that person's face. Offer the sugar cubes as a handy means of demonstration.

Ask one of the guests to select a cube for the test from among those you have set in front of you. Tell him to hold the lump of sugar against his face for an instant and then to replace it among the others. Either turn your back or leave the table while this operation is carried out. When he lifts the sugar cube, the very small pinch of salt you have deposited on its top will spill off, and the white tablecloth will camouflage the grains of salt.

When the now saltless cube is back among the salted ones, proceed to examine them for those personal vibrations you previously described. Lightly touching the lumps with one finger, feel for the

invisible mounds of salt; when you come to the cube whose surface is completely smooth, the vibrations will be loud and clear.

TWO BITS WORTH OF TEARS

It may be impossible to wring blood from a stone, but with this trick you prove to your audience that you can squeeze water out of a coin. Have someone lend you a quarter, rub it up and down with your right hand on the back of your raised, left forearm, and then give it a squeeze. Your audience will be taken aback to see actual teardrops falling from the coin.

The secret is that you have hidden a small, wetted wad of absorbent tissue paper behind your left ear. While your left forearm is raised and the attention of the audience is drawn to the movement of the coin in your right hand, you take the wad of tissue in your left hand, whose position during the rubbing is very close to your ear. Conceal it between your forefinger and middle finger. Then move the coin to your left hand, positioning it between the thumb and forefinger so as to press the tissue against the back of the coin.

With your palm turned toward the audience, give the quarter a squeeze, and the hidden tissue behind it will release a few drops of water. Transfer the coin to your right hand before turning it over to someone for inspection; casually lower your left arm and covertly slip the tissue into one of your pockets.

GLASS LIGHTNING

Handling two glasses at a time, in three lightning moves you change the positions of three glasses placed on a table; no one in the audience is able to follow your hands and duplicate the arrangement you make with the glasses.

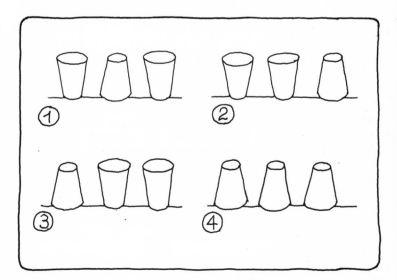

Set the glasses in a row with the middle glass turned upside down. Suppose the glasses to be numbered one, two, and three, from left to right. Tell the audience that by turning two glasses over at a time you will have them all resting upside down in three movements. To do this, first turn over numbers two and three, then turn the first and third glasses, and finally turn numbers two and three again. The speed of your gestures effectively hides the sequence.

THE PERPLEXING PULSE

This trick calls for a dramatic prologue in which you relate the strange teachings you've encountered while studying magic, how simple tricks led to more complex undertakings, and how you recently discovered a most peculiar and mystifying technique—one that alters life itself.

Explain that you have come into possession of an ancient book found in a dusty corner of a secondhand bookshop, which contained the writings of a strange, disturbing man of the seventeenth century who succeeded in stopping life itself for short periods of time.

Accuse your audience of being skeptical and offer to prove that his death-defying technique works. Ask someone from the audience to find your pulse and verify that it beats. Once the volunteer has found it, ask him to continue holding his fingers there until he feels the pulse stop. Explain that it's vital for him to shout out the instant it does stop.

Following your instructions, the volunteer will find your pulse and shortly thereafter, as he feels your pulse stop beating, will shout out in disbelief.

The secret of this illusion lies in the small rubber ball you have placed under your shirt in the center of your armpit. After the volunteer finds your pulse, you slowly press your arm against your body. The pressure of the ball on this area will stop the pulse from beating. As soon as the volunteer verifies that your pulse has stopped, move your arm away from your body, allowing the ball to fall down to your belt.

THE ROPE-KERCHIEF ENIGMA

Ask your audience if they have ever seen a solid pass through another solid. Tell them that not only have you seen it, you're actually prepared to demonstrate the feat for them right now.

Pull out a handkerchief with one hand and a fifteen-foot-long, thin, soft rope with the other hand. Bring them together in a dramatic gesture, saying, "I can cause this rope to pass right through this handkerchief."

Join your hands together, palm-to-palm. Turn to someone in the audience and ask him to tie the handkerchief tightly around your wrists. Then instruct him to put the rope between your tied hands so that it rests on the handkerchief with half the rope behind your tied hands, the other half in front of your hands.

Once this is done, ask your volunteer to pick up both ends of the

rope and stand directly in front of you, still holding the two ends of the rope which now encircles the tied handkerchief. Take a moment to concentrate and then request that he pull both parts of the rope toward his body. To everyone's amazement, the rope will come forward freely at his pull. Invite the audience to inspect both the handkerchief, which is still tightly binding your hands, and the rope, which is still intact.

The way you work the trick is as follows: As the handkerchief is being placed around your wrists, make sure you cup your hands a little, leaving space between your palms. Utilize the moment of concentration; use the fingers of your right hand to push the rope off all of the fingers of your left hand (see diagram). Once you've placed the rope on the outside of your left hand, it will slide out easily when pulled.

LUMBER IS LIMBER

This is a simple example of an illusion. The only prop needed is a new pencil. Tell the audience you've noticed that brand-new pencils are not quite fully rigid. As you were about to sharpen one the other day, you go on, you realized that it seemed flexible and, sure enough, upon investigation you discovered it did indeed bend.

Offer to prove what you've just asserted. Take out a new, unsharpened pencil, and pass it around, asking if everyone agrees that it is just an ordinary wooden pencil. After they hand it back to you, take hold of it about one-third from either end with the thumb and index finger of your right hand. Holding it very loosely between those two fingers, jerk your right hand up and down. Use fast, short flicks of the hand and as it travels through the air, the pencil will give the illusion of bending at each end, almost as if it were made of rubber.

There's no trick involved here; it just works that way.

SMASH THE GLASS!

The most appropriate setting for this trick is at the table after the finish of a meal or snack. With your family and/or friends still sitting around, with the dishes still on the table, pick up an empty glass and, holding it high in the air, declare that you can make any coin disappear with the aid of this completely innocent glass.

Take a coin, place it on the table in front of you, and invert the glass over the coin. Act bewildered for a few seconds and then remember that a piece of newspaper is also needed. Drape the sheet of newspaper over the glass, molding it to the shape of the glass. Work on this until you have made a tight, glass-shaped form easy to recognize by the others. Stare at the newspaper-covered glass and declare dramatically that the coin has now disappeared. Lifting both the glass and the newspaper around it, bring it to the edge of the table in front of you and look surprised to find the coin still there on the table.

Repeat your actions again, lifting both the glass and the newspaper and again bring them in front of you. Look even more amazed this time—incredulous even. The coin is still there!

Request the help of the two people sitting at your right and left. Ask each person to hold the newspaper edge nearest him. Hold your hand over the glass-shaped newspaper and then, quickly and sharply, bring your hand down fast and heavy on the glass!

The surprise of all those watching when your hand hits without any accompanying sound of broken glass is this trick's real goal. Yes, the glass has completely disappeared. Or has it? Surreptitiously lower your hand beneath the table and slyly produce the smashed glass—intact and unharmed.

Effective? Yes. Difficult? No. As you stare down at the coin still on the table after your second attempt, you simply drop the glass into your lap. There is nothing beneath the glass-shaped newspaper when you smash down on it. And the glass is there, in your lap, waiting to be produced, giving a very dramatic finish to your trick.

THE MAGIC KEY RING

Introduce this trick by asking, ''Is it possible for two pieces of string to join together and become just one?'' And answer quickly by saying, ''Yes, when the two strings have been touched by a key ring.''

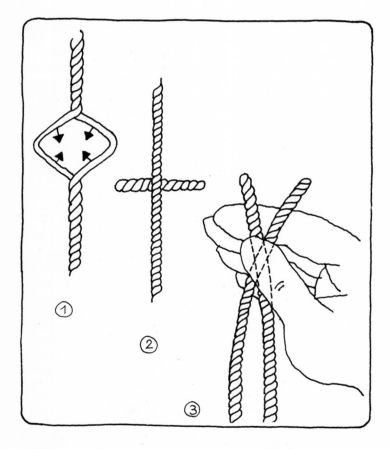

Offer to explain this puzzle by doing it. Take two pieces of string out of your pocket with your right hand and ask someone from the audience to lend you a key ring, a key ring that will join these two pieces of string together. Continue to hold the two pieces of string between your thumb and first two fingers of your right hand (see diagram 3) as your left hand places the bottom end of either of the strings into the open center of the offered key ring. With the string

imprisoned in the key ring's opening, you move the key ring up and into the palm of your right hand. Ask two people to assist you; tell each to take the bottom end of a different string and pull them toward themselves and away from you. You soon open your hand and release its contents—not only have the two strings joined and become one, but the key ring is now riding on the center of the single length of string.

This trick calls for a special string, one that consists of 8, 10, or 12 intertwining strands of soft cotton. Prepare for this trick beforehand in the following way: separate about four inches of the string into two equal strands of thickness in the center of its thirty-inch length, creating a diamondlike shape (see diagram 1). Now twist each of these two sidepieces so that they each resemble the full thickness of the string. Now you have created a crosslike effect, with the two short arms at right angles to the string itself (see diagram 2). Put the thumb and index finger of your right hand on the point where they all cross. Pull the two short ends up and above the top of your hand. Arrange the two longer pieces to look like the bottoms of two pieces of string held in your hand (see diagram 3). Keep the back of your right hand toward the audience at all times. They will see only what appears to be two pieces of string, the short tops protruding at the top of your hand, the rest of the two strings dangling from the bottom of your hand. Remember, this is always the way you show the string(s), starting with its removal from your pocket.

The rest of the trick is relatively easy. When the key ring is put onto either of the bottom ends of string, use your left hand to run it up to and into your right palm. When the two people are asked to pull hard on their string ends, the entire string straightens out, and the audience will see the key ring riding the center of the now magically joined single string.

MAGIC NUMBER

Here is a purely mental card trick that can be performed even over the telephone. Call a friend and ask him to think of a card. Tell him to write down both the suit of the card and its number; for a jack he lists eleven, for a queen, twelve, and for a king, thirteen.

Then you assign him a little arithmetic, which he can do on paper or in his head. He multiplies the number of the card by two, and to this figure he adds three; then he multiplies that sum by five; to that sum he now adds one if his card is a club, two if it is a diamond, three if it is a heart, and four if it is a spade. When he gives you his final figure—and this is the only number he divulges to you—you are immediately able to name his card.

You do this by subtracting the number fifteen from his total, and no matter what card he has selected you will get a two- or three-digit figure whose first digit (first two digits for tens through kings) gives the numerical value of his card and whose last digit reveals the card's suit (1, clubs; 2. diamonds; 3, hearts; 4, spades).

Here's an example. Your friend selects the six of hearts. He multiplies the 6 by two and gets 12. He then adds 3, getting 15. He then multiplies the 15 by 5, getting 75. Since his suit was hearts, he adds 3, giving him a total of 78, which is the number he gives you.

You subtract 15 from the number 78 he gives you, getting 63. The first number tells you his card was a six, the second number indicates his suit was hearts. You inform him that his card was the six of hearts.

THE FLOATING CUBE GAME

This sleight of hand, although basically simple, must be studied and perfected before being performed. It is well worth the effort since it is unusually successful in bewildering an audience.

Take four paper-wrapped sugar cubes from the sugar bowl and place them on the table. Move them so that they form the four corners of an imaginary five-inch square. Let's label their original positions as follows:

TL (for top left)	TR (for top right)
BL (for bottom left)	BR (for bottom right)

There is a secret fifth sugar cube, which the audience never sees. This sugar cube is positioned in your left hand at the start and is held there by the pressure of your thumb against your palm. Remember, practice the following moves so that your hands dart about quickly, surely, and skillfully. The smoother the moves, the more impressive the trick.

Place your left hand containing the hidden fifth cube over the TL cube and your empty right hand over the BR cube. Twitch your fingers around a little to divert the audience. Your right hand picks up and palms the BR cube while your left hand puts down the fifth cube at TL. You pick up your hands and the audience sees two cubes at TL and none at BR.

Move your now empty left hand to BL as you place your right hand over TL's two cubes. Divert the watchers again by moving your fingers around, and release the palmed cube from your right hand at TL while palming the BL cube in your left hand. Remove your hands and the audience now sees three cubes at TL and none at BL.

Put your left hand with its palmed cube over TL and add it to the three already there, as your empty hand palms the final cube at TR. Lift your hands and let the audience see that all four cubes are now at TL while all the other corners are empty. Remember that you still have a sugar cube secreted in your right palm.

Pick up the four assembled cubes with your right hand (you'll actually add the fifth cube to the four as you do so). Place all of them back in the sugar bowl.

FOR WHOM THE BELL TOLLS

This intriguing deception calls for enough practice to enable you to perform it both quickly and smoothly, so that all your moves seem to flow. The trick requires an opaque cloth about thirty inches square and a small bell with a handle.

Standing behind a table, face the audience and put the bell down directly in front of you. Ring it several times to establish its tone. Tell the audience that they will hear the bell ring again, but this time mysteriously, without any human contact.

Take out the cloth and hold it up in two hands so the audience can see the front of it. Then turn it around, moving your left hand forward and to the right, in front of your right hand, and your right hand to the left, behind your left hand. In fact, bring your right hand far enough to the left to touch your left shoulder.

While you are holding the cloth in this position, the audience will hear the clear sound of the bell ringing. Move your hands back to their original position and again show the front side of the cloth to the audience, verifying that there is nothing on either side of the cloth to have caused the bell to ring.

Nothing the audience can see, that is. Actually, there is a tiny bent pin that you've skillfully hidden beforehand in the upper right-hand corner of the cloth. When you bring your right hand over to your left shoulder, you quickly hook the point of that pin onto the material on that shoulder. Your right hand, now free, and hidden by the cloth, darts to the bell, shakes it, and quickly returns to your left shoulder, unhooks the pin, and, holding the corner again, now turns the cloth around to show the bewildered audience that there's nothing to account for the ringing bell.

LIT AND RELIT

Here's a trick that requires just an ordinary book of matches and a candle. Light the candle and after it has burned for a minute or so, light a fresh match. Blow out the candle and bring the burning match a few inches above the candle. A flame from the burning match will seem to jump to and relight the candle.

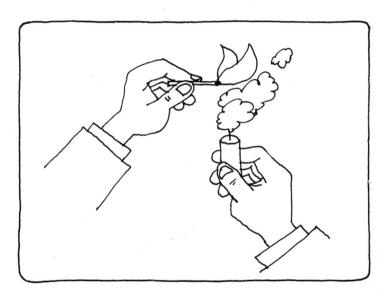

You can repeat this several times. The secret is to place the flame of the burning match directly in the column of smoke rising from the blown-out candle. You will have to experiment to determine exactly how far above the candle the match should be held. The traveling of the flame down along the column of smoke to the candle seems like a startling bit of magic.

THE REAPPEARING THIMBLE

Urge the audience to examine carefully both the thimble and the man's handkerchief you are going to pass around. Place the thimble on top of the index finger of your right hand. Hold your right hand up, the palm facing you, with only the thimble-covered index finger pointing up; the other fingers of the right hand are to be folded into your palm.

Use your left hand to drape the handkerchief over your right hand. As you do this, quickly and inconspicuously lower the right index finger and extend your right middle finger in its place. Bring your left hand back to the audience, in front of the handkerchief, and move the index finger wearing the thimble out from behind the handkerchief and toward your body and up behind your handkerchief-covered middle finger. Your left hand will conceal this movement from the audience. Encircle your right index and middle fingers with your left fingers. Lift the thimble off your right index finger with the left hand. Your right index finger returns to the cover of the handkerchief. Your left hand places the thimble on the handkerchief-covered extended right middle finger.

When you remove your left hand, the audience sees the thimble, now mysteriously on the outside of the handkerchief, riding on top of what they assume is still your index finger. The thimble has apparently penetrated the handkerchief.

THEY CAN'T CUT IT

A modest version of sawing a woman in two, this fascinating trick will produce a reaction almost equal to that which greets the more spectacular version.

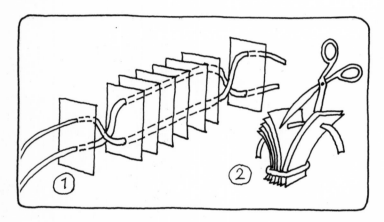

To prepare for the trick, punch two holes in each of ten playing cards. Locate the holes close to the narrow ends of the cards, halfway across each end. Run a length of string straight through each row of matching holes (see diagram 1).

The secret of the trick lies in the last preparatory step. Push the cards together and turn both the top card and the bottom card around end to end. Now, although the two lengths of string still appear to pass straight through both sets of holes, they in fact cross over above the bottom card and below the top card (see diagram 1). The ends of the string hang free as you introduce the trick.

Keeping the cards in a tight stack, move them back and forth on the lengths of string to convince your audience that the cards are really strung as they appear to be. They move easily and give no sign of trickery. Ask a volunteer to select one of the two pieces of string to be cut. Tie the two ends of the other piece of string loosely around the card ends. At the untied end, spread the cards apart from the center, and ask your volunteer to take a pair of scissors and cut the string between the cards (see diagram 2).

When the string has been cut, square up the cards. Give the stack several taps, announcing that by this means you will permanently rejoin the ends of the severed string. Offer the strand at the end of the deck to your volunteer, and tell him to pull the restored string all the way through the set of cards. Since the string lengths were crisscrossed under the top card and above the bottom

card, he will not actually be pulling on the severed string at all. But in the eyes of the audience, it will appear that the severed piece has been mysteriously rejoined.

CATCH AS CATCH CAN

Before performing this simple juggling act, demonstrate the positions of the objects to your audience. Pick up an empty water glass in one hand, as you would to take a drink, and place one sugar cube between your thumb and forefinger of the hand holding the glass (see diagram 1). Have it tightly pressed against the glass. Balance a second sugar cube on top of the first, and then ask members of the group if they think they can throw the lumps in the air, one at a time, and catch them both in the glass. If anyone makes the attempt, he will fail because your instruction has misled him.

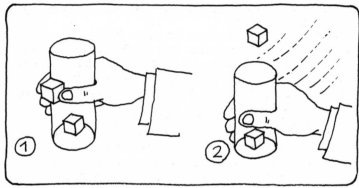

Take the glass and the cubes and proceed to perform the feat successfully. The upper cube is easily thrown up and caught, as any volunteer will have learned; it is the cube pressed against the glass that proved to be a stumbling block. You succeed in catching this one simply by releasing it from your thumb and forefinger and dropping your hand quickly; before the cube starts its fall, you can easily move the glass underneath it for the capture (see diagram 2).

MONEY! MONEY! MONEY!

How would you like to multiply money? You take out a dollar bill, hold it up to the audience, snap it several times to prove it is a single dollar bill, and then, suddenly produce many more dollar bills.

Effective? Yes. Yet this simple sleight of hand calls for a minimum of practice to perform smoothly and effortlessly.

The additional dollar bills (start with six bills and increase the number after practice if you wish) have been rolled together beforehand into a tight roll of bills and hidden in the folds of your sleeve at your right elbow.

Show your hands empty except for the single bill held in your left hand at your fingertips. Pull up your left sleeve with your right hand. Take the dollar bill in your right hand and pull up your right sleeve with your left hand. (As you do so take hold of the roll of bills hidden in the folds of your right sleeve.) Bring your two hands together and behind the single bill immediately unroll the bills and fan them out. Show the audience all of the magically produced dollar bills.

THE PENETRATING TOOTHPICK

You can create the optical illusion that a toothpick is going through the solid side of a safety pin.

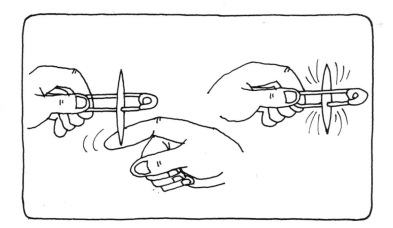

Pass an ordinary safety pin and a toothpick around to the audience for inspection. Open the safety pin and run the point through the center of the toothpick. Holding either end of the safety pin tightly with the thumb and index finger of your left hand, use the right hand to center the toothpick on its prong. Close the safety pin, and using a finger of the right hand, move the toothpick against the other bar until the toothpick touches it.

Then, again holding the safety pin in your left hand, use the index finger of your right hand to snap the toothpick away from the bar it is resting against. This will cause the toothpick to spin and hit the opposite bar. Do this several times, snapping the toothpick each time it returns near its starting position.

You will discover that each snap of your right index finger causes a rapid turning of the toothpick. This fast movement creates the illusion that the toothpick penetrates the safety pin bar. It would be wise to prepare the center hole in the toothpick beforehand so the trick is performed smoothly.

CARD CONCENTRATION

Display five cards to the audience, fanning them as you would a poker hand. Tell one person to mentally select a single card. Place the cards you have displayed in one of your jacket pockets.

Before you begin the trick, place four cards in this pocket; these should be the four cards in the deck that most closely resemble the ones you will exhibit to the audience. The two sets should correspond in color and numbers, so that only the suits are different. For instance, display the four of hearts, the five of diamonds, the six of hearts, the seven of diamonds, and the eight of hearts, and pocket in advance the four of diamonds, the five of hearts, the six of diamonds, and the seven of hearts. The order in which the displayed cards lie in your pocket is very important since you will have to count them with your fingers, so keep this group in numerical sequence.

As you put the cards that were shown into your pocket, separate them with a pack of cigarettes from the group you have previously concealed there. Remove your hand from the pocket and pause

briefly to give an impression of concentration. Then reach back inside your pocket and take out the four cards you planted secretly, one at a time, announcing that these cards do not include the one chosen by your volunteer. Place them facedown on the table, and then ask the volunteer to announce his card's identity.

Have your hand in your pocket as he tells the name of his card. Locate the card by feeling for its place in the sequence, and produce it for the audience. Then turn up the four non-chosen cards in an offhand manner but do not call special attention to them. The difference in the suits of the cards belonging to the two sets will be missed by the volunteer for two reasons: the numbers and the color are the same in both, and his mind is focused exclusively on a single card.

PUT YOUR FOOT IN IT

Show the audience a file card measuring five inches in length and three inches in width, and make the dubious claim that you can put your entire body through it. Wait for the expressions of disbelief to subside and then proceed to do just what you said you could.

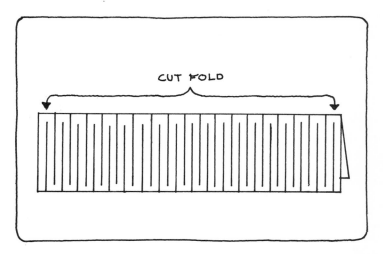

CUT FOLD

Fold the card in half, lengthwise. Use a scissors to make the following series of precision cuts (see diagram). First, cut a slit along the fold itself, leaving one-eighth inch of uncut card at each end. Then, holding the folded card together, make thirty-nine cuts perpendicular to the fold as shown in the diagram.

At one end of the folded card cut down through the fold to a point that is one-eighth inch in from the edge of the card's border. Start your second cut one-eighth inch away from the first, and cut from the border upward toward the fold, leaving one-eighth inch between the end of your cut and the fold. Each successive cut should be one-eighth inch away from its predecessor. And each cut should alternate, from the fold down to the last one-eighth inch from the border end, and from the border up to the last one-eighth inch of the fold.

When you finish cutting and spread out the card, your audience will see a circular zig-zig strip, one-eighth-inch wide and easily big enough when opened to accommodate your body. Your claim will be satisfied just as soon as you slip it over your head and shoulders and slide it down your body to the floor.

THE DISSOLVING COIN

Tell the audience that you are able by magical means to make a coin dissolve in water. Pick up a glass of water, stare at it, and then announce dramatically that you can prove your point with this glass of water. Ask if anyone is willing to take a chance on sacrificing a small coin to the experiment.

Once someone has volunteered, take out a men's handkerchief and ask your volunteer to place his coin in the center. Have him hold onto the coin through the material of the handkerchief. Place the glass of water flat on the palm of your left hand, and ask your volunteer to drape the handkerchief over the glass while still holding onto the coin inside the handkerchief. Tell him he is to release both the coin and the handkerchief at your command.

Just before you give the command, move your left hand up by squeezing your fingers together tightly enough to tilt the glass away from the path the coin will take after dropping. The coin will now hit the side of the glass and fall into your left hand; however, the sound of the coin hitting the glass will mislead the audience into assuming it fell into the glass.

Take both the glass and the handkerchief draped over it to a nearby table and place them on the top of the table. As you do this, subtly drop the coin into your pocket. After you have set the handkerchief-draped glass on the table, announce that the coin should have dissolved by now and ask your volunteer to remove the handkerchief. Enjoy everyone's surprise as they look into the glass and find it coinless.

SUGAR, SUGAR, BURNING BRIGHT

Bring out a bowl full of paper-wrapped sugar cubes and a book of matches, and place them on the table. Suggest that the audience inspect both the sugar cubes and the matches in order to assure themselves that they are innocent in every respect.

Once they indicate they are so satisfied, challenge one of them to unwrap a cube of sugar and burn it, using any match he wishes to select.

After the first person fails, encourage some of the others to try their luck at burning the sugar cube. No one will succeed in setting a cube of sugar on fire.

When they finally give up and demand to see you do it, ask one of them to unwrap and hand you any sugar cube he wishes. Then ask him to select any match he likes for you to use. Light the match and hold the flame to the end of the sugar cube, and watch the astonished faces in the audience as it burns.

The secret to your success is that you previously prepared an ash tray with a layer of cigarette or cigar ashes. Before lighting your match, you secretly pressed one end of the sugar cube into the ashes. The flame, when held against the deposit of ashes on the sugar cube, will make the sugar burn.

BREAKOUT!

This is a simple yet effective deception—a perfect trick with which to baffle a friend. All you need is a small rubber band that you claim can in no way be imprisoned. You lock it up inside the fingers of both hands and watch the look on your friend's face as it escapes.

Start by putting your two index fingers inside the rubber band and twirling it around those two fingers several times, palms toward you (see diagram 1). Then lock it up twice by putting the index finger and thumb of each hand around the rubber band at either end. It is now double-locked (see diagram 2). Bring the four fingers involved inside the rubber band and place them together—lo and behold, the rubber band escapes by dropping down, free as a bird.

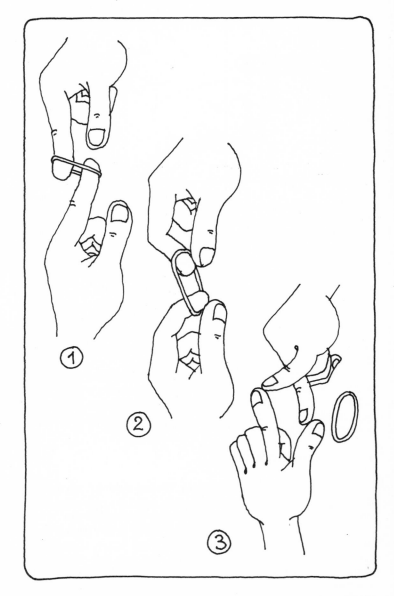

It is important to remember to keep your palms toward your body as you first twirl the rubber band around. Bring your thumbs up, imprisoning the section of rubber band between the thumb and index finger of each hand. Then, you put your four fingers together, pushing each index finger hard against the thumb of the opposite hand. This push will open the lock wide enough for the rubber band to fall through (see diagram 3).

It looks simple; yet, without the secret, your friend will be unable to do it.

GEORGE WASHINGTON MOVES!

You can turn the Father of Our Country over on his head in a series of simple folds, refolds, and unfolds. Practice the moves described and illustrated here until you have them down pat. The trick should be performed smoothly and surely, allowing the audience to see every move you make.

Hold up a one-dollar bill so that your audience may see that George Washington's picture on the front is in an upright position. Ask them to watch carefully as you turn him upside down without ever turning the bill over.

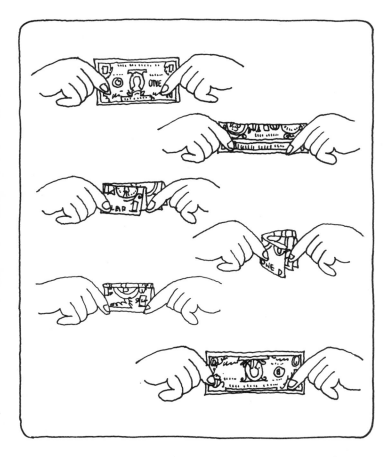

First, fold the top of the bill in half lengthwise by bringing the top front edge down to meet the bottom. The president's face is now on the inside of the fold.

Second, fold the bill in half again sideways by taking your right-hand edge and bringing it over to your left-hand edge.

Again fold the right-hand edge over to the left.

You now have the bill folded in eighths and are ready for the decisive move. This fourth step is done by subtly turning the entire folded bill toward the right so that the solid edge is now on your left-hand side.

Now for the unfolding. You open the bill once by moving the back half toward your left. Once again unfold the bill toward your left. The bill should now have only a single horizontal fold in it.

Finally, turn the front half up and open it, revealing the upside-down first president—as promised.

THE QUICK COUNT

Have a volunteer shuffle a deck of cards as many times as he wishes. Ask for the deck and, when it is in your hand, quickly but smoothly tilt it just enough to give you a glimpse of the card on the bottom. Then pull out one card at a time from the bottom of the deck and place each facedown onto the table. Count to yourself as you put each card down. Tell the volunteer he can stop you anytime he wishes. When he does, tell him to look at the last card placed on the pile and remember it. When he has done this and returned that card to the pile of cards, place the remainder of the deck from your hand on top of the pile on the table.

Hand the complete deck to the volunteer and tell him he can cut the deck as many times as he wants. The one condition you impose is that he make single cuts only, breaking the deck into two parts and then closing it before a further cut is made; if the deck is divided into more than two piles before it is closed, the original sequence of cards will be disturbed and your count will be useless.

Take back the deck and spread the cards out in your hand, holding them as you would for a card game, with the new bottom card at the extreme right of the fan. Locate the original bottom card and count to the left until you reach the number you counted before. If you come to the card at the far left before your count is finished, pick up the count with the card on the far right and continue counting to the left until you hit the right number. Your volunteer's card will always be "down for the count."

A WAY WITH MATCHES

You need two matches, two hands, and one boast for this trick. The boast is that you can make solid objects pass through one another.

Using either wooden or paper matches, place one match between the thumb and index finger of your right hand, the other match between the thumb and index finger of your left hand. Hold them up and show the audience that each match is firmly posi-

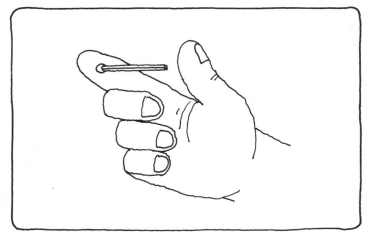

tioned between the fingers, in effect locking it in place.

Quickly move one hand toward the other and let one match pass through the other match—and then out again. Do this quickly and do it several times, back and forth, in and out. Stop and offer your audience another look at the locked-in matches. Continue passing them through again and again until you've proven your boast.

The trick is actually quite simple. You wet the tip of your right index finger just before placing the sulphur end of the match on it. This causes the match to adhere to that finger (see diagram), allowing you to lift it slightly so that the other match may slip through the opening just above the right thumb and appear to pass through without effort.

UNLOCKING THE ANSWERS

Set the tone for this trick by expressing your belief that our subconscious contains the answers to even the most difficult of questions.

Take a foot-long piece of colored string out of your pocket. Announce to the audience that this string, together with a person's key, can unlock the answer to any question he dares to ask.

Solicit a volunteer from the audience and ask him to hand you the most valuable key he possesses. Knot the key to one end of the string and hand the other end of the string to him. Explain that he is to hold his right hand straight out, gripping his end of the string tightly. Emphasize that he is to hold the string out as far as humanly possible, letting the key dangle toward the floor.

Tell him he may now ask any question he wishes answered but explain that he must phrase the question so that it can be answered with a yes or no. Tell him that if the key moves back and forth in a straight line, the answer is yes, but if the key moves in a circle, the answer is no.

There's no explaining this trick but rest assured that if the volunteer holds the key out as far as possible and concentrates, the key will indeed move after each question, usually giving him the answer he most wants to hear.

ORANGE MAGIC

A coin, covered by your hand for just a second, disappears into thin air. This phenomenon is verified by your audience as you turn your hands over several times to prove them innocent of any guile. From a bowl of ordinary oranges, a volunteer selects one orange at random. Picking up a knife from the table, slice the orange in half and show the audience that the coin has been transported to a hiding place inside the fruit.

The coin is made to vanish by the following ingenious method. Run a very strong thread, fastened at one end to a metal disk slightly smaller in size than a quarter, up under your left jacket sleeve. Bring the thread across the back of the jacket, running it through a safety pin attached to the middle of the lining, and carry it down through the right sleeve. When you put on the jacket, choose a spot on your right wrist that is high enough to be covered by the jacket sleeve, and wind the thread around your wrist and tie it securely. Adjust the length of the thread so that when your arms are bent the disk can just reach your left fingers but when you straighten both arms the disk should go up your left sleeve.

On one side of the metal disk apply a bit of soft soap. Beforehand press the disk's soaped surface against the coin. Show the audience the coin and then vanish it. Since the coin will then stick to the disk, both will disappear up your sleeve when you straighten and spread your arms apart quickly.

There is another secret weapon in your arsenal. To the knife you will use on the orange, you have stuck beforehand a twin of the coin you intend to vanish up your sleeve; the blade must be wide enough to conceal the coin behind it while you are cutting. Have this knife in readiness near the bowl of oranges, resting so that the quarter is underneath the blade.

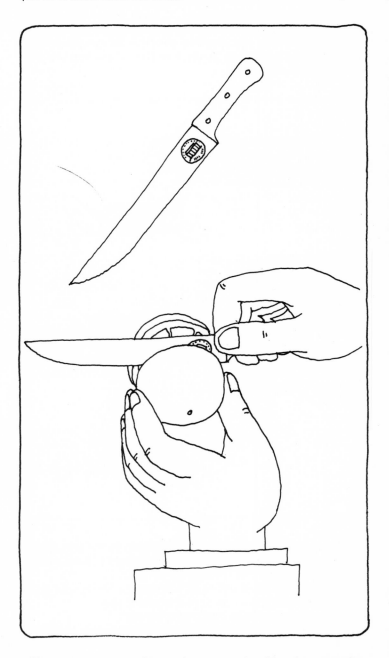

Now you are prepared to work your wonder. After the orange has been selected and inspected by the audience for suspicious imperfections, make a slice with your right hand, always keeping the clear side of the blade toward the audience. Use your right thumb to detach the coin from the knife as the blade passes into the fruit. Withdraw the knife and display the coin in its remarkable hiding place.

DISAPPEARING AND REAPPEARING

Show a pencil to the people in the room. Then tear off a piece of newspaper or provide a sheet from a writing pad, and roll the pencil up in the paper. Claiming that the pencil is no longer inside the rolled paper, tear the roll across in several places and stuff the shreds into one of your pockets. From another pocket, produce the missing pencil.

How is it done? Beforehand you have obtained two identical round pencils. Glue yellow glossy gift paper around one sharpened pencil. Place it inside your breast pocket. Make a tube of another piece of the same paper (same size as real pencil). Insert and glue a cut-off point end of this second pencil in one end of the tube and its eraser end in the other end of the tube. This give you two pencils: one real, full pencil and the fake pencil.

In front of the audience, handle your counterfeit pencil as if it were real. Roll it up in the newsprint or writing paper and proceed to rip. The tube containing the pencil stub and eraser end tears along with the outer sheet, and the two stub ends remain hidden as you crumple the shredded paper around them. Pocket the torn bits and stubs together, and produce the real pencil from your other pocket, where you'd placed it in advance.

THE MATCHED CIGARETTE

This trick calls for a bit of acting, preferably without words. Play the role of someone in great need of a cigarette. Exaggerate the motions of taking out materials for rolling yourself a cigarette. Pretend to put the invisible cigarette between your lips upon completing it.

Take out a real, small box of wooden matches from your pocket, open the box, and remove a match. Strike the match and raise the lit match in your cupped hands up towards your mouth as if you were lighting the imaginary cigarette. When you bring the match down, you will have a real cigarette in your mouth, already lit. Take a puff and blow the smoke at the audience.

Here is the preparation necessary to make the trick work sucessfully: cut away about one-third of either end of the inner drawer of the match box. Remove enough of the wooden matches to make room for a cigarette. Insert the cigarette into the box and allow an inch of the cigarette to protrude through the cut-away section (see diagram). Cut off any excess.

When you pull the box of matches from your pocket, cup your hand so that the audience cannot see the inch of cigarette extending from the box. Take out a match, again not letting the audience see the cigarette inside the box. Bring the box towards your mouth as you bring up the lit match. Put the protruding end of the cigarette between your lips. Continue to hide the bottom of your face as you do this. Lower the match box with your left hand as you put the burning match to your cigarette with your right hand. Enjoy the look of surprise on the faces of your audience as you light up the real cigarette now in your mouth.

THE GHOSTLESS SEANCE

This trick requires a silent partner, a lightweight bridge table, and an impressionable audience.

Announce that, in your opinion, spiritualists have no monoply on creating ghostly effects. Admit that making a table rise does call for tremendous concentration, but confess in a confidential tone that you've been able to raise a table several times recently without calling for any ghosts. Go on to say that in fact you now feel confident enough of this new ability to perform that very feat right now.

To prove your boast, invite three to five people to sit around the bridge table, making sure that your partner is seated directly opposite you. Have the lights dimmed. Tell everyone to place both hands flat on the edge of the table, palms down, directly in front of themselves.

Close your eyes in deep concentration for a few seconds, murmur a provocative sound, and, lo and behold, the table will indeed begin to rise and float.

The reason the table rises, of course, is that both you and your silent partner have prepared yourselves beforehand. You have both tied a flat stick, one inch wide by ten to twelve inches long, to the underpart of your right arms, placing the sticks so that one short end is on the wrist line. The sticks are concealed under your jackets. When you murmur, both you and your partner subtly move each of your sticks forward, hooking them under the table edge in front of you—and lifting. Presto! The table rises.

TOUCH AND TELL

With this compelling trick you can demonstrate your telepathic wizardry. Using an accomplice and a prearranged signal code, you will be able to discover the identity of a card that was touched by a member of the group during your absence from the room.

From a deck remove nine cards; their suits may be mixed but the numbers must read in order from ace through nine. Place the cards on a table in any sequence with their faces showing, and then pass the rest of the deck to your silent partner. Ask someone to touch one of the cards while you are out of the room. Say that you will be able to see his choice with your mind's eye.

When you return to the table, a sign from your accomplice enables you to vindicate your claim to clairvoyance. The deck held by your partner is used to convey the necessary information; the position in which his thumb rests on the back of the top card constitutes a signal that refers to an imaginary grid of numbers into which you have divided the card's area. The imaginary grid

represents the nine cards on the table in three rows of three. The row imagined on the top third of the card goes from ace to three, the middle row goes from four to six, and the bottom row from seven to nine.

Having observed the spectator's selection, your partner positions the end of his thumb over the correct imaginary box. When you return to the room, he holds the deck so that you can read the signal, and you promptly identify the chosen card. See diagram as an example of how your partner would indicate the five had been touched.

THE REARRANGEMENT

There's often a need for a fast, easy trick, one that calls for no elaborate props or preparation. Here's one that fills the bill.

Take out a nickel, a dime, and a quarter. Put them down in that order, left to right, so that each touches the one next to it. Ask if anyone can manage to put the nickel between the dime and the quarter without ever touching the dime or moving the quarter.

Make the volunteers stick to the stated rules, and the odds are that they will be unable to solve the problem. When your turn comes, simply put the tip of your left index finger firmly on the center of the quarter, use your right index finger to move the nickel several inches to the right of the right-hand side of the quarter, and hit that right-hand edge of the quarter with the nickel, fast and hard!

That sharp, striking motion will force the dime to move away from the quarter—far enough away for you to then move the nickel into the newly created space between the quarter and the dime.

INTO THIN AIR

The props and preparation necessary to perform this classic trick are well worth it since the effect on the audience is usually one of total bewilderment.

The main prop is an elastic cord attached to a safety pin at one end and at the other end to a small metal disk the size of a nickel. The metal disk has a hole at its edge through which it is tied to the elastic cord. The cord is pinned inside your jacket, near your right shoulder, and run down through your right sleeve, so that the metal disk at the other end is positioned several inches above the sleeve's edge and out of sight. Before the performance, you completely coat one side of the disk with soap.

Hold the coin in your right hand and, stooping a little, place it near the top of your right thigh. Gather up the pants material around the coin with your left hand—enough material to completely cover the coin. After a moment straighten up and show both your empty hands to the audience; the coin has disappeared.

The way the trick works is this: Attach a coin to the soaped side of the disk ahead of time. Hold the coin (and disk hidden behind it) at your right fingertips. Show it to the audience (your fingers and hands hide the elastic cord). Place the disk on your right trouser leg. Your left hand pulls some fabric over the coin. The right fingers release the coin and it flies up your sleeve.

CONCENTRATION-POWER

This trick is best performed at a party or with a group of friends. Preplan by selecting the initials of one of the people who will be attending. Write the initials on a two-inch-square piece of paper. Fold it into quarters and hide it by tucking it behind the sweatband of the hat you will be wearing that night. Remember to have several dozen more identical pieces of paper with you when you go to the party.

Once at the party, pick an appropriate time and start discussing the power of mass concentration. Tell everyone how you've been able to receive short messages when a group of people concentrate on them collectively. Say that, for instance, in a roomful of people such as this, you can receive a set of initials, if enough people think of them at the same time.

Suggest that everyone call out his own initials, one at a time, while you write them down, each on different slips of paper. Fold all the slips of paper in quarters and put them into your hat. Have someone shake the hat and, without looking, pick one out. The one you pick, of course, is the one you have hidden under the sweatband. Hand that slip, still sight unseen, to the group and ask them all to read and concentrate on those, and only those, initials. Tell them you will not only receive the initials but will make them appear in a strange and mysterious fashion.

Insist dramatically that they put the piece of paper with the initials on it into a nearby ash tray and burn it! As they are burning it, roll up your right sleeve. Ask one of them to take some of the ashes from the ash tray and rub them on the underpart of your right arm. As the ashes are applied to your arm, the correct initials will mysteriously appear there.

Impossible? No. Simple. Just before you left for the party, you wrote the preselected initials on the underpart of your right arm, using the edge of a thin piece of soap. The ashes will adhere to the soaped areas, thus causing the initials to appear.

SQUEEZED OUT OF SIGHT

This trick requires a small glass, a small, hard sponge-rubber ball that will fit tightly into the mouth of the glass, a piece of black elastic cord about twenty to twenty-four inches long, and a mirror to practice in front of. The practice is well worth doing, for this can be an unusually impressive trick, one that will truly mystify your audience. Attach one end of the elastic to the rubber ball and the other end to a safety pin. Attach the safety pin to the lining of your jacket just under the right shoulder. Adjust the length of the cord so that the rubber ball hangs three inches above the bottom of your jacket, out of sight of your audience.

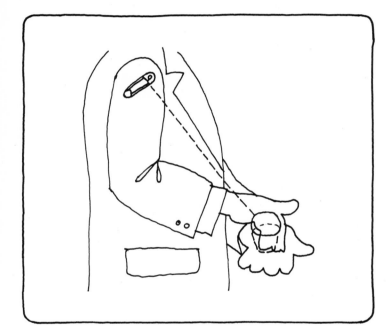

Secretly take hold of the ball with your right hand. Hold it with your second finger pressing the ball into your palm. Pick up the glass partially filled with liquid in your left hand. Press the ball into the mouth of the glass with your right hand. Lower your hands while doing this and hide the ball with the back of your right hand. Cup your left hand under the glass and your right hand on top. Pretend to squeeze the glass between your hands but actually release the glass and the elastic will snap the ball and the attached glass back under your jacket out of sight. Open your hands wide and hold them up so everyone can see that they are—empty. The glass and its contents have been squeezed into oblivion.

PSYCHIC COMMUNICATION

Introduce this trick by saying that you have mastered the mysterious process of psychic communication. Ask members of the group to lend you three specific items, such as a pen, a key, and a ring. Set these on a table and ask someone to touch one of the three items while you are out of the room.

When you are called back into the room, ask if anyone has a pencil. As soon as you are given a pencil, take out a sheet of paper and write down the name of the item that was touched while you were out of the room. You do this quickly, acting as if thought-waves are your only aid—or so it appears to the audience.

The truth is the person who happened to have a pencil to lend you is your accomplice. The two of you have assigned a code to each item beforehand. He has three pencils of appreciably different lengths, each pencil assigned to one of the three items. Your partner hands you the pencil assigned to the selected item. You now know which is the correct name to write. After each demonstration, you return the pencil to your accomplice. When the act is repeated and another item is chosen, your audience will not see that your accomplice hands you a different pencil.

JUST PASSING THROUGH

Hold up a handkerchief to the audience and show them both sides. Tell them the handkerchief has an invisible hole in it somewhere near its center. Invite the audience to inspect the handkerchief. After everyone admits they cannot see the hole, offer to prove the hole exists by passing a coin through it.

Ask someone in the audience to lend you a coin, preferably a quarter. Have them mark the coin in some way, with a crayon or marking pencil perhaps. Take the marked coin and hold it straight up in your left hand so that everyone can see you are holding it only by its bottom edge. Using your right hand, drape the open handkerchief over the coin, making sure that the center of the handkerchief covers the top of the coin. Let the handkerchief fall over the coin so that half the handkerchief falls forward toward the audience and the back half falls on your left hand, behind the coin. The left thumb takes a nip in the cloth of the handkerchief behind the coin.

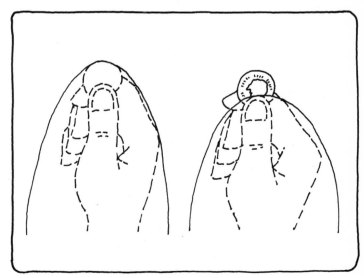

Pause for a few seconds. Then use your right hand to pull back the front half of the handkerchief toward your body, showing the coin to the audience again and proving that it hasn't disappeared in any devious manner. As you show the coin this time, both halves of the handkerchief are lying on your left hand.

Having satisfied the audience that the coin is indeed still there, raise your left hand and wrist over, throwing both halves of the handkerchief forward in front of the coin. From that position it will appear as if you had returned only the front half of the handkerchief to its original position. Actually you have thrown both halves over and are now holding the coin under a double fold of the handkerchief.

With the help of your right hand, slowly, teasingly, work the coin up into view. To the audience it will seem to be emerging from a hole in the center of the handkerchief. Continue to do this until most of the coin shows. Then pluck the coin up with your right hand, and offer both the coin and the handkerchief to the audience for their inspection.

SELECT ANY CARD AT ALL

For this trick you will need a pack of playing cards with a picture or an asymmetrical design on the back. Before you do the trick, arrange the entire deck so that the designs on the backs of the cards all face in the same direction.

Have someone select a card from the deck. While he is looking at it, turn the deck around end for end. When the card is inserted into the deck, the selected card will be the only one with its back design turned around the opposite way from all of the other cards.

Keep shuffling until you've established that the cards have been well mixed. Hold the deck facedown in your hand, and deal one card at a time from the top of the deck onto the table faceup. Watch for the card with the reversed back design. When it appears, throw it out with a dramatic gesture—proof that you have successfully fulfilled your promise.

In case the only deck of cards available has a symmetrical design on the back, simply square the deck tightly beforehand, and mark one of the short ends with several up-and-down pencil marks. The trick remains the same, except that now you look for the break in the pencil marks to show you which card was selected by your volunteer.

THE MATCHBOOK FLIP

Here is a trick whose very simplicity will help to confound your victim. Using only an empty matchbook, with nothing up your sleeve or anywhere else, you make the matchbook turn a flip in the air; but when someone else tries to get the same result by copying your simple maneuver, he will fail every time.

The secret of the trick is in plain view, and for that very reason it goes unnoticed. Bend the closed matchbook so that its front and back covers together form a single gentle curve. Stand it on a table upside down with the striking surface at the top. Press lightly on the top of the matchbook with one finger and give it the order to turn a flip. Helped by a slight downward push of your finger, the

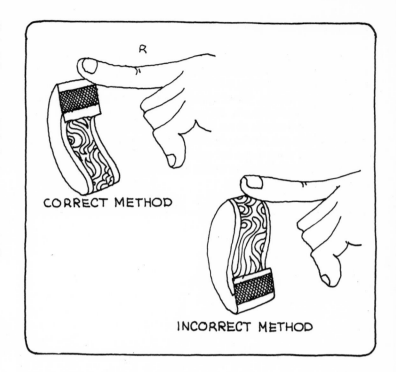

CORRECT METHOD

INCORRECT METHOD

matchbook will neatly carry out your command.

Tell your audience that you believe none of them can duplicate this effect. When someone comes forward to challenge you, place the matchbook in front of him on the table—right side up, with the striking surface at the bottom. To prevent him from turning the matchbook over, keep your finger on top of it until his finger is in position for the attempt. His confidence will be rewarded by a flop, not a flip; now that the matchbook is resting on its heavy end, it has lost its acrobatic talents.

THE MULTIPLE CARD-FINDER

If you follow this method, you will unfailingly locate any card a volunteer removes from your deck and replaces—without ever seeing the card's face.

Prepare the deck in advance. Disregarding suit, place all of the odd-numbered cards (kings, jacks, nines, sevens, fives, threes, and aces) together in the top half of the deck. Collect all of the cards with even numbers (queens, tens, eights, sixes, fours, and twos) in the bottom half of the deck. Holding the entire deck of cards in your hands, spread out the top half containing the odd cards and have one card selected.

While the volunteer is looking at his card, continue fanning the cards out in your two hands so that when he is ready to reinsert his card into the deck, the bottom of the deck containing the even cards is in front of him. He will slip his card into this bottom half of the deck.

Square up the cards. Have the deck cut several times. Pick up the deck and fan them out facing you. Look for the odd card among the even cards and produce it—triumphantly.

LIGHTER THAN AIR

Tell everyone in the room that you have discovered a means of defying the law of gravity. Say that by force of concentration alone you have succeeded in restraining unbalanced objects from falling. Demonstrate with a pack of cigarettes you have prepared in advance and placed in your shirt pocket.

To get the pack ready, take out all of the cigarettes and put five or six pennies into the empty pack, letting them rest on their flat sides at the bottom. So that the pack will appear full to the audience, insert just enough cigarettes to fill the opening where the foil has been torn away. Leave one cigarette slightly protruding from the pack so that you can easily take hold of it. After making your claim to have mastered the laws of nature, casually bring the prepared pack out of your pocket. Place the package on a table, aligning its opened top with the table edge, and then pause briefly to give the effect of serious concentration.

Announce that you are ready to challenge the laws of nature, and begin to withdraw the slightly protruding cigarette from the pack. To prevent a tell-tale jingle of coins, do this without tapping the pack at the bottom or on the side. As you bring the cigarette forward gingerly, it will pull the pack along behind it. When approximately three-quarters of the pack is hanging out over the edge of the table, gently remove your cigarette from the pack. The pack, which now appears to be lighter than air, is prevented from falling by the weight of the pennies, confounding all believers in gravity.

STANDING A DRINK

Everyone knows the old trick of balancing an egg on its end by hardboiling it first and slightly crushing the tip, but you will outdo this feat by far when you demonstrate your ability to balance a full

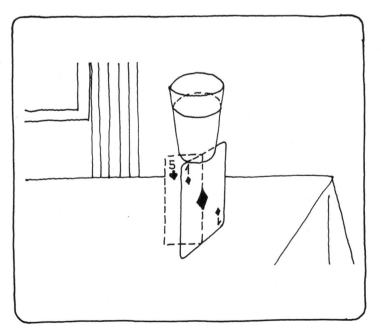

glass of water on the edge of a card that is itself mysteriously balanced.

To prepare, you must fix a stable base for the glass of water. Take a card and bend it lengthwise exactly in half. Then carefully glue the front of one half of the card to the back of another card, press the loose half flush against the second card (see diagram), and place this double card at the bottom of the deck.

Stand back a distance from your audience and use a table whose height and angle will make it impossible for the audience to see the special easeled card you are using. Shuffle the deck, taking care not to disturb the special flapped card. When you are finished shuffling, pull out the prepared card and hold it upright on the table, concealing its face while moving the flap out with your thumb until it lies at a right angle to the unbent card. Position the card so that it stands between the audience and you.

Now, with all of the facial concentration you can muster, pick up a nearby tumbler filled with water and place it atop the card(s) so that its bottom is centered on the point where the loose flap meets the face of the front card. It stands, apparently on the edge of a single card. While the audience is still recovering from their surprise, you remove the glass, straighten the flap, and insert the double card back into the deck.

BEFORE INFLATION

Here's a fast follow-up to any other trick involving the use of a pencil.

Pull out a dollar bill and fold it in half lengthwise. Pretend to attack the pencil with the folded bill. Act as if you really wanted to break the pencil in half. After several futile attempts, turn to the audience and insist that the bill could break the pencil if only the pencil weren't resting on a surface. Say that you know you could break it if someone would pick the pencil up and hold it by both ends, giving you a crack at its vulnerable middle.

Ask a volunteer to stand directly in front of you so that you get a direct hit at the pencil. Strike the pencil with the folded edge of the dollar bill several times. Let your frustration visibly grow until finally you hit the pencil once again, really hard, and sucessfully break it in half.

The trick is simple. Just insert your index finger into the crease of the folded dollar bill immediately before your final strike. Bring your finger down hard and sharp, across the center of the pencil, and it will break.

MAGAZINE CHARMER

In this trick you will appear to charm a magazine that is rolled around a double string into moving up and down, while you touch only the ends of the string.

To prepare for your mysterious demonstration, roll the magazine into the shape of a tube. With paper clips, fasten the tube securely together at the top and the bottom. Take a piece of string about four feet long, double it, and drop the loop into the end of the tube that will face the floor during your performance. Hook the loop over the bottom paper clip and let the ends of the string fall freely out the bottom of the tube.

Take one end of another four-foot-long piece of string and pass it into the tube through the opening at the top; run it under the string hooked to the paper clip and back out through the top of the tube. You now have what looks like one double string running clear through the magazine (see diagrams).

Begin your performance with the magazine at the lower end of its run; the string that is hooked onto the paper clip will then cross the loop of the other string close to the top of the tube. Take care that you do not make the clipped string visible to the audience by pulling it too far toward the magazine's upper end. By pulling on the

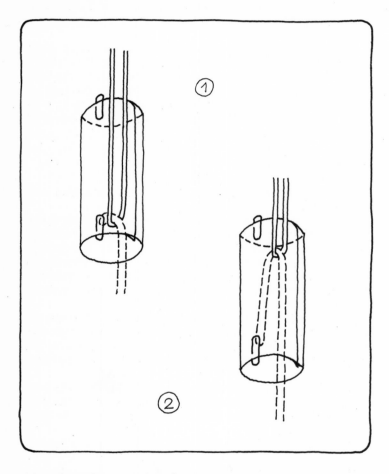

strings from the top and the bottom, the magazine will rise. If you pull on the upper string and the lower string is relaxed, and you ever so slowly allow your hands to come slightly together, the magazine will descend.

BEATING THE SHELL GAME

Money disappears readily enough in the ordinary course of things, but with this trick, you will be able to find an invisible nickel.

Place a nickel on a light-colored mat or cloth. Then produce three small paper or plastic cups that will fit snugly over the coin; cream containers for individual cups of coffee are about the right size. Tell a volunteer to hide the nickel under one of the cups while you are out of the room. When you return, hold a finger in the air just above each cup (pretending that you can feel "vibrations" from the coin through the cup). At the same time you look for the hair. After a few seconds point to the one that is covering the coin.

How does it work? Beforehand you have glued to one side of the nickel a dark hair long enough to protrude beyond the rim of the cup when the nickel is covered by it. When you put the nickel down on the table, make sure the hair is on its underside. You, and not the audience, will spot the hair protruding from under the correct cup.

SEEING HANDS

Announce that your nose can correctly pick out any specific brand of cigarette, even when mixed up along with other various brands. Offer to demonstrate its unusual capacity by collecting a half-dozen cigarettes, each one of a different brand, from the people in the room. Ask a volunteer to name any one of these brands, and declare that your nose will be able to single out the specified brand while a blindfold prevents your seeing the cigarette your nose is smelling.

After the volunteer makes his choice, drop the cigarettes one by one into a bowl. If there are filter tips among the cigarettes, pick them up by the end opposite the filter. As you take the selected cigarette between your fingers, gently and unnoticeably squeeze it at the end, thus flattening it slightly so that you will be able to feel this alteration in shape when you have the blindfold on (or bend the center of the cigarette slightly).

When the cigarettes are all in the bowl, ask someone to tie a folded handkerchief or scarf over your eyes. Then bring each cigarette up to your nose and smell it—until you come to the one whose tip you flattened or whose center you bent. Hold this cigarette up proudly and announce its brand name. Your audience will credit your nose with 20:20 smellavision.

THE IMPOSSIBLE KNOT

Take out a large men's handkerchief. Dare anyone in the audience to tie a knot in the center of the handkerchief while holding two opposite corners, one in each hand. Regardless of how many people try, they will find it impossible to do.

Announce that you alone can tie the impossible knot, and proceed as follows: lay the handkerchief down flat on a table, with one of its corners pointed toward you. Use diagonally opposite corners of the handkerchief.

Cross arms by putting right hand on top of left upper arm; then tuck left hand over the right arm and in under the right elbow. Pick up the opposite corners of the handkerchief, one in each hand, hold them securely, and unfold your arms. This automatically ties a knot in the handkerchief without letting go of the corners.

CHANGING ACES

Here's a very simple but effective trick. Prepare a deck of cards, all facedown, with the ace of spades on top and the ace of hearts directly under it. Remember, all the cards must be facedown. Announce that you're prepared to demonstrate a unique technique for changing the suit of a playing card.

Take out the prepared deck of cards, turn the top card over, and show the audience that it is the ace of spades. Place the card back on top of the deck but this time let it face up. Tell the audience that by simply throwing the deck of cards down on the floor, you will change the ace of spades into the ace of hearts right before their very eyes.

Just before throwing the deck down to the floor, push the top two cards—the ace of spades, now faceup and the ace of hearts, facedown—over the side of the deck about a half inch. Air pressure will force the two top cards to turn completely over. The ace of hearts will land on top of the deck faceup, while the ace of spades will land facedown with the rest of the deck. To the audience it will look as if the ace of spades changed into the ace of hearts in mid-air.

It's important to remember to throw the pack down firmly, but not too hard. Practice this throw by yourself several times before performing the trick in front of an audience.

TOUCH-UP

Lay five quarters on top of a table and challenge anyone to move the five quarters around until each quarter is touching each of the other quarters.

Most people will find the solution difficult because we all tend to

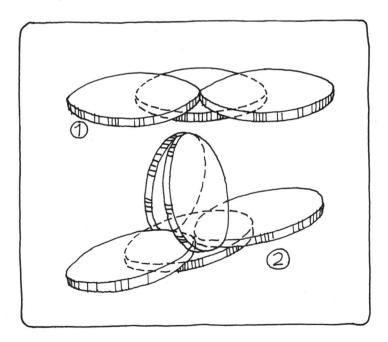

move the quarters in a flat plane. To solve this puzzle, however, one must consider all three dimensions.

First place one quarter down flat on the tabletop. Lay two quarters on top of this quarter, one to the left and one to the right of the base quarter, with the inside edges of both top quarters touching each other just above the center of the bottom quarter.

You now have three quarters, each touching one another. The one at the bottom touches the two above it and the two above it touch each other where they meet in the center (see diagram 1).

Now for the clincher—you take to the air. Prop the fourth and fifth quarters in the two arcs of space remaining on the bottom quarter between the two touching quarters. Remember to prop these last two quarters forward so that they rest on the bottom quarter, touch the already-touching second and third quarters, and meet and touch each other.

It's hard to visualize, so study the accompanying diagrams for clarification.

THE RABBIT RUBBER BAND

You can perform a simple, yet amusing feat with just an ordinary rubber band. As you take the rubber band out, tell the audience you own a rubber band that can't seem to make up its own mind—it keeps darting about trying to find a comfortable set of fingers.

Hold up your left hand with all the fingers extended, palm toward you, and place the rubber band over your index and middle fingers. The rubber band should be large enough to encompass all four fingers in a snug fit, so that when it is on only two fingers, the excess will fall into the palm of your hand.

Slap the part of the rubber band lying in the palm of your hand twice as you say, "Now will you stay here or what?" As you give it a final slap, bring all fingers down towards your palm, and slip the rubber band lying in your palm over the tops of all four fingers. Do this quickly, pause, and then straighten out the four fingers to their original position—the rubber band will now be encircling the other two fingers of that hand.

ESCAPING BOX

For this trick you need nimble fingers and the kind of cardboard container in which kitchen-type wooden matches are sold. With the proper preparation, the match box will appear to the audience to slip free of a string you have run beneath its outside cover.

You will find that the cover of the match box is fastened on one of the sides of the box, where two layers of cardboard are glued together. After removing the drawer from the box, your job consists of pulling these layers apart and then sticking them back together with chewing gum spotted strategically so that the side of the box is closed and will not resist a light pull on the outer layer.

In front of your audience, produce the apparently perfect match box with its drawer in place. Remove the drawer and run a long piece of string through the box, letting about ten inches of string protrude from each end. Replace the drawer and tell the audience that you will now coerce the match box into slipping off the string, without either breaking the string or moving the drawer.

Ask someone to hold the ends of the string. Then place a scarf over the match box. Reach under the scarf and quickly pull the outer layer of the cover away from the inner layer, thus creating an

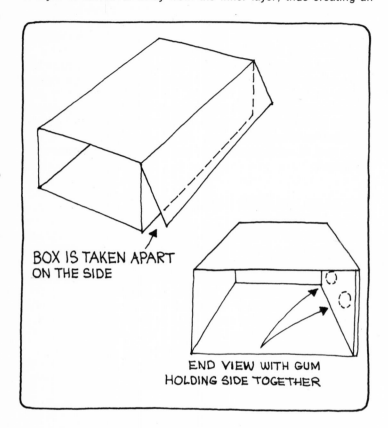

BOX IS TAKEN APART ON THE SIDE

END VIEW WITH GUM HOLDING SIDE TOGETHER

opening in the side of the box. Move the drawer just far enough to let the string pass out through the opening, and then reattach the two layers. Whisk the scarf away and let your audience observe the uncut string and the intact match box.

THE PAPER BRIDGE

This trick requires three ordinary drinking glasses, an 8½-by-11-inch sheet of plain paper, plus a bit of ingenuity.

Place two of the glasses about five inches apart, lay the sheet of paper on top of them, and challenge anyone to place the third glass in the center of the piece of paper without having if fall off. The trick is to turn the sheet of paper into a bridge strong enough to hold the glass.

When everyone has given up, simply pick up the sheet of paper and fold it, lengthwise, in as many accordion pleats as you can make. The folds will reinforce the strength of the paper. Place the paper back on top of the two glasses, and set the third glass on the paper bridge, which is now sufficiently sturdy to carry the weight.

THE BURNING QUESTION

This trick calls for a highly dramatic presentation. Inform your audience that after much experimentation you have finally perfected the ability to read and answer any written question—sight unseen!

Produce a piece of paper 3″ × 3″. Draw a circle 1½″ in diameter in its center and hand it to a volunteer, who will test your ability by writing down a secret question. Explain that it is necessary for him to write the question inside the circle; otherwise the words turn fuzzy and indistinct before they can be fully transmitted to your mind.

Make a point of looking away from him as he writes down his question. When he's finished, ask him to fold the paper in half (with the question on the inside), and then in half again in the other direction so that the question is completely hidden from your view. Take the folded sheet from him and rip it in half. Surreptitiously place the

piece containing the circle at the bottom and tear the paper in half again the other way. Palm the section containing the circle in your right hand and tear the remaining pieces of paper once or twice again.

Walk over to an ash tray, which you have placed beforehand in a far corner of the room or stage. Throw the scraps of paper into it and put a match to them. Turn your body away from the audience slightly and gaze into the flame. Open the hand containing the encircled question, unfold it, and read the question quickly. Don't worry about getting the question letter-perfect; all you need is its gist. Quickly think up a fitting answer and deliver it to the mystified audience.

The reason the trick works is because of the way the paper was folded. The first tear tore off only the blank top and bottom of the sheet, leaving the piece with the question in the center. The second tear tore off only the blank sides, leaving you with the encircled question to palm and later read.

LET FREEDOM RING

Hold up the ring you are wearing and talk about its very unusual quality. At this point, take out a piece of string about twenty-four inches long, and pass it around so that the audience has a chance to inspect it. When it has been examined by several people, remove

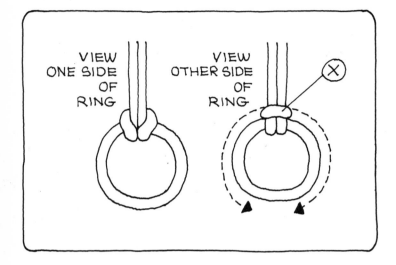

your ring from your finger and also send it around for inspection. When both the string and the ring have been returned to you, fold the string in half and run the ends of the string through the ring. Then bring the ends of the string over the outside of the ring and through the loop formed by the center of the string. Tighten the string on the ring. It will look something like a knot on the ring (see diagram). Hold the string by the two ends, letting the ring held by the "loop-knot" dangle in the air, above the floor.

Ask for as many rings as the audience will volunteer. As each ring is offered to you, place the ring's center opening over the two string ends held by your hand at the top. Use your fingers to bring the ring down the length of string gently, until it rests on top of your ring. Repeat this for each additional ring offered, resting each new ring on top of the others.

After you have carefully piled all the rings on top of your ring, ask someone to hold the two string ends at the top, thus preventing your ring from using the only possible escape route.

Take out a large handkerchief and drape it over the bottom section of the string, containing all the rings. Slip your hand under the handkerchief and shortly withdraw it—holding all of the rings.

This trick is impressive yet its secret is simple: The loop-knot around your ring is really a type of slip knot. Study the diagrams and you will see that once your hand is under the handkerchief, you simply pull to one side the string that runs across the ring (see X on diagram), and it will slide around and out of the ring allowing all the rings to fall freely into your cupped hand.

THE RESTORATION

Take out a sheet of cigarette paper (this is easily obtained in any tobacco shop). Hold it up in your left hand and snap it once or twice to establish that it is only a single piece of paper. Then tear it in half by ripping it once across in either direction. Hold up each half in different hands to prove you have really torn it. Put the two pieces together, one on top of the other, and rip them in half again and then again.

Gather the pieces together, press them into a small ball, and slowly unravel it before the people's eyes—into its original untorn state.

This interesting sleight of hand requires an identical piece of cigarette paper and some practice. Before starting the trick, roll the second sheet of cigarette paper into a similarly shaped ball and place it between your right index and middle fingers; it remains hidden between those two fingers as you rip up the other cigarette paper in front of the audience. As you roll the torn pieces together into a ball, press the prepared ball against the torn paper ball. Pressed tightly together the two balls will seem to be one. Lift your right hand to your lips as if to moisten them before opening the whole paper, and secretly put the ripped paper ball into your mouth under cover of your right-hand fingers.

Once the ball of torn paper is in your mouth, return your right hand to the prepared ball now waiting in your left hand, and slowly, using both hands, unfold the "restored" cigarette paper.

SPECIAL DELIVERY

This impressive trick is done with a business card that has had a hole punched out of its center, a small envelope that has also had a

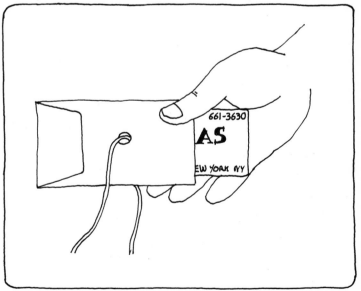

hole punched through it, and a piece of string about 2 feet in length. The envelope should be only slightly larger than the business card and of the type that has its flap located at one of the narrow ends. In advance, make a clean razor slit through the end of the envelope opposite the flap.

Take the envelope in your left hand. Hold it so that you conceal from the audience the end of the envelope with the slit in it. Insert the business card through the regular flap opening, and surreptitiously push it down through the slit until half its length ends up hidden in the palm of your left hand (see diagram). Lick the gummed flap and seal the envelope.

Announce that you are going to thread both the card and the envelope onto the string. Push the string through the holes of the envelope and supposedly through the card as well. Actually, because of the card's position, the string will not touch it at all. After you have run the string through the envelope, use your right thumb to push the protruding card back inside the envelope. The card will push the center of the string ahead of it, deep into the envelope.

Ask for two volunteers to hold the opposite ends of the string. Tear off the slit end of the envelope and pull out the card, free from the string but still intact. Place the torn-off slit end of the envelope into your pocket. Leave the envelope threaded on the string held by the volunteers. Allow the audience to examine the card, envelope, and string. By tearing off the slit end of the envelope you have eliminated any telltale evidence of the modus operandi.

A SIMPLE ESCAPE

Here's a simple trick, one that you might use to entertain youngsters after dinner. Clear off a space in front of you and ask the young people to watch as you set up the trick. Promise that you will show them how it's done—unless one of them can do it first.

Take out three coins—two fifty-cent pieces and one dime—and pass them around so that everyone can see for themselves that they are not trick coins. Get an empty glass and put it on the tablecloth at your side while they are inspecting the three coins.

When everyone has agreed that the three coins are ordinary, place the two fifty-cent pieces down on the tablecloth in front of you, with about an inch of space between the two coins. Place the dime on the table in the space left between the two fifty-cent pieces. Turn the glass over, placing the rim of the glass on top of both fifty-cent pieces.

Now deliver the challenge: ask them to remove the dime from beneath the glass—without touching any of the three coins or the glass.

Their attempts will vary, often producing laughter and frustration, but they will not succeed. When they've given up, show them the simple solution. Put the nail of your right index finger on the tablecloth directly in front of the glass in a direct line with the dime, and scratch at the tablecloth. This scratching will make the dime move slowly towards you until it has completely escaped from beneath the glass.

ONE-HAND KNOT

With three simple movements of one hand, you can dramatically tie a knot in the middle of a piece of rope.

Drape a short length of rope over your right hand, running it up between your fourth and little fingers, then across your palm, and finally over the base of your index finger so that it drops behind your hand at a spot above the crotch of your thumb.

With the rope in this position (see diagrams), reach down

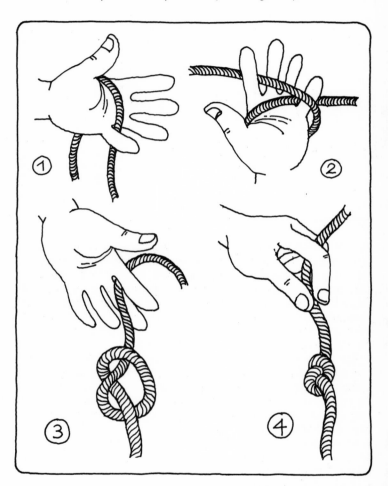

quickly, with your right hand to scoop up the end of rope that hangs from the back of your hand. Catch this end of the rope between your middle and index fingers. Then turn your palm down and shake loose the end of the rope that is pinched between your fourth and little fingers; this motion will form a slack knot in the middle of the rope. Bring your thumb over the end you are holding and give the rope a sharp snap. The knot will pull tight, and your agility will be much admired.

NO NEED FOR SHERLOCK HOLMES

You pick up a glass, hold it in the air, and claim that it can speak to you. Pass it around as you continue talking, so that everyone can see for themselves that it looks like an ordinary glass.

Ask that any small object—a ring, a wristwatch, or a key case—be put on the table. Place the glass alongside it, so that the bottom of the glass touches the object, but just barely. Announce that you will leave the room and that while you are gone, someone should pocket the object. When you come back in, you will ask each person to touch the glass—and the glass will then tell you who it was that pocketed the object.

Leave the room and wait to be called back in. Once you are back in the room, walk over, turn the glass over, and stare at it dramatically. Ask each person in the room to touch the top of the glass. After everyone has touched the glass, approach the person who pocketed the object and point to him.

The trick requires a confederate, who is in the room all the time. When you have each person touch the top of the glass, your confederate subtly manages to touch the glass immediately after the person who pocketed the object. With this clue, you are easily able to point him out.

NO HOLDING POWER

Remove a pencil from the outside top pocket of your jacket with your left hand and bring it forward toward the audience, holding it vertically by the point at the bottom of the pencil. Say that you can make the pencil stand in midair after removing your left hand— by placing two fingers against, not holding, the top of the pencil.

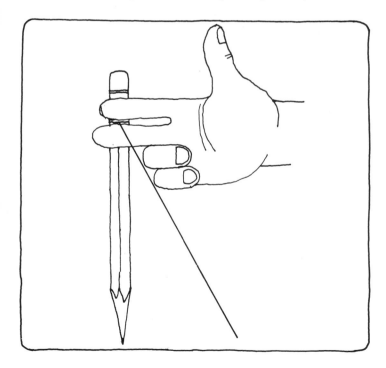

Bring your right hand forward and slowly place the backs of your index and middle fingers against the pencil top facing you. Once those two fingers are positioned there, obviously unable to hold the pencil up by themselves, slowly allow your left hand to release its hold on the pencil point.

Watch everyone's amazement as the pencil continues to hang in midair. Since the two fingers of your right hand are simply resting against one side of the pencil top, they have absolutely no holding power—yet the pencil continues to just stand there, in the middle of the air.

To perform this trick successfully, you must wear a very dark jacket, use a very dark pencil, and have worked with a very dark piece of thread beforehand. Before putting the pencil in your jacket pocket, fasten one end of the thread to the underside of your right-hand lapel with the aid of a small safety pin. Form a loop in the other end of the thread and put the loop around the top of the pencil, leaving about seventeen inches of slack between the lapel and the pocketed pencil. Allow the slack thread to just fall against your jacket.

When you first bring the pencil out of your jacket pocket, move it forward toward the audience until the entire length of thread is taut, pulled from your lapel to its midair position. When you place the fingers of your right hand against the pencil top, simply slip your fingers on either side of the thread, tightly holding the thread between them. Then, when you remove your left hand, the full length of thread is held taut and applies enough pressure to continue holding the pencil up in midair. The two fingers just anchor the thread so the pencil won't fall down.

CHANGING COLORS

Ask to borrow a hat from someone in the audience. Take three cards out of your pocket and show the color of each card as you gently drop it into the hat. Show and insert first a white card, then a blue card, and finally a black card.

Don't touch the cards; just stare into the hat for a few seconds. Then, rolling up your sleeves, put your right hand into the hat and lift out one card timidly with the tips of your fingers. Show it to the audience; it's the blue card. Put it into your pocket.

Slowly slip your hand into the hat again and lift up the second card. Let both of its sides be seen as you show it to the audience. It's the white card. Put it into your pocket.

Now, put your hands on your hips and stare down into the hat, as you ask the audience, "Which color card is still in the hat?" They will of course, answer, "Black."

Shake your head as you pull out—a blue card. Show the audience that both its sides are blue. If the audience now insists on seeing the two cards in your pocket, take two cards out and show both sides of both of them. One is white on both sides, the other is black on both sides.

Impossible? Not really—since, unbeknownst to the audience, you've had four cards all the time.

Before beginning the trick, you had secreted one extra card in your pocket. The card is black on both sides. The three other cards you pull out are: a two-sided white card, a two-sided blue card, and a third card that has one blue side and one black side. When you put this card into the hat you only show its black side; when you pull it out, you only show its blue side. When the audience asks to see the two cards you put into your pocket, you pull out the two-sided white card and the unused, two-sided black card. This last card is the extra card that's been in your pocket all along and that you switched with the blue/black card as you pocketed it.

E S P?

Two people are needed to perform this diverting trick. One announces that the two of them have recently discovered that they are endowed with an unusual rapport, extrasensory perception or ESP. They have been testing themselves and are amazed by this ability to mentally transmit words, thoughts, and especially numbers to each other.

To prove it, one leaves the room while the other remains and is given a two- or three-digit number by a member of the audience to transmit by telepathy. Both the partners are blindfolded. Before the first man is called back into the room, his partner turns his chair around dramatically, placing his back to the audience.

The man outside is led back into the room and over to his seated colleague. He puts the fingertips of both hands on his partner's temples, concentrates for a short time, and then calls out clearly the correct number.

The secret of this trick is that the number is transmitted simply by having the seated person clench his jaw the proper number of times. The number twenty-seven, for instance, would call for a clench, then a clench, then a pause; then seven clenches. One to nine are easy, but don't forget to agree that zero calls for ten clenches in a row.

FOUR CARDS IN ONE

Using a special card with unusual arrangements of round spots on both of its sides, you can give your audience the impression that you are manipulating a card that actually has four sides. The card is marked exactly as diagram 1 shows: the sides carry two and five spots, respectively.

After holding one side of the card up to the audience, you then turn it around in your hand in a sequence of moves, and the card will appear to reveal four sides that are marked in order: a one-spot, a four, a three, and a six (see diagram 2). During this operation your fingers are cleverly positioned to conceal, as required, either spots or empty spaces.

First, the side showing two spots is exhibited; the lower spot is hidden by your fingers, and the audience perceives the card to have one spot. Flipping the card over carefully, you cover the middle spot on the right half of the side carrying five spots, and the card appears to have four spots.

In each of your next two movements, you must both turn the card over front to back and reverse it top to bottom. With the two spots in the upper half of the card and your finger covering the blank space at the bottom, it seems to have three spots. On your

final turn you hide the blank area in the left center of the side with five spots, so that the card apears to have six spots. Precise manipulation is the key to this effect, and you will need to practice before a mirror until you can almost convince yourself that you are holding a strange four-sided card.

THE TRAVELING MAGIC BALL

Here's a trick that you can perform with a minimum of preparation. It can be done either by yourself or with the aid of a friend. The trick is best presented before a group of people sitting around a table covered with a tablecloth. This is ideal to do after dinner.

Prepare for this trick beforehand by obtaining a strong thread or string, and tie the end of the string to a ring about the size of a key ring. Place this ring near the center of the table, under the tablecloth, and have the string run across the table, also under the cloth, so that its end is near your partner, who is seated at the opposite side of the table.

Announce to the group that you have a magic ball. Produce a golf ball or a small wooden ball and place it over the center of the concealed ring. Staring at it with a fixed look, order it to move. Move it does, as your partner pulls the string, because it is riding on the unseen ring.

The ball will move away from you and toward your partner. If you are doing the trick alone, simply run the string under the table, and back to where your hand can pull it.

If someone insists on examining the ball before the trick is completed, tell them to feel free to do so but warn them that this will break the spell. As soon as you lift the ball to give to a spectator to examine, the string should be pulled out the rest of the way from under the tablecloth, leaving no evidence of the ring that actually moved the ball.

ACE PERFORMANCE

Holding a man's soft hat, ask a volunteer to shuffle a deck of cards and return them to you. Drop the cards into the hat, holding it at arm's length to prove to the audience that you can't see inside it. Shake the hat thoroughly to scramble the cards, and announce that you are going to reach in and come up with all four aces.

An instant's sleight of hand does the trick. In advance, fasten the four aces together with a small paper clip and stick them in the sweatband of the hat. Place the hat with its brim down on a table or chair. Have the deck of cards shuffled. Then pick up the hat, turn it brim uppermost, hold the hat above everyone's eye level, and ask the volunteer to reach up and drop the deck into the hat.

After the rest of the cards have been mixed in the hat, reach under the sweatband, remove the clip, and bring out the four aces, leaving the clip hidden inside of the sweatband.

WHOLE AGAIN

Sew a one-fourth-inch hem on each of the four sides of a dark-colored handkerchief, concealing a toothpick inside one of the four hemmed sides (be sure the hem is closely stitched). Hold the top two corners in your hands, and show both sides of the handkerchief to your audience. Place a toothpick in the center of the handkerchief. Fold the handkerchief in half and then in half once again (be sure both folds are made in the same direction). Now fold the handkerchief once more, but this time in the opposite direction.

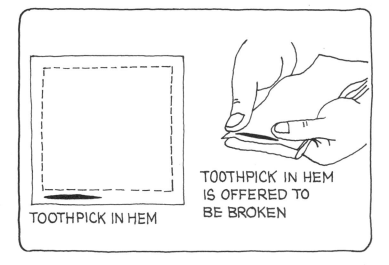

TOOTHPICK IN HEM

TOOTHPICK IN HEM IS OFFERED TO BE BROKEN

Holding the toothpick in the handkerchief's folds, offer it to a volunteer and ask him to break the toothpick in half, even in thirds. After he has done this, take back the handkerchief, say a few magic words, and shake open the handkerchief—the toothpick, still intact, will fall to the table.

The secret to the trick is the duplicate toothpick you have concealed beforehand inside the hem of the handkerchief. After you fold the handkerchief, you offer your volunteer the toothpick hidden in the hem to break, not the one folded inside the handkerchief; that one falls out whole when you shake open the handkerchief.

TALENTED TOE

In this trick you perform the remarkable feat of cutting a deck of cards with your toe in order to locate a card selected in secret by a volunteer.

While you are facing away, a volunteer shuffles the deck thoroughly and then cuts it into four separate stacks, which are laid out in a row on a table. He then chooses a single card from the middle of one of the stacks, makes a mental note of its suit and number, and places it at the top of any stack. What you do when facing away from the audience is to reach into one of your pockets, where you have previously dropped a small portion of salt, and take a bit of salt between your thumb and forefinger.

Approach the table and ask your volunteer to point out the stack with his card at the top. After he points to his stack, ask that that pile be placed on top of another pile. Then ask that a third pile be placed on top of the selected card. As you instruct him to do this, bring your hand (holding a very, very small pinch of salt) over his selected card and surreptitiously drop the salt on his card as you gesture in instructing him to place the third pile on top of his card. Finally have the fourth pile placed on top of all the cards. Then have the deck placed on the floor.

When you give the end of the deck a sharp kick with the toe of your shoe, the presence of the salt will cause the cards to divide so as to leave the volunteer's card at the top of the lower part of the deck on the floor.

ONE DOLLAR AND TEN CENTS

Tell the audience that you know how to use money to make money. Ask for a collective (and temporary) contribution of ten one-dollar bills. Lay the bills out on a table, with their green sides showing and the portraits of Washington turned down. Approach the table with your secret weapon—a dime concealed in your right hand.

Tell a volunteer to take one of the bills from the table, copy its serial number, and then turn the dollar over and hand it to you. Take the bill and quickly crumple it, letting the dime slip down from your hand into the folds. Wad the bill around the dime and place it in a bowl.

Then crumple and wad the other nine bills, taking care not to make them noticeably smaller than the one in which the coin is concealed. Place them in the bowl with the first bill and shake the bowl a few times to scramble the bills.

With an air of concentration, handle all of the bills before you finally pick up the right one, which you will find when you feel the coin through the paper. As you unfold the bill, let the dime fall into your hand with a flourish and read aloud the bill's serial number.

LOOP THE LOOP

Bore a small hole just below the eraser of a new, unsharpened pencil. Run a piece of string through the hole (a needle will help you push it through) and tie the string into a loop by making a knot. Make sure that the loop, when fully extended, is slightly shorter than the length of the pencil (see diagram).

You now need a willing victim, one wearing a jacket. Place the loop over your right hand so that the pencil just hangs, dangling down in the air (see diagram). With this same left hand, take some of the material of your volunteer's jacket near one of the buttonholes. Put the loop over it, making sure that this handful of material includes the buttonhole. With your left hand, hold the pencil horizontal to the floor, aimed at the buttonhole.

Pull back enough material around the buttonhole so that you can push the front of the pencil through the buttonhole with your left hand. Once the pencil has been put through the buttonhole, pull the pencil down, tightening the string so that the loop is now tied around the edge of the buttonhole, with the pencil and the rest of the string hanging down the front of the person wearing the jacket.

Chide the volunteer gently, asking him to give you back your pencil. Try as hard as he may, he will not be able to free the imprisoned pencil.

Wait until he's given up, and then remove the pencil by simply reversing all the steps you used in first putting the pencil through the buttonhole.

THE COMIC STRIP TREE

More a clever manipulation than a trick, this effective creation of a colorful, tall tree is a real crowd pleaser.

Collect six sheets of your tabloid-sized Sunday Comic Section. Unfold the sheets and lay them out flat. Take one sheet and, holding the narrower end towards you, roll almost its entire length into a tube, leaving only the last few inches flat. Overlap the first few inches of a second sheet with the unrolled section of the first sheet

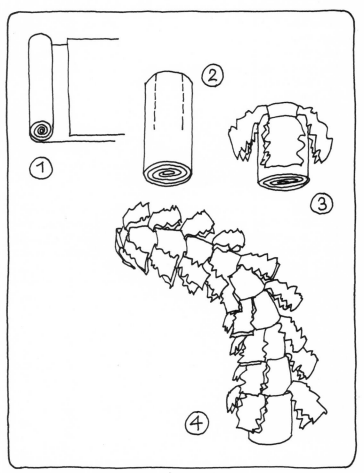

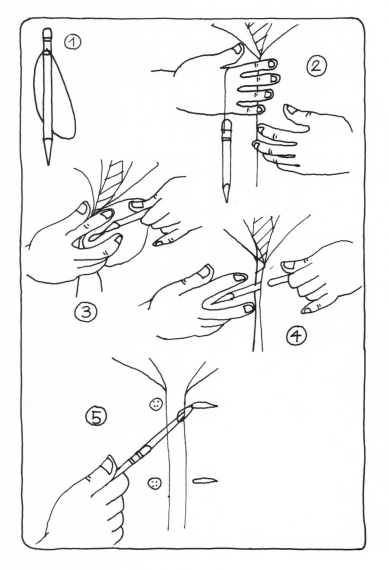

(see diagram 1), and continue rolling into a tube. Again leave a few inches of the second sheet unrolled, overlap it with the first few inches of the third sheet, and continue to roll.

Do this with all six sheets, always overlapping the last few inches of one sheet with the first few inches of the next sheet. When all six sheets have been rolled into a tube of colored paper, cut four slits in the top of the tube, about half way down the length of the tube (see diagram 2). Pull each of the four slits down and against the base of the tube, letting them rest against the sides (see diagram 3).

Hold the base of the tube tightly in your left hand. Put several fingers of your right hand into the opening at the top, grasp the inside sheets of paper, and pull them up, and up, and up, until you've grown a colorful tree even taller than yourself (see diagram 4).

PENETRATING THOUGHTS

With a pocket dictionary lying casually on a table, propose an experiment in thought transmission. Have a volunteer call out a number to indicate a page. Ask another volunteer to wait until you are out of the room before picking up and opening the dictionary. Ask him to turn to the page number just called out and to write the top word on that page on a piece of paper which he is to then fold up and place in his pocket. When he has done this, he is to call you back into the room.

Go to the designated room, where you will have secretly placed a second copy of the pocket dictionary beforehand. Locate the selected page and read the top word before being called back by the group. Say that you have definitely been receiving his thought-wave; the signals were at first rather blurred but are now becoming clearer and clearer.

With an air of deep concentration, pronounce the first syllable of the selected word to give the impression that it is slowly emerging in your conscious mind; then say the complete word, demonstrating to everyone's satisfaction that thoughts can indeed pass through solid walls.

THE FLYING CARD

For this spectacular exercise in playing-card gymnastics the corner of a card must be secretly bent after it has been selected by a spectator. Fan a deck of cards in your hand, holding it so that the faces of the cards are visible to the spectator while you see only their backs. Ask that a single card be touched by your volunteer, and then remove this card with its back still facing you. Show the card to the people in the room, telling everyone to keep its identity in mind, and then, as you reinsert it into the deck, secretly bend one of its corners slightly.

Shuffle the deck until the card with the bent corner is on the bottom of the deck. Then take a man's felt hat with a creased crown, and hold it above your head with the brim uppermost. Reach the deck over the hat and drop the cards into the upturned crown, making sure that the bent card falls on one side of the crease while the rest of the cards fall on the opposite side. Against the underside of the crown where the bent card lies, give the hat a sharp snap of your finger, and the card will take a flying leap in the air. When you pick it up to show the audience, quickly straighten the bent corner.

THE SELF-MENDING STRING

Pass a three-foot length of string to your audience and ask them to inspect it carefully. Ask them to return it once they are convinced that it is just an ordinary, conventional piece of string.

Tie the two ends of the string into a knot, creating a circle of string. Hold the string as shown in diagram 1 with the knot in your left hand. Move your right hand to the left as shown in diagram 2. As you do this, let the slack center section of the string fall loosely between your hands.

Put the string resting in your right hand into your left hand, letting the center of the string continue to dangle. Now move your right hand down and collect the center of the loose middle dangling above the floor. Do this deftly and smoothly so that the audience will not see the interlocking loops that have been created by the

turning of your right hand. Hold the loops under the thumb of your right hand as you now pull the string tightly between your two hands.

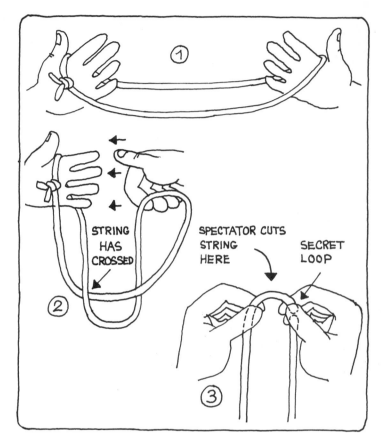

Drop the string in your left hand. It will fall, showing the audience that the knot is still there. With the left hand take hold of the double string again to the left of your right hand (see diagram 3). Ask a spectator to cut both strands of string at the point between your hands with a pair of scissors. Continue to hide the loop and tiny piece of interlocking string under your right thumb as you let the rest of the string fall.

Now for the mending operation. Put the ends of the string still in your right hand into your mouth. The audience assumes that you have mouthed only two cut ends of string but you have really mouthed the loop and its tiny interlocking section of cut string. Use your tongue to remove the tiny piece from around the loop. Hide it in a corner of your mouth as you proudly remove the miraculously mended string, a single strand in one continuous piece.

COLOR SENSE

This trick, requiring a small package of crayons, will demonstrate to the audience your remarkable powers of clairvoyance. Say that you are able to visualize the color of an object even though you never set eyes on it; you can do this, you say, by using the color concentration you've recently developed.

Bring out the pack of crayons and hand it to someone; then turn around so that your back is toward him and place your hands behind your back. Ask him to choose any one of the crayons from the pack and to put that crayon into one of your hands. Face the audience and declare that, without having seen the crayon, which is still being held behind your back, you will form an accurate mental image of its color and will soon name it.

While you are speaking to the group, lightly run your fingernail along the edge of the crayon, collecting some of it under your fingernail. Then raise the hand with the marked nail in front of your face, leaving the crayon in the other hand behind your back. As you place the hand with the marked fingernail over your eyes, as if to shield your mind from any distraction, notice the color of the crayon under your fingernail. After a few seconds of pretended concentration, call out the correct color, justifying your claim to clairvoyance.

SLICING THE DECK

Tell the audience that you have a secret method of identifying cards by means of dividing the deck with a dull butter knife. Take the deck in your left hand and hold it in a horizontal position in front of you, with one of its narrow ends facing you.

Pick up a dinner butter knife of silver or silver plate and insert the blade of the knife horizontally into the end of the deck near you. Three inconspicuous movements, almost simultaneously performed, will reveal to you the identity of the card resting on top of the knife blade.

As the knife slides between two cards of the deck, tilt the blade up slightly. The knife's weight will press the lower cards down just far enough to let you glimpse in the blade a reflection of the index corner of the card directly above.

READING A CLOSED BOOK

Have someone in the room be given a playing card to insert between the pages of a book you are holding. After a few seconds'

thought announce the numbers of the pages lying on both sides of the card. Then recite a few lines printed at the top of the two pages.

The trick works because the book you offer to the volunteer has been covered with a blank paper jacket, and thus it can be turned end on end without anyone's knowledge. Before you introduce the trick, place between the book's pages a duplicate of the card you later give to the volunteer; note the page numbers marked by your card and memorize several lines at the head of both pages. Offer the book for the volunteer's card with the card you previously inserted protruding slightly from the end of the book away from the audience.

Have your volunteer place his card between any two pages at the end of the book opposite your card; tell him to leave it protruding slightly beyond the edge. As soon as he does this, walk to a table and pick up a pad, give it to the volunteer and ask him to make a note of the top lines and page numbers his card is between. As you do this shove his card down so that it is hidden from view and switch the ends of the book so that your card now protrudes. He will record from the pages divided by your previously inserted card.

Facing the audience, put the book on the table and give the correct page numbers. When he opens the book to the pages marked by your card, your mental mastery is confirmed. As a climax to your feat, quote the lines you have memorized.

COUPLED FOR MONEY

This dramatic effect will baffle any audience. It requires the use of a dollar bill and two small paper clips.

Fold the bill across into the shape of an ''S'' and divide it into three segments of equal width. At the top edges of the folded bill, clip together (about one-half inch from their ends) the two segments nearest you on the right side, and then the center and front segments (the parts facing the audience) on the left side.

Take the clipped bill in your two hands and pull sharply. The paper clips jump into the air, interlocked. The pull forces them together so tightly that one of the clips is hooked between the open-ended double wire of the other.

THE "DEAD NAME" GAME

Take out a piece of paper about eight inches square. Fold it in thirds horizontally and then in thirds vertically. Tear the sheet apart along all the folds you've made, and you will have nine small squares, all approximately the same size.

Hand the center square to someone and ask him to write on it the name of a famous dead person. Hand out the other eight squares to various people, and ask them each to write on their squares the name of a living person.

When they are finished writing out the names, ask them to blindfold you and then to drop their unfolded squares of paper into the hat you are holding.

Still blindfolded, ask someone to guide your hand into the hat—but only after they've shaken up the contents to mix the papers to their complete satisfaction. When your hand is lowered into the hat, touch the various squares until you find the one containing the name of the famous dead person. Take it out and offer it to someone nearby. Ask him to please read the name he sees on the paper out loud. It is, of course, the correct name.

With some dramatic embellishments, this performance can be very effective. How do you pull out the correct square? Simple. Remember that it was the center piece of paper that you handed to the person who was to write the dead name on it. The center square is the only square with four rough edges. The other eight pieces of paper all have at least one smooth edge. You simply feel for the only square in the hat without a single smooth edge, and that one will contain the dead person's name.

THE NOISY EMPTY BOX

Show the audience three small match boxes. Open one and show that it's empty. Do the same with the second one. Hold up the third box and shake it—the noise of the matches rattling around in the box establishes that this box is indeed half full.

Put the third box down on the table between the other two, and move them all around quickly: here, there, back and forth, around and about, mixing them up repeatedly. Finally, you stop and ask if anyone has been able to follow the box half full of matches. Challenge anyone that says he did to point to it. Once he has made a selection, pick up the box and open it. It will be empty. You pick up any one of the remaining two boxes and shake it—the matches rattle!

Put the boxes back down and repeat the fast, here-and-there shuffle. This time ask someone else to do the guessing. Where is the half-full box of matches now? Again let them point to the one they've selected, again open the drawer of the box—again it will be empty. You take either one of the two remaining boxes and shake it—see, this is the one with the matches.

You can repeat the trick as many times as you and your audience desire. They will never guess the correct box simply because all three boxes on the table are empty. The half-full box is just above your right wrist, held there by a rubber band or string. It, and only it, shakes whenever you want it to—simply by jiggling your arm. You use your left hand to move and open up the empty boxes and your right hand only when you want to shake the box containing some matches.

THE TWIST

This is more a game than a trick and is suitable for a small group of friends. You will need twice as many crayons as there are people present since you begin the game by giving two crayons to each person, including yourself.

Ask the group to listen and watch carefully as you describe and demonstrate each move. Put one crayon into the valley between your left thumb and left index finger and the other crayon between your right thumb and index finger, and hold them there. Take the thumb and index finger of your right hand and place them on the two ends of the crayon in your left hand. And put the thumb and index finger of your left hand on the ends of the crayon in your right hand.

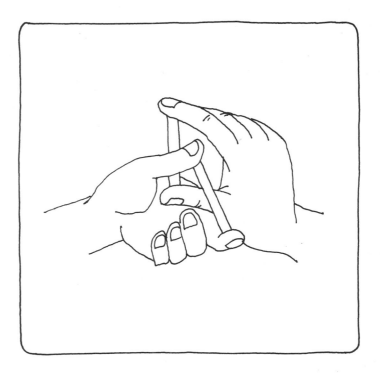

Lift the crayons up and announce the object of the game: to separate your hands without letting go of the crayons. Watch your friends as they struggle without success. They will soon discover that each crayon forms part of a triangle that prevents the other crayon from escaping. They have created two interlocking prisons made up of fingers and crayons.

When everyone has given up, demonstrate the twist that guarantees a successful solution.

Position the two crayons exactly as you first described. Take the thumb and index finger of your right hand and place them at the ends of the crayon in your left hand—but now for the twist. Move the fingers of your left hand under your right thumb and towards your body as you slip your left thumb into the palm of your right hand. Place the thumb on the end of the crayon in your right palm. Bring the left index finger around so that it can be placed on the other end of the crayon in your right hand (see diagram). In this position, the hands are free of each other and can easily be separated, each hand onto its own crayon.

Bibliography

Magic and the Occult

Baldwin, Gordon. *Schemers, Dreamers and Medicine Men.* New York: Four Winds, 1971.

Bonewits, P.E.I. *Real Magic.* New York: Coward, McCann & Geoghegan, 1970.

Brown, Slater. *The Heydey of Spiritualism.* New York: Hawthorn Books, 1970.

Butler, E.M. *Ritual Magic.* New York: Noonday Press, 1959.

Cavendish, Richard. *The Black Arts.* New York: Capricorn, 1967.

Cohen, Daniel. *Masters of the Occult.* New York: Dodd, Mead & Co., 1971.

DeGivry, Grillot. *Witchcraft, Magic and Alchemy.* New York: Bonanza, n.d.

Gibson, Walter. *Witchcraft.* New York: Grosset & Dunlap, 1973.

Hill, Douglas, et al. *Witchcraft, Magic and the Supernatural.* London: Octopus Books, 1974.

Murray, Margaret. *The God of the Witches.* New York: Anchor Books, 1960.

———. *The Witch-Cult in Western Europe.* Oxford: Oxford University Press, Clarendon Press, 1967.

Paine, Lauran. *Witches in Fact and Fantasy.* New York: Taplinger Publishing Co., 1971

Rachleff, Owen. *The Occult Conceit.* New York: Cowles, 1971.

Rhodes, H.T.F. *The Satanic Mass.* New York: Citadel Press, 1955.

Robbins, R.H. *The Encyclopedia of Witchcraft and Demonology.* New York: Crown Publishers, 1959.

Rony, Jerome-Antoine. *A History of Magic.* New York: Walker & Co., 1950.

Russell, Jeffrey. *Witchcraft in the Middle Ages.* Ithaca: Cornell University Press, 1972.

Summers, Montague. *Witchcraft and Black Magic.* New York: Causeway Books, 1974.

Thorndike, Lynn. *A History of Magic and Experimental Science.* 8 vols. New York: Columbia University Press, 1923-58.

Underwood, Peter. *Into the Occult.* New York: Drake Publishers, 1973.

Waite, Arthur E. *The Book of Ceremonial Magic.* New York: University Books, 1961.

Wheatley, Dennis. *The Devil and All His Works.* New York: American Heritage Publishing Co., 1971.

Zolar. *The History of Astrology.* New York: Arco Publishing Co., 1972.

Conjuring

Blackstone, Harry. *Blackstone's Modern Card Tricks and Secrets of Magic.* (2 vols. in 1). New York: Garden City Publishing Co., 1941.

———. *Blackstone's Tricks Anyone Can Do.* New York: Garden City Publishing Co., 1948.

Christopher, Milbourne. *The Illustrated History of Magic.* New York: Thomas Y Crowell Co., 1973.

———. *Houdini: The Untold Story.* New York: Thomas Y. Crowell Co., 1973.

Curry, Paul. *Magician's Magic.* New York: Franklin Watts, 1965.

Dexter, Will. *This Is Magic.* New York: Citadel Press, 1958.

———. *101 Magic Tricks for Amateurs.* New York: Arco Publishing Co., 1958.

Fischer, Ottokar. *Illustrated Magic.* New York: Macmillan, 1931.

Gibson, Walter. *The Master Magicians.* New York: Doubleday & Co., 1966.

———. *Professional Tricks for Amateur Magicians.* Englewood Cliffs, N.J.: Prentice-Hall, 1947.

Gibson, Walter, and Morris Young. *Houdini's Fabulous Magic.* Philadelphia: Chilton Co., 1961.

Hay, Henry. *The American Magician's Handbook.* New York: Thomas Y. Crowell Co., 1972.

Hocus Pocus Junior (pseud.). *The Anatomy of Legerdemain; or, The Art of Juggling.* 1634. Reprint (of 8th ed., 1675). New York: John McAndle, 1950.

Houdini, Harry. *A Magician Among the Spirits.* New York: Harper & Brothers, 1924.

———. *The Unmasking of Robert-Houdin.* New York: Publishers' Printing Co., 1908.

Hugard, Jean. *Encyclopedia of Card Tricks.* New York: Max Holden, 1937.

Hunt, Kari and Douglas. *The Art of Magic.* New York: Atheneum Publishers, 1967.

Lewis, Angelo (Professor Hoffmann). *Modern Magic.* London: George Routledge & Sons, 1878.

———. *More Magic.* London: George Routledge & Sons, 1889.

———. *Later Magic.* New York: E.P. Dutton & Co., 1935.

Maskelyne, Nevil, and David Devant. *Our Magic.* 2nd rev. ed. Berkeley Heights, N.J.: Fleming Book Co., 1946.

Mulholland, John. *Magic of the World.* New York: Charles Scribner's Sons, 1965.

———. *Quicker Than the Eye.* Indianapolis: Bobbs-Merrill Co., 1932.

———. *The Story of Magic.* New York: Loring & Mussey, 1935.

Robert-Houdin, Jean Eugène. *Memoirs of Robert-Houdin.* Translated by Lascelles Wraxall. New introduction and notes by Milbourne Christopher. New York: Dover Publications, 1964.

Sachs, Edwin. *Sleight of Hand.* Berkeley Heights, N.J.: Fleming Book Co., 1946.

Scarne, John. *Scarne on Card Tricks.* New York: Crown Publishers, 1950.

———. *The Odds Against Me.* New York: Simon & Schuster, 1966.

Severn, Bill. *Magic and Magicians.* New York: David McKay Co., 1958.

———. *Bill Severn's Big Book of Magic.* New York: David McKay Co., 1973.

Thurston, Howard. *My Life of Magic.* Philadelphia: Dorrance & Co., 1929.

———. *300 Card Tricks You Can Do.* New York: Pocket Books, 1948.

Index

INDEX

A

Aaron, 21
Aeromancy, 31
Agoston, Chevalier, 113
Albini, 108
Alchemy, 30-31
Alexander, Herr, 113
Anatomy of Legerdemain, The (Hocus Pocus Junior), 45, 54
Anderson, John Henry ,(Great Wizard of the North), 68-70, 113, 191, 203
Animal magnetism, 33
Ankele, Robert, 113
Arrow, dancing, 40-41
Art of Juggling, The, 45
Astrology, 11, 17, 22, 23, 30, 31
Automata, 52-53, 56, 57, 60, 64-65, 79

B

Balsamo, Giuseppe, 54
Bancroft, 113
Basch, William, 113
Beck, Martin, 98
Becker, Rudolph, 113
Bellachini, 113
Bellini, 113
Bertram, Charles, 113
Black Art illusion, 74, 86
Black books, 25-26
Black magic, 14, 22, 26, 32, 33, 41, 42, 44, 45, 47, 59
Black Mass, 24
Blackstone, Harry, 105, 106-10, 111, 143, 179
Blackstone, Harry, Jr., 113
Blitz, Antonio, 68, 69, 70, 79, 113, 191
Bodkins, 43
Bosco, Giovanni Bartolomeo, 61, 63, 113
Bouton, Henri, *see* Blackstone, Harry
Bouton, Peter, 108
Breslaw, Philip, 45-46, 57
Buatier de Kolta, Joseph, 74, 75, 81, 83, 86, 113, 179, 203
Bullet Catch, 69, 87

C

Cabala, 24-25, 32
Cabalism, 24
Cagliostro, Count Alessandro di, 54-55, 76, 113
Card tricks, 87, 88, 89, 90, 92, 97, 104-105
Cardini, 104-105, 110, 115, 116
Cartomancy, 31
Chaldeans, 17, 18, 22
Chess-playing automaton, 52-53
Chimney, human, 48, 49
Chinese Water Torture Cell, 98, 100, 101, 102
Ching Ling Foo, 87
Chiromancy, 22, 31, 32
Christianity, 23-24, 26, 41-42
Christopher, Milbourne, 113, 143
Chung Ling Soo, 85, 87, 203
Circe, 22, 28
Circle, magic, 25

Clairaudience, 33
Clairvoyance, 33
Clavicula Salomonis, 25
Cleromancy, 31
Compendium Maleficarum, 29
Comte, Louis, 61, 64
Comus, 55, 59
Conjurer Unmasked, The (Decremps), 56, 57
Contagious magic, 14, 17, 22
Cooke George, 78-80, 81
Crystal Cash Box, 67
Crystallomancy, 31
Cups-and-balls tricks, 21, 39, 40, 45, 61, 62, 63, 64
Cut-and-restored-rope trick, 45
Czeiler, Franz, *see* Tihanyi

D

D'Alvini, 113
Dancing arrow, 40-41
"Dancing" handkerchief, 109
Dante, 191
Davenport Brothers (Ira and William), 77, 78-79, 80, 83, 84, 143, 203
Decapitation mystery, 36, 42-43, 63, 72, 73, 114
Decremps, Henri, 56, 57
Dedi, 35-39, 42
Definition of magic, 11
Delf, Mickey, 113
De Thorn, 113
Devant, David, 79, 80, 81, 113, 179
Devil, 23-24, 29, 45, 59
Discoverie of Witchcraft, The (Scot), 44, 45
Doebler, Ludwig, 113
Doors, trumpeting, 38, 39
Downs, Thomas Nelson (King of Koins), 85, 113, 155
Duck, automatic, 52
Ducrot, Frank, 165
Dunninger, Joseph, 105, 111, 131
Duval, Ade, 179

E

Eastern magic, 48
Egypt, ancient, magic and, 18, 21, 35
Elliot, J. William, 113
Escapes, Houdini's, 96, 97-101
Ethereal Suspension illusion, 67, 79
Extrasensory perception, 33, 111
Eye-lift, Hindu, 48, 49, 50

F

Faith healing, 33
Fakirs, Hindu, 48-49, 50-51, 68
Faust, Johann, 25
Fawkes, Isaacs, 45, 46, 59
Fay, William (Professor Fay), 83, 84
Fertile Crescent, 17, 18
Floating Lady illusion, 93
Flosso, Al, 155

Flowing Coconut illusion, 91, 92
Flute player, automatic, 52
Fowler, Gus, 104
Fox, Imro, 113
Frikell, Wiljalba, 104, 113, 191

G

Geomancy, 31
Germain, Karl, 131
Gnosticism, 22, 24
Gods and goddesses, 18, 21, 22, 23
Goldin, Horace, 103-104, 113, 165
Great Raymond, 165
Greece, ancient, magic and, 22
Grimoires, 25, 33
Growth-of-flowers illusion, 84, 85
Guibal, Monsieur, 113
Gwynne, Jack, 110, 115

H

Handkerchief tricks, 65, 108-109
Harms, Jacoby, 113
Hartz, Joseph Michael, 68, 70, 104, 113, 191
Haruspicy, 31
Hayman, Jack, 96-97
Hayman, Joe, 97
Healing, faith, 33
Hecate, 22, 28
Heller, Robert, 68, 70, 83, 113, 131
Henning, Doug, 113
Herrmann, Madame Adelaide, 74-76, 90
Herrmann, Alexander, 71-76, 81, 84, 85, 86-87, 88, 89-90, 113, 171
Herrmann, Carl, 71-74, 76, 113, 155
Herrmann, Leon, 90, 113
Herrmann, Samuel, 71
Hero of Alexander, 38-39
Heubeck, George 113
Hiam, Henry, 113
High priests, 18, 38
Hinricks, J., 113
History of magic, 12-33
Hi-watari, ritual of, 51
Hocus Pocus Junior, 45
Hoffman, Charles, 171
Hoffmann, Professor, 81, 89
Hofzinser, Johann Nepomuk, 104, 116
Holden, Dr., 113
Houdini, Bessie, 98
Houdini, Harry, 93, 94-102, 116, 143, 155, 203
Hughes, I.H., 82
Hypnosis, 33

I

Ichi, Ten, 143
Imitative magic, 14, 17
Indian Rope trick, 50-51, 92, 110
Indians, American, magic and, 40-41
Inexhaustible Bottle trick, 67
Inquisition, 26, 28, 29, 30
International Brotherhood of Magicians, 52
Israelites, 21-22

J

Jacobs, George, 47
Jadoo wallahs, 48, 50
Jambres (Egyptian court magician), 21
Jannes (Egyptian court magician), 21
Jansen, Harry Alvin, see Dante
Jon, Fin, 113

K

Kaps, Fred, 113
Katterfelto, Gustavus, 46, 59
Keating, Fred, 111
Kellar, Harry, 82-87, 93, 97, 108, 113, 143, 203
Keller, Heinrich, see Kellar, Harry
Kempelen, Baron Wolfgang von, 52
Key of Solomon, 25
Khufu, Pharaoh, 35-37
Kreskin (George Kresge, Jr.), 131

L

Lechner, Ernst, 113
Leipzig, Nate, 104, 110, 116
Le Roy, Jean Servais, 113, 116, 155
Levitation, 48, 49, 50, 67-68, 79, 80, 93, 108, 110, 111
Levitation Extraordinary, 79, 80
Levitation of Princess Karnac, 93
Lewis, Angelo, 81
Liebholz, Professor, 113
Linking Ring, The (publication), 52
Linking Rings trick, 52
Lorraine, Sid, 113
Löwenstern, Johann Kunckel von, 31
Lyle, Cecil, 165

M

Macallister, Andrew, 113
Maggi, Vito, 113
Magicians
    first, 35-37
    master, 59-114
    tribal, 14, 28, 40-41
Mandeville, Sir John, 48
Manfre, Blaise, 171
Marchand, Floram, 171
Maro, E., 113
Martyn, Topper, 113
Maskelyne, John Nevil, 77, 78-81, 97, 113, 179, 203
Medea, 22, 28
Mediums, 77, 86, 102
Mellini, H., 113
Mental magic, 105, 111, 113
Mephistopheles, 25
Mesmer, Franz Anton, 32-33
Mesmerism, 33
Metamorphosis, 96, 97, 101
Metoposcopy, 32
Meyer, Jacob, see Philadelphia, Jacob
Miser's Dream trick, 85
Modern Magic (Hoffmann), 81, 89
Mulholland, John, 111
Myths, 17, 18, 21, 22, 51, 93

N

Necromancy, 21, 22
Nix, Dr., 113
Numerology, 11, 17, 22, 31

O

Oracles, 38

P

Pact (with Satan), 26, 29
Paracelsus, 30, 31
Patrizio, Signor, 113
Pepper, John Henry, 77
Pepper's Ghost illusion, 77, 86
Philadelphia, Jacob, 47-48, 59
Philippe, 61, 63, 64, 203
Philosopher's stone, 30
Physiognomy, 32
Piddington, Sidney and Lesley, 131
Pinetti, Giovanni Giuseppe, 54, 55-57, 59, 66, 131, 171
Pitchford, Richard Valentine, see Cardini
Plate, Adrien, 113
Playing cards, 31
Poe, Edgar Allan, 53
Polo, Marco, 48, 51
Powell, Frederick Eugene, 113, 171
Prehistoric man, magic and, 12-17
Primitive magic, 12-17
Puritans, witches and, 29-30

R

Religion, magic and, 11, 12, 17, 18, 21, 22
Rhabdomancy, 31
Rising Card trick, 88, 89, 90
Rituals, magic, 14, 17, 18, 21, 22, 40, 51-52
Rix, Claude, 113
Roberth, Professor, 113
Robert-Houdin, Emile, 66
Robert-Houdin, Eugenè, 66, 67-68
Robert-Houdin, Jean Eugenè, 60-70, 72, 76, 78, 79, 96, 113, 131, 155, 179, 203
Robinson, Bill, 203
Robinson, William, 85-87, 90, 113
Rome, ancient, magic and, 22-23
Rope tricks, 45, 50-51, 92, 110
Rossner, Max, 113
Rouclere, Harry, 113
Roger, Jean, 171

S

Sabbat, 29
St. Roman, 113
Sanchez, Antonio Navas, 113
Satanism, 24, 27
Satanists, 28, 29
Sawing a woman in half illusion, 103, 108, 111, 113, 114
Scarne, John, 111, 116
Schlumberger, Wilhelm, 53
Science, magic and, 22, 32, 52
Scot, Reginald, 44, 45, 131, 143
Seancès, spirit, 21, 77, 102
Second Sight deception, 66
Seeman, Baron, 113

Selbit, P.T., 103-104
Siegfried and Roy, 113
Sleight of hand, 38, 45, 47, 48, 54, 59, 63, 68, 71, 72, 74, 76, 89, 92, 104, 110, 113
Smith, Albert E., 113
Soothsayers, 38
Sorcar, Protul Chandra, 111, 113
Sorcery, 26, 30, 42
Spells, magic, 26
Spirits, 13-14, 18, 22, 24, 25, 76-77, 78
Spiritualism, 33, 76-77, 86, 102
Stag dance, 14, 17
Statue, wine-pouring, 38, 39
Stevenson, 113
Strickland, William, 113
Substitution Trunk escape, 96
Sunetaro, Soto, 113
Superstitions, 17, 23, 38, 76
Symbols, magic, 25, 26
Szandor La Vey, Anton, 28

T

Taboos, 14, 17
Talma, Mercedes, 155
Tarbell, Harlan, 143
Tarot, cards, 31-32
Telepathy, 33, 111
Television, magic and, 111, 113, 114
Temple vessels, ever-full, 38, 39
Theurgy, 24
Thompson, Charles, 113
Thought transference, 111
Throwaway tricks, 65
Thurston, Howard, 84, 86, 88-93, 116
Tihanyi, 191
Torture tricks, 43, 45
Tribal magicians, 14, 28, 40-41
Tricks
    Ace Performance, 259
    Aces High, 122
    All Purpose Production, 200
    All Thumbs, 152
    Amazing Coin Drop, 236
    Any Number Will Play, 235
    Beating the Shell Game, 252
    Before Inflation, 251
    Belts of the Orient Magic Lesson, 214
    Bewitched Bottle, The, 233
    Book Telepathy Experiment, 132
    Bottomless Change Purse, The, 232
    Bracelet Knot, 146
    Breakout!, 244
    Burning Question, The, 254
    Burnt Match Relighted, 237
    Candy from Confetti, 198
    Card Concentration, 243
    Card in an Orange, 117
    Card Stabbing, 124
    Catch as Catch Can, 242
    Changing Aces, 253
    Changing Colors, 257
    Clairvoyance Extraordinaire, 134
    Color-Changing Handkerchiefs, 184
    Color Sense, 261
    Color Vibration, 235

Tricks (continued)

Combination Puzzles, 236
Comic Strip Tree, The, 260
Concentration-Power, 248
Coupled for Money, 262
Cups and Balls, 224
Currency Caper, 156
Cut to the Quick, 254
Cylinder-Box Rabbit Production, 192
"Dead Name" Game, The, 263
Deck of Many Tricks, 126
Devil's Black Mark, 210
Dice Divination, 138
Disappearing and Reappearing, 247
Disappearing Candle, 228
Dissolving Coin, The, 244
Do As I Do, 120
Escaping Box, 253
ESP?, 258
ESP Mail Prediction, 136
Floating Ball, 204
Floating Cube Game, The, 241
Flying Card, The, 261
Flying Handkerchief, 188
Forty-Niner, The, 237
For Whom the Bell Tolls, 241
Four Cards in One, 258
Genie Pencil, 206
George Washington Moves!, 245
Ghostless Séance, The, 247
Glass Lightning, 238
Goldfish Bowl Production, 194
Grab Bag, The, 232
Handkerchief-Prison Break, The, 237
Hanky Panky, 186
High Roller, 234
His Master's Voice, 236
Impossible Knot, The, 252
Into Thin Air, 248
Just Passing Through, 249
Knife through Handkerchief, 230
Let Freedom Ring, 255
Lighter Than Air, 251
Lit and Relit, 241
Loop the Loop, 259
Lumber Is Limber, 239
Magazine Charmer, 251
Magic Hat, 168
Magic Key Ring, The, 240
Magic Number, 240
Magic Paddle, 219
Magic Photography, 140

Matchbook Flip, The, 250
Matched Cigarette, The, 247
Migrating Coins, 162
Milk to Flowers, 174
Mini-Weighing Mystery, 220
Money! Money! Money!, 242
Multiple Card-Finder, The, 250
Needle Trick, 212
Next of Boxes, 216
Newspaper-Handkerchief Production, 196
Newspaper Plus, 166
No Holding Power, 257
Noisy Empty Box, The, 263
No Need for Sherlock Holmes, 257
One Dollar and Ten Cents, 259
One-Hand Knot, 256
One-Two-One Rope, 144
Orange Magic, 246
Paper Bridge, The, 254
Penetrating Thoughts, 261
Penetrating Toothpick, The, 243
Perplexing Pulse, The, 239
Ping-Pong on a Tightrope, 233
Psychic Communication, 249
Put Your Foot in It, 243
Quadruple Your Money, 160
Quick Count, The, 245
Rabbit Rubber Band, The, 253
Rainbow Liquids, 172
Reading a Closed Book, 262
Reappearing Thimble, The, 241
Rearrangement, The, 248
Restoration, The, 255
Ring and String, 222
Rising Cards, 128
Rope-Kerchief Enigma, The, 239
Rope Penetration, 148
Rope-Tie Escape, 150
Séance Sorcery, 208
Seeing Hands, 252
Select Any Card at All, 250
Self-Mending String, The, 261
Simple Escape, A, 256
Slicing the Deck, 262
Smash the Glass!, 239
Special Delivery, 255
Spooky Scarf, 190
Squeezed Out of Sight, 249
Standing a Drink, 251
String the Bracelet, 232

Sugar, Sugar, Burning Bright, 244
Sure Sinker, A, 235
Sweet Deceit, A, 238
Talented Toe, 259
Telephone Telepathy, 142
They Can't Cut It, 242
To Be or Knot to Be, 235
Touch and Tell, 247
Touch-up, 253
Traveling Coin, 158
Traveling Knots, 182
Traveling Magic Ball, The, 258
Tricky Disks, 233
Twist, The, 263
Two Bits Worth of Tears, 238
Unlocking the Answers, 246
Vanishing Handkerchief, 180
Vintage Magic, 176
Way with Matches, A, 245
Which is Mutt and Which is Jeff?, 237
Whole Again, 259
X-Ray Vision, 233
Trumpeting doors, 38-39

V

Vanishing Birdcage trick, 74, 81, 83, 108
Vanishing Lady illusion, 75-76, 81
Vaucanson, Jacques de, 52
Vigenère, Blaise de, 31
Virgil the Great, 111
Voodoo, 17

W

Walsh, Patrick, 113
Weiss, Ehrich, see Houdini, Harry
Weiss, Theodore, 96, 97
Werner, F.J., 113
Westcar, Henry, 35
Western magic, 48
White, George, 91
White magic, 14
Wiccas, 28-29
Wilson, Mark, 113
Witch doctors, 17
Witchcraft, 28-30, 42, 44, 47
Witches, 27, 28-30, 32
Witches' sabbath, see Sabbat

Z

Zig Zag Woman illusion, 114

Photo Credits

Page 10, clockwise from top left: The American Museum of Natural History; Walter Hampden Memorial Library; Thomas Höpker, W. Camp; Photographie Giraudon; Jack and Betty Cheetham, Magnum; Library of Congress; Walter Hampden Memorial Library. Page 10, top center: Bettman Archive. Page 10, center: Walter Hampden Memorial Library. Page 12, left: Jeffrey Foxx. Page 12, top center: Hans Hoefer. Page 12, bottom center: Thomas Höpker, W. Camp. Page 13, clockwise from top left: Bettmann Archive; Jack and Betty Cheetham, Magnum; Auckland Institute and Museum; Thomas Höpker, W. Camp; Jack and Betty Cheetham, Magnum; Bishop Museum; Jack and Betty Cheetham, Magnum. Pages 14 and 15: The American Museum of Natural History. Page 16: Dr. William E. Mitchell. Page 17: The American Museum of Natural History. Page 19, bottom: Mueum Boymans-van Beuningen. Page 20: Photographie Giraudon. Page 22: Michael Holford Photographs. Page 23, bottom: Kunglinga Biblioteket. Page 24: Gabinetto delle Stampe. Page 26: Guidotti: Madeline Grimoldi. Pages 27 and 28: Jack and Betty Cheetham, Magnum. Page 29: New York Public Library Picture Collection. Page 30: Culver Pictures. Page 31: Visconti-Sforza tarocchi cards, reprinted by U.S. Games Systems, Inc., New York, and Grafica Gutenberg, Gorle, Italy. Pages 32 and 33: Culver Pictures. Page 34, bottom right: Rudi Haas. Page 34, left: Baich-Haas for Indian Affairs. Page 34, top right: Richard Iden. Page 40: Photographie Giraudon. Page 42: Walter Hampden Memorial Library. Page 44, left: Irving Desfor. Page 44, right: Library of Congress. Page 46: New York Public Library Prints Division, Astor, Lenox and Tilden Foundations. Page 47, top: Library of Congress. Page 47, bottom: Bettmann Archive. Page 51: Patricia A. Freeman. Page 54: New York Public Library Rare Book Division. Pages 55 and 56: Library of Congress. Page 57, right: Walter Hampden Memorial Library. Page 58: Walter Hampden Memorial Library. Page 59: New York Public Library Picture Collection. Page 61, bottom: Irving Desfor. Page 63: Roger-Viollet. Page 67: New York Public Library Picture Collection. Page 70: New York Public Library Picture Collection. Page 71, top: Library of Congress. Page 71, bottom: Walter Hampden Memorial Library. Pages 72, 73, 74, 76: Walter Hampden Memorial Library. Page 78: New York Public Library Picture Collection. Page 79: Walter Hampden Memorial Library. Page 81: Radio Times Hulton Picture Library. Pages 82, 86, 88, 90, 92: Walter Hampden Memorial Library. Page 94: Culver Pictures. Page 95: Walter Hampden Memorial Library. Page 97, left: Culver Pictures. Page 97, right: Walter Hampden Memorial Library. Page 98: Culver Pictures. Page 99: Walter Hampden Memorial Library. Page 100: Bettmann Archive. Page 102: United Press International. Page 103: Walter Hampden Memorial Library. Page 104, left: courtesy Mrs. Cardini. Page 104, right: Irving Desfor. Page 105: Irving Desfor. Page 108: Walter Hampden Memorial Library. Page 109, left: Acme. Page 109, right: United Press International. Page 112: Walter Hampden Memorial Library. Page 114: courtesy The Dime Savings Bank of New York and Doremus & Co.

Creative Direction and Design Studio: Panullo Associates
Photo Research: Yvonne R. Freund
Design and Styling of
"Another 100 Mystifying Tricks You Can Perform:
Harold Franklin

Acknowledgments

We wish to acknowledge the valuable assistance and cooperation given us on this project by Mr. Louis A. Rachow, Curator and Librarian of the Walter Hampden Memorial Library, and Mr. Irving Desfor of New York.